LEAHY'S LADS

LEAHY'S LADS

THE STORY OF THE FAMOUS NOTRE DAME FOOTBALL TEAMS OF THE 1940s

BY JACK CONNOR

This is the story of the players and coaches of the Notre Dame football teams of the 1940s offering a behind-the-scenes view of what it was like to play in that golden era of college football. Featuring Frank Leahy, Moose Krause, and the other coaches, and such great players of that day as Bob Dove, Bernie Crimmins, Angelo Bertelli, Creighton Miller, Bob Kelly, Elmer Angsman, Johnny Lujack, George Connor, Bill Fischer, Marty Wendell, Emil "Red" Sitko, Leon Hart, Jim Martin, Jerry Groom, Bob Williams, the incomparable Ziggie Czarobski, and the rest of the teammates.

Diamond Communications, Inc.
South Bend, Indiana
1994

Leahy's Lads

Copyright © 1994 by Jack Connor

10 9 8 7 6 5 4 3 2 1

Manufactured in the United States of America

Diamond Communications, Inc.
Post Office Box 88
South Bend, Indiana 46624-0088
(219) 299-9278
FAX (219) 299-9296

Library of Congress Cataloging-in-Publication Data

Connor, Jack, 1928-
    Leahy's lads : the story of the famous Notre Dame football
teams of the 1940's / by Jack Connor.
        p. cm.
    ISBN 0-912083-75-1 : $24.95
    1. Leahy, Frank 1908-1973. 2. Football coaches–United
States–Biography. 3. University of Notre Dame–Football–
History–20th century. I. Title.
GV939.L35C65 1994
796.332'092–dc20
[b]   94-20706
                                                            CIP

CONTENTS

ACKNOWLEDGMENTS...ix
FOREWORD xi
PROLOGUE...xv

1. LEAHY'S EARLY YEARS 1

2. NOTRE DAME 9
   The Players 10
   Bob Dove..12
   Angelo Bertelli 16
   Bernie Crimmins 18

3. THE FIRST LEAHY SEASON—1941 20
   Creighton Miller 20
   War 33

4. THE 1942 SEASON 35
   Lou Rymkus 36

5. THE 1943 SEASON—
   LEAHY'S FIRST NATIONAL CHAMPIONSHIP 53
   John Lujack 54
   Bob Kelly 57

6. THE UNAPPRECIATED YEARS, 1944-1945......80
   The 1944 Season 81
   Zeke O'Connor..82
   John "Tree" Adams 84

7. THE 1945 SEASON 96
   Frank Tripucka 98
   Bill "Moose" Fischer 100

8. THE POST-WAR YEARS 114
   The 1946 Team 118
   Ziggie Czarobski 119
   George Connor 122
   Unlimited Talent 128
   Leon Hart 129
   Noon Meetings 137

9. THE 1946 SEASON—
   LEAHY'S SECOND NATIONAL CHAMPIONSHIP 150

10. THE 1947 SEASON—
   LEAHY'S THIRD NATIONAL CHAMPIONSHIP 183
      George, Ziggie, and Weight 183
      The 1947 Team 187
      George Strohmeyer 189
      The Pep Rallies 196

11. ZIGGIE AND FUN AFTER THE SEASON 221
      The East-West Game 221
      The Old-Timers' Game 223
      The Senior Prom 225

12. THE 1948 SEASON 228
      Jerry "Boomer" Groom 230

13. THE 1949 SEASON—
   LEAHY'S FOURTH NATIONAL CHAMPIONSHIP 246
      Bob Williams 249
      The Old-Timers' Game 263

14. LOOKING BACK 265
      Frank Leahy 265
      Moose Krause 286
      Other Coaches 289
      The Players—Life After Football 292

15. ZIGGIE AND REUNIONS 295

EPILOGUE 312

LEAHY'S LADS, 1941-1949
      Team Rosters 315

ABOUT THE AUTHOR 325

DEDICATION

This book is dedicated to all of the Notre Dame players and coaches of the 1940s. It is their love for each other, and for Notre Dame, that gave me the inspiration to undertake this endeavor. It has been their trust in me and their encouragement that has given me the confidence to complete it.

In particular, I dedicate this book to five of the deceased teammates and coaches: my brother, Chuck Connor, and four of my brothers in spirit, Ziggie Czarobski, Moose Krause, Red Sitko, and Msgr. Mike Hart. Although each of these men were different in so many ways, they shared the common values of a love of life, a love of Notre Dame, and a love of their neighbor. The example they gave by so generously giving to others has been, and continues to be, a source of inspiration for me and many of my teammates.

For Alice.
Because of her, I have come to know the beauty of a sunset,
the vivid colors of the autumn leaves, the goodness of others, and that
anything is possible—even writing a book.

Acknowledgments

As with any worthwhile endeavor I undertake, it has been my wife Alice who has been my guiding light. She has graciously put up with my trips, the late nights at my word processor, and my moods as I pondered some problem. She helped me with the manuscript by giving me her wise council, and in so many other countless ways. But most of all, it has been her love, support, and constant encouragement during the several years it took to write this book which has been my inspiration to complete it.

Our four children, Kevin Connor, Terri Connor Brankin, Kacky Connor Buell, and Pattie Connor Beem were sources of continual encouragement and help as were their spouses. I owe special debts to Kevin, who is my attorney, a sometimes editor, and a full-time advisor; and to Terri, who was my computer expert, my proofreader, and special advisor on all kinds of matters.

Outside of my immediate family, my best friend in life, my brother George, was essential to the writing of this book. He is blessed with a great memory, is a wonderful storyteller, cares deeply about all the teammates and coaches, and shared all this with me along with his love and encouragement.

My sister, Mary Ellen, a retired school teacher who lives in Cleveland, was also very much a part of the enterprise. We kept the postman busy as we mailed drafts of the manuscript back and forth as I sought her always valuable advice and council. As it has been since we were kids, she was always there with her sound advice, her love, and her encouragement.

In the course of researching this book, I either interviewed or have on tape from the many teammate gatherings the following: Moose Krause, Bernie Crimmins, Johnny Druze, Wally Ziemba, Lou Holtz, Angelo Bertelli, Johnny Lujack, Creighton Miller, George Connor, Jack Leahy, Bob Kelly, Zeke O'Connor, Lou Rymkus, Bob Dove, Jerry Groom, Bob Williams, Jim Mello, John Panelli, Leon Hart, Marty Wendell, Bob McBride, Cornie Clatt, Elmer Angsman, Ed Mieszkowski, Joe Signaigo, Fr. John Smyth, Bill Fischer, Jim Martin, Frank Tripucka, Walter Grothaus, Blackie Johnston, Rodney Johnson, Art Statuto, Mike Romano, Buddy Romano, Dore Sitko, Doris Czarobski, Jim Nerad, and Mike Smith. My profound thanks to all these magnificent people for giving their time and sharing their memories with me.

In preparing to write this book, I mailed a little over 100 detailed questionnaires to all the living players who received their monogram from 1941 to 1949. I was very pleasantly surprised by the over 70 percent response from these players, some of whom I had never met.

Knowing so many of the players from the teams of the 1940s as I do, it should not have come as a surprise to me how generous these men were with their time. Yet, it still amazes me how supportive they are for any teammate that needs help or assistance of any kind. They gave their thoughts about playing at Notre Dame, oftentimes adding pages of additional information and stories. I extend to all these players my deepest thanks.

There are several dear friends who helped me in various ways and have my profound gratitude. These include: Richard Cordasco, for helping me with some of the interviews; Buddy Romano, Michael Romano, and Tom Gallagher, each of whom read the manuscript at every phase and offered their suggestions and constant encouragement. A special thanks to my dear friend, Jack Leahy, for his stories about his uncle, Frank Leahy, and his consent to use the Leahy name in the title, as well as for his support and encouragement.

I owe a debt of gratitude to John Heisler, the sports information director at Notre Dame, for so generously allowing me to use the Notre Dame files; to Lou Holtz for graciously writing the Foreword; to Moose Krause for allowing me, while a guest in his booth at the Notre Dame games, to tape many of the marvelous stories that were told by him and his guests; to Mary Stimming, who helped edit my work; and to Bud Maloney, a retired sportswriter and dear friend, for putting in an enormous amount of time in performing his editing magic, and advising me on all sports matters. To all these marvelous people, I will be forever grateful.

A special thank-you to Doris Czarobski, for not only her permission, but her encouragement to write a book that would feature Ziggie.

Finally, my thanks to Jim Langford for his editorial direction and to my publisher, Jill Langford of Diamond Communications, for enthusiastically agreeing to publish and promote the sale of *Leahy's Lads*.

Foreword

When Frank Leahy won his first national championship as Notre Dame's head football coach in 1943, I was six years old. While I was growing up in East Liverpool, Ohio, Leahy's teams in the late 1940s went through 39 games without a loss.

In those days, I attended St. Aloysius grade school where we marched into and out of the building to the Notre Dame Victory March that played on the juke box in the foyer. The impressions Notre Dame made on me 50 years ago remain today.

I grew up following Notre Dame because so many people close to me—especially members of my family—held Notre Dame in such high esteem. I would have loved to have attended Notre Dame, but I never did well enough academically to qualify and certainly wasn't enough of an athlete to have an opportunity to earn a scholarship.

But that didn't mean I didn't keep up with the Irish teams through the years. In fact, after I got into coaching, I was as interested in finding out the Notre Dame scores on Saturdays as anything else that happened. And that never changed.

When I left Arkansas after the 1983 season, I had no idea what might happen. I ended up becoming head coach at the University of Minnesota, and the two years we spent there were an experience I'll never forget. When I signed the contract at Minnesota, I included a clause that gave me the opportunity to come to Notre Dame if that job opened up.

There was no particular reason to include that clause. It wasn't as if I really expected anything to come of it. In fact, I absolutely fell in love with Minnesota, the people there and the enthusiasm and commitment they made to the program. But I had reached a point in my career where, if for any reason, any kind of opportunity at Notre

Dame appeared on the horizon, I wanted to be in a position to look at it. That's how strongly I felt about Notre Dame after all those years.

When Gerry Faust resigned in November of 1985, I remembered that Gene Corrigan, who had been at Virginia when I coached at William & Mary and North Carolina State, was the athletic director at Notre Dame. When I ended up accepting the job in South Bend, it was the thrill of a lifetime.

I've always been enthralled by Leahy and the success he had at Notre Dame. When I first arrived on campus beginning with the 1986 season, I savored the opportunity to learn more about him because it helped me understand what being the football coach at Notre Dame was all about.

On one occasion, I had difficulty finding a copy of the Leahy biography *Shake Down the Thunder*, by longtime *San Francisco Examiner* sportswriter Wells Twombley. I happened to mention it once on my radio show and, within a week, I received approximately 20 copies in the mail. One woman asked me to please read the book and send it back within the month because she had checked it out of the library.

Once I came to Notre Dame, I had occasion to spend time with some of the individuals who played on those Leahy teams that I'd followed back in the '40s. Ziggie Czarobski, in the early '70s, first organized a reunion of players from the Leahy years, and the tradition has continued yearly even after his death. Football weekends at Notre Dame are extremely hectic for me, but I've tried to make a point of accepting the invitation to visit with this group for a few minutes because I think they are a special group of Notre Dame people.

As a history major in college, I've always been interested in what makes people and organizations successful. One of the questions I always asked of Angelo Bertelli, Leon Hart, John Lujack, Creighton Miller, George Connor, John Lattner, and all the other players from the Leahy era was this one: What made you so successful?

Naturally, Leahy's name usually was woven into the response in some fashion, and there's no doubt Notre Dame had its share of quality football players during those years. But I never cease to be amazed at the affection and camaraderie those players have for one another and, especially, for Leahy. Maybe it was Leahy himself, maybe it was because his tenure at Notre Dame surrounded the war years, maybe it was the players.

What they accomplished on the football field was nothing short of amazing. They dominated the college football scene and they actually went four consecutive years from '46 to '49 without losing a game.

I've read as much as I can read about Knute Rockne and Leahy. I've had the pleasure of spending a good deal of time with Ara Parseghian and, to a lesser extent, with Dan Devine. It doesn't take long to understand that being at Notre Dame and having the success those individuals had in the '40s really was something extra special.

What's more incredible to me is the feeling these men have for each other today and the importance those experiences hold for them—even though it's been more than 40 years since they played at Notre Dame.

I've had the great pleasure of becoming good friends with George and Jack Connor over the last eight years. What Jack has done here is detail the glory years of the Leahy era in such a way that you can't help but feel that you know these individuals personally. He paints vivid portraits of the men themselves, of Notre Dame football through that decade—and of what it was like to play for Leahy.

Whether you're a die-hard Notre Damer, a history buff when it comes to college football, or simply a casual fan, I think you'll be intrigued by *Leahy's Lads*. It portrays in an intimate fashion what the Notre Dame spirit is all about.

Lou Holtz
Head Football Coach
University of Notre Dame
March 1994

"The men, the times, and the place conspired together, albeit unknowingly, to produce a very unique group of very special people. The 'group' has had, and still has, I dare say, an influence quite beyond Saturday's gridiron. The care and concern for one another, the bonds of friendship, all surpass the superb teamship on the field and the joy of many victories. It's the stuff that builds ties that bind and brings pleasure to friendship."

Msgr. Michael (Father Mike) Hart,
Chaplain to the Teammates
of the Ziggie Reunion Group
November 3, 1989

PROLOGUE

It was early June and a beautiful summer day in 1984 when my brother George and I were making our annual drive from Chicago to South Bend to attend the Notre Dame Monogram Club dinner.

The Monogram Club reunion is always a special day for the two of us because it gives us the opportunity to share each other's company. It is even more special because it's the day when Notre Dame's best athletes, in all sports and from every year, gather on the familiar setting of the Notre Dame campus with former teammates and lifelong friends. George and I would have the opportunity to renew old friendships and mingle with all the great players of former years—such marvelous guys as Moose Krause, Mario "Motts" Tonelli, John McHale, Johnny Lattner, Marty O'Connor, Leo Klier, and so many more.

This year, however, was different. Our dear pal Ziggie Czarobski, affectionately called by his playing number "76," was dying of colon cancer. He was scheduled to be honored at the dinner that evening as the Monogram Man of the Year.

As we drove the familiar Indiana Toll Road to South Bend, George and I discussed the upcoming evening and voiced our apprehension as to whether "76" could hold up. We knew from having seen him a few days before that he was beginning to fail, so we were concerned that he might not be able to physically weather the proceedings, let alone the emotional toll of the evening.

We went straight to the Athletic and Convocation Center and we arrived just in time for the Mass being celebrated by Father Riehle, the Monogram Club's executive director. As we slipped into the back of the room, there was a wave from Elmer Angsman, the great halfback from the 1944-45 teams; a smile and nod from Johnny Jordan, Notre Dame's famous basketball coach from former years; and a firm arm squeeze by big Mike Smith (Mr. New Orleans), one of Krause's basketball players from the 1940s (and for many years the executive director of the Sugar Bowl).

During the Mass I found my attention wandering, and I looked over the crowded room. Four hundred men who had played varsity sports from the 1930s to the previous year were in attendance.

The track men seemed smaller, and some of the football players looked bigger (particularly in the middle), the baseball players not so lean, and the basketball players not as tall as I remembered them. Yet despite the physical changes which had occurred since their varsity days, they continued to hold one thing in common: They were proud men. Even given the limitations that come with age, they all carried themselves with a certain dignity that you see only in people who know they have earned their way. And these men earned their way by performing in their chosen sport, when it counted, against the best of their day.

Any fidgeting ceased when Father Riehle began his homily. It was a homily which captured the spirit of the evening. He told these men they helped create the folklore of Notre Dame sports, but, more importantly, they had carried the lessons taught at Notre Dame—about love of God and love of their neighbor—into their families and everyday lives. He urged us to strive to do better with the same intensity that made us strive for perfection on the athletic field.

We filed out of Mass to a room where a cocktail party was just beginning. The mood switched from the reflective to one of fun, laughter, and noisy greetings.

After many handshakes, bear hugs, and all forms of welcome, the crowd settled into groups of four or five with the usual seeking out of a special friend.

"Have you seen Boomer?"

"Where is Bertelli?"

"Is Ed Mieszkowski here?"

The inquiries about a specific player were different in each little group, but the questions that seemed to be voiced in every group were: "Is Ziggie here yet?" "Will he be able to accept the award?" "What's the latest on him?" "Has anybody seen him recently?"

Amid all the noise and happy confusion, my brother caught my eye and nodded towards the door. I knew exactly what he meant and what he wanted to do without any words spoken between us. He wanted to see firsthand if Ziggie was on the way and if he needed any help. We went down the stairs to the entrance of the Convocation Center just in time to see a car pull up with Ziggie in it. As soon as it stopped, his lifelong pal, Jim Nerad, stepped out and said, "Zig needs a wheelchair."

Fortunately, Bill Fischer (a Hall of Fame guard who was captain of the 1948 team), the current president of the Monogram Club and our host for the evening, had anticipated this possibility and had one waiting just inside the door. We helped Ziggie into the wheelchair and Nerad wheeled him to the elevator that took us to the entrance of the Monogram Room where the party was being held. As Ziggie was wheeled in and the crowd realized he was there, a momentary hush fell over the room. As quickly as the silence descended it lifted again as, one by one, those gathered came to Ziggie and gave him their greetings.

George and I joined in conversation with a group that included Johnny Lujack, Creighton Miller, Mike and Buddy Romano, Billy Hassett, and Leo Barnhorst. Fischer came up to us with a problem made obvious by the look on his face.

Fischer said, "Fellas, I've got a problem and I need your help. I have just seen Ziggie and I know I can't present the award to him tonight without breaking down. Can you guys help? George, how about you? You're his closest friend."

"I'd probably break down too," George replied.

Turning to Lujack, Fischer asked, "How about you, John?"

Lujack hesitated and said, "I can't do it either."

All eyes then turned to Miller who, like George and Lujack, was an experienced speaker and a close friend of Ziggie's.

Miller said, "I couldn't do it either, but I have an idea. Why don't we split it up so each of us takes a part of the presentation and in that way maybe we can all get through it?"

It was agreed to present the award that way. The four—Bill Fischer, George Connor, John Lujack, and Creighton Miller—huddled together and after several minutes had worked out a plan whereby all of them would participate in the award ceremony.

As the dinner plates were cleared away, the award program began. Soon it was time for the Man of the Year Award. The four presenters took their places at the mike. Fischer introduced the other three and told the audience that Lujack would lead off. Lujack set the tone when he said, "Our goal tonight, Zig, is to make you laugh because your whole life has been dedicated to making people laugh."

The presenters played their parts to perfection and worked together as if they had rehearsed for days. They balanced a degree of seriousness, as befitted the award, with a light touch designed to produce the promised laughter as Lujack, Miller, and Connor regaled Ziggie with their many stories. They kidded "76" with such lines as, "Ziggie was at Notre Dame for two terms—Roosevelt's and Truman's." "He claimed he would have been Phi Beta Kappa at Notre Dame if it wasn't for his grades." They had Ziggie laughing so hard that it was impossible not to be caught up in the spirit of the night.

When Ziggie was called to the mike to receive his award and make his response, he was greeted not only by a standing ovation, but by loud chants of "Ziggie, Ziggie, Ziggie," which lasted for several minutes. As he was wheeled to the microphone, the audience realized that Ziggie was going to attempt to stand. The group grew very quiet and nervous as they watched this dying man grip the handrail of the wheelchair and push up with those once mighty arms and lift himself to his feet.

As was his custom when he spoke, he wrapped his still chubby hands around the mike and began in a surprisingly strong voice, "You know, I have been getting a lot of awards lately. You would think I was going someplace."

The crowd broke out in loud laughter, much of it a nervous release—happy that he was able to respond, but still a little apprehensive of how long he would last. Ziggie quickly added, "I was a little sick for a while and had to spend some time in the hospital. One night after the visitors had left, I was looking for something to read and spotted this book. So I grabbed it and started thumbing through it. It was a Bible. You know, it had the same old stories—they never change anything. So I went to the back page and there was a handwritten message which said, 'If you have a problem, call 376-9500.' So, I figured I had a problem and called the number. The voice that answered said, 'Romano Brothers Liquors, your order please?'"

This was classic Ziggie and it brought down the house with laughter.

Anyone who ever knew Ziggie and heard him speak will tell you there was no one better at playing a crowd than Ziggie. He knew he had us that night. He proceeded to entertain us with story after story.

We forgot he was sick, he forgot he was sick, and it was one of those moments that you wish you could freeze, frame, and capture forever.

But after a while, when he had finished yet another story, his legs began to buckle and he had to sit back in his wheelchair. He quickly grabbed the mike with one hand and said, "Fellas, it's been one helluva party so far, let's get to the bar and have another drink."

One helluva party though it was, Ziggie wore himself out and had to leave. As he was being wheeled out to the exit many of the guys wanted to say goodbye to their pal number "76," but Ziggie wanted no part of final farewells. As he sensed someone about to get sentimental, he would immediately say, "Good to see you. I'll see you at the reunion this fall."

His friends quickly caught on and gave him a handshake or hug, and, with a smile, said, "Take care, Zig. I'll see you soon."

As they turned away from their farewells, each one had tears in his eyes. Those who did not live in the Chicago area knew they would never see him alive again.

There was comfort in knowing that Ziggie had just given the performance of his life. He was dying, obviously in pain and very weak, yet he had tapped that loving heart one more time to give his pals his final gift—a vintage Ziggie performance. It was truly a night to remember.

Ziggie died one month later. Appropriately, "76" was buried in the seventh month on the sixth day (7/6/84).

As George and I began our drive home later that night, George settled comfortably in the passenger seat next to me, took a puff on his newly lit cigar, and said in a soft and gentle way, "Some night, huh brother?" He paused and added, "We are really lucky guys."

I was so filled with the emotion of the evening all I could say was, "Some night, we sure are lucky."

Yes, we were lucky. Lucky to be alive when our pal was dying, lucky to be Ziggie's close friends, and unbelievably lucky to be part of such a gathering where the kind of love and affection exhibited that night between grown men was not an exception, but occurred every time we got together.

Very few, if any of us, had any idea when we entered Notre Dame that years later we would be so blessed as to be part of such a group. It is no wonder that our annual football team reunion is eagerly anticipated by all the teammates. We look forward to being together, not only for the pleasure of being with old pals and sharing laughter as we tell our stories, but, more importantly, so that we can be nourished by the spirit that comes from a group in which this type of love is always present.

Somehow the funny stories, Ziggie's role in our lives, Frank Leahy's and the other coaches' influence, and, most of all, the mutual love we have for each other had to be preserved in writing. I realized that night someone had to write a book to tell about this amazing group of men, but I did not know who it would be. The seed of an idea was planted.

In the months and years that followed I taped as many of the teammate gatherings as possible with the thought that someone could use the information for a book. A typical gathering occurred in June of 1988 when we were sitting around the table with Moose Krause at the South Bend Country Club after a round of golf. Present were a group of Leahy's "Lads," players from the Notre Dame teams of the 1940s: George Connor, Creighton Miller, John Lujack, Jerry Groom, Mike and Buddy Romano, Elmer Angsman, and me. We were engaged in our favorite pastime—telling Ziggie stories and other stories about our days on Cartier Field under Coach Leahy, Krause, and the other assistant coaches.

When it was Moose Krause's turn, he told of the day when Coach Leahy was leaving the locker room for the practice field and he spotted Ziggie taking a shower. Leahy said, "Hmmm Zygmont, practice begins in 15 minutes. You'll be late."

Ziggie replied, "Coach, I have never been late for practice. I'll be on time."

As the coach began to leave, he turned and asked, "Zygmont, why are you taking a shower before practice?"

Ziggie quickly answered, "Coach, it gets too damn crowded after practice."

As it had so many times in the past, this brought a gale of laughter from the group and somebody said, maybe for the hundredth time, "Somebody has to write the book." We all agreed that, yes, somebody had to write a book to preserve all the stories that we have been telling and retelling for years, but, as was the case when it had been said before, the "somebody" was never identified.

In 1989, during the Notre Dame-Michigan State game weekend, these and other teammates gathered for our yearly reunion, now affectionately called the "Ziggie Reunion" in honor of our departed teammate and spiritual leader. Again the stories and laughter abounded throughout the weekend and the inevitable refrain was repeated again, "Somebody has to write a book."

Driving alone back home to Chicago from the weekend, I reflected on my blessings to be a part of such a great group of people, and I recalled the laughs and tears we shared at the reunion. I actually laughed out loud as I thought of some of the stories and heard myself say, "Somebody has to write the book."

After driving for several minutes without any particular thought in mind, there seemed to be a voice in my head—a very loud voice—that said quite clearly, "You write the book!" I was stunned not only by the force and suddenness of the thought, but also by the very idea that I could or should write a book. We had always said the "somebody" should either be a sportswriter or journalist, somebody with a background as a writer, and hopefully someone with name recognition to add credibility to the enterprise. I quickly dismissed the idea and attributed my crazy thoughts to being overstimulated by the excitement of the weekend.

As the days passed and I settled down to my normal work schedule, the thought returned. At first it was occasional, then it progressed to a constant nagging, "Write the book, write the book." As I drove back and forth to work and to other appointments, I had the same debate with myself.

"You can't write a book, the idea is ridiculous. It has to be a professional, someone with experience in writing." The response was, "We have been saying that for years and we are no closer now to finding someone than we were two years ago. If we keep talking and not doing anything, these stories will never be told outside our group and when we depart this world, a part of Notre Dame history will be lost forever. Write the book."

To escape the now-constant torment of my internal debate, I sat down at the word processor in my converted home office and began to record some of the stories and sketch an outline for a book. My hope was that I would not be able to think of anything to write and I could then put this crazy idea to rest once and for all.

Much to my surprise the words seemed to write themselves. The excitement grew as the various stories filled my mind. I wrote an outline for the book and the idea of visiting my teammates to interview them with tape recorder in hand took shape. I finally concluded, rightly or wrongly, and no doubt with a great deal of rationalization, that maybe I should write the book.

I informed Alice and our four grown children (Kevin, Terri, Kacky, and Pattie) of my decision. Since this was my first attempt at such an endeavor, the kids would have been justified in asking skeptically, "Dad's writing a book?" But they didn't. Instead, the enterprise became a family undertaking with everyone pitching in to help. The project seemed to take on a life of its own. It became known around the Connor household as "The Book."

One Sunday night, after about four years of work, I completed the manuscript. That same night, Chicago's south side, where we live, experienced an unbelievable lightning storm. I happened to be talking to our youngest daughter, Pattie, the following day and told her I had completed "The Book" the night before. She responded, "Wasn't it nice of Moose and Ziggie to arrange a fireworks display to help you celebrate?"

What follows is not a football book in the usual sense, or a book of just anecdotes without the "feel" of having been there, but rather it is a people book. It is a book about the players and coaches and the stories they tell of what it was like to be a part of the teams of the 1940s. It tells what has happened to them since those times and why the teammates and coaches meet every year to share each other's company.

To me it is a history of the times. But on another level, it is a love story—about the love of teammates for each other, and their individual and collective love for the school of Our Lady.

Chapter One

LEAHY'S EARLY YEARS

Our story begins in the spring of 1941 when Frank Leahy, at the age of 33, took over as the head football coach and athletic director at the University of Notre Dame. He came well prepared to take on this new assignment.

Frank Leahy seemed destined to be a head football coach from his early days in Winner, South Dakota. He displayed an intense desire to learn all he could about the game which would dominate his life. His football education began early in Winner, where, as a halfback, he was fortunate to have Earl Walsh as his football coach. Walsh played three years under Knute Rockne and was the famous George Gipp's understudy on the 1920 Notre Dame National Championship team. Walsh knew fundamental football and he imparted his knowledge of the lessons learned from Rockne to the young, eager Leahy.

After earning letters in football, baseball, and basketball at Winner High School for three years, Leahy and his family moved to Omaha, Nebraska. Leahy attended Central High School in Omaha his senior year where George Schmidt, the former Nebraska star, moved Frank to tackle. He again earned letters in all three sports, captaining all three teams.

Leahy also gained a reputation as an excellent amateur boxer and he seriously considered a professional boxing career. But an after-dinner talk by Knute Rockne and discussions with his former coach, Earl Walsh, persuaded Leahy to accept a Notre Dame scholarship. He entered Notre Dame in the fall of 1927. When Leahy filled out a questionnaire for the freshman football team, one of the questions was, "Why did you come to Notre Dame?" Leahy answered simply, "Because of Rock."

As a freshman he played under Tommy Mills, who, later as head

1

coach of Georgetown University, gave Leahy his first coaching job. From the beginning of his college football career at Notre Dame, Leahy showed an intelligence peculiarly suited for the game of football. This ability combined with a winning attitude made Leahy one of Rockne's favorites. Perhaps Rockne saw some of himself in the young man: Both had keen football minds, were completely dedicated to the sport, had a competitive desire to win, and both had been boxers when they were younger.

As a junior Leahy enjoyed the ultimate experience—starting right tackle on the team that went on to win the National Championship. (This team was captained by John Law, who later earned fame as the warden of Sing Sing Prison.) Unfortunately, before the 1930 season began, Leahy suffered a severe knee injury that forced him to miss his entire senior season. He did, however, have the opportunity to assist with coaching the line and to spend a considerable amount of time watching Rockne and his assistants coach the ends and tackles. In so doing, he gained a knowledge of play at all positions that he could not have absorbed had he competed as a tackle.

Another consolation for the injury was that, after the season ended, Rockne asked Leahy to go with him to the Mayo Clinic in Rochester, Minnesota. Leahy could have his bad knee examined while Rockne was being treated for his chronic phlebitis. During their stay at the clinic, Leahy had the opportunity to spend time with Rockne as they shared a two-bed room.

Years later Leahy recalled that time for a group of sportswriters: "During the week we were there, Rock did practically all the talking. For instance, he'd say, 'Frank, do you remember this play that happened in the Southern Cal game last fall?' And Rock would explain the situation. Then we would discuss that play for as much as a full morning.

"In the week I was confined to a hospital bed I learned more about football and the technique of coaching than in all my previous college playing. Right there I decided to go into coaching. When I told Rock of my choice, he said, 'I think you've made a wise one, and I'm going to start to work on getting you a job as soon as we get back to South Bend.'"

Rockne did as he promised and went a step further. When talking to the press about his stay at the Mayo Clinic, Rockne said, "We have an injured tackle on the squad named Frank Leahy who has all the earmarks of a coach. He may not be in the headlines now, but he'll be on everybody's tongue in the years to come."

Leahy graduated from Notre Dame in 1931 and began furthering his football education by serving as an assistant coach at Georgetown University and Michigan State University. While he was an assistant line coach at Michigan State under Jimmy Crowley (of Four Horsemen fame), Crowley took the head coaching job at Fordham University and he took his young assistant with him to help coach the line.

The Fordham experience was the perfect next step for Leahy's continuing football education as it gave him the opportunity to continue his training under Crowley and to work with some outstanding players. During his stay at Fordham, the famous "Seven Blocks of Granite" played. Among these seven several stand out. For example, Alex Wojciechowicz, the great center, would go on to a long and successful professional career with the Philadelphia Eagles. (In 1968 he earned election into the Pro Football Hall of Fame in Canton, Ohio.) Also on the line for this famous seven was a short, but powerfully built guard named Vince Lombardi. Lombardi became known as a builder of men and, as every football fan knows, became a legend by leading the Green Bay Packers to five National Football League titles. Not many people would question that three of the best coaches in the annals of football were Rockne, Leahy, and Lombardi. It is interesting to note that Leahy was Rockne's pupil and Lombardi was Leahy's pupil. Each of these men were different in their style of coaching, yet all three were superb teachers. Leahy, above all else, was a student of the game of football as well as a teacher.

A third member of that line and the captain of the "Seven Blocks of Granite" team was a man who would be associated with Leahy to the end of his coaching career, Johnny Druze. Druze was a great high school athlete. At Irvington High School in Irvington, New Jersey, he won letters in basketball, baseball, and football all four years, was captain of all three sports in his senior year, and was named to the All-State team in baseball and football.

Crowley's assistant coaches at Fordham were all Notre Dame men: Earl Walsh (ND 1922) was the backfield coach, Glen "Judge" Carberry (ND 1923) handled the tackles, Frank Leahy (ND 1931) coached the centers and guards, and Hughie Devore (ND 1934) was the new freshmen coach. Working side by side with such colleagues contributed to Leahy's growing talents as a coach.

3

According to Druze, it was Hughie Devore who initiated the custom of the position coach personally playing against his players in one-on-one drills—which would become a hallmark of future Leahy-coached teams. Devore started this practice with the freshmen. He would work first with the ends, then the tackles, and on down the line. As Druze says, "Crowley must have said something to Devore because he would go up to the varsity practice and do the same with them. Eventually, Carberry and Leahy started to do the same thing."

The importance of this method of coaching—whereby the assistant coaches would, without the benefit of football equipment, take on each player in a one-on-one blocking drill—cannot be overemphasized. The drill ran like this: An assistant coach, for instance the guard coach, would call out the name of one of the guards (usually the best). That player would line up in his three-point stance in front of the assistant coach who took on the part of the defensive player. With the rest of the guards looking on, the coach would announce the snap count, for example, "on two." The coach would then, acting as a back, call out the signals, "Ready, set, down, hut one, hut two," and the player would drive into the coach as if he were in a live scrimmage or a game. The coach would ward off the block as an actual defensive player would.

You might think that the coach was at a tremendous disadvantage in this drill because he was not protected by pads and was facing a big, young, well-conditioned player. However, some of Leahy's later assistants, such as Moose Krause and Wally Ziemba, were as big, if not bigger, than the players they were facing. Also, all the assistant coaches were in top physical condition themselves and were not too many years older than the players.

Moreover, in conducting this drill the coaches had two advantages over the players. First, they were masters of the correct technique for warding off a blocker and, most importantly of all, they cheated on the count. This means that when they barked out the signals and got to "hut one," they hit the player who was prepared to hit "on two." With this advantage, more often than not, the coach would get the best of the player and succeed in throwing him to the ground.

The assistant coaches had to be in top physical shape to do this, particularly since the coaches conducted this drill not just with one player, but, at least once a week, with all the players in his position, which most times meant roughly 14 players.

The significance of this drill is that it gave the assistant coach direct, first-hand experience of the blocking ability of each player in his group. The coach could personally assess each player's ability to get off the ball, how hard he hit, his technique, and the player's determination to stay with the block. This information was vital to the assistant coaches in rating each player under his charge. This daily rating of each player by the assistants would become a regular part of Leahy's coaching procedure when he later coached at Boston College and at Notre Dame.

"I didn't get to know Leahy very well then," says Druze. "He was mainly concerned with the guards and tackles. I played under Hugh Devore, who had become the varsity end coach. We all used to watch when Leahy would take on Wojciechowicz, who was a real fighter. It was always quite a battle. You could see Leahy's legs go up in the air and come down, but he would go right back at it and give Wojie a great battle. That's what made Wojie so great—and All-American in college and a Hall of Fame player in the pros."

Years later Wojciechowicz confirmed how tough Leahy was as an assistant coach. He told of the day he and Leahy were squaring off on the field as Leahy attempted to demonstrate some fine point about Woj's play. On the charge Woj caught Leahy on the lip with a shoulder and, besides causing a deep cut, loosened one of Leahy's teeth. Woj stopped, figuring the session had been concluded. But, he recalled, Leahy merely spat out a bloody tooth and said, "Okay, lad, let's try again."

Leahy was married in Druze's senior year. Leahy and his wife, Floss, occasionally invited Druze and one of his teammates to dinner at their place in the Bronx. As Druze tells it, "I got to know Frank fairly well on a personal level. Even then Leahy was quiet, reserved, very polite, very formal, and well mannered."

Leahy's six years as an assistant coach at Fordham were formative ones for the future head coach of Notre Dame. He learned a great deal about both the fine points of the game and how to impart this knowledge to his players. Because of the excellent record of the Fordham teams during those years and the outstanding line play, Leahy received attention on a national level as an excellent prospect for a head coaching position.

Several offers to become a head coach did come in. The one

5

from Boston College was the opportunity he was looking for. In 1939, he signed a two-year contract and became the head football coach of the Jesuit school in Boston.

His first priority as coach was to enlist the services of some top-flight assistants. He knew the type of assistant he wanted—bright, tough young men who were capable enough athletes themselves to take on the players in one-on-one drills. He had learned at Fordham that these drills were an excellent teaching tool and were invaluable in assessing a player's potential.

His first selection was his former player at Fordham, John Druze. Druze had just finished a year of pro football with the Brooklyn Dodgers when he got a wire from Leahy asking him to go with him as his tackle and end coach. Leahy then hired a coach from Texas as his backfield coach, Ed "Tex" McKeever. Eventually, Leahy completed his staff by hiring John Del Isola (who had played for the New York Giants). After a year, Del Isola left and Leahy hired Joe McArdle, another of his former Fordham players who played in 1932, 1933, and 1934. McArdle, like Druze, was to stay with Leahy through his coaching career.

Leahy and his staff had the good fortune at Boston College to inherit a talented freshman team and some outstanding players from the varsity team. From the beginning, Leahy had the nucleus of an excellent team. Leahy and his staff went right to work on honing the skills of their players and, as Leahy so often did, switched the positions of some of the players to maximize their skills.

The team responded to the new coach by going undefeated in 1939—Leahy's first year as a head coach. In the post-season, the team played in the Cotton Bowl, but lost to Clemson, 9-6.

The following year the team won all but one game and was invited to play in the Sugar Bowl against a powerful University of Tennessee team. Boston College defeated General Robert Neyland's unbeaten and untied Volunteers by the score of 19-13 in what was considered to be one of the great upsets of modern times.

With only two losses in two years and two post-season bowl invitations, Leahy was offered and signed a five-year contract to continue to coach at Boston College. On the day he signed the contract, John Curley, the graduate manager of athletics said, "If Notre Dame ever asks you back, Frank, we'll be happy to hand you your release." In commenting about that remark years later, Leahy said, "Little did he or I know that BC would have a chance to live up to that statement less than two weeks later."

Days later, Notre Dame announced that Elmer Layden had re-signed at Notre Dame to accept a five-year contract as president of the National Football League. On the list of potential successors were: Frank Leahy of Boston College, Clipper Smith of Villanova, Jimmy Crowley of Fordham, Buck Shaw of Santa Clara, Harry Stuhldreher of Wisconsin, Frank Thomas of Alabama, and Gus Dorais of Detroit.

Within another week, Leahy received a call at his Waban, Massachusetts, home offering him the job. Arrangements were made for a meeting between Leahy and Frank Cavanaugh in Albany, New York, to discuss the details of the offer. A few days later, Leahy asked Druze if he could take him for a ride the next day. Druze, not knowing what the request was about, told Leahy that his then-fiancee, Rose, was in town and he was showing her around. Then he asked, "What did you have in mind?"

To this Leahy replied, "Oh, no never mind John, you take care of Rose—show her the area."

Little did Druze know that Notre Dame had offered Leahy the head coaching job and he wanted Druze to drive him to Albany for the prearranged meeting with Father Cavanaugh.

Leahy did commit to coach at Notre Dame during his meeting with Father Cavanaugh, but the news was not released to the press until several days later. In the meantime, Druze drove Rose back to Irvington where he was going to stay for a few days to scout some football prospects for the upcoming Boston College season. While Druze was there, he received a telegram from Leahy asking him to telephone him. (Leahy sent the telegram because he knew Druze's parents' house was without a telephone.) Druze immediately placed a call to Leahy, who said, "John, I have an opportunity to go out to the Midwest."

"The Midwest?"

"Ah, yes, it's a school in the Midwest—it's a big institution."

"You mean Notre Dame?"

"Yes, Notre Dame. Would you like to come with me?"

It took Druze all of a second to respond, "Coach, don't say anymore. I'm with you all the way."

Leahy, then talked to McKeever and McArdle, who also agreed to accompany him to Notre Dame.

When the story finally broke in the Boston newspapers that

Leahy was leaving Boston College to take the head coaching job at Notre Dame, the Boston press was not very pleased with Leahy and wrote about him accordingly. The writers and the BC alumni were mad at Leahy because he had promised to stay at Boston College for another five years and they felt betrayed that he was leaving to coach someone else. However, whether they knew it or chose to ignore it, Leahy carried with him a letter of release from the Rev. Francis J. Murphy, president of Boston College, so he felt no guilt in leaving BC to return to his alma mater.

In a matter of days after the announcement, Leahy was back on the Notre Dame campus to meet with Fr. Hugh O'Donnell to sign the contract making him the head football coach and athletic director. Years later, Leahy characterized that meeting by saying, "That was my greatest day in football."

Druze laughed when he recalled for me some of the lighter moments of their days at Boston College: "All of the coaches, with the exception of McKeever, lived in a rooming house and I was the only one who had a car. It got to the point that I had to wait for everything. I had to wait for the guys to get up and have breakfast and then drive them out to the school. Then I had to wait after practice until everyone was ready to drive home.

"Leahy didn't have too many clothes at the time and what he had were kind of old-fashioned. I, on the other hand, was the type of guy who liked to dress well. I had new suits and ties and things like that. As time went along, Leahy fell into the habit of borrowing my shirt or a tie. He would say, 'Oh, John, you wear nice shirts and ties, would there be the possibility of borrowing a shirt?' I would say, 'Sure, go ahead, Coach.' So he would borrow a shirt and never return it. It got to be a habit." Druze added that he was happy when Bernie Crimmins joined the coaching staff after the war. Crimmins, like Druze, was a good dresser and was also about the same size as Leahy. Much to Druze's delight, Crimmins became the new part-time supplier of clothes for the coach.

Frank Leahy was ready to move on. He had served his apprenticeship as an assistant coach for eight years at three different schools and had been a successful head coach for two years. He had learned his craft well, paid his dues, and was now ready to test his football mettle as the head football coach at Notre Dame.

8

Chapter Two

NOTRE DAME

Frank Leahy arrived on the Notre Dame campus in February 1941 eager to assume his duties as head football coach. His dream of one day returning to his alma mater was fulfilled. Leahy had been away from Notre Dame only 10 years when he assumed his new duties, but he brought to his new coaching assignment experience gathered through years of hard work and study as a player, an assistant coach, and a head coach.

He knew the kind of team he would like to field. He wanted a team that was in better physical condition than any of his opponents, one that would play touch football, one well drilled in the fundamentals of blocking and tackling—in short, a team composed of players ready to play all-out on every play. He liked the running game, but he also wanted to find a passer who could break the game open and devastate the spirit of the other team.

Like any good coach, Leahy knew he had to shape his team according to the talent available to him. Thus his first task was to evaluate the players returning for the 1941 season. Leahy had always exhibited a remarkable capacity for grading the talent of a player and, if necessary, switching a player's position in order to field the best 11 players.

On St. Patrick's Day, March 17, 1941, on the opening day of spring practice, Leahy and his staff made their first public appearance as coaches at Notre Dame. It was a cold, blustery day. All the sportswriters gathered around Leahy and his assistants outside Cartier Field before practice began. Leahy had on a sweatsuit with a hood, which served as his only protection against the biting wind. In contrast, Druze, McArdle, McKeever, and Bill Cerney wore big Mackinaw coats over their warm Notre Dame sweaters. (Cerney, a holdover from Layden, had been added to the staff to help coach the backs.) Leahy talked to the writers about his assessment of the team he was about to coach and his plans for their training during spring practice. He then looked at the assistant coaches and said, "My coaching staff, they believe in warmth. See what nice jackets they have on." The coaches got the hint and immediately shed the jackets they were wearing. From that day on, the assistant coaches always wore what Leahy wore.

In the weeks before that first day of practice the coaching staff had studied the previous year's game films until they had a good idea of the talent at hand. The first few days of practice were devoted to finding out if their evaluations were correct. To accomplish this, each coach went one-on-one against each of his players. For example, Druze was in charge of the tackles and ends. He had them line up from goal line to goal line and proceeded to spend three or four minutes with each man. It was amazing what could be learned in so short a time about the potential of each player, especially the linemen.

From conducting this drill for two years at Boston College and while recruiting, these coaches had developed a knack for sizing up a player in a short period of time. They looked for several things: How did the player set up in his stance? How quickly did he get off the ball? How hard was his initial thump? Did he drive his legs? How was his technique? How strong was he? As the coaches went down the line they made mental notes about each player that they would pass on to Leahy that evening when they reviewed the day's practice. This individual review of the team personnel by the assistant coaches in their evening meeting would become a daily routine as long as Leahy coached.

The Players

Leahy had inherited from his predecessor, Elmer Layden, a talented group of football players. On paper it looked as though there were only four first-string players from the 1940 season returning for the 1941 season: Bob Dove at end, Paul Lillis at tackle, Bob Hargrave at quarterback, and Steve Juzwik at halfback. But also returning was a cadre of seasoned, tough players who had seen a lot of action the previous year. This group included Bernie Crimmins, Wally Ziemba, Bill Earley, Lou Rymkus, Jim Brutz, Jack Barry, Ray Ebli, Harry

Wright, Bob Maddock, Joe Laiber, George Murphy, John Kovatch, Larry Sullivan, and the elusive running back, Dippy Evans. In addition there were some outstanding sophomores such as Angelo Bertelli, Creighton Miller, Bob McBride, Pat Filley, Matt Bolger, and Pete Ashbaugh to complement the many veterans.

These players had been recruited and coached by Layden. They had to make big adjustments to the methods of Frank Leahy after having played for Layden. Layden was a strong coach who demanded the best from his players. Leahy demanded perfection. Although some of the players might have questioned Leahy's methods, few, if any, doubted his ability to teach the techniques of each position, his skills as a psychologist, or his genius for producing a winning team.

As Bob Hargrave, the quarterback of the 1940 team who received honorable mention on the All-American team that year, puts it, "Frank Leahy was a tough taskmaster. He was not always easy to play for. At times I doubted his tactics, but I later found that, in his own way, he did have the best interests of Notre Dame and his 'Lads' at heart."

Ray Ebli, a veteran senior tackle known as "Lil Abner," said about Leahy, "He was a taskmaster, a perfectionist, a good teacher of techniques. His practices were always filled with tension as compared to a more relaxed atmosphere under Elmer Layden."

In comparing Layden with Leahy, Bernie Crimmins said, "I'd have to say Elmer was more of a diplomat. He stressed a lot of the things Frank did and he believed in contact on the practice field, but not as much as Frank. Frank thought you had to have a tremendous amount [of contact] and I agreed with him—that you have to prepare well. I believe Frank's teams were a little better conditioned than Elmer's were. Both were excellent coaches, but as for the importance of getting all the details, Frank stressed more. So, I'd say the two biggest differences were there was more contact and more attention to details under Leahy. Another thing is that Frank had the ability to get more out of an athlete. He could convince folks to do far beyond what they thought they were capable of doing."

Larry Sullivan, another tackle who played under both Layden and Leahy, contrasted the two by saying, "They were two different personalities and those who had the opportunity and pleasure to be associated with both of them gained immeasurably. Their goals were identical but their approach was vastly different. Coach Layden could be a leader of the Diplomatic Corps. Coach Leahy could be the leader of the Gung-Ho troops, but outwardly he had a silver tongue with gents and lads."

This use of "gents and lads" by Leahy was something the players had to get accustomed to (as did all the players on all the Leahy teams that followed). Leahy had a very distinct way of speaking which sounded very formal. When talking to or about one of his players, he used the player's full first name instead of the commonly used nickname. For example, Jim would be James and Bob would be Robert, and so on. Sometimes he would use the person's full name when he wanted to emphasize a point, and, more often than not, would start his comment with, "Oh." For example, he might say, "Oh, Robert Dove, you missed that block. Let's run that play over again and see if Robert Dove wants to block that tackle." When he spoke to or about the team as a whole, he would call them "Gents" or "Lads." When he spoke to the assistant coaches in front of the players, he always addressed them as coach—"Coach McArdle, let's see if your guards can block" was a comment that was heard quite often. He insisted that all the players call the assistant coaches, "Coach." It goes without saying that he was called "Coach."

As for the players themselves, there were some outstanding ones on that 1941 squad who would gain football fame playing under Leahy.

Bob Dove

Dove, a junior end in 1941, was recruited for Notre Dame by Benny Barrett (who himself had played for Elmer Layden at Duquesne University). Dove had won All-City honors playing end for South High School in Youngstown, Ohio. When Dove made a trip to South Bend, he was given a tour that included a stop at Breen-Phillips Hall, which had just been completed. A student guide took Dove into a big room that had a private shower, a setup which looked very nice to Dove. He asked the student, "Is this a freshman hall?" "Yeah, this is a freshman hall," replied his escort. Dove went back to Youngstown very pleased with his visit.

Shortly thereafter, Dove decided to go to Notre Dame. When he first arrived on campus to begin the school year in the late summer of 1939, he was greeted by one of the Holy Cross Brothers who directed him to the Administration Building. On the main floor he encountered Brother Pat who inquired if he was a freshman, and Dove acknowledged that he was. Brother Pat directed him down a hall where they made a left turn down another hall lined with big green lockers. Brother Pat stopped in front of one of the lockers and said, "This is your locker where you will keep your clothes."

Brother Pat then took Dove into a room where there were 169 sinks and stopped in front of sink number 163 and said, "This is your sink where you can keep your shaving gear." By this time Dove was looking at Brother Pat wondering if all this was some kind of joke. Brother Pat took Dove to the steps that led to a large room called Bronson Hall where there were rows of large green desks with open tops and he pointed out the one that Dove would use.

Brother Pat then took Dove to the long dormitory above to an area they called "the sheets." This was an area where the pipe network with white canvas sheets formed a small "room"—complete with a single bed, a little carpet about one foot by one foot so your feet would not get cold when you got up in the morning. Brother Pat said, "This is where you sleep, but you can't get in here until after 8 o'clock in the evening and it's closed after 10 o'clock in the morning."

A little later that day Dove ran into the student who had taken him to Breen-Phillips Hall on his visit and asked, "How about that Breen-Phillips where I stayed and that nice room I used?" The student laughed and said, "That was the rector's room." Dove's vision of a pleasant room with a shower quickly vanished as he learned he was to be a resident of Bronson Hall, not the posh Breen-Phillips, and certainly not of the rector's room.

Dove's surprises as a new student at Notre Dame were not over. He was handed a slip of paper and told to report to Mr. Z., the chief assistant to Mr. Lovely who was in charge of the dining hall where all the students ate their meals. Dove was wearing a new grey gabardine suit given to him by his uncle before departing Youngstown. When Dove arrived at the dining hall, Mr. Z. said, "Where have you been? Get over there and rack those dishes." Dove quickly learned that in those days a full athletic scholarship meant that for your room and board you had to wait on tables three meals a day, seven days a week or rack dishes once a day, seven days a week. Dove had his choice, so he chose to be a "racker." Dove went back and changed clothes to begin his job.

Nor was Dove's first day of football practice too pleasant. Like all freshman players, he met for the first time Notre Dame's equipment manager, John "Mac" McAllister. Mac had been at Notre Dame since the Rockne days. There was no question that Mac ran his equipment room as he pleased. One of his treats in life was making life miserable for incoming freshman ballplayers.

On Dove's first day of practice he drew his equipment from Mac without incident, or so he thought. He put his football gear on the bench in front of his locker and began to get dressed for practice. When he turned around to get his socks, he found there were none there. Mystified, he returned to Mac and said, "You didn't give me any socks."

Mac shouted back, "What do you mean I didn't give you any socks? You're not getting another pair."

So Dove, not knowing whether Mac gave him socks or whether they had been "borrowed" by someone, dressed in his football gear without any socks.

During practice after going through several drills, Dove started to limp a little. The end coach, Joe Benda, asked, "Dove, what's the matter with you?"

"I think I'm getting a blister on my foot," replied Dove.

The coach looked down at Dove's feet and demanded, "Where are your socks?"

Dove answered, "He said he gave me some and I'm not getting another pair."

Steaming, Benda ordered, "You go back in there and tell McAllister to give you some socks."

Dove got his socks and returned to the practice field where he ended up the day on the ninth string out of 11. Dove did not have any more equipment problems, or any other problems, that year.

George Murphy, who would captain the 1942 team, and Dove worked their way from that ninth string on the freshman team to the first team by the end of the year.

As a sophomore, Dove became a regular on the varsity after the second game of the year against Georgia Tech. During that game Dove went downfield from his left-end position on a kickoff. At about the 20-yard line he had a perfect shot at Johnny Bosch, Georgia Tech's elusive halfback, and hit him with what Dove thought was a great tackle. As Dove tells it, "I don't know what happened. He must have shot straight up in the air, because the next thing I knew, he was

14

gone and I slid right on my belly. Well, I figured the big eye [the camera] was on me, so I jumped up and started running. Our safety man, Steve Bagarus, was using the sidelines and jockeying for position on Bosch, who might have slowed down a little, then cut and ran by Bagarus, who jumped and went in front of me. I stepped over him, caught my toe, and on the five-yard line I missed Bosch again as he ran in the end zone for a touchdown."

The following Monday when Coach Layden was showing the team the movies from that game, he gave the regulars hell for their spiritless play. At the point where Dove's missed tackles were about to be shown, Layden said, "I want you to watch this next play." Dove, knowing what was coming, sank as low in his seat as he could. Layden went on, "I want you to watch this next play. Put it on slow and I want you to see something. There is a sophomore out there playing and I want you to notice something. Who was the first man to come downfield and miss Johnny Bosch? I want you to notice on the five-yard line—who was the last man to miss him? The same sophomore." Layden looked at Dove and said, "Dove, when we go out on the field this afternoon, you start on the first team."

The following week the *South Bend Tribune* reported that Dove was the first sophomore to start a game for a Notre Dame team in 11 years. Dove smiles when he recalls that he made the first team by missing two tackles on the same play. Dove started the rest of the games that year.

It did not take long before the coaching staff knew who the best players were. Leahy believed—as did his mentor, Knute Rockne—in putting the best 11 men on the field, even if he had to switch the positions of some of his players. Switching a player's position was something Leahy would do throughout his coaching career. Leahy saw many moves he wanted to make.

Wally Ziemba was a big rough player who earned his monogram as a sophomore on the 1940 team as a backup tackle to Paul Lillis, who was returning as a senior and was the captain-elect of the team. Ziemba, at 6-feet-4 and 245 pounds, was too good a player not to be in the staring lineup, so Leahy switched him to center. (In 1946, when Ziemba was on the coaching staff, he asked Leahy why he had switched him to center in 1941. Leahy said, "Walter, you had such a big backside that putting you at center spread the line out.")

Leahy's second significant move was shifting Harry "The Horse" Wright, who had been a reverse fullback the previous year, to quarterback. He saw in Wright a smart, determined player who was an excellent blocker and had the kind of football mind that Leahy liked as a signal caller.

The team seemed to be shaping up according to Leahy's plan. There was, however, one notable exception. Leahy had still not found that combination tailback and passer he sought. However, he did have his eye on a sophomore named Angelo Bertelli from West Springfield, Massachusetts. Leahy knew Bertelli well from his high school days at Cathedral High in Springfield when he tried to recruit him to attend Boston College. In Leahy's mind, Bertelli was in the image of Charlie O'Rourke, the tailback who was so successful for him at Boston College. Leahy wanted a strong passing attack, so after keeping his eye on Bertelli for some time, he made his decision and moved Bertelli from the lowly seventh team to the starting left halfback (tailback). It could be said that Bertelli got the break of his life when Frank Leahy was made the new head football coach at Notre Dame to succeed Elmer Layden.

Prior to his move to first string, Angelo wondered at times if he would ever play for Notre Dame. His freshman year had not been an easy one.

Angelo Bertelli

Bertelli transferred from West Lafayette High to Cathedral High (the only Catholic school in the area). This proved to be a milestone in his football career. As Bertelli recalls it, "Milt Piepul, who was captain of the 1940 Notre Dame team, was also a Cathedral man. Piepul was from Thompsonville, Connecticut, and I was from West Springfield, so we were both transplanted football players who went to Cathedral because it was the best in the area and had the best coach, Billy Wise [who played for Holy Cross]. Transferring from West Lafayette to Cathedral was one of the best things I ever did in my life. It gave me the opportunity to play with some real good football players and we won the Western Massachusetts championship two years in a row."

In his senior year, Bertelli was named the most valuable football player in Western Massachusetts and was dubbed "The Springfield Rifle" for his passing ability. His fellow Cathedral man, Milt Piepul, talked to Layden about Bertelli. It was not long before Bertelli was offered a football scholarship at Notre Dame. He was delighted to receive the offer, but hesitated at accepting it because he thought, considering all of the excellent football talent already at Notre Dame, he might be just another of the many, many accomplished backs.

Moreover, in addition to playing football, Bertelli was an excellent hockey player. He grew up across the street from the home of a minor league hockey team, the Springfield Indians, so it was natural that the boys in that area grew up playing a lot of hockey. Because of his love of hockey, Bertelli gave serious consideration to the scholarship offers he received from some of the eastern schools that played hockey (such as Dartmouth, Boston College, and Cornell). But, in the end, Bertelli decided he wanted to go the football route and opted to accept the offer from Notre Dame.

Bert did not have an enjoyable freshman year at Notre Dame in 1940. He says, "When I first came on the campus, I was lonely. I would sit in the stands and watch the varsity play and count the number of left halfbacks who were returning the next year and there were four. I was running on the fourth string on the freshman team and they only kept about six teams, so I said, 'Where am I going?'

"I was afraid to go home at Christmastime because when you leave western Massachusetts as the most valuable player, everybody in your hometown and in that area is saying Bertelli is at Notre Dame and will be playing next year. I was very disillusioned and very disappointed the fall of my freshman year. I just couldn't see how I was going to move up and possibly play. There are an awful lot of people that get lost in the shuffle."

During the early days of spring practice under Leahy, things had not changed. This led Bertelli to continue to question his future as a Notre Dame football player. Then Bertelli was "discovered" by Leahy. But it did not happen immediately according to Bertelli. "I don't think he [Leahy] realized for a while that I was there. I was just there—no one even knew my name or anything about me, but I was there going to practice every day. Running on the seventh team you get disillusioned. Then almost overnight he seemed to say, "We've got to go along with someone who throws the ball,' and thank God he did."

Bertelli not only started that year, but passed for over 1,000 yards, earning him second place in the balloting for the Heisman Award as the outstanding college football player in the nation.

Through the years a myth has developed concerning Bertelli's running ability. I have read articles about Bertelli that state he was the worst runner Leahy ever saw. This is pure nonsense. In truth, Bertelli was a complete football player and not just a passer. One only has to examine his defensive accomplishments in 1941 and 1942 to realize he was quick on his feet and could run with the best of the day. As a ball carrier he was above average, but few teams had such extraordinary running backs as Dippy Evans, Steve Juzwik, and Creighton Miller. Leahy did the wise thing in making the other backs the key runners.

The coaches spent the remainder of the spring practice working with the players on their fundamentals and trying to blend the players into a unit that could compete as a team. In those days players had to play both on offense and defense, so Leahy worked the team hard, mindful that conditioning would play a big part in any game. By the end of spring practice the team was beginning to look like the type of team Leahy envisioned. He had already shifted the positions of 13 of the players, but there was one more move that Leahy knew he had to make to have the team he wanted.

Bernie Crimmins played fullback in spring practice, his first under Leahy, and was even allowed to play baseball when Leahy would let him out of football practice. After spring practice ended, Crimmins was called into Leahy's office and was informed that Leahy was going to make him a "glorified fullback."

"What's that?" asked Crimmins.

Leahy answered, "Instead of carrying the ball, you're going to lead the ball carriers."

Crimmins recalls that Leahy told him he would continue to play lineback on defense. "There was a lot of footwork he wanted me to get down. He came to Louisville that summer and took me to the park one day and showed me how to pull out and things of that nature. He told me, 'You work on that now.'"

Bernie Crimmins

Crimmins was from Louisville, Kentucky, where he attended St. Xavier's High School. While there, he starred in football, baseball, and basketball. Crimmins was recruited by many Big Ten schools as well as quite a few of the schools in the Southern Conference. Being from Louisville, the University of Kentucky wanted very much to have Crimmins play there. The governor of Kentucky let his feelings about the matter be known to Crimmins and his family. Notre Dame was also very interested in Crimmins and this was passed on to him through George Keogan, Notre Dame's basketball coach.

Crimmins laughed when he recounted to me how the decision was made as to which college he would attend. "I was confused for a while as to where I wanted to go. I visited a few campuses and they all treated me very well. Then one night I was sitting at the dinner table with my brothers and my father. My brothers were ribbing me about whether I was going to Kentucky because the governor was try-ing to get me to go there. So, after about a half hour or so of every-body ribbing me about this and that, all at once Dad hit his hand on the table and said, 'He's going to Notre Dame.' And that was that. I went to Notre Dame."

Crimmins would earn All-American honors in 1941, his last foot-ball season at Notre Dame. Before graduation the following spring, he also captained the Notre Dame baseball team. In 1946, after the war, Bernie returned to Notre Dame as one of Leahy's assistant coaches, a position he held until 1951 when he went to the University of Indiana as the head football coach.

Leahy's kind of team was now in place and set to begin the 1941 season—Leahy's first at Notre Dame.

Chapter Three

THE FIRST LEAHY SEASON—1941

Creighton Miller was one of the players who reported back to school from summer vacation to start summer practice. Miller, who would become one of the greatest backs in Notre Dame's history, did not get along very well with Leahy at first. Their initial stormy relationship was precipitated by Miller missing spring practice. The tension between them would last until the start of the 1943 season.

Creighton Miller

Creighton Miller was from Cleveland, Ohio. When he was a freshman in high school, changes in his father's company caused his family to relocate to Wilmington, Delaware, along with one hundred other families. About those days Miller said, "I went to a small school on the outskirts of town which really wasn't a first-class athletic school. I played junior varsity ball my freshman year and played half the year on the varsity. I weighed 132 pounds then and by my senior year weighed about 175. My brother Tom was a year ahead of me and in his last two years we had very good seasons."

When it came time to select a college, Miller did not have much of a choice. As he said, "My father was a starting halfback at Notre Dame in 1907, 1908, and 1909. My uncle Walter was the starting fullback with George Gipp. My uncle Don was one of the Four Horsemen. So, when it came time for me to go to college, my father didn't ask me what college I wanted to attend. He told me what time the train left for South Bend.

"I had never been to Notre Dame before I arrived on campus that first day. When I stood out on Cartier Field and watched a practice, I never thought I would play because they all looked so big and brawny."

Miller tells how his problems with Leahy began: "I went home at Christmas and didn't feel too well. Doctors found my blood pressure was elevated, so my doctor told me 'no exercise.' In the spring of my freshman year Leahy said, 'You have to come out for practice.' I said, 'I can't. I can't get medical approval.' So that started a very tense relationship with Leahy. He thought I was conning him and didn't want to come out for spring practice, when the fact was I was dying to try and make the team and I knew I would have a very bad time if I didn't. So that's how I got off on the wrong foot with Leahy.

"I kept going to this doctor. They didn't know too much about blood pressure in those days. He told me not to exercise and I followed his orders, but one weekend I played six sets of tennis and went water skiing. I had an appointment on Monday to see him. He said, 'Your blood pressure is so much lower I can't believe it—I don't know about this. I'm sending you to the University of Pennsylvania to the best cardiologist I know.'

"I went there around August 1st, just before summer practice. Other than that weekend when I had exercised, I had not even walked fast for eight months. During the exam my blood pressure was up and the cardiologist said, 'I'm all through with you.' I was sitting in the waiting room and he walks out very casually and throws that measuring thing on me so fast and checked my blood pressure. It was normal. This guy was a good psychologist. He said, 'I think you can play ball.' Three years later he was listening to one of the games and wrote a letter to me saying, 'I'm glad to hear you are playing.' I wrote back and said, 'If it weren't for you, I would probably still be walking slow and taking my pulse in church.'"

As the rest of the team reported for summer practice, Leahy checked their hands to see if there were callouses. If they lacked them, that was proof they had not been doing manual work. Miller remembers, "My hands looked like a girl's hands because I hadn't even walked fast for eight months. So Leahy decides that this is a guy that really needs a lot of extra work. He went after me physically and I wasn't able to do it."

The featured headline in the sports section of the *South Bend Tribune* on September 10, 1941, the day Notre Dame officially opened practice for the start of the season, read, "ND Launches New Era in Football." The article pointed out that Leahy would concentrate on offense. Leahy was quoted as saying, "If we have possession of the ball most of the afternoon, the other team isn't going to give our defense much to worry about." The reporter pointed out that the 1941 Notre Dame varsity squad would be the smallest one (in number of players) since the World War (World War I).

As daily practices continued, the consenus among the sportswriters of the day seemed to be that the 1941 team was an average team. They cited the lack of depth and inexperience among the starters as their reasons for the average rating. They pointed out that Ziemba was new at center, the guards lacked any meaningful playing time, and Bertelli was untested at tailback.

As the day of the first game approached, the writers acknowledged that, due to the hard work of the coaching staff, the reserves appeared to be faster and more consistent than in the spring. The writers urged Notre Dame fans to reserve judgment and be patient until the season progressed.

In the meantime, Leahy's practices continued to be very regimented. He knew what he wanted to accomplish in every minute. He used to say, "We don't care what formation we play against, you still have to block and tackle and that's what we're going to work on." During the day, Leahy worked the team hard in preparation for the season opener. At night, he and his coaches met in Breen-Phillips Hall. At nine o'clock, as the players came from the Huddle (ND's snack shop) just before it closed for the night, they would see the lights in the coaches room and knew the coaches were still working.

Often, what the coaches were working on was the team's offense. Leahy, always the innovator, had altered the offense in many ways, five of which had been written about by the press. First, he instituted a line shift, whereby the linemen would position themselves about a foot behind the tip of the ball and take three small steps in rhythm with the backs, always ending up with a balanced line. This maneuver, according to Leahy, would make the linemen feel more a part of the offense and they would obtain better blocking angles as they shifted.

Secondly, he developed what is known as the "Lopsided T." This formation had the quarterback, prior to the shift into the Notre Dame box, line up behind one of the guards as opposed to lining up behind the center. This allowed the center to snap the ball directly to any of the three other backs. Leahy expected to use this formation about one-third of the time.

The third change involved shifting the wingbacks wider than usual so the back could give better help to the end in blocking the defensive tackle.

Fourth, Leahy implemented the use of shorter and more precise pass patterns, such as button-hooks and quick passes over the middle and in the flat. Included among these improvements of the short routes was "the pocket" pass-protection scheme, which is still so talked about in today's game.

The last published change Leahy put in the offense was the "man in motion." Leahy's idea in using this unexpected maneuver was to catch the opposition by surprise and thus unprepared.

The one change not publicized was Leahy's plan to make the fullback the main running threat. He wanted Bertelli at tailback (left halfback) for his passing skills. When Bertelli did handle the ball, it was either to hand off to one of the other backs or to throw the ball. This innovative move would prove to be a stroke of genius as the season unfolded.

Arizona

On September 27, 1941, the Notre Dame football team, under new head football coach Frank Leahy, opened the season at home against the University of Arizona. This game would make the first time in Notre Dame's football history that it would play the Arizona Wildcats. (ND did not play them again until 1980.)

The Arizona team was coached by Miles W. Casteel, who had been an assistant with Leahy under Jimmy Crowley at Michigan State in 1932. There were many times these two had plotted together against an opponent. Now they would use their skills to battle each other.

To the delight of the home crowd, and Notre Dame fans everywhere, their team defeated Arizona, 38-7. The lead article on the sports page of the *South Bend Tribune* the next day read, "The winner from Winner, South Dakota started winning for Notre Dame Saturday."

It was a strong victory for Notre Dame as the team scored in every period, showing a balanced attack with three scores on runs and three on passes. The game was highlighted by a 75-yard run from scrimmage by Dippy Evans and an 11-of-14 passing day for 145 yards by the sophomore, Angelo Bertelli. In addition to this, the writers commented on the superior physical condition of the Notre Dame team and of its coordinated line play. The writers particularly praised four sophomores: Bertelli, Creighton Miller, Bob McBride, and Matt Bolger.

Leahy, true to the form that would become familiar, said, "I am not satisfied with the team's performance. They will have to do much better if we want to beat Indiana."

Indiana

In the second game, despite Leahy's pessimism in front of the press, Notre Dame defeated Indiana University, 19-6. Evans scored all three of Notre Dame's touchdowns while Bertelli had another excellent day completing seven of 14 passes for 133 yards. An important insight to the success of the Notre Dame team was offered by two of the Indiana players in post-game interviews. Billy Hillenbrand, one of Indiana's great backs, said, "Notre Dame is the blockingest team I ever saw." In the same vein, the captain of the Hoosier team, Gene White, said, "They really block and keep after a man until he is down."

Georgia Tech

The Indiana game was followed by an away game against Georgia Tech coached by Bill Alexander. It was a rugged game with plenty of hard hitting, but Notre Dame won, 20-0. Early in the game, Paul Lillis, the captain and right tackle, received a hard blow to the head that caused a concussion. Lou Rymkus, a junior from Chicago's Tilden Tech High School, went into replace Lillis. Just before halftime Rymkus caught an elbow in the face that caused a serious gash inside his mouth. The blood came pouring out, but Rymkus continued to play. Not until halftime did Rymkus receive a dozen stitches in his mouth. With Lillis out for the game, Rymkus started the second half. Later in the half, the guard opposite Rymkus hit him in the mouth. Rymkus, who had been a heavyweight wrestling champion in high school, picked him up and threw him in Tech's backfield and added an elbow of his own as he flattened the guy. Rymkus had no more trouble with that player, but the blood from his mouth began to flow again, so, with three minutes to play, Leahy took him out for good.

As Rymkus was walking off the field, Leahy put his arm around him and said, "Lou Rymkus, you're a battler." The name stuck. Years later when he was earning All-Pro honors with the Cleveland Browns, he was known as Lou "The Battler" Rymkus.

While he was preparing for the Georgia game, Leahy had worried about the offensive schemes used by Coach Alexander, who was known to blow a game wide open with his razzle-dazzle offense. He was well known for his wide-open aerial attack. Aware of this, Leahy devised a four-man line in which the two guards would drop off the line and stand in tandem behind the line. This gave the appearance of a middle that was very congested. This move was used during the game and is recorded as a first in major college football. It apparently worked—Notre Dame's defense smothered six of Georgia's passes.

Notre Dame not only stopped Tech's passing game, but also Georgia's two fine running backs, Davy Eldridge and Johnny Bosch. One of the highlights of the game was the running of Steve Juzwik, who scored twice for the Irish. One of his scores was on a 67-yard reverse, during which he amazed the fans and the press with his speed on those "chubby legs" as one writer described them.

Despite the team's undefeated record, Leahy continued to work his players hard in practice. He also continued giving Miller extra work and riding him with caustic remarks. Finally, in one scrimmage, Miller reached the end of his physical endurance.

"One day I was either going to pass out or sit down," Creighton recalled. "I sat right down on the field in the middle of a scrimmage. Leahy got the whole team, not just the ones in the scrimmage, but everybody on the squad around me. He said, 'We're going to wait until fluff duff gets rested.' He tried to embarrass me, but he kind of made a hero out of me because all the guys were ticked off at him because he was kicking the hell out of everybody. That first year, I understand, he worked us harder than any of his other teams. When I sat down, the guys thought this was pretty good, not that I was a fluff duff.

"From then on I figured out the way to handle Leahy. Some weeks later he called me 'fluff duff' in his office and I said, 'You know, Coach, I like that name. Some of the other guys would like a name like that.'

He said, 'You know that name is not meant to commend you. It's meant to inspire you to do better—it's meant to be insulting.'

"I said, 'Well, whatever it's meant to be, I like it.' He didn't know how to handle that."

25

Carnegie Tech

The fans who gathered in Pitt Stadium to watch the Fighting Irish play the Tartans of Carnegie Tech thought they would see a lopsided score of 50 or 60-0.

The once-powerful teams of Carnegie Tech were a thing of the past. They already had been defeated by such unlikely winners as Muhlenberg College and Westminster College. It was expected that the undefeated Notre Dame team would demolish Tech in the last game ever played between these two schools. Notre Dame did gain 297 yards on the ground while holding Carnegie Tech to a mere 14. And, Notre Dame controlled the ball most of the game. Yet, despite the fact they won the game, 16-0, the offense had difficulty scoring. On several occasions Carnegie Tech did not allow Notre Dame to score when the Irish were inside the five-yard line. This humiliating experience lead to one of Leahy's more famous drills.

The team returned from Pittsburgh to South Bend by train on Sunday morning. Leahy put the word out before the train arrived at the station that no one was to leave the train until he said so. The team soon found out why. Leahy ordered them to go directly to the stadium to get dressed in full practice gear and to report to Cartier Field for a workout.

As soon as the squad was assembled on the field, Leahy put the ball on the five-yard line with the first team on offense and told the rest of the team to alternate on defense. The object of the drill was for the first team to score using straight ahead plays with "wedge" blocking. Wedge blocking is a blocking scheme in which the offensive line closes any gaps so that the linemen are shoulder to shoulder; they charge straight ahead blocking anyone in their path. In reality, from a defensive point of view, it is more like facing seven crazed bulls charging straight ahead, trampling anyone, or anything, that is in the way, rather than a coordinated blocking scheme. Leahy had the team do this drill for about an hour and a half while repeatedly asking the first team, "Can you score next week when we get in close?"

During the Illinois game the following week, the Notre Dame team had the ball on the opponent's five-yard line, first down and goal. As they huddled, and before the quarterback could call the play, Jim Brutz (a senior tackle) said to his teammates, "For God's sake, let's push them out of here and score. I don't want to go through that

crazy drill again." The Notre Dame line set down in its wedge blocking formation. When the ball was snapped, they charged ahead like
seven wild men and succeeded in driving the Illinois defensive linemen almost out of the end zone. The ball carrier scored an easy
touchdown. Coach Leahy, as the team was learning, did have a way
of making his point.

Illinois

Although Illinois scored first after intercepting a Bertelli pass,
Notre Dame had little trouble in its fifth game, crushing the University of Illinois, 49-14, at home for its fifth straight victory. Juzwik
scored the first of seven Irish touchdowns on a 12-yard sweep and
later scored on a 13-yard pass from Bertelli. Evans scored from the
six-yard line for a 21-7 halftime lead. After an Illinois touchdown the
Irish roared back with four unanswered touchdowns. Evans scored
three times, twice on passes from Bertelli and once on a short plunge.
Miller scored the final touchdown on a pass from Dick Creevy. This
triumph set the stage for the much-awaited game against Army.

Army

Of all the coaches who took over new jobs at major schools that
year, only the teams coached by Red Blaik of Army and Frank Leahy
of Notre Dame remained unbeaten. A story is told about Blaik's first
talk with the Army team after taking over as head coach. During the
course of his talk about the tackle position and how it wins or loses
games, he caught one of the players gazing out the window. Blaik
said, "Hey, you over there by the window!"

"Yes, sir," was the reply.

"Where are most football games lost?"

"Right here at West Point, sir," the player answered.

Such was the attitude of the Army teams prior to Blaik's arrival at
West Point.

Blaik did an amazing job of changing the mental attitude of the
team that would face Notre Dame. It was undefeated and was now
confident that it could upset the Irish.

Leahy drilled his team relentlessly during the week before the big
game. There was no way he was going to let the team's success to

27

date make his players overconfident. He told them, "We'll be hit hard and hit often and the only way we can survive is to be more rugged than our opponent."

The one thing Leahy feared was to play on a muddy field. With Bertelli, now recognized as one of the premier passers in the country, Leahy relied on the passing game to open the defense, which in turn allowed Evans and Juzwik to make their slashing runs. To his dismay, it started to rain the Friday night preceding the game and rained continuously throughout the game. The field at Yankee Stadium was a quagmire, which nullified the passing attack of both teams and made it impossible for the backs to get the proper footing.

There were no obvious scoring opportunities as each team played conservative football. The game ended in a 0-0 tie.

Navy

Despite identical records and the fact that Navy was favored to hand Notre Dame its first defeat of the season, the Irish beat the Middies in Baltimore by a score of 20-13.

The game was a struggle that was in doubt up to the end, but when the game was over, Notre Dame had proven to be the superior team. Leahy played only 21 men that day, but each was sensational. Evans, Juzwik, Bertelli, and a few others played almost the entire game. Only Bill Earley and Bob Hargrave gave the ball carriers any relief. Leahy's theory that year was that he would rather play a tired regular than a fresh reserve.

Bertelli was outstanding. He completed 13 passes for 232 yards. He earned the name of "Mr. Accuracy" from the sportswriters. Evans, who scored two touchdowns, and Juzwik both exhibited speed around end, consistently gaining good yardage. The defensive end play of Dove, Kovatch, Barry, Murphy, and Bolger was amazing as they continually crashed into Navy's blockers and set up the linebacker trio of Ziemba, Wright, and Crimmins to stop the Sailors' speedy backs. The victory over Navy kept the Irish in the dwindling ranks of undefeated teams.

Only two games away from becoming the first undefeated Notre Dame team since 1930, the Irish began preparations to play their traditional rival, Northwestern University, in Evanston, Illinois.

During the week before the game, Miller and Leahy went at each other again. Miller remembers vividly what happened. "It was Thanksgiving and for some reason I was late for practice. With the whole team around, he asked me why I was late. I said, 'My clock was wrong.' Leahy said, 'I don't believe that.'

"I said, 'That's unfair for you to tell me that you don't believe me.' So I sort of took him on. The other guys approved because everybody was so tired from all the work. We didn't have any rules about drinking or smoking—everyone was too tired to do either one. I wasn't on a scholarship; my father was paying my brother's and my way. So I could take him [Leahy] on, sort of as a spokesman for guys that couldn't afford to do that. He told me later, after I was through playing, that he kind of liked that, that some player would stand up to him."

Miller put it best when he said, "It was hard to stand up to him. My own personal opinion is that as many tough guys as you know around here, I always thought that Leahy was tougher than any of them. Physically and mentally, you take the toughest guy on our team, and Leahy was tougher."

Leahy came by his toughness naturally. When he was growing up, Frank Leahy and his three brothers loved to fight, and they did a lot of it, either in the ring, around town, or with each other. Frank's younger brother, Tom, once estimated that he had about 900 fights. His pals used to arrange fights for him around town and then bet money on the outcome. They always won. One day at home, Tom told his father, Frank, Sr., "There isn't anyone left to fight, so I guess I can beat anyone in town."

Frank, Sr., said, "Except one."

"Who is that?" Tom asked.

"Me," replied the father.

As was the custom with Tom's fights, the two made a wager. If Tom won, he would never have to do any chores around the house. If he lost, he would have to dig a latrine at a designated spot on their property. With the bet settled, Tom and Frank, Sr., went at it. In just 30 seconds, Frank, Sr., had Tom pinned and admitting defeat. Later in the day, the father sat on a chair with a wide-brim hat to shield his face from the heat of the sun to watch Tom dig the latrine. When he reached the agreed upon six-foot depth, Tom asked, "I did what you asked. Am I through now?"

Frank, Sr., replied, "Tom, make it two feet wider."

Maybe Leahy's toughness came with the genes.

Leahy *was* tough—as the players knew only too well. He had definite standards by which he acted in his role as head coach concerning his relations with his players, particularly during the football season. He used to quote that trite expression, "Familiarity breeds contempt," and he lived by that in his dealings with the players. He did not eat with them, drink with them, or fraternize with them in any way. Leahy not only talked in a very formal way, but he kept his interaction with the players on a formal basis.

Leahy was indeed difficult to talk to. If you were summoned to his office or the coaches' room, you knew it was to talk about some football matter he had in mind. You could be sure the conversation would be brief and to the point. He wasted very few words in any individual meeting. He was in charge in all meetings and, more often than not, the player's response to whatever he said was, "Yes, Coach," or "No, Coach," thus ending the conversation, if it could be called that.

Leahy was equally demanding on the field. He did not just want each player to play well, he wanted the best each player had to give, and he wanted—or demanded—it all the time. He did not tolerate nonsense on the field. He had his idea of how football should be played and, if you wanted to play for him, you had better understand what that was—and play accordingly. He had absolutely no time for a player who was the least bit timid in blocking or tackling, who did not think, who committed dumb mistakes, who was late for practice, or who did not put forth his best effort at all times.

Like many coaches, Leahy had an intolerance for injuries. He acted at times as if it was the player's fault for being injured. Once a player was injured, he expected that player to set some kind of record for healing so he could be back playing as soon as possible. Especially in his early years of coaching, Leahy believed that he could work his teams as hard as he wanted without the players suffering any ill effects from the long difficult practices, where vicious hitting was the norm. As Miller puts it, "He had a philosophy that everyone was a workhorse, there weren't any racehorses. I always objected to that philosophy because not everyone is a workhorse. You can't run a racehorse into the ground and leave it out on the practice field."

Northwestern

Northwestern was a great spoiler whose whole season could be made by knocking off Notre Dame. Having lost to Michigan and Minnesota, the Wildcats' coach, Lynn "Pappy" Waldorf, wanted nothing more than to do just that. With 19 veterans back from the previous year's team and with the famous Bill DeCorrevont, the soon-to-be famous sophomore Otto Graham in the backfield, and big Don Clawson, beating Notre Dame was a real possibility.

Notre Dame squeezed by the Wildcats on a Bertelli pass and a sensational catch by Matt Bolger. Juzwik added the winning point as the Irish won, 7-6.

To Northwestern's credit, it won the statistical battle. The Wildcats showed great heart when they roared back to score following Notre Dame's touchdown. On the extra-point try, Ziemba broke through and blocked what would have been the game-tying kick.

Notre Dame also showed heart as Evans, Juzwik, and Bob Maddock played 60 minutes of football while Bertelli was out of the game only on kickoffs. Several other members of the team played nearly the whole game. John Kovatch played so well on defense that he earned a starting role for the upcoming final game against the University of Southern California.

However, the Notre Dame team came out of the Northwestern game badly battered. In the backfield, Juzwik, Evans, and Wright were hurting, as were Dove, Crimmins, and many others in the line. Despite their injuries, their spirits were high. They knew they had only one more competitor to face, and a victory would mean an undefeated season. In addition, this final game would be the last as a Notre Dame player for 19 members of the squad. They wanted to make it one they would enjoy remembering.

Southern California

And indeed it was. The Irish beat the Trojans, 20-18, in a hard-fought contest. The Trojans scored first and last, but the weary Irish were up to the challenge as Bertelli completed 13 of 21 passes to finish the best year ever for a Notre Dame passer. There was inspired running as Evans scored twice and Juzwik once. Maddock again played 60 minutes while Captain Lillis, Dove, Kovatch, and Wright played over three quarters of the game. Brutz was cited by the press for his masterful job on both offense and defense.

After the game, Leahy summed up the season when he said, "If ever a group of boys deserved an undefeated season, these boys did. They fully deserved what they got and I'm very happy for their sake and for Notre Dame's. The team spirit was wonderful all year. The boys worked hard and they fought every inch of the way all season."

· In reminiscing about the 1941 season, Angelo Bertelli said, "It ended up that the 1941 season, which was my sophomore year, we still had the single wing, still the leather helmet, and we were undefeated—the first undefeated Notre Dame team since Rockne's 1930 National Championship season. We were tied by Army in the rain in New York. We ended up third in the nation. Minnesota won the National Championship for the second year in a row with Bruce Smith and some other great players.

"Although I wasn't much of a runner, Leahy was so innovative, I would be at the tailback position or fullback, and when I wasn't faking or handing off, I would just go back and throw a pass. Otherwise, a tailback in the single wing is a guy that always runs—I never ran. I was always giving the ball to someone else, either to Dippy Evans or Steve Juzwik.

"Thank God Leahy came along with that great coaching staff of Johnny Druze, Ed McKeever, and Joe McArdle. It was a great year and Frank Leahy did the job, without question."

It was, indeed, a great year for a team that was considered average at the beginning of the season and that started the season with only four returning regulars and a new head coach. The 8-0-1 record of the 1941 team was a remarkable accomplishment and a very auspicious start for the young head football coach, Frank Leahy.

As individual honors for the season were announced, Brutz, the senior left tackle, was named Notre Dame's most valuable player. Crimmins, the converted back playing this first season as a guard, and Dove, junior left end, were named to almost everyone's All-American team.

Lillis, the captain of the team and right tackle, was named a second team All-America. Bertelli, the sophomore left halfback, led the team in passing with 1,027 yards and eight touchdowns—earning him second place in the Heisman balloting as the nation's outstanding player. Evans, the fullback (who Creighton Miller claims was one of Notre Dame's most underrated backs) led the team in scoring. Juzwik, the shifty-running right halfback, led the team in receiving and punt returns. Maddock was the iron man with 413¾ total minutes of playing time, which meant an average of almost 50 minutes per game.

Leahy, in only his third year as head coach and after only one season at Notre Dame, was named Coach of the Year by the American Football Coaches Association. He also received the honor of an invitation by Arch Ward, the sports editor of the *Chicago Tribune*, to be one of the coaches for the 1942 College All-Star team.

Later in the year when the 1942 College All-Star squad was named, Lillis, Hargrave, Crimmins, Juzwik, Brutz, Maddock, and Kovatch were elected to represent the University of Notre Dame. Minnesota, the '41 National Champion, also had seven players selected. No other school approached these totals.

War

The glories of this season, however, were soon overshadowed by larger events.

On December 7, 1941, 15 days after Notre Dame's victory over USC, Japan atacked the U.S. Naval base at Pearl Harbor, triggering the entry of the United States into World War II. This event, which plunged the nation into war, would forever change the lives of all players and students across the country. The Notre Dame team proved no exception.

Until late 1941, Notre Dame's campus, like most college campuses, reflected the peacetime atmosphere that the U.S. had maintained since the outbreak of hostilities in Europe. One of the few concessions to the war was the establishment by the Navy of a Naval Reserve Officers' Training Program on campus earlier in the year. This was all soon to change. Before a year had passed, the University went from a civilian campus to that of a semi-military base. Instead of wearing corduroy pants and open-necked shirts, now roughly 50 percent of the students were outfitted in the uniform of one of the military services that had an officers' candidate program on campus.

Many of the seniors from the 1941 team would soon be called to active duty. The Navy became the post of several Notre Dame seniors: Lt. (JG) Jack Barry was with the first wave at Omaha Beach on D-Day; Lt. Comdr. Jim Brutz served four and a half years; both Crimmins and Lillis would skipper PT boats and be decorated for heroism; Ebli and Hargrave would both serve over four years as officers. Many other players would soon follow into military service.

As with all other college coaches, Leahy had a new set of concerns in preparing his team for the 1942 football season. The usual concerns of recruiting, players' academic standings, and replacing graduating seniors were overshadowed by concern over whether his players and coaches would be called to active military service.

In the meantime, Leahy, never one to linger over success, was already to work planning for the big changes he would make before the 1942 football season. His mind was made up. Even though he had just concluded a successful undefeated season, he intended to abandon the traditional Notre Dame box formation in favor of the new version of the T-formation as pioneered by George Halas, the coach of the Chicago Bears, and Clark Shaughnessy, coach at Stanford University.

Chapter Four

THE 1942 SEASON

As Leahy looked ahead to the 1942 season, he knew that there was an enormous amount of work to do to be ready for the fall opener. He did not mind the work—he thrived on it. What bothered him were the uncertainties. Could the team learn and perfect the new T-formation he was initiating? Could the backfield be realigned to fit the T-formation? Could he fill the voids at the guard and tackle positions created by the loss of all his starters? He worried that there might not be sufficient time to resolve all the problems before the season opener.

He knew he needed help from people who knew the T. This would require hiring a new coach and getting outside help, but that could be done. His one consolation was that he harbored no anxieties about the suitability of the main ingredient of the T—the quarterback. Angelo Bertelli had demonstrated he was the best passer in the country. Leahy knew Bertelli was bright, a hard worker, and could learn the intricate moves the new system demanded of a quarterback. Indeed, one of the main reasons Leahy had decided on the T was to take advantage of Bertelli's passing ability for the next two years.

In assessing the rest of the team, the end position looked good despite the loss of Matt Bolger, John Kovatch, and Jack Barry. All-American Bob Dove was back as was George Murphy. There were also some promising freshmen coming up in the form of John Yonakor, Jack Zilly, and Paul Limont.

At tackle he was losing both starters, Jim Brutz and Paul Lillis, but replacing them was a talented group that included Lou Rymkus, Bob Neff, Larry Sullivan, and freshmen Jim White, Ziggie Czarobski, and Luke Higgins.

Lou Rymkus

Rymkus, who would become the starting left tackle, was a classic case of a poor boy from a small town making good. Raised in Carbondale, a southern Illinois coal mining town, Rymkus graduated from grammar school in 1934 when the mines closed down because of the depression. Rymkus' father had died when he was six years old, so he, his mother, and his older brother left Carbondale and headed for Chicago in search of employment and comfort from relatives there.

Upon arrival, they moved in with Rymkus' aunt on the south side of Chicago, and Rymkus and his brother looked for jobs. At this time going to high school was not an option. Lou's brother found employment at the Chicago Stockyards. With his brother employed and housing assured by the aunt, Rymkus was persuaded to attend Tilden Tech. There he met Les Harvey, Tilden's football coach. Seeing Rymkus, 6 feet tall and 220 pounds, Coach Harvey immediately recruited him for the football team. By the latter half of his first season, Rymkus became a first-string tackle.

In his sophomore year, he made the All-State team—as he did the next two years. In his senior year he also won the City of Chicago Championship and the State Heavyweight Championship in wrestling.

Rymkus was heavily recruited by Purdue, Northwestern, and Wisconsin. During a visit to Purdue, the wrestling coach asked Rymkus if he would mind working out with their two top heavyweight wrestlers. Rymkus not only obliged the coach, but pinned both of their best wrestlers in less than two minutes. The coach was so impressed he didn't want Rymkus to leave the campus for fear he might go to another school.

This fear proved to be well founded. During his final season at Tilden, Rymkus played a game in Mishawaka, Indiana, which is near South Bend. Some Notre Dame coaches saw him play, were impressed with what they saw, and invited him to visit the Notre Dame campus. This visit to Notre Dame determined Rymkus' future. Immediately at ease with the players and coaches, Rymkus decided to attend Notre Dame and prove his mettle on the football field.

"I used to listen to the Notre Dame games when I was 12, 13 years old," recalls Rymkus. "Being from the coal mines of southern Illinois near Carbondale, I had only one pair of shoes and pants, yet I sat around and visited with the guys and they were real nice to me. I liked the atmosphere and everything about the school. I figured that's where I wanted to go—Notre Dame. It really was a stroke of God that I ended up there and got to play for Elmer Layden and later, Frank Leahy."

Rymkus, who was hampered by injuries his junior year (1941), became the starting left tackle, earning recognition by his teammates as the most valuable player on the 1942 team. Bob Neff, also a senior with two years of experience, became the starting right tackle.

The guard position presented Leahy with his most serious problem. He was losing his two starting guards, Iron Man Bob Maddock and the All-American Bernie Crimmins. In addition, he was losing Joe Laiber and Will Riordan. This left only Bob McBride and Pat Filley with any game time.

The center position was the strongest. All three centers had returned: Wally Ziemba, Tom Brock, and John Lanahan. And a great freshman prospect, Herb Coleman, was slated for play in the new season.

In the backfield, Leahy was losing only one starter, Steve Juzwik, but he would also miss backups Jack Warner and Bob Hargrave who were big contributors to the success of the 1941 team. He knew he had two outstanding runners in Dippy Evans and Creighton Miller who would complement Bertelli's passing. And the returning Tom Miller, Bill Earley, Pete Ashbaugh, and the talented Bob Livingstone, who was moving up from the freshman squad, would further strengthen the team. The fact that in Cornie Clatt, Gerry Cowhig, and Jim Mello he had perhaps the best trio of fullbacks ever on the freshman team gave him comfort. Harry Wright, the rugged blocking quarterback from the 1941 team, was also back, but, with the new T, Wright would have to be shifted to another position. He was too good not to be a starter.

Leahy had only three assistant coaches during the 1941 season: John Druze handled the tackles and ends, Ed McKeever the backfield, and Joe McArdle the guards and centers. Switching to the T-formation required a tremendous amount of individual coaching. In order to handle it, Leahy had to add to his staff.

He was fortunate in luring Moose Krause from Holy Cross College in Worcester, Massachusetts, back to his alma mater, Notre Dame, to take over the duties as coach of the tackles.

There is a story of Krause's return to Notre Dame as a coach that George Connor loves to tell. (Krause would later become Connor's tackle coach after the war in 1946.)

As Connor tells it, "Moose was on the coaching staff at Holy Cross and spent quite a bit of time at our house in Chicago recruiting me to go to Holy Cross. I remember his final words to me. 'George, I'll guarantee you one thing young man, I'll be with you night and day for four years.' Then while I'm on the train heading east going to Worcester, Massachusetts, to enroll at Holy Cross, my coach, the Moose, was on a train going the opposite way headed for South Bend."

To Krause's delight, George has embellished the story through the years to add, "Moose was working for a lawn sprinkling company that summer and, since he spent so much time at our house, he sold my dad one of the lawn sprinklers. Using the sprinkler that summer ruined our grass and it took five years before our lawn was back to normal—but at least my brothers and I did not have to mow the lawn."

Druze says that one of the things that made Leahy so successful was he always went with the times. Leahy believed that the T-formation was the offense of the future, plus he wanted to take greater advantage of Bertelli's passing ability. The question was how do you use the T? How do you get the information about the handoffs and the execution between the center and the quarterback? Druze tells what happened early in 1942:

"I was recruiting in the East and got a call from Leahy telling me to meet him in New York because he was with Sid Luckman, the All-Pro quarterback from the Chicago Bears. Leahy said, 'I'm going to have Sid up in our room, and we are going to go over the execution between the center and the quarterback and get the theory of how it works.'

"That's exactly what we did. I would play the part of the center snapping the ball back to Sid and Sid would hand off to the back played by Leahy. Then we would change positions and Leahy would be the center and give the ball back to Sid at quarterback. Then Leahy would play the part of the quarterback and so on. We kept doing this until we understood the moves of each position."

To make sure they had a continuing tutor in the intricacies of the T-formation, Leahy hired Bob Snyder, a former Chicago Bear quarterback, as a backfield coach. In addition, Luckman had agreed to spend

38

some time at Notre Dame in the spring to continue to impart some of his knowledge of the T to the coaches and players.

At the start of spring practice, Leahy initiated some shifts in the positions of certain players that he had been thinking about. Dove, who had just made most All-America teams as Notre Dame's left end, was called into Leahy's office to have a chat with the coach. Leahy explained to Dove that they were losing both starting guards, Crimmins and Maddock, for the 1942 season and that he wanted him to shift to guard. Dove was shocked to think that he would have to change positions for his senior year, particularly after making All-America the previous year. Leahy, sensing Dove's hesitance to make the move, gave him a pep talk about how he could help the team and that he was the only one who could make the switch. Dove, with some reluctance, agreed to play guard in spring practice that year.

Leahy's next move was to switch Wright, the blocking quarterback from the previous year's team, to guard. With the great results he achieved by shifting Crimmins from fullback to guard the year before, this seemed a natural move to make. He needed Wright in the starting lineup.

With the new T-formation, the fullback would no longer be the main running threat as it had been the previous year. Accordingly, Leahy shifted Evans to left halfback and Miller to right half. This alignment gave Leahy a potent backfield of Bertelli at quarterback, Evans and Miller at halfback, and Clatt at fullback.

It was a grueling spring practice. The quarterbacks and centers worked on the snap endlessly—the quarterbacks practiced their spins, reverse pivots, and handoffs until they became second nature. Leahy was careful not to overload the offense with too many plays. They stayed mainly with quick dives, around end, and the other bread-and-butter plays. The linemen were drilled constantly on their blocking assignments. With the new T, Leahy worked the team very hard in perfecting his style of pass blocking to make sure Bertelli would be well protected.

On the last day of spring practice, Druze was given an unforgettable assignment: "I had to meet George Halas, the owner and coach of the Bears, at the train station in South Bend. He was coming down for the Old-Timers' Game. As we drove to school we were talking about Leahy, and he made the statement that he admired Coach Leahy for doing what he was doing in making the change to the T-formation. He said it is very hard to be successful in one system and then change to a new one, but he was sure that Leahy had the ability to do it."

At the conclusion of spring practice Leahy made one prediction to the press. He said that Dove would make the All-America team at guard as he had done the previous year at end. Given what happened that season—Dove did not play one down as a guard—Leahy would never again make such a prediction.

Before the start of the season, Druze and McArdle, Leahy's two trusted assistants, were commissioned in the Navy and called to active duty. Both returned after the war in time for the 1946 season. Leahy added Wayne Millner, the All-American end from the 1933, 1934, and 1935 Notre Dame teams, to his staff for the upcoming season.

The team was scheduled to open the season on September 26th against a very solid Wisconsin team at Camp Randall Field in Madison, Wisconsin. The Badgers were coached by Harry Stuhldreher, one of the famous Four Horsemen. He always fielded a competitive team, and this year was no different. Stuhldreher had some terrific players in Dave Schreiner at end, Fred Negus at center, and Elroy "Crazy Legs" Hirsch and Pat Harder in the backfield.

Leahy knew he would face a tough opponent, but after a rigorous spring practice devoted to the switch to the T and an intense summer session, Leahy was sure his team was sufficiently expert in the new formation for the 1942 season.

There were other problems. Notre Dame's best back from the 1941 team, Dippy Evans, had torn a cartilage in his knee during the early fall practice and was out for the season. (Ironically, he injured it out in the open field without anyone touching him.) He was replaced in the lineup by the promising sophomore, Bob Livingstone. Many of the players were hurting in one way or another and not at their best physically. Especially worrisome was Miller's bout with a bad ankle. Some critics attributed the injuries to the constant scrimmages Leahy conducted in the pre-season practices.

About four days before the opening game, another problem presented itself. Leahy sent word to Dove to meet him in his office. Bob entered and Leahy announced, "Oh, Robert Dove, you are a better guard than you are an end, but Robert, I'm going to have to switch you back to end." Leahy went on to explain that Zilly, scheduled to

40

start at end, had become ineligible and that he did not feel Yonakor, who showed great promise, was quite ready to assume a starting role.

A stunned Dove replied, "Coach, we're going to play in four days and I have never run any of the plays at end since we switched to the T."

Leahy called Druze over, the end coach, who was on the other side of the room. "Coach Druze, I want you to work an hour each day with Robert and to give him your play book so he can become familiar with the new blocking assignments."

He turned back to Dove and said, "Don't worry, Robert, I won't play you very much on Saturday in the Wisconsin game, so you don't have to worry." (Dove played all but the first four minutes of the game.)

With that late move, the Notre Dame first team was: at end, Dove and Murphy; at tackle, Rymkus and Neff; at guard, McBride and Wright; at center, Ziemba; at quarterback, Bertelli; at halfback, Miller and Livingstone; at fullback, Corwin Clatt.

Wisconsin

Leahy was always a detailed planner, but there was one thing about the opening game that even he could not anticipate—his star quarterback, Bertelli, missed the train going to Madison.

The team had stayed in Chicago on Friday night in order to get an early start to Madison. On Saturday morning they went to Union Station to get a special train that would take them directly to the rail-road siding next to the field in Madison. The station was crowded with students and other fans who were taking trains to the game. With all the people and so many students, the station was a very noisy and congested place.

While the Notre Dame team and coaches were milling around the station waiting for the call to board the train, Bertelli was sitting off to the side reading a Chicago newspaper. The place he picked to sit and read was close to a concession stand that partially blocked his view of the tracks and his teammates. The announcement came that the Notre Dame football special was boarding on track 23. The play-ers and coaches grabbed their bags and headed for the gate to board, but with the noise and confusion, Bertelli did not hear the announce-ment, nor did he notice that his teammates were leaving the area to board the train. So he continued to read his paper.

Instead of all the players boarding at one car as they were sup-posed to do, they entered from various cars. The student manager responsible for counting the players as they boarded, got confused and did not get an accurate player count. The train pulled out of the station and headed for Madison with Bertelli in the station still read-ing his newspaper.

Shortly after his team departed, Bertelli heard an announcement for the boarding of a Notre Dame special and he boarded that train thinking it was the team train—but it was a special for the Notre Dame students. He went immediately to the observation car in the rear of the train and settled back to read his newspaper. A few min-utes later, the conductor asked Bertelli for his ticket. Bertelli said, "I'm with the football team. They don't give us tickets."

The conductor quickly realized what the problem was and said, "You're with the football team? Son, your train pulled out about 10 minutes ago."

In the meantime, on the train that carried the football team, the players and the coaches were settled in their seats. McKeever, the backfield coach, took a walk through the cars and was the first of the coaches to realize Bertelli was missing. He had the conductor send a message to investigate. After many communications between the football train, the station, and other trains, it was determined that Bertelli was aboard the student train headed for Madison and due to arrive at a different siding and much later than the team train. McKeever had the unenviable task of breaking the news to Leahy.

As McKeever approached the seats where Leahy was sitting, Leahy said, "Ed, get the quarterbacks up here."

The other quarterbacks, including big John Creevey, Bertelli's understudy that year, gathered around the coaches. Leahy looked around and said, "Ed, where is Angelo?"

McKeever was forced to inform Leahy. "Coach, we have one player missing. Don't worry, Coach, Bertelli is missing, but we have messages back to the other trains."

Leahy jumped up and shouted, "Stop the train—stop the train— Ed, stop the train!" Then Leahy spotted the emergency stop cord overhead and lunged for it. McKeever, using his athletic skills, tack-led Leahy and held him down to prevent him from pulling the cord.

For the remainder of the trip to Madison, Leahy was a nervous wreck. He could be seen muttering to himself and grimacing as if in terrible pain.

Dove recalls what happened when the team arrived at the stadium and went into the locker room. "I can remember getting dressed for the game while Leahy is outside questioning people as they passed by, 'Have you seen Angelo Bertelli? Have you seen Angelo?' We got dressed and went out on the field and Leahy remained outside looking for Bertelli. We worked out and came back to the locker room, and still no Leahy or Bertelli. Now, we go back on the field to start the game and Leahy is still outside looking for Bertelli, stopping strangers and asking, 'Have you seen Angelo?' Finally Angelo's train arrives and Leahy spots him running from the train siding to the stadium. He rushed Bertelli into the locker room to get dressed for the game."

Bertelli did make it to the field in time, but his missing the train was an omen of what was to follow. The Irish could not put it together that day. Just when it seemed they had some momentum there would be an interception or a fumble. Bertelli's passes were intercepted twice by the Badgers, and twice the Notre Dame backs fumbled inside Wisconsin's 10-yard line. Notre Dame did score when Mello ran over from the three, and was leading, 7-0, when Elroy Hirsch ran 40 yards for a Wisconsin score. The conversion was successful and the game ended in a disappointing 7-7 tie.

Leahy was very disheartened. This was Notre Dame's first game with the new T-formation. He had hoped to unveil to the public a potent new offense that would carry Notre Dame football to new heights. He was deeply disappointed and despondent. It was not only his state of mind that was troubled, but it was becoming obvious to everyone that he was working himself too hard and was physically spent.

Georgia Tech

Leahy worked the team hard in practice the week following the Wisconsin game to prepare for the upcoming Georgia Tech team. However, no amount of work could spark the team to produce the explosive type of offense that Leahy, the other coaches, and many of the fans expected to see. Tom Miller scored for the Irish in the final period on a seven-yard run, but it was not enough—Notre Dame went down in defeat, 13-6.

In practice the week before the Georgia Tech game, Leahy inserted a special play that had Jim Mello throwing a pass from his fullback position. During the week before the game, Leahy complimented Mello on his passing, telling him he looked like Sid Luckman, the star quarterback of the Chicago Bears.

Just a few seconds before the half ended with Notre Dame behind, 7-0, Bertelli called for the special play. Georgia Tech's defense took the bait and John Yonakor was wide open in the end zone. As Mello remembers, "I can picture my friends in Rhode Island, so proud to see Jim Mello throw his first pass in college for a touchdown. Oh God, I'm so thrilled! I throw the ball, it slips from my hand and flutters through the air like a wounded duck and is intercepted by Georgia Tech and the half ends.

"As I entered the locker room Leahy spots me and yells out, 'James Mello, you poop! If you ever throw another pass for Notre Dame, even in practice, I'm going to ship you back to West Warwick, Rhode Island, on the fastest New England Express train I can find.' Needless to say, I became strictly a blocking and running back and my old high school 'triple threat' days were over."

It was the kind of game the players on that Notre Dame team do not care to recall. They do, however, like to recall an incident from that game.

While reviewing the scouting report for the Georgia Tech game, Leahy noticed that on occasion the Georgia Tech defense would line up in an odd formation that he was sure Notre Dame could exploit. Leahy even asked Druze (who had scouted the game), "Oh John, are you sure they line up in that formation?"

Druze replied, "Not often, but they do get in that formation on occasion."

"We can get 30 or 40 yards if they try that against us," commented Leahy.

During practice that week he inserted a special play to use against that particular Georgia Tech defense. The keys to making the play successful were, first, to make sure Bertelli called an audible when the defense was spotted to alert the team to the special play; second, for Bob Neff, playing right tackle, to execute a shield block on the defensive player to his left. Neff's block would allow Creighton Miller to burst into the secondary where there was no defensive player for about 20 yards. It was definitely a play that had big yardage potential—and with Miller in the open, anything could happen.

Late in the first quarter the Notre Dame coaches on the sideline

44

spotted the odd defense. They immediately signaled for Bertelli to call the special play. Bertelli caught the signal and shouted the audible.

Miller took the handoff as planned and was immediately creamed by the Georgia Tech defensive player that Neff was supposed to block. Russell (Pete) Ashbaugh, whom Leahy liked to have next to him on the bench, jumped up and hollered, "Neff, you sonofabitch, you missed your block!"

Leahy turned to Ashbaugh and said, "Russell, we do not use profanity at the school of Our Lady. Neff is one of your teammates, and you should always treat all of your teammates with respect. I do not want to hear any more profanity."

In the middle of the second quarter, Georgia Tech's defense again lined up in that odd formation and Bertelli spotted the defense when he lined up behind the center. He gave the appropriate audible and handed off to Miller, who was hit again behind the line in a bone-crushing tackle by Neff's man. Leahy was furious. He shouted, "Who missed that block?"

Somebody yelled, "Neff." Leahy turned to Ashbaugh and said, "Oh, Russell, you were right. Neff is a sonofabitch."

The loss to Georgia Tech was more than Leahy could handle. It seemed to drain the last bit of reserve from him as he was now totally exhausted and needed rest. At the insistence of his doctor, and with the concurrence of his wife, Floss, Leahy went to the Mayo Clinic in Rochester, Minnesota, for treatment of his spinal arthritis and a complete rest. Little did he realize that being away would enable him to take an objective look at the team and develop a solution for the team's offensive problems.

The coach could no more stop thinking of football than he could stop breathing. He was in regular contact by phone with McKeever, who had been designated to coach the team in "Frank's" absence. Leahy, with time on his hands, reviewed in his mind what plays they had run during the previous season when they had been undefeated. He questioned why, with a potentially more explosive offense using the T-formation, the current team could not seem to get the offense moving as he knew it should. Then it came to him. Why had he not recognized the flaw before?

In 1941, Wright, playing quarterback, called the plays. He was aggressive and daring in his play selection. He knew when to have

45

Bertelli throw the ball—oftentimes unexpectedly. This type of play-calling kept the defense perplexed, thus enhancing the running game and contributing to a potent offensive attack. He realized that, on the current team, Bertelli was not calling the plays properly. Instead of calling his own plays, he was, for the most part, giving the ball to someone else. Leahy decided to let Wright, who was now a guard, call the plays as he did the year before. Leahy could not wait to call McKeever with a set of instructions to be implemented immediately so as to be in place for the game against Stanford.

Leahy's idea was right on the money. Wright knew from the previous year what a weapon Bertelli was and he knew how to use this powerful weapon. With Wright now calling the plays Notre Dame defeated Stanford, coached by Leahy's former teammate, Marchy Schwartz, 27-0, with Bertelli throwing four touchdown passes. Of his 20 attempts, Bertelli completed 14—nine of them in a row. Notre Dame's offense was now on the right track. With Wright calling the plays, Bertelli was throwing more passes—play-calling was the key.

With Leahy still at the Mayo Clinic, McKeever guided the team to two more victories with the rejuvenated offense. In a major upset, Notre Dame beat Iowa Pre-Flight, 28-0, at home and Illinois on the road, 21-14.

Iowa Seahawks

The favored Iowa Seahawks (Pre-Flight) were loaded with outstanding players, many of whom were former All-Americans plus a number of players from the pro ranks. Since every able-bodied man under the age of 30 was called into some branch of the military during the war years, many of the service teams had veteran football players on their roster. These included players who had played several years of college football, as well as some professional players.

In the first quarter, the Seahawks lived up to their reputation as they dominated the game but could not score. In the second quarter, Notre Dame's offense exploded for two scores in less than two minutes. After a 47-yard pass to Livingstone, Clatt plunged from close in for the first touchdown. After the kickoff, Clatt intercepted a pass and ran 40 yards for another touchdown. The final two tallies were scored by Cowhig on short runs.

Creighton Miller vividly remembers one incident from the Iowa Pre-Flight game.

"John Peasenelli, a reserve back, had not seen any playing time during the year and, being the character he was, he didn't bother to put on any pads when he dressed for the game that day against the Seahawks. As the game was winding down, and with Notre Dame leading, 28-0, Coach McKeever substituted freely in order to give the reserves some playing time. One of the assistant coaches discovered that John was the only player that had not been in the game. Peasenelli was sent in to the delight of his teammates, who knew that he wasn't wearing any protective equipment.

"Peasenelli carried the ball only once and gained 25 yards when the coach learned he wasn't wearing any pads, not even wearing an athletic supporter. He was immediately yanked from the game, but he had the last laugh: with his one carry, John was the leading rusher for the game in terms of average yards gained per carry.

"Later that season during a practice session on Cartier Field, the first string decided to have some fun with Peasenelli, who was returning punts during a kicking drill. They decided the next time John fielded the ball they would let him return it all the way for a touchdown.

"Peasenelli caught the next punt and started upfield. Bodies were flying all over the place in what the first team hoped looked like a valiant try to stop him. Peasenelli crossed the goal line for a touchdown to the amazement of everyone except the one that mattered most— Coach Leahy. He knew too much football to be deceived by the charade of missed tackles. Coach Leahy was not very happy about what he just witnessed. As punishment, Leahy ordered each player on the first team to run 36 times around Cartier Field—which translates into nine miles of laps after practice."

Illinois

Notre Dame beat a previously undefeated Illinois team with a come-from-behind rally to win, 21-14. Clatt scored on a five-yard run for a first-quarter tie, 7-7. Ashbaugh returned a punt 40 yards, enabling Bertelli to score on a quarterback sneak and tie the score, 14-14, in the third period. In the final quarter, Cowhig scored the winning touchdown from the one-yard line after Notre Dame had marched 77 yards on runs by Clatt, Livingstone, Ashbaugh, and Cowhig.

Navy

Leahy returned from the Mayo Clinic to coach the next game against Navy. Despite the rain, sleet, and mud, Notre Dame managed a touchdown and field goal to defeat the Navy, 9-0. Bertelli scored from in close after a pass to Dove set up the score. John Creevey connected on a 17-yard field goal to end the scoring. It was a hard-fought, conservative game as Bertelli only threw two passes because of foul weather.

Army

Before a capacity crowd in Yankee Stadium, Notre Dame defeated an excellent Army team, 13-0. It was Notre Dame's ground game and its aggressive defensive play that spelled the difference. After a scoreless first half, Ashbaugh recovered a fumble on Army's 35-yard line. Clatt and Dick Creevy ran it to the 15 where Creevy went off tackle for the first score. In the final period, Bertelli threw to Murphy, Notre Dame's right end and captain. The ball was tipped by a defensive player, but Murphy retrieved it for a 17-yard touchdown. The difference of the game was the play of the Notre Dame line, which was superb the entire afternoon.

Michigan

The Irish team was now 5-1-1 with four very difficult games to play—the toughest being its next opponent, Michigan. Despite leading by a point at halftime and playing at home, Notre Dame could not contain the well-coordinated Michigan running attack as the Wolverines defeated the Irish, 32-20.

Notre Dame opened the scoring on a Bertelli-to-Dove pass good for seven yards. Michigan came right back and scored after a sustained drive. An Irish fumble led to Michigan's second touchdown. Before the half, Michigan returned the favor as a fumble led to Notre Dame's second touchdown on a three-yard plunge by Miller. Michigan dominated play in the third quarter, scoring three times. The Irish fans got their hopes up early in the fourth quarter when Miller raced 14 yards for a touchdown, but Irish mistakes and the running of

Michigan's Tom Kuzma, Paul White, and George Ceithaml were too much for Notre Dame to handle as the Irish lost their second game of the season.

Northwestern

Notre Dame got back on the winning track the next week, defeating an Otto Graham-led Northwestern team, 27-20. Ed Hirsch plunged over for the Wildcats, giving them an early lead. Notre Dame responded with a 60-yard drive that Clatt finished with a five-yard plunge for a score. After an interception, Northwestern put on an 80-yard drive, making the score, 13-6, in its favor. Clatt scored again on a short plunge. Notre Dame took command of the game when it mounted a 79-yard drive that saw Miller, Clatt, and Livingstone take the ball to the Wildcat four-yard line. Bertelli hit Livingstone for the final touchdown.

Southern California

The Southern California game was a bitterly contested one. Several players were ejected as these two old rivals battled hard the entire game. The Irish were too much for the Trojans that day, beating them, 13-0. With the ball on the USC 48, Bertelli passed to Miller who caught it on the 25 and evaded the secondary on some nice running to score the first touchdown of the day. Later, Notre Dame put together an 80-yard drive that Bertelli engineered, hitting Dove twice, as well as connecting with Murphy and Clatt. He passed to Livingstone for the touchdown.

Great Lakes

In the final game of the long season (11 games), Notre Dame ended as it began, with a tie. Great Lakes, like many other service teams, had an all-star cast of players who had been unscored upon in its previous six games, making the Irish the underdogs.

The game seemed to be unfolding as anticipated with Great Lakes taking a 13-0 halftime lead. After three and a half minutes of the second half, in a dramatic comeback, the Irish had tied the score. Clatt exploded for an 82-yard touchdown run aided by a great block

49

from the All-American left end, Bob Dove. A few plays later, Miller, with a dazzling demonstration of open-field running, ran 68 yards for a touchdown. The Irish dominated the second half but could not manage to take the lead. They had high hopes when, in the final minutes of play, they marched 62 yards to put John Creevey in field goal position. On the last play, Creevey's kick was short as time ran out.

It was a great comeback for the Notre Dame team against a favored Great Lakes 11. Although it was not a victory, it was an impressive showing that allowed the Notre Dame players and coaches to end the season on a high note.

Bertelli, Dove, and Wright made the All-America team. Dove was also named the 1942 Lineman of the Year by the Washington, D.C., Touchdown Club. Bertelli was sixth in the Heisman balloting for the outstanding player in the country. He led the team in passing, completing 72 of 159 attempts for a total of 1,039 yards and 10 touchdowns. On defense, he also led the team in interceptions with eight, which was a school record that would stand for 20 years until Tom McDonald intercepted nine for the Irish in 1962. Because of his value to the team and the fear of injury, Leahy held Bertelli out on defense the following season (1943).

Rymkus was elected the most valuable player on the 1942 team by an almost unanimous vote of his teammates. Clatt led the team in rushing with 698 yards in 138 carries, and he tied Miller for the team lead in scoring. Livingstone topped the team in receiving and kickoff return average. Ashbaugh led in the punt return average category.

Many of the seniors, as well as others on the 1942 team, were called to active duty shortly after the season ended. Some of these players played service ball before going overseas or to other duties, and some hoped to play professional football after the war. Others knew they had played their last game.

Bob McBride, who had joined the Army, was captured by German forces at the Battle of the Bulge. After four months as a prisoner of war, he was released. He was later awarded the Silver Star and Purple Heart for his military service. Tom Miller was called to the Navy where he served in the Pacific as a lieutenant on an ammunition ship.

Dove was sent to the El Toro Marine base in California where he played ball for that team in 1943. Four teammates from the 1942 team, Murphy (captain and end), Neff (tackle), John Lanahan (center), and Larry Sullivan (tackle), all played for the Marine Corps team at Camp Lejuene during the 1943 season. Even there there remained a connection to Notre Dame. The coach of the team was Jack Chevigny, who played under Rockne in 1927 and 1928 and later became Rockne's backfield coach. After Rockne's death he became the coach at the University of Texas. (At the close of the 1943 season, Chevigny was sent overseas and was killed in action on Iwo Jima.) Lanahan later went to Saipan. Murphy, Neff, and Sullivan were sent to Okinawa and assigned to the same rifle battalion. Murphy was killed in action on Okinawa. Neff and Sullivan were both wounded.

Most of the players from the 1942 team who were not already in the service at the end of the season enlisted in some branch of the military after the season was over. As Creighton Miller puts it, "Everybody got into something. We didn't wait to be drafted. Everybody wanted to get in this thing, and, not only that, you didn't mind being called up, except you didn't want to miss the season like Bertelli did getting called in the middle of the season."

Miller entered the Army in the spring of 1943. He was assigned to Fort Dix where he was given a physical exam. The doctor examining Miller said, "You're not going to get in the Army." (His blood pressure was not acceptable.)

Miller shot back, "I'm already in the Army."

"Well, you're not going to be for long," the doctor replied.

Miller, who was officially in the Army for four days, was put in the base hospital where he stayed for six weeks until they could process his discharge.

Arch Ward, the sports editor for the *Chicago Tribune*, invited him to play in the August All-Star Game. Usually one had to be a senior in college to be invited, but with the war on, this rule was temporarily lifted. Other non-seniors, such as Otto Graham of Northwestern and Charlie Trippi of Georgia, were also invited to play.

Miller went to the All-Star camp, but could not pass the physical there either. Ward asked Miller to have dinner with him at his place. During the course of the dinner, Ward told Miller that he, too, had high blood pressure, and that he did not think it was a good idea for Miller to play in the game. Miller heeded Ward's advice and left camp.

On the way home Miller stopped in South Bend to pay a visit to Leahy. While he was in the Army, Miller had been getting weekly communications from Leahy, including pictures of Notre Dame and

51

notes telling him what a nice place Notre Dame was—all the material that would be sent to a possible recruit. Of course, the funny thing about it is that Miller had already been at Notre Dame for three years. However, Leahy was well aware of the fact that he was under no obligation to return to Notre Dame and, with all the players going into the service, Leahy desperately wanted him to return for another year.

When Miller arrived at the athletic offices at Notre Dame, Leahy was delighted to see him. During the conversation, Miller told Leahy that he was going to try and play the 1943 season. Leahy said, "That's great."

In recalling that time, Miller says, "Leahy figured if the Army won't take this guy, there must be something wrong with him. So he sat down with me and said, 'I'm willing to listen to you.' I said, 'I want to play ball. You be fair with me and I'll be fair with you and give you everything I've got. When I'm so tired that I can't go anymore—don't push me and I'll give you one hundred percent.' From that day on, we never had any problems. He never gave me an extra five laps because he thought I was goofing off. Up until then, I was considered a guy that was putting him on. I never did go out for spring practice. If you're a coach, that's pretty tough to have a guy that doesn't show up for spring practice."

In hindsight, that meeting between Leahy and Miller was of enormous importance to the fortunes of the team for the coming season. With their new understanding, both Leahy and Miller would now know what to expect of each other. Miller could play all out, as he always did, but with the difference that he now knew he would get some rest when needed. It is a shame such a meeting did not take place years before, but as Miller comments, "That's what we should have done before, but he was a hard guy to talk to, especially if you're 19 years old."

For Leahy's part, having Miller available on such good terms lifted a burden from his shoulders in planning for the season ahead. It also may have taught him invaluable lessons—that each player is unique, and that if one is not able to physically withstand the same amount as another, it does not mean that the first is not giving his all in practice or a game.

Chapter Five

The 1943 Season—Leahy's First National Championship

From the viewpoint of returning players the outlook for the upcoming season was dim. The Notre Dame team had lost nine of its starting 11 players and 22 of 32 monogram winners from the 1942 squad to either graduation or the service. However, all colleges across the country were in the same predicament. With the war in full tilt, the military was claiming young men everywhere as soon as they reached draft age.

Compared with many universities, Notre Dame was fortunate. The Navy had designated Notre Dame one of the colleges that would serve as a training base for its officer candidate programs. These programs allowed some of the students to stay at Notre Dame until their training was completed, and it also brought in some military transfer players that Notre Dame would otherwise not have had.

All the starters on the line from the previous year were gone. This included two-time All-American end Bob Dove and the All-American play-calling guard, Harry Wright.

In the backfield, the Irish had lost starters Bob Livingstone and Cornie Clatt as well as Tom Miller, Dippy Evans, Bill Earley, and Pete Ashbaugh. However, returning from the 1942 team, were All-American quarterback Angelo Bertelli, the starting right halfback, Creighton Miller, and Jim Mello, who had won a monogram at fullback the previous year. If Leahy could have had his pick of which two starters would return from the 1942 team, he would have chosen Bertelli and Miller. They would form the nucleus of a great team.

Returning monogram winners on the line included John Yonakor, Jim White, Pat Filley, Bernie Meter, Herb Coleman, Ziggie Czarobski, and Paul Limont. Yonakor, White, Filley, and Coleman would go on to win All-American honors that season, as would Bertelli and Miller.

Added to this group were juniors John (Tree) Adams and Jack Zilly and a group of talented sophomores who joined the varsity from the previous year's freshman team, including Jim Flanagan, Gasper Urban, Joe Signaigo, Frank Dancewicz, Fred Earley, and Johnny Lujack.

In 1942, because of the war, many schools had adopted the rule declaring freshmen eligible to play varsity sports. Notre Dame, following the conferences in the Midwest, adopted the rule in 1943. Military transfer students were eligible immediately.

The freshman rule helped Leahy by adding several talented youngsters—Bob Kelly, Bob Hanlon, George Sullivan, Art Statuto, Bob Palladino, and Fred Earley—to the team. A group of seasoned players who had received military transfers from other schools completed the team. These transfer players were in one of the many officer candidate programs now dominating the campus at Notre Dame. Included in this group were two players who would become starters, Julie Rykovich, a back from the University of Illinois, and John Perko, a guard from the University of Minnesota. In addition, Ray Kuffel, an end from Marquette, and Vic Kulbitski, a fullback from Minnesota, would see a lot of action as valuable additions to the team.

All coaches dream of being able to coach a great player—that nearly perfect player who is gifted with ability beyond the normal and who uses that ability to the fullest. Leahy was fortunate to have coached several such players. One of the sophomores moving up to the varsity was John Lujack. He had already established himself as a player with great potential by his play on the freshman team. He would eventually become one of the greatest players ever to play for Notre Dame.

John Lujack

Lujack's hometown was Connellsville, Pennsylvania, located about 50 miles south of Pittsburgh and about 35 miles from Morgantown, West Virginia. John was the youngest of the four Lujack boys. His three older brothers preceded him at Connellsville High. There was a Lujack on the varsity team for 14 consecutive years and each participated in football, basketball, and track. Each captained the football and basketball teams.

When Lujack told his Notre Dame teammate Miller that he was

an All-County player in Pennsylvania, Miller, who loved to tease Lujack, retorted, "Yeah, that wasn't so hot... I found out your high school was the only one in the county. If you made your high school team, you made All-County."

In Lujack's words, "I had no plans for college. I was hoping I could go to college, but I wasn't sure what college was about. I didn't feel I was all that terrific, but my senior year everyone started talking about where I was going to school and I didn't have any idea. There was a guy named Henry Opperman who was a great fan, semi-alumni of Notre Dame, I guess. He got ahold of Leahy and McKeever, the backfield coach at Notre Dame, and I remember Ed McKeever coming to Connellsville and meeting my parents.

"Pretty soon I went out to Notre Dame and I remember having a workout. I ran, passed the ball, and punted. Later I was told through somebody that I had a scholarship at Notre Dame. I couldn't believe it. I was really surprised because I didn't think I was good enough for this tremendously talented university.

"Meantime, I got an appointment to West Point. I was never interested in going to West Point, particularly in view of the fact you had to go there for four years and then sign up for four years afterward. When I was accepted at Notre Dame, that settled everything as far as I was concerned. It's a place I had always wanted to go. I can remember as a little kid listening to Notre Dame football on the radio, never dreaming I'd have a chance to go. That ended my looking around."

It ended Lujack's looking around, but it did not end the talk in Connellsville. Congressman Jay Buell Snyder had announced Lujack's appointment to West Point at his graduation ceremonies and succeeded in having the whole community talk about where Lujack should go to college. Most of them thought Lujack was crazy not to accept the appointment. His mom and dad were under a lot of pressure, but they left the decision to Lujack and he had made his choice—Notre Dame over West Point.

Before Lujack reported to Notre Dame in the fall of 1942, he accepted a summer job from Hughie Mulligan, the Chicago president of the Asbestos Workers. Mulligan had been putting Notre Dame players to work in the summer since the Rockne days, when he secured a job for the young Frank Leahy. Lujack was delighted to work covering pipes in one of the buildings at the Great Lakes Naval Training

Center. It offered a needed escape from the controversy that was still swirling in Connellsville about his refusal of the appointment to West Point. When he would call home, his parents would ask, "Son, are you sure you're making the right decision?"

As Lujack says, "I could feel their pressure, but I was at peace with my decision, so I was feeling no pressure."

In the fall of 1942, Lujack reported for his first practice at Notre Dame. Freshmen were not eligible to play on the varsity in that year. (The wartime policy allowing freshmen to play was not yet operative.) Like so many before him and many to follow, Lujack was issued the solid green, itchy jersey with no number. When the freshman team was assembled on the field, Jake Kline, the freshmen coach, ordered, "Linemen, get over here, and backs, get over there."

Lujack wanted to get one thing clear that first day and not make an error. He wanted to make sure he knew where the backs went and where the linemen went so he would end up with the backs. Not until he was certain where the backs were to go did he make his move. This put him in the front row of backs. Thus, when Leahy called for a defensive team to scrimmage the varsity and Jake Kline said, "You, you, you and you," pointing to the players nearest him, Lujack was the first "you" to be selected.

Since this was the first year of the T-formation, none of the freshmen had played against a team using this formation. As Lujack tells it, "I played safety and every time I looked up, here comes one of those charging halfbacks on those quick openers and they were coming right at me. I knew that at 165 pounds I was going to get killed that day, but I wasn't really sure how. I made up my mind then and there that I was going to go in the right direction, because if I was going to be carried out and live the rest of my life in the infirmary, at least they'd say he was really charging forward."

Lujack started to make some tackles—then a lot of them. Practice was stopped several times as Leahy asked from his perch atop the tower in the center of the practice field, "Who made that tackle?"

At first, the coach nearest to Lujack, Ed McKeever, said, "Son, what's your name?"

"Lujack," he answered. Then the coach would holler to Leahy, "Lujack made the tackle."

Lujack made so many tackles that first day that the coaches quickly learned who he was and what he could do. At the beginning of the second day's practice one of the coaches asked, "Lujack, where are you?" Lujack raised his hand. The coach continued, "Lujack, you, you and you," pointing to other players, "get in on defense." Lujack had made his mark on defense.

When it came time for the freshman team to scrimmage the varsity offensively, in their traditional role of assuming the identity of next week's opposing team, Lujack was again selected. If Notre Dame was playing a single-wing team, Lujack was the tailback, which is the position he played in high school. If the varsity were playing a T-formation team, Lujack was the quarterback. As he recalls, "That's how I got noticed at Notre Dame."

In the spring of 1943, nobody, including Frank Leahy, was sure what kind of football team Notre Dame would field. Leahy was not sure how long it would be before Bertelli would be called up by the Marines (the call came after six games); he did not know how Lujack was going to fare with no prior varsity experience; and he did not know how long Yonakor, White, Coleman, and others would be there because they were in various officer programs and were subject to transfer at any time.

With the uncertainty of who would be available to play, it became very difficult to plan ahead. Then unexpectedly, Leahy, the players, and Notre Dame became beneficiaries of a change in Naval policy that would prove to be a big factor in their success. It was Bob Kelly's father, U.S. Congressman Edward A. Kelly, who was partly responsible for the change.

As a congressman, Kelly's father was used to dealing with powerful men. He was the type of man who never backed down from a fight and certainly knew how to use his own power when the occasion called for it. As we look at young Kelly's career we get a glimpse of the father and how he accomplished what he did.

Bob Kelly

Bob Kelly was a 17-year-old All-State halfback from Leo High School on Chicago's south side. He, along with Bob Hanlon, starred on Leo's Chicago City Championship team in 1942. Kelly was heavily recruited by many schools, particularly by Ed McKeever and Frank Leahy of Notre Dame, and by Andy Gustufson and Earl Blaik of Army. Freshmen were eligible to play varsity ball that year providing they earned the prescribed minimum credit hours (about a semester).

57

The schools wanted Kelly to leave before graduation to enroll in college in time to get enough credits to be eligible by the fall season. After some heavy pressure by McKeever, the principal of Leo High consented to let Kelly leave Leo in January.

Kelly's father told him that one way or another he was going in the service and, if he had to be in the military, it was better to have the class ring from West Point. Although Kelly liked Notre Dame, he decided that he would accept the West Point appointment that had been offered him.

In January of 1943, Kelly and his father took a train to West Point where they were met by Army's coach, Earl "Red" Blaik. Coach Blaik invited Kelly and his father to his house, where they had a long discussion about West Point and the football program Kelly would soon join. Blaik explained that Kelly would be with 12 other incoming freshmen at a prep school in Peekskill, New York. The group included Barney Poole and Felix "Doc" Blanchard (both of whom would later become great players at Army). At the prep school, Kelly would be tutored, along with the others, on how to pass the mandatory West Point entrance exam. Naturally, there would be time to practice with the varsity football team.

Kelly says that talking to Blaik was like talking to Leahy. "Blaik was Frank Leahy junior—the same personality. They looked a lot alike physically and facially. When you talked to him, other than Leahy's speech mannerisms, he was another Leahy."

After visiting with Blaik, Kelly's father said, "I am going to take you to New York to see my good friend Dinty Moore at his restaurant where we can have a good dinner."

After their session at Dinty's restaurant, they stayed the night at a nearby hotel. As Kelly says, "It's the only night of my life I couldn't sleep. In the middle of the night I woke my dad and said, 'Dad, I don't want to go there [West Point]. I want to go to Notre Dame.'"

Kelly's father went along with his decision, but he thought it was very important that Kelly have everything properly settled, so he went back with him to South Bend instead of going on to Washington, D.C., as originally planned. As events unfolded, it proved to be a very wise decision.

The congressman sent a wire ahead to the Notre Dame Athletic Department telling McKeever they would arrive in South Bend the next morning. While they were still on the train, Kelly received a telegram from McKeever that said, in effect, "Suggest you stay at

West Point a year or two and give it a try." Kelly's father wired back that they were arriving in the morning and would like an appointment with him.

When they arrived, McKeever and Fr. John Cavanaugh were at the station to meet them. They drove immediately to the Oliver Hotel where Father Cavanaugh had a suite. Father Cavanaugh and McKeever told Kelly and his father that the reason Kelly would not be allowed to enroll at Notre Dame was because Blaik, who was irate over Kelly's abrupt decision to leave West Point and go to Notre Dame, had called to tell these men that if they took Kelly, he (Blaik) would break the Army-Notre Dame series. Father Cavanaugh said, "We can't take you at Notre Dame. We can't afford to lose that revenue."

Fortunately, Kelly's father was there to hear all this. Congressman Kelly patiently listened to the discussion, then spoke up, "You're telling me that Bob can't come to Notre Dame because of this football business?"

Father Cavanaugh explained that it was his opinion that Blaik was still mad at Notre Dame for what he thought was another ballplayer "stolen" from the Point—meaning Lujack. Kelly's father said, "Father Cavanaugh, may I use your phone?"

Father Cavanaugh replied, "Certainly."

Kelly's father placed a call to Blaik at West Point. When he got Blaik on the line, he said, "My son can go wherever he wants to and you, as a military man, are not going to dictate where he can or cannot go. If you do, you won't be at West Point much longer."

Congressman Kelly did not let up as he continued for several minutes to tell Blaik exactly how he felt about the situation. Blaik probably had not had a dressing down like that since his plebe days at the Point. There was not much Blaik could do to defend himself or his position because he knew only too well that Congressman Kelly was a senior member of the Interstate Commerce Committee and wielded great power in all matters before Congress, including military appropriations. Blaik quickly, and wisely, changed his position, informing Kelly's father that Kelly could certainly go wherever he wanted and there were no hard feelings.

Congressman Kelly said, "That's fine, now I'm going to put Father Cavanaugh on the line and I want you to repeat that for him."

Father Cavanaugh took the phone and talked with Blaik for about 10 minutes. When he got off the phone, he turned to Kelly and said, "Bob, you can come to Notre Dame."

With the matter settled, Congressman Kelly went back to Washington, D.C., while Kelly, McKeever, and Father Cavanaugh drove out to the campus to enroll Kelly in the January semester. Father Cavanaugh commented as they were parting on campus, "Bob, your father is quite a man."

That June, during the semester break (schools were on a tri-semester schedule because of the war), any players not already in the military enlisted in some branch of the service. Leahy told the players to sign up for the Navy V-12 program because it was the best as far as getting the opportunity to stay in school the longest. Artie Donovan, who would become a Pro Hall of Fame tackle with the Baltimore Colts, was on the squad that spring and was one of the players who enlisted in one of the programs. Donovan and a few others signed up for the Army A-12 program instead of the recommended V-12 program, and they were called up right away. Kelly signed on to the V-12 program as Leahy had advised.

During the semester break between June and July, Kelly got his orders to report to John Carroll University for training. Jim White, the left tackle, got the same news. Yonakor received his orders to report to Miami of Ohio with the Marines and several others received transfer orders. Leahy called Congressman Kelly to complain to him how awful it was that so many players were being transferred. Congressman Kelly told him that these were military orders and nothing could be done, but he promised Leahy he would look into it.

Congressman Kelly called "BuPers" (the Bureau of Personnel) and talked to the admiral in charge. He very cordially explained who he was. He asked the admiral why the Navy would take boys out of a school they were presently attending and send them to another school when the programs were identical. He went on to tell the admiral that it did not appear to make much sense.

The admiral explained that, in effect, everyone had a number in a pool and the military merely took a handful of numbers from the pool and sent that group to a selected school without regard to where the men were presently stationed. They kept doing this until everyone was assigned.

When Congressman Kelly heard how the system worked, he jumped on the admiral and told him that the method of taking a boy from his own school and sending him away when there was no reason for it, "stinks to high heaven." He went on to say, "They should be able to go to school where they started." He told the admiral it was bad for the morale of the young men and cost the taxpayers untold wasted millions of dollars, and that the matter should be looked into.

The admiral promised to do so. Evidently, the Navy concluded that its policy did not make much sense because several days later Kelly, White, and all the others who had received transfer orders, were issued new orders reassigning them to Notre Dame. It was a tremendous break for the Notre Dame team and other schools that had been similarly hit by the former transfer policy.

As it turned out, Notre Dame was able to play a powerful 11 composed of: Yonakor and Limont at end, White and Czarobski at tackle, Perko and Filley at guard, Coleman at center, Bertelli at quarterback, Miller and Rykovich at halfback, and Mello at fullback.

The backups behind this starting 11 were players who could not only be counted on to fill in whenever needed, but were of the caliber that, when they were playing, there was no notable difference in the quality of play.

Kuffel and Zilly at end could have started on almost any other college team. They would play important roles in the team's fortunes as the year progressed. Other reserves such as Sullivan, Meter, Urban, Adams, Szymanski, and Signaigo would all play prominently on the line for Notre Dame that season.

In the backfield, Lujack, who later in the season replaced Bertelli as the starting quarterback, did yeoman work that year. He was the backup quarterback to Bertelli; the backup left halfback to Miller; and a full-time defensive halfback. As an 18-year-old sophomore, Lujack played more minutes that year than at any time in his illustrious career.

Kelly became the understudy to Rykovich at right half, and Kulbitski backed up Mello. Hanlon filled in at both halfback and fullback, while Dancewicz, Terlep, Davis, Palladino, and Nemeth also played well when called upon.

Going into the season, Leahy had some new faces on his coaching staff. Hughie Devore, Leahy's coaching friend from his Fordham days, replaced Druze as the end coach, and Wally Ziemba, who had been discharged from the Marines because of bad knees, replaced

61

McArdle as the center and guard coach. Both Druze and McArdle had received their orders to report for duty as officers in the Navy.

Leahy knew he had a solid team with which to face Pittsburgh in the opening game on September 25, 1943. But, being a worrier, he could remember being tied by Wisconsin in the previous year's opener. He worked the team hard in practice the weeks before the game to make sure he had not overlooked any element of the detailed plans he always had for every game.

Pittsburgh

Miller, who has a great sense of humor and a fondness for giving his friend Lujack a rough time, loves to tell the story of what happened in the opening minutes of the Pitt game.

"Before the game, Coach Leahy informed Bertelli, who was the number one quarterback and the Heisman trophy winner that year, that he was going to start Lujack at quarterback. Leahy explained that many of Lujack's family and friends from nearby Connellsville would be at the game and he thought it would be good for Lujack's morale to play at the beginning of the game. He promised Bertelli that he would take Lujack out after the first Notre Dame possession and let Bertelli continue as the number one quarterback.

"During Notre Dame's first possession of the ball, we quickly got to Pitt's four-yard line where it was first down and goal. Lujack was still very nervous as he called a '22 on three.' This was a simple play where the quarterback handed off to the two-back, me, who would go straight ahead through the two hole on the count of three. At the snap of the ball, I ran straight ahead, through a huge hole, into the end zone, but there was one thing wrong—I didn't have the ball. It seems that Lujack had spun the wrong way and failed to make the handoff.

"When we got back to the huddle, I said, 'Lujack, I am really a Notre Dame player and on the same team with you—just hand me the ball.' Lujack called the same play and I ran through a big hole into the end zone, but again I did not have the ball. Lujack had turned the wrong way for the second time.

"I got Lujack aside and said, 'John, see the number on my jersey—it's number 37—my name is Creighton Miller and I am the number two back on this team. Believe me, I'm a Notre Dame man. My father was a starting back on the 1906, 1907, and 1908 Notre Dame teams, my uncle Wally was the fullback with George Gipp, and my uncle Don was one of the Four Horsemen. I am truly a Notre Dame man and a member of this team—so just give me the damn ball.

"Lujack called the play for the third time. This time he handed me the ball and I scored an easy touchdown."

As a postscript to the story: After the game, some of the sportswriters raved about Lujack's clever deception in faking the ball to Miller on two consecutive plays to set up the "trick play" for him to score an easy touchdown.

The Irish went on to overwhelm a very young Pitt team by a score of 41-0. A record opening crowd of 60,000 in Pittsburgh watched a Notre Dame team that was called "a power-laden, smooth-functioning, predominantly veteran outfit." Notre Dame's fleet backs, Miller, Rykovich, Lujack, Hanlon, and Bertelli could not be stopped. They were so effective in running the ball that Bertelli only passed six times, completing three.

Notre Dame spoiled the debut of Clark Shaughnessy as the head football coach at Pitt. Shaughnessy, who was one of the masters of the T-formation, watched as Notre Dame ran the T as he would have liked to see his team do it. His only comment about his Pitt team was, "They're a fine high school team."

Georgia Tech

In its home opener, Notre Dame completely outplayed Georgia Tech, crushing the Engineers, 55-13. It was the worst defeat for Tech since it had been beaten by Florida, 55-7, in 1929. The Irish more than atoned for the previous year's defeat.

Notre Dame's offensive attack amassed 418 yards compared with Tech's 98. Bertelli threw seven times, completing six of them, three for touchdowns. "Mr. Accurate," as he was dubbed by the sportswriters, hit three different receivers, Rykovich, Miller, and Kuffel, for scores.

On the ground, the Irish launched a potent attack with Mello leading the way with 167 yards in 18 carries. Rykovich gained 66 yards, as Mello and Rykovich took over as workhorses for the steady Miller, who had scored twice against Pitt.

The backfield of Bertelli, Miller, Mello, and Rykovich was developing into one of the best in the country.

Michigan

With just two games under its belt, Notre Dame was already ranked as the number one team in the country. The team's third game of the season against Michigan at Ann Arbor was billed as one of the greatest and most important games of the college season. Michigan, ranked number two in the nation, had a veteran team with a backfield of Bill Daley, Elroy Hirsch, Paul White, and Bob Wiese. Its line was equally talented with such players as Fred Negus, Merv Pregulman, and Bob Hanzlik. The game was a sellout, with an estimated capacity crowd of over 86,000 expected.

Bertelli tells about an incident that occurred the night before the game.

"I was with a group of players who were hanging around the hotel lobby. The game is completely sold out and you can't get a ticket anywhere. It's time to go to bed because Leahy is going to have a bed check. As we were going up the elevator, Scrapiron Young, the team trainer, says, 'It's too bad somebody doesn't have tickets. There is a guy in the lobby offering one hundred dollars for four to the game.' My mind started to work. I thought, 'I'll go and talk to Coach Leahy and maybe I can possibly get four tickets from him and make myself a quick hundred dollars.'

"I went to the coaches' room and told Leahy, 'There are four young guys in the service of our country who are here who have not seen me play since high school and have never seen Notre Dame play, and they would sure like to.'

"Leahy says, 'Impossible, impossible. You know how things are—it's just impossible. There is no way you can get any tickets.'

"I said, 'Okay, good night, Coach.' As I started to walk out the door the coach calls me back and says, 'Oh, Angelo, are you sure they are in the service of our country?'

" 'Yes, Coach.'

" 'Are you sure they have never seen Notre Dame play?'

" 'Yes, Coach.'

"Leahy came up with the four tickets. I went down to the lobby, found the guy, sold him the four tickets, went back to my room, and never slept better in my life."

Coach Leahy gave an odd pep talk to the team in the locker room the following day. "Lads," Leahy began, "Michigan is one of the 48 states of our great country. It is a beautiful state with magnificent lakes, splendid trees, picturesque hamlets, with excellent universities and colleges. [By this time Ziggie Czarobski is poking the player next to him with his elbow, which is quickly passed to the next player and around the room, as if to say, 'Here he goes again.'] We are in one of those towns today, at the site of the University of Michigan, to play a football game against a team composed of players from that fine institution.

"You will notice when we go out on the playing field that the players from Michigan wear different color jerseys than we do. I want to tell you that those people wearing a different color jersey are unfriendly—they are here to do harm to you, they do not like you. So when you encounter one of those players, you must attack him before he attacks you..."

And attack they did as the Notre Dame team dominated the Michigan team from the very start of the game. The Irish victory by a 35-12 score was the worst defeat for the Wolverines in six years. It was only the second time Notre Dame had defeated Michigan in their 10 games dating back to 1887, Notre Dame's first football season.

Oddly enough, in the 1909 victory over Michigan 34 years before, Harry "Red" Miller, Creighton's father, starred for the Irish. Miller upheld the family tradition as he dazzled the crowd with some brilliant running, scoring two of Notre Dame's touchdowns. Miller reminiscing about that game said, "It was one of those days when our line just blew everybody out. The holes were unbelievable. Our line just pulverized their line, and they had some damn good players. Our line had one great day."

A strange incident occurred that day in '43. The third quarter seemed endless to both the Michigan and Notre Dame players. The referee finally stopped play and the officials huddled in the center of the field for what seemed an eternity. They finally concluded that the clock was wrong. The teams had already played 23 minutes in what had to be the longest quarter in football history. By mutual agreement between the two coaches, the last quarter was only seven minutes. With the game on ice, Leahy yanked all the starters to give them a much-needed rest and to give the reserves some playing time.

One of the reserves that saw action that day was a freshman

65

tackle, Ed Mieszkowski, from Chicago's Tilden Tech. He was an eye-witness to a incident that would have far-reaching effects for both Notre Dame and Michigan.

As Mieszkowski was leaving the field after the game, he saw Frank Leahy and Fritz Crisler, the head coach of Michigan, approach each other at the center of the field for the traditional post-game handshake. He recalled what happened. "When they were about five yards apart, Crisler, who has that cigar hanging out of his mouth, stopped and said, 'Leahy, this was the rottenest, dirtiest football game I have ever seen and if I have anything to say about it, Michigan will never play Notre Dame again.' With that, Crisler turned around and walked away."

Years later, when Mieszkowski was coaching football at Mt. Carmel High School in Chicago, he told the story to a prominent Michigan alumnus who was recruiting players at Mt. Carmel to attend Michigan. Mieszkowski recalled, "The guy didn't believe me, but several days later he called me at Mt. Carmel and said he had asked Crisler about the incident with Leahy. The guy said, 'I asked him [Crisler] if it was true, and he asked me where I heard it, and when I told him, he admitted it was true.'" (Michigan did not play Notre Dame again until 1978. There are confirmed reports that Crisler also led a campaign to have all Big Ten schools boycott Notre Dame. Red Mackey, the athletic director of Purdue, put an end to the attempted boycott when he said no to Crisler.)

Wisconsin

The Irish breezed by the Wisconsin Badgers at Madison by a score of 55-0. Notre Dame scored on its first possession and hit pay dirt seven more times as Miller scored twice, and Rykovich, Bertelli, Lujack, Mello, Yonakor, and Mike Lyden each scored once. Keeping their aerial attack under wraps, Bertelli only tried six passes, connecting on four for 104 yards.

Several of the Notre Dame halfbacks were injured during the course of the game. Leahy decided to put Elmer Angsman, a sophomore reserve who had not played much, in the game. As Angsman was running on the field, Leahy hollered to Bertelli, "Don't give the ball to Angsman! Don't give the ball to Angsman!"

In the huddle Bertelli said to Angsman, "Do you know what a 27-slant is?"

"Sure," replied Angsman, "that's the off-tackle play."

Bertelli said, "OK, we'll call that—when you get to the hole, cut inside because the linebacker is drifting outside. It should work."

Angsman took the handoff, cut in as Bertelli had instructed, and got 18 yards. Leahy loved to tell this story in later years to demonstrate the point that coaches are not always right.

Illinois

Notre Dame's fifth game of the season was at home against a weak Illinois team, its ranks depleted by the transfer of all its 1942 stars to other schools. Illinois was hopelessly outclassed as Notre Dame won, 47-0. Leahy used his regulars only in the first quarter and five minutes into the second half. He used all 42 players to try to hold the score down.

Navy

I recently asked Creighton Miller about reports that he had stopped short of the goal line on one of his runs. He laughed and said, "Yes, I did. Here is what happened.

"It was the Navy game in 1943. The night before the game in Cleveland, I was rooming with Bertelli and Lujack. We were kidding about different things and I said, 'If I get a chance to score tomorrow, I am not going to run through the whole end zone. I am going to stop as soon as I cross the goal line.

"During the game I was running in for a score and I thought I'll have some great fun with my roommates by doing exactly what I said the night before and stop as soon as I cross the goal line. I glanced to the side to see where the goal-line marker was and, for some reason, instead of being right on the sidelines, the marker was set about 10 yards back, so my perspective was off. What I thought was the goal line was really the five-yard line. When I crossed it, I immediately stopped, only to be tackled by a Navy player pursuing the play. [Miller was hit from behind by Jim Pettit at about the three and fell over the goal line. The officials ruled it a touchdown.]

"Our bench went wild. They thought that Navy should be penalized for hitting me after I scored. The referee made the right call.

"Watching the movies the following Monday it was very clear that

I stopped just past the five-yard line. Leahy wasn't too happy with me to say the least."

That game, against a powerful Navy team ranked number three in the country, was played before a capacity crowd of 82,000 in Cleveland's Memorial Stadium. From the very outset there was no doubt of the outcome as Notre Dame overpowered Navy for a 33-6 win. It was the highest score ever achieved against the Midshipmen in the history of the classic rivalry between these two schools.

The Irish were known for their potent offensive attack, but they also showed how well they could play defense. Navy's net yards rushing were a minus seven, forcing the Middies to pass 39 times, five of which were intercepted.

Miller continued his scoring spree with two touchdowns, but it was Bertelli's day. The game marked Bertelli's last appearance in a Notre Dame uniform. He had received his orders to report to the Marine Corps camp at Parris Island, South Carolina, to begin his Marine training. Bertelli bowed out in a manner befitting the way he had played his entire career at Notre Dame. He scored one of the Irish touchdowns himself and figured in nearly every other scoring play.

In all of Notre Dame's history there was no finer passer than Angelo Bertelli. This modest, well-liked player would make history at the end of the season by becoming the first Notre Dame player ever to receive the Heisman Award as the outstanding college football player in the country.

Lujack, Bertelli's replacement at quarterback, became, at 18 years of age, the youngest player ever to call plays for Notre Dame. Although only a sophomore, Lujack had as much game time in the first six games as anyone on the team.

Leahy, true to his pre-season understanding with Miller, gave him a rest every time he made a long run and there were many of them. Lujack would then go in the game for Miller at left halfback. According to Creighton, "Lujack cheered for me every time I carried the ball, hoping I would make a long run so he could get in the game at halfback. Lujack actually would have preferred to run with the ball. That was much more exciting to him than being a T quarterback. Lujack played more minutes that year than any other year. Leahy didn't want Bertelli in on defense except when they needed him. So our defensive backfield was Julie Rykovich, Lujack, and myself—we were going both ways."

Army

Leahy took his undefeated team to New York to play its seventh game against an undefeated Army team in Yankee Stadium. If Coach Blaik's Cadets thought they were getting some relief because they would face Lujack at quarterback instead of Bertelli, they were in for a terrible surprise. Lujack, playing his first game as the starting quarterback, was nothing short of sensational as he tossed two touchdown passes to Yonakor to open the scoring and scored the third touchdown himself on a quarterback sneak. Earley scored the fourth touchdown on a sweep around end to make the final score, Notre Dame 26, Army 0.

Kelly, the 17-year-old halfback from Chicago, started his first game for the Irish in place of Rykovich at right half. Miller, aware that it was Kelly's first game in Yankee Stadium, said, "Now, Bob, don't be nervous."

Kelly shot back, "Who's nervous?"

He was not nervous. What Miller and some others did not realize was that Kelly had played in Chicago high school city championship games three years in a row to crowds in excess of 80,000 fans. Despite his age, playing before big crowds was nothing new to Kelly.

There were a number of standout players in the game. Miller gained 94 yards on 20 carries and played 58 minutes. Yonakor caught some great passes; Kelly, Mello, and Kulbitski had some good runs; White, the left tackle, stole the ball from Davis near the Army goal line which "broke the game wide open," according to Coach Blaik of Army. The victory made it seven in a row for Leahy's lads.

Northwestern

The Notre Dame team stayed overnight at the Palmer House in Chicago before the short trip the next day to Evanston to play the Nothwestern Wildcats at Dyche Stadium. Miller and Kelly were assigned to be roommates. Kelly describes what happened the night before the game:

"Creighty and I were in our room at about 10 o'clock when there was a knock on the door. It was Otto Graham, the star halfback for Northwestern, looking for Creighton. After I was introduced to Graham, the two of them sat around and talked for about an hour and a half. They had met at the All-Star camp the previous August. I just sat there and listened to them, amazed that the best player from each school would calmly sit and visit with each other the night before the big game. Here I am, just 17 years old, I kept wondering what Leahy would say if he found Otto Graham in our room talking to Creighton."

It was a surprisingly balmy November day that Saturday as the Notre Dame team prepared to battle for its eighth straight victory. Before the game even got underway, Miller provided some extra color.

He had obtained four tickets for good friends who lived in nearby Winnetka. During the pre-game warm-up Miller spotted his friends in 50-yard-line seats situated close to the playing field. When Leahy gave the signal for the team to return to the visiting locker room, Miller went over to the stands to say a quick hello. In the meantime, the Notre Dame team exited the field via an unusual exit route peculiar to Dyche Stadium. To get to the locker rooms below the stands it was necessary to first exit the field at the 10-yard line, go up the steps to a ramp, then take the ramp down below the stands to the unmarked visiting team locker room.

When Miller had finished his short visit with his friends, he glanced to where the players had been only to find they were already out of sight. He now had to make a decision. If he went back on the field to the 10-yard line, all the people in the stands would see the recognizable number 37 on his jersey and wonder what Creighton Miller was doing alone on the field. He thought that would be embarrassing, so he opted to take the closest ramp which was higher up on the 50-yard line.

This ramp took him underneath the stands, but the problem now was to locate the correct door. To his dismay, there were numerous unmarked doors. He tried a couple of doors, knocked on them, but no luck. He hurriedly knocked on a few more doors with no success. By this time, Miller is starting to get panicky as he can imagine what Leahy must be thinking about his absence such a short time before kickoff.

He had an idea. He would ask a concessionaire for directions. Surely, one of these guys would know where the visiting locker room was located. As he anxiously looked for a stand he could not help but notice that people were looking at him in a strange way. He recalls thinking, "I am sure these people are wondering what kind of jerk wears a football uniform to a game."

He spotted a hot dog stand and with no pretense of politeness pushed his way through the crowd to the head of the line. He asked the man working the stand if he knew where the visiting locker room was. The attendant, thinking Miller was a weird fan dressed as a player, replied, "That uniform don't cut any mustard with me fella, get back to the end of the line." Miller went to the end of the line to wait his turn. As he was about third in line he saw Fr. John Cavanaugh, the vice president of Notre Dame in charge of athletics, approaching him. He tried to hide behind one of the fans, but Father Cavanaugh had already spotted him. Father Cavanaugh inquired what Miller was doing standing in a hot dog line just before game time. As Miller started to explain, Father Cavanaugh cut him short and turned to the distinguished-looking gentleman with him, the president of Northwestern, and said, "Remember our conversation at lunch yesterday when I predicted that Northwestern should do well against Notre Dame? Well, here we have one of our starting halfbacks in a hot dog line with just five minutes to game time. See what I mean?"

To Miller's relief, a student manager whom Leahy had sent looking for the missing Miller, suddenly appeared and told Miller that Leahy wanted him right away. The manager escorted him to the visiting team locker room. As soon as they entered the room, Leahy rushed up to Miller and asked, "Oh, Creighton Miller, where have you been? Where could you possibly go with that uniform on?" Before he could answer, Leahy hastily added, "No, don't tell me. Just don't say anything. I don't think I want to know. I just don't want to know."

Miller had a much easier time on the playing field than he did under the stands as he gained 151 yards running and scored a touchdown as Notre Dame rolled over Northwestern by a 25-6 score. Lujack, starting his second game at quarterback, played another outstanding game. Kelly, subbing for Rykovich, scored two touchdowns and Rykovich scored the fourth.

The Irish were clearly the number one team in the country with only two more games to win to become the first Notre Dame team since the days of Knute Rockne to go through a season undefeated and untied.

Iowa Pre-Flight

The upcoming game at home against Iowa Pre-Flight was, without question, the big game of the year. The Iowa Seahawks were

71

coached by Don Faurot of Missouri and loaded with college stars and seasoned pro players. They had Jimmy Smith, the former Illinois star at quarterback, Dick Todd of the Washington Redskins at halfback, along with the elusive Art Guepe of Marquette and Bus Mertes of Iowa to complement them in the backfield. In the line there were such standouts as Perry Schwartz, the former California All-American, Vince Banonis, the All-Pro center from the Chicago Cardinals, Nick Kerasiotis from the Chicago Bears, and Notre Dame's own George Tobin. They were a team to be reckoned with as their undefeated season to date clearly indicated.

Coach Leahy desperately wanted to win this game. To get his team in the right frame of mind, Leahy decided to take his players to the gravesite of the legendary Knute Rockne. Lujack describes their strange visit.

"As the team knelt around the grave Coach Leahy said, 'Lads, bow your heads and say a silent prayer to Rock that he will be with us tomorrow and help us defeat this great team.'

"After about a minute, I got off my knees and walked about 10 yards away to the grave of the revered Notre Dame basketball coach, George Keogan, to pay my respects.

"Leahy raised his head and spotted me at Keogan's grave and said in that disapproving tone we all knew so well, 'John Lujack, this is not the time for that. You get back over here, this is the football season.' "

Maybe Rockne did hear them because Notre Dame won a come-from-behind contest by the slim margin of 14-13. It all came down to Earley's dramatic extra point that spelled victory for the still-undefeated Irish. Just the previous week in Notre Dame's 25-7 win over Northwestern, Earley had missed three of four conversion attempts, but when it counted most, his kick was perfect.

The Seahawks scored first when Guepe went eight yards to score standing up in the first period. Notre Dame took the second-half kickoff and did not surrender the ball until it had scored a touchdown. Eighteen-year-old Earley tied the game at 7-7 with his extra-point kick.

The two teams lived up to their billing as number one and two in the nation. They battled each other until early in the fourth quarter when the Seahawks capitalized on a Notre Dame fumble and scored on a pass to go ahead, 13-7. They failed to convert when Barney McGarry, substituting for the injured Monk Maznicki (their regular placekicker) hit the upright with his kick.

The Irish took the ensuing kickoff down the field to score, setting up the potential winning kick by Earley. With eight minutes left to play, the tough Seahawks marched to Notre Dame's 17-yard line where they attempted a field goal that fell short, thereby ending the scoring threat.

After the game, the injured Maznicki, who had played for Leahy at Boston College, went to the Notre Dame dressing room to congratulate his former coach. He told Leahy, "You wouldn't have won the game if I were playing." And he might have been right as Maznicki was one of the best when it came to kicking extra points and field goals.

All of the Notre Dame players played well. Lujack played 60 minutes of gruelling football. At one point Lujack made a one-handed interception of a Seahawk pass that astounded the capacity crowd.

Leahy was highly pleased that his team had made it nine victories in a row by winning over the previously undefeated Seahawks in one of the most spectacular games ever seen at Notre Dame. Some of the sportswriters tried to get him to compare the 1943 team with some of Rockne's great teams, but Leahy tactfully avoided the comparison. Instead, he took the opportunity to graciously praise his present team when he said, "These boys, with so many other things on their minds in these terrible times, have done nobly. They have splendid team spirit and enthusiasm, they are an extremely easy squad to handle and coach, and they respond promptly and eagerly to coaching. There isn't a fat-headed kid on the entire squad; every one of them has realized, from the first game right up to now, that the only way to win football games is to forget your press raves and go out there every Saturday afternoon and give it everything you've got. That's what these boys have done for me and for themselves, that's what they did against the Seahawks, and I'm extremely proud of them.

"Also, don't forget the splendid job of coaching done by Ed McKeever, Ed Krause, Hughie Devore, Wally Ziemba, and Jake Kline. Each has contributed mightily to our success and I am as proud of the unselfish loyalty and devotion of my assistants as I am of the players themselves. It took a perfect combination to achieve the success we have attained this year."

Great Lakes

The final game of the year against the Great Lakes Blue Jackets put an end to the dream of an unbeaten and untied season when

Great Lakes scored in the final 30 seconds of play to defeat Notre Dame, 19-14. Steve Lach, the former Duke University and Chicago Cardinal star, threw a fantastic desperation pass 46 yards into the arms of Paul Anderson for the go-ahead touchdown. As Lujack, who was playing defensive halfback, describes the play, "It looked like he was going to be tackled and then he started around end—we all moved up and he threw it over our heads for the touchdown."

One of the stars of the game was Emil "Red" Sitko, who had played on the freshman team at Notre Dame the previous year along with Mike Romano, now his Great Lakes teammate. Also on the team with Sitko were two other Notre Damers, Steve Juzwik and Pete Kelly. As a halfback for the Great Lakes team, Sitko gained 114 yards on 17 carries. Sitko, who would return to Notre Dame after the war, would become one of Notre Dame's all-time greats as a running back. Eventually, his prowess earned him induction to the College Football Hall of Fame.

After the game, Romano and Sitko went to the Notre Dame bus to see some of their former teammates. When they encountered a saddened Leahy, the coach said, "Oh, Emil, my school lost today."

Sitko responded, "It's my school too, Coach."

At the Marine base, Parris Island, Bertelli was listening to the game in a Quonset hut together with three or four other Notre Dame men. When they heard Great Lakes score the last minute winning touchdown, they left the hut with tears in their eyes. As fate would have it, just then a fellow Marine came up to Bertelli with a telegram informing him that he had won the Heisman Trophy as the outstanding player in the nation.

Despite this disappointing finish, Notre Dame was awarded the National Championship for its great play throughout the season. It helped ease the hurt the players felt after the loss that marred their record. There was no question in their minds that they were the best team in the nation.

The 1943 team led the nation in total offense with an average of 418 yards per game. The Irish were also first nationally in rushing offense, with an average of 313.7 yards per game.

In addition to the team honors, six players were named to All-America teams: Angelo Bertelli, Creighton Miller, Jim White, Herb Coleman, John Yonakor, and the captain, Pat Filley.

Bertelli capped a sensational three-year career by winning the Heisman Award. It was a tribute to Bertelli's great career to win the award after having played in only six games during the 1943 season. In speaking of Bertelli, Bob Kelly said, "Bertelli was a great quarterback. He had a touch like a feather. He was a very good ball handler and a great faker. He was the best I ever played with. John Lujack was also great and a better all-around player."

Lujack, who was Notre Dame's second Heisman Award winner, says of Bertelli, "I've been a great admirer of his for a long time. In fact, every time I'm around him I say something nice about him, and he thinks I'm kidding him, but I think Bertelli is as classy a person now as he was then. He was as sharp a passer as Notre Dame has ever had. He could throw the ball with great accuracy. He had so much control over the ball, much more than I ever thought of having."

Creighton Miller lead the nation in rushing with 911 yards in 151 carries. He was fourth in the Heisman voting. He led the team in scoring with 13 touchdowns and in kickoff and punt return averages. He also led the team with six interceptions.

When his fellow players talk about Miller, they use nothing but superlatives to describe his play. Bertelli says, "Creighton Miller was one of the best runners I have ever seen. He had the quickest start—he would just burst in there. The T-formation in those days was not like the T-formation you see in the pros or in college today. Everything today is options along the line and big splits in the line. The T-formation of 1942 and 1943 was closed—all the linemen were closed—everything was faking by the quarterback and quick hand-offs. Creighton Miller could hit in there like you wouldn't believe. Bob Kelly was another one who could do the same thing. There was another back that could really hit in there, Elmer Angsman. You could tell he was going to be a great one as he later showed with the Chicago Cardinals. It is hard to believe that anyone could be better or have better moves than Creighton Miller."

Kelly, Miller's teammate in 1943, adds, "Creighton Miller was the best back I have ever seen in my life. He could do everything. He had the size, the speed, and was a great inside runner. If you needed five yards or three yards, he would hit anything to get you the yardage. He was also a good defensive back."

All Miller's teammates believe that he was the best runner they have ever seen. Lujack summed it up best when he said, "Creighty is the finest running back I have ever played with, college or pro. I have been back here at Notre Dame watching an awful lot of games and I have not seen anybody that I thought could measure up to Creighton Miller. Creighty was a dash champion. He could run the hundred in about 9.6 seconds. Keep in mind this is back in 1943. He weighed 195 pounds and he might have been the trickiest back. You run into a lot of fast halfbacks, but they're not maneuverable, they're not tricky. Creighty could head-fake you and hip-fake you, and he had bow legs and it just seemed like legs were coming at you from all directions—then suddenly he would dart past you and you didn't know what happened. A pass catcher? He had the softest hands—anything that was near him he had, then he would just go."

Miller, in addition to being one of Notre Dame's all-time greats in football, also earned his monogram in track. He tells it this way:

"Babe Murphy was our sprinter at Notre Dame. His best time in the 100-yard dash was 9.5 seconds. One day at track practice, just as a joke, I said, 'Babe, I think I can beat you. I'll bet you a milkshake I can beat you.' I went in and put a uniform on and got some track shoes. We ran a 60-yard dash and I was timed by the coach, Doc Handy, at 6.2 seconds and I beat him. Handy asked if I would come out for the track team and I said no. I said I don't like practice. We had just gotten through with football—it was in January. He said, 'How about running just in the meets?'

"I said, 'No practice?'

"He replied, 'No practice.'

"I might win a dual meet indoors, that was about the best I could do. But I did win enough points to win my letter, so I became a monogram man in track. At the Michigan State relays some guy got sick, so Doc Handy came up to me and said, 'There's a medley relay; do you know what a medley is?'

"I said, 'Sure that's where guys run different distances.'

"He asked, 'Would you run the 220?'

"I said, 'You're sure it isn't the 440? I'm not running the 440, the track is 440.'

"He said, 'No, it's 220.'

"I said, 'If it turns out to be 440, I'm giving you the baton when I come around the first time.' "

The remaining four All-Americans played on the line that was rated as one of the best in the nation.

Jim White, the left tackle, had been outstanding on offense and defense throughout the entire season. He was known as an aggressive, tough player who often spent a good part of the game in the other team's backfield. His stealing the ball from Davis in the Army game played a crucial role in the outcome of that important game. He went on to become the captain of the New York Giants after the war.

White, who was a fast, rugged, hard-charging tackle, would fight like hell during the practice scrimmages to get to the ball carrier or passer. Not wanting to get his quarterback, Angelo Bertelli, hurt in practice, Leahy had Bertelli don a red shirt to alert the oncharging linemen that they were not to tackle him. Several times during the scrimmage, Jim White broke through the line headed for Bertelli, but Leahy would blow his whistle and say, "James White, don't hit our quarterback." This frustrated White, so to at least get some satisfaction, he started to call Bertelli, "Precious." Even after the two were out of school, White's usual good-natured greeting to Bertelli was, "How are you, Precious?"

Herb Coleman, at center, was an outstanding blocker who consistently opened big holes for Miller, Mello, Rykovich, Kelly, and all the backs. He was not exceptionally heavy, but he made up for it with his quickness and ability to move his man out of the play.

John Yonakor, at 6-feet-5 and 235 pounds, was one of Bertelli's and Lujack's favorite targets when the game situation called for a clutch play. He had good hands, excellent speed, and body control for a man of his size. He led the team in receiving with 323 yards and four touchdowns.

Pat Filley, at left guard, was a wonder at 5 feet, 8 inches and about 185 pounds. His teammates say he was quick and tough. He had a way of getting to the defensive man's body, and once he did, that man was out of the play.

The whole team played exceptional and consistent football. All the players talk about what a great year Ziggie Czarobski had both as a player and in keeping the team entertained. Miller says, "Ziggie was a better player than a lot of people gave him credit for. Because he was so funny and such a great personality it sort of overshadowed his ability, but he was good. He was a funny guy that kept everyone loose, but he was real serious during a game. He was one of those classic guys that wherever he went people would follow him around. On the campus you could always see two or three guys walking with him—he always had an entourage."

77

Bertelli echoed the feelings about Czarobski when he said, "Ziggie's humor on the practice field, even when Leahy would have him run laps after practice, kept us loose. He was so much a part of our group and was Notre Dame all the way."

Lujack filled in for the departed Bertelli in a masterful way. Lujack's contribution to the success of the team was enormous. He played the entire season on defense as well as playing halfback and quarterback before his starting assignment at quarterback in the Army game. He averaged 43 minutes a game and missed only four minutes of playing time the last four games of the season.

When asked about this, Lujack said, "I loved playing both ways. I never wanted to come out of the game. If I could play 60 minutes—that was fine. I just wanted to be in there—I loved it. Somebody asked me, 'Did you enjoy playing offense more than defense?' and I don't know. I just liked them both and wanted to do both. I know that I never wanted to come out of a football game—I just hated it."

In assessing the merits of the 1943 team Lujack said, "I think that the 1943 team offensively was maybe the best of the three teams I played on [1943, 1946, 1947]. The 1946 team defensively was just tremendous. Our opponents only scored four touchdowns and never made an extra-point try, but I think the '43 team was as good an offensive team as I have ever been on."

Frank Leahy, who never seemed to take the time to enjoy his successes, would have two years away from coaching to think about 1943. He was called into active duty as a lieutenant in the Navy. Given the way he usually operated, he probably was thinking more about the future and planning for the teams after the war than he thought about the past.

Meanwhile, the players who were in one of the military programs and had not finished their sophomore years continued on with college life. Lujack, who was in the Navy V-12 program, went out for the basketball squad and made the first team. He played in Madison Square Garden, which was a thrill, and was a teammate of one of Notre Dame's great basketball stars, Leo Klier.

That spring John went out for track and specialized in the high jump and the javelin, easily winning his monogram. Then he went out for baseball and lettered in that. In his first game, he had a triple and two singles to go three-for-four. With the baseball game still going on, he did the high jump and the javelin for the track team. John's roommate, Tom Sheehan, the catcher on the baseball team, said, "John, if you get dressed real fast, I think there's is a swimming meet at the Rock."

Lujack won four letters his sophomore year and was only the third Notre Dame man ever to accomplish this feat, and the first one to do so at Notre Dame in over 30 years. George Ratterman, another quarterback and a teammate of Lujack's in 1946, would also win letters in four different sports a few years later.

Chapter Six

THE UNAPPRECIATED YEARS, 1944-1945

When one reads the various books, articles, or publicity items written about Notre Dame football, it becomes apparent that, as compared to other years, little is written about the 1944 and 1945 football teams. It gives one the feeling that football was either not played at Notre Dame during those years, or, at best, the teams were not very good.

One obvious reason for this is that the country's attention was on the war. The U.S. war effort was at its height both in Europe and in the Pacific theater of operations. As a result, most young men who would normally have been in college and eligible to play football were serving in some branch of the service, as were many of the big name college coaches.

Notre Dame, like so many schools, had to field a team composed of mostly young players just out of high school. It was a common occurrence in the 1944 season to have from five to eight freshmen in the starting lineup. My research on the teams of 1944 and 1945 has convinced me that these teams, admittedly manned by young players, were well coached, fiercely competitive, and achieved remarkable results given their youth and inexperience.

As evidence of the ability of the players on these teams, one only has to look at the roster of the teams after the war, when the football talent at Notre Dame was so abundant, to discover that the 1944-45 teams were well represented. Such players as Bill Fischer, John Mastrangelo, Marty Wendell, Fred Rovai, Bill Walsh, Zeke O'Connor, Walter Grothaus, Bob Skoglund, Jim Dailer, John Panelli, Jack Fallon, George Ratterman, Frank Tripucka, Terry Brennan, and Bill Gompers all began their Notre Dame football careers by playing on one of these teams.

The combined record of these two teams is 15-4-1, which is an outstanding record by any standard. Perhaps the losses to Army in those years by such lopsided scores of 59-0 and 48-0 is the key reason why the 1944 and 1945 seasons are not given their just due. Zeke O'Connor, the starting left end on the 1944 team, said, "Losing to Army by such a big score put a stigma on this team that has lasted through the years."

To understand how these losses could occur one should be aware of the times in which the games were played and the football talent on hand at the respective schools. As was pointed out before, Notre Dame, like most schools, had to rely on mostly younger players, freshmen and sophomores, to field a team. On the other hand, the U.S. Military Academy Cadets, because they were training to be future Army officers, remained at that school for at least three years. Thus the Academy could field a team of seasoned players. The same held true for the U.S. Naval Academy. Great Lakes, Iowa Pre-Flight, and other service teams were loaded with college and pro stars. These teams resembled All-Star teams.

In looking at Notre Dame's four losses in these two years, it is interesting to note that two were to Army, one to Navy, and one to the Great Lakes Training Center—all service-related teams. The one tie was with Navy. In other words, when Notre Dame played teams other than "service" teams in 1944-45, the Irish were undefeated.

This explanation is not meant as an excuse for the defeats, or in any way to downgrade the tremendous accomplishments of these service teams—it is given so that the reader may have a better understanding and appreciation of the accomplishments of the young Notre Dame players of 1944 and 1945.

The 1944 Season

With Frank Leahy, Johnny Druze, and Joe McArdle in the U.S. Navy, only Ed McKeever was left from the original coaching staff that started at Notre Dame in 1941. Moose Krause, who joined the coaching staff in 1942, was now in the Marine Corps.

Ed McKeever had been Leahy's top assistant, so it naturally followed that he would be selected as the new head football coach at Notre Dame. The 34-year-old McKeever was an excellent coach. He had coached the backs for Leahy during Leahy's two-year stint as head coach at Boston College and then for three years at Notre

Dame. Not only did he know the intricacies of the T-formation and had been responsible for many of the pass patterns that played a big role in the success of Bertelli and Lujack, he knew how to impart his knowledge to the players.

McKeever's staff included holdovers from the previous year, Hughie Devore, Wally Ziemba, and Jake Kline, with new additions of Adam Walsh, Clem Crowe, and Creighton Miller.

If Leahy and his staff thought they had problems in planning ahead as to which players would be available to play in 1943, they should have faced the problems of player availability that McKeever and his assistants faced for the 1944 season. It became an almost day-to-day thing for the coaches in trying to guess which players would be in school and available to play football. Without freshmen being allowed to play, most schools, including Notre Dame, could not have fielded a team.

Zeke O'Connor

One of the freshmen who started for Notre Dame that season was William "Zeke" O'Connor. O'Connor was typical of so many who, at age 17 or 18, found themselves playing on a big-time college football team years before they ever dreamed they would.

O'Connor lived in the Bronx and attended Mount St. Michael High School. He played football, basketball, and baseball while in high school and did very well in all three. In his junior and senior years, O'Connor made the equivalent of the All-State basketball team. In football as a junior, he was first string end, where he played next to Artie Donovan (who would go on to become a professional Hall-of-Fame player with the Baltimore Colts). In his senior year, O'Connor's team won the area All-Catholic title, which entitled it to play in a first-ever game against the Chicago Catholic League Champions. The game was billed as the national championship of high school football.

Mount St. Michael's opponent that early day in December 1943 at the Polo Grounds in New York was St. George High School from Evanston, Illinois. In reminiscing about the game, O'Connor said, "It was a great game—cold as it could be. We lost to St. George, 25-20. We had the ball on the one-foot line when the game ended and we still had downs left. So it really was an exciting game."

St. George had a hard-running fullback, who also was sensational as a linebacker, by the name of Marty Wendell. Wendell and O'Connor played on opposite teams that day, but soon they would be teammates; they played together as freshmen on the 1944 Notre Dame team, then on the same Great Lakes Naval Training Center team in 1945, and again at Notre Dame in 1946 and 1947.

O'Connor always thought he would like to attend either the University of Southern California or West Point. However, when he was recruited by Hughie Devore to attend Notre Dame, his dad, a New York City policeman, and his coach, Howie Smith (a Notre Dame man), persuaded him to go to Notre Dame. O'Connor said, "I've never regretted that decision. It was the best thing that could have happened to me."

O'Connor was not due to graduate from high school until June of 1944, but because of the war, he, along with three others who were also going to Notre Dame, were given a special exam that allowed them to graduate in January.

When O'Connor arrived on the Notre Dame campus from New York in January 1944, it was during a tri-semester break. As O'Connor recalls, "Boy, I'll tell you that was impressive. I had never been out here before. What a thrill to see the campus. It was beautiful. It's hard to say that military uniforms are beautiful, but at that time they had the officers' candidate school for the Marine Corps, the Navy V-12 program, and the V-5 program for future Navy pilots, plus an ROTC program. All these men were in uniform and at 8 A.M. the quadrangle would be filled with men in uniform lining up—it was really impressive."

O'Connor, who was 6 feet, 4 inches, had a reputation as a very good basketball player, so even though the Notre Dame basketball team only had two more games to play, he was asked to join the team. Thus, on a Wednesday morning, O'Connor registered for school, and on that Wednesday night he played in a varsity basketball game. He might have set some kind of record by playing in a varsity game the same day he registered and without ever having been to class! As O'Connor describes it, "What a thrill! Here I am 17 years old and wearing a Notre Dame uniform."

O'Connor enjoyed an excellent spring football practice. One day, at a practice with Frank Leahy looking on (he was visiting while on leave), O'Connor caught Leahy's eye. O'Connor caught a pass, then shed a defender who tried to tackle him and raced another 40 yards for a touchdown. Leahy, from the sidelines, hollered so everyone could hear, "Oh, William O'Connor, that's the way to play."

O'Connor's work earned him the starting left-end position as well as the George Herring Award for the most improved player in spring practice.

Pittsburgh

One indication of the effect the war had on the 1944 Notre Dame team is how the squad that went to Pittsburgh for its first game traveled in two groups on different days. Twenty-four civilian members of the football squad arrived in Pittsburgh one day ahead of 10 servicemen teammates, V-12 Navy men, who had to take a later train because they were restricted to 48 hours of absence from their station (Notre Dame).

The starting lineup for Notre Dame was composed of:

At end: Bill "Zeke" O'Connor, 18, V-12, and Bob Skoglund, 19, ROTC student. At tackle: George Sullivan, 18, V-12, and John "Tree" Adams, 22, 4-F. At guard: John Mastrangelo, 18, civilian, and Fred Rovai, 21, 1-C. At center: Ralph Stewart, 20, V-12. At quarterback: Frank "Boley" Dancewicz, 19, 4-F. At halfback: Chick Maggioli, 22, Marine trainee, and Bob Kelly, 19, V-12. At fullback: Elmer Angsman, 18, civilian.

The starting lineup averaged 19 years of age. Only Kelly, Adams, Sullivan, Dancewicz, and Pat Filley had previously won ND monograms. That was an all-time low for returning lettermen. Filley, who captained the 1943 team, had just been released from the service because of his bad knees and, due to limited practice time, was not expected to play very much.

John "Tree" Adams

Everyone called the starting right tackle, John Adams, "Tree." Adams was a big man even by today's standards. He was about 6 feet, 8 inches and weighed about 260 pounds. Adams was very fast of foot for his size, and a very tough player, yet, off the field he was a gentle giant. He had an enormous head which looked even bigger with his football helmet on. No one knows for sure, but guesses at his hat size range from $8\frac{1}{4}$ to $8\frac{3}{4}$. Notre Dame did not have a helmet to fit him. Scrapiron Young, the team trainer, constructed a custom one by splitting two regular helmets in sections and placing them on Adam's head. When the desired fit was obtained and the helmets temporarily taped together, the trainer had someone sew the parts into a permanent helmet.

One day in practice, Adams really tested the strength of his unique helmet. Adams made a bet with one of the other tackles that he could run through the seven-foot wooden fence that surrounded Cartier Field. As Wally Ziemba, the center coach, tells the story, "Adams took about six or seven strides and, with that huge helmet, went headfirst through the fence, shattering about seven of the slats. The crazy thing is the bet was for 50 cents—I don't think Adams ever collected."

Playing against Adams in practice was no fun. Bob Welch, a reserve guard, recently recalled one particular day playing against him. "It was a very hot summer afternoon in 1944, near the end of a tough practice, that one of the coaches decided that Tree Adams and I should go one-on-one. John on offense, me on defense. We went at each other with everything we had. I cannot remember if the whole team looked on, but I do remember that all the linemen were there. John was a better football player than I was, but I was determined to do my best. We were both near exhaustion when Moose Krause, who was calling the hikes, said, and this is exactly what he said, 'That-a-boy Welch, you will make Tree an All-American.' In spite of myself, I had to laugh and I can remember muttering, 'Yes and I hope I live to see it.' "

On October 1, 1944, the Sunday following the game, the sports page of the *South Bend Tribune* carried the headline "ND Crushes Pitt, 58-0." Pitt could not seem to do anything right—four passes were intercepted which Notre Dame quickly converted into touchdowns; three Pitt fumbles were recovered by the alert Irish defenders and also turned into touchdowns.

Kelly, at halfback for Notre Dame, put on a one-man show. He scored Notre Dame's first four touchdowns and kicked two extra points. He accounted for all of Notre Dame's first 26 points. On the second play after the second-half kickoff, Kelly ran 65 yards for a score that had the fans gasping as he burst through the line, eluded two secondary defenders, then headed for the sidelines where he was hit, only to regain his stride, reverse his field, and sprint untouched the rest of the way into the end zone. At this point, Coach McKeever decided Kelly had done enough. He sat out the rest of the game.

Notre Dame's passing and rushing totaled 622 yards. The whole team played steady football, particularly Dancewicz and his 17-year-old understudy, Joe Gasparella, who was making his debut as a college player.

Tulane

McKeever announced that he was promoting the recently turned 18-year-old Johnny Ray, former center for John Adams High in South Bend, to starting center for his fine play against Pitt. McKeever also planned to start 17-year-old Tom Guthrie at right end against Tulane. With O'Connor, age 18, and Guthrie, age 17, at ends, they became the two youngest starting ends ever used by Notre Dame.

Before a home crowd of 45,000, the young Notre Dame team racked up its second straight shutout in triumphing over Tulane, 26-0. Notre Dame kept the Green Wave off balance all day by mixing its passing and running games. Dancewicz's and Gasparella's outstanding work at quarterback was complemented by the excellent running of Kelly, Angsman, Maggioli, and Steve Nemeth. On the line, Rovai, Adams, Mastrangelo, and Sullivan were equally outstanding. Ray, starting his first game at center, completely justified McKeever's faith in him as he played an exceptional game.

Dartmouth

For their third game, the undefeated, unscored-upon Irish traveled to Boston to play Dartmouth in Fenway Park. Dartmouth must have wished the Irish had stayed at home. Notre Dame trounced a completely outmanned Dartmouth team by a score of 64-0. It was the most points scored by a Notre Dame team since 1932, and the most points scored against Dartmouth since Harvard defeated the Indians, 78-0, in 1884.

The first play from scrimmage set the tone for the day when Kelly bulled his way through the line for a 51-yard touchdown run. Notre Dame scored nine more touchdowns as Angsman, John Corbisiero,

Gasparella, Nunzio Marino, George Terlep, Nemeth, and Ed Clasby each scored once, and Dancewicz scored twice. One can only wonder what the score might have been had the regulars, who played only 10 to 17 minutes, played the full game. As the Irish prepared for their next game, they were ranked as the number one team in the nation.

Wisconsin

Kelly, the explosive sophomore runner, again ignited the Irish attack when he sprinted 52 yards for a touchdown on the second play of the game. (Oddly enough, in the previous game against Dartmouth, Kelly ran 51 yards for a touchdown on the first play from scrimmage.) He scored again on a four-yard burst through the middle. Angsman ran 35 yards for a touchdown and midway through the third quarter Dancewicz passed 35 yards to Maggioli for the final Notre Dame score. After shutting out Pittsburgh, Tulane, and Dartmouth, the Irish were scored upon for the first time when Earl "Jug" Girard, a freshman standout, passed 14 yards to Jack Mead in the third quarter. Wisconsin scored again in the fourth period to make the final score Notre Dame 28, Wisconsin 13.

Illinois

In preparing for the upcoming Illinois game, McKeever planned to use two 18-year-old freshman backs, John Corbisiero from Medford, Massachusetts, and Marty Wendell from St. George High in Evanston, Illinois, to stop a backfield rated the swiftest in the game. Corbisiero had played in each of the four previous games and had proved his worth as a defensive back. Wendell, as a Navy trainee, had just become eligible.

The one player Notre Dame had to stop was Claude "Buddy" Young, a sprint champion. He was the fastest player in football. Paul Patterson, also in the backfield for the Illini, was another speedster who had to be watched.

The first time Young got his hands on the football, he raced 74 yards for a touchdown to the delight of the huge homecoming crowd at Memorial Stadium in Champaign. The Irish came right back and scored when they capitalized on an Illini fumble at the Illinois 16. Kelly got the touchdown from the three-yard line six plays later, but Notre Dame failed on a pass conversion attempt, leaving the score, 7-6.

Later in the first half, Young started on one of his patented runs when Adams, the mammoth Notre Dame right tackle, scooped him off the ground and, at the same instant, Wendell, from his line-backer position, hit Young so hard it looked like he had cut him in half. Those who witnessed that play say it was one of the hardest hits ever seen.

The Illinois public-address announcer said at halftime that Young had been kicked in the head and would not play the second half. The Notre Dame players who were there attributed Young's sitting out the second half to Wendell's bone-crushing hit.

Young's absence was a major factor in Notre Dame's holding the speedy Illinois backfield scoreless the rest of the day. Maggioli, play-ing his last game for the Irish before going to Marine training, took a lateral from Kelly and galloped 65 yards for the winning touchdown in the last quarter, making the final score Notre Dame 13, Illinois 7.

Navy

Going into the Navy game, Notre Dame was rated the number two team in the nation. Navy was rated number six. The Midship-men were reported to have the best line in the country.

With Maggioli lost to the service, Terlep was scheduled to start in his final game of the season before shipping off to Midshipmen school. Expecting to see some action was Jim Brennan, the little half-back from Marquette Prep in Milwaukee.

Before 67,000 fans in Municipal Stadium in Baltimore, the Navy team crushed the previously unbeaten Irish, 32-13. The Middies scored twice in the first quarter and again in the third before Notre Dame could manage to score. The Navy's line was too much for Notre Dame. It overpowered the less experienced Notre Dame line and forced Dancewicz to pass 32 times. It was Navy's first victory over Notre Dame since 1936, and Notre Dame's first loss of the sea-son. This defeat marked the first time a Notre Dame team was beaten by a regular college team since the Michigan game in 1942.

Army

Bruised and battered from the pounding they took at the hands of the older and more experienced Navy team, the Irish prepared for the next game against a seasoned Army team. McKeever had to find a replacement for Terlep at left halfback. He, like Maggioli before him, had been called to active duty.

The two possible replacements for the left halfback position were a pair of V-12 freshmen, Bill Chandler from Chicago and Jim Brennan. A third possibility was Nunzio Marino, who had looked very good in scrimmages.

One bit of good news for McKeever was the return of Frank Szymanski, a tough and experienced linebacker from the 1943 team, who had recently been given a medical discharge by the Navy. His return would add a new dimension to Notre Dame's defense.

By game time, McKeever had decided on a lineup of O'Connor and Guthrie at end, Sullivan and Adams at tackle, Filley (captain) and Rovai at guard, Szymanski at center, and Dancewicz, Marino, Kelly, and Angsman in the backfield.

The 31st annual meeting of these two rivals, played at Yankee Stadium before 76,000 fans, was a disastrous outing as the Notre Dame team suffered its worst-ever defeat, 59-0.

Army's experience, speed, and overall play was too much for Notre Dame, which did not register a first down until the score was 32-0 in favor of Army.

Early in the game, Army drove close to Notre Dame's goal line. Syzmanski, who only had about a week of practice, almost single-handedly stopped the Cadets for three downs, and again on the fourth. But the officials called an offside penalty against Notre Dame and this enabled Army to score.

In the second period, Doc Blanchard, Army's 215-pound plebe fullback (who would win the Heisman Award in 1945), ran an end sweep. Seeing Blanchard, the head linesman froze, so Blanchard wisely used him as a blocker. Thus, when Wendell, playing a linebacker spot, came up to make the tackle, he found the linesman in his way. As any player who has played with or against Wendell knows, anyone who got in his way was trampled, and that is exactly what happened. He took the ball carrier and the official in one hit right in front of the Army bench. The official, Dave Reise, suffered a dislocated left shoulder and was unable to continue.

With Reise out for the remainder of the game, the coaches, Blaik and McKeever, had to agree to continue play with only three officials. During the discussion to agree to this, McKeever said to Blaik, "Hey,

89

Red, how about letting us use some of your players that you're not using today so we can give you a game?"

Blaik just kept his stone face and made no reply.

Lt. Frank Leahy listened to the game in Honolulu where he was stationed with the Navy. Leahy was quoted in an interview after the game as saying, "It sounded to me like everything Army did was right and everything we did was wrong. The Army victory was not unexpected—they have a wonderful team. But I can't get over the size of the score. It shouldn't be."

Since Leahy had said in reference to the score, "It shouldn't be," one can only imagine what he must have thought when he later learned what happened. Red Blaik had kept his first two teams in action until the score had mounted to 52-0 in the final quarter. Only then did Blaik put in his third team with Arnold Tucker, Army's best passer, at quarterback. Tucker threw nine passes in the final 10 minutes in an obvious attempt to score again.

Perhaps Leahy regretted, if only for a moment, telling his team the year before, when the roles were reversed, to confine the offense to a selected list of fundamental plays in order to hold the score down. Notre Dame won that game, 26-0. No doubt Leahy would remember Blaik's piling on the score when the teams would play after the war. (Coaches have very good memories, particularly when they think the opposing coach took advantage of a situation.)

Northwestern

A demoralized Notre Dame team caused McKeever to again revamp his starting lineup for the Northwestern game. With Captain Filley out for the season, and Rovai, Kelly, and fullback Angsman on the injured list, McKeever was forced to start freshmen to fill these gaps. George Martz and Joe Westenkircher were slated to start at guards, with Brennan and Marino at halfbacks and the second-string quarterback, Gasparella, at fullback.

As if injuries were not burdensome enough, McKeever also lost the services of Ray (the center who had started until the return of Szymanski) and Corbisiero (the number two fullback). Both of the players had received their orders to report for active military service.

As the team was warming up before the game, Kelly noticed that

Devore would periodically stop his walk around the field and dig his toe into the ground, pause, look at the turf, and then tap the ground back in place. Kelly got his pal Szymanski's attention and said, "Frank, what's Hughie doing kicking holes in the ground?"

"I don't know," replied Szymanski, "I've seen him do that before, but I can't figure it out. Let's watch him."

They saw Devore stop at one spot, dig in his toe until he peeled back a flap of turf, get on one knee, then stand up and tap the flap back to its original position. Now their curiosity was really aroused. After the game they asked Devore about his routine with the turf. "Oh that," he answered, "I'm just finding the right spot to bury the scapular medal. I figure we can use all the help we can get." (At the Mass before each game, the players and coaches are given scapular medals. Traditionally the players tape the medal to some part of the uniform.)

Something must have worked as Notre Dame, before a home crowd, bounced back from the defeat by Army to defeat the Northwestern Wildcats, 21-0. Jim Brennan, the 18-year-old freshman starting his first game for Notre Dame, raced for 40 yards to score with the game only three minutes old. Seven minutes later, Brennan ran 29 yards to score his second touchdown. Wendell scored the final touchdown in the third quarter on a three-yard plunge. Nemeth converted all the extra-point tries.

Georgia Tech

With only two games remaining in the season, the Irish had to face two formidable opponents: the favored Georgia Tech team, which had beaten Navy, and the always tough Great Lakes Training Center.

Yet, before a surprised crowd in Atlanta, Notre Dame beat Georgia Tech, 21-0. This prompted McKeever to proclaim, "We played our best game of the year."

Jim Brennan scored twice as he gained 86 yards in 16 carries. Kelly, his ankle healed, scored on a 35-yard run after receiving a pass from Dancewicz. McKeever had praise for many of the players, but he singled out Szymanski, Kelly, and Wendell, in particular, for their excellent play. "Szymanski and Wendell were great as linebackers

91

against Tech. They really jarred those Tech ball carriers, and Kelly played his best game of the season, too. He was particularly strong on pass defense, which is one reason why Tech completed only nine of 29 forward passes."

In his sports column in the *South Bend Tribune,* Jim Costin told of what happened to Szymanski, Notre Dame's star center, after the game. Frank Broyles, Georgia Tech's star fullback, said to him, "Ah don't see how in the world you-all lost to Navy."

"And I don't see," replied Szymanski in his best Detroit accent, "how you-all BEAT Navy."

Great Lakes

In taking on Great Lakes, the Notre Dame team would see some familiar faces on the other side of the line. Jim Mello, the starting fullback on the 1943 Notre Dame National Championship team, was Great Lakes' leading ground gainer and leading scorer. Other Great Lakes players with Notre Dame backgrounds included Bob Hanlon, Bob Palladino, Frank Sullivan, and Don Lesher.

Great Lakes got off to a good start, making five first downs in the first quarter on some great running by Mello. Great Lakes punched across Notre Dame's goal line early in the second quarter to make the score, 7-0. But Notre Dame came back and scored when Kelly made a sensational catch of a Dancewicz pass in the end zone. It was all Notre Dame after that as the Irish went on to defeat the Blue Jackets, 28-7.

A jubilant Coach McKeever had high praise for all his players, especially Brennan, Wendell, Kelly, Sullivan, and Dancewicz.

The Notre Dame team closed a great season. It had won eight out of 10 match-ups. It beat all seven college opponents handily, then trounced a very strong Great Lakes team. The Irish lost only to Navy and to Army, which had beaten Navy to become the 1945 National Champion.

The team's success was a great tribute to the 34-year-old McKeever. He did a great job of coaching a team that had practically no experienced players and frequently had to start six, seven, or eight freshmen. McKeever had the benefit of excellent help from his assistant coaches, Hughie Devore, Adam Walsh, Jake Kline, Wally Ziemba, and Creighton Miller.

The team had every reason to be very proud of its record and of its fighting spirit in coming back from successive Saturday defeats by Navy and Army. As one sportswriter put it, "They turned what could have been a disastrous season into one of the most brilliant in Notre Dame's history." In the final Associated Press poll, Notre Dame was ranked ninth.

In addition to the fine job turned in by the Notre Dame coaches and the team as a whole, there were some superb performances by individual players. Kelly had an amazing year in which he led the team in rushing—681 yards; led the team in receiving—283 yards; and led the team in scoring with 84 points on 13 touchdowns and six extra points, putting him in a tie for second place among the nation's scorers. This was a Notre Dame record which would stand for 34 years until Vagas Ferguson surpassed it in 1979. Kelly led the team in punt return average, kickoff return average, and kicked off until he hurt his leg. He came in sixth in the Heisman Award balloting, and he was named to several All-America teams.

Dancewicz did an outstanding job of directing the team on offense and led the team in passing with 989 yards and nine touchdowns. He also made a major contribution on defense.

Angsman, Gasparella, Maggioli, Jim Brennan, Corbisiero, Wendell, Terlep, and all the backs had terrific years. Wendell and Angsman had particularly great seasons as stalwarts on defense.

On the line, mention has to be made of the play of George Sullivan who, at one time or another, played both right and left end and right and left tackle, and played each position as if it was the one he had trained for all his football career.

Filley, the captain of the team, made several All-America teams, as he had the previous season. He was playing on bad knees but never let up until after the Army game when he was forced to the sidelines for the season.

But, without doubt, the most dominant defensive player for the last four games was Szymanski, who joined the team just before the Army game. He hit as hard as any linebacker in college football. The experience he gained from playing on the 1943 team enabled him to be where the ball was better than some of the younger players.

The men on the line—Zeke O'Connor, Bob Skoglund, George Benigni, Tom Guthrie, Doug Waybright, Tree Adams, Art Mergenthal, Ken Schuster, John Mastrangelo, George Martz, Art

Statuto, Joe Westenkircher, Jim Dailer, Pete Berezney, Jack Fallon, Mike Davlin, and Mark Limont—could all be proud of the way they played and their role in making the season a successful one. Davlin, at age 16, was the youngest player in Notre Dame history to win a monogram.

On December 6, 1944, just six days after the season ended, Fr. John J. Cavanaugh, vice president of the university and chairman of the faculty board in charge of athletics, announced that Ed McKeever would remain as head football coach and director of athletics for the coming year.

The news was not unexpected and was greeted by wide acceptance on the part of all Notre Dame fans. There had been reports that the popular McKeever might take the head coaching job at Fordham that was rumored to have been offered him. Cavanaugh's announcement quashed all speculation that McKeever would go elsewhere.

McKeever loved Notre Dame and he'd had every intention of continuing his career there. However, one of those unpredictable events occurred that made him change his mind.

At the annual football banquet, the president of Notre Dame, Fr. J. Hugh O'Donnell, addressed the large and enthusiastic audience. The main theme of his talk was the tradition of excellence in sports, particularly in football, at Notre Dame. He told how Frank Leahy came to Notre Dame in 1941, had great teams for three years, and won the National Championship in 1943. He went on to paint a picture of what it would be like when Leahy returned to the university at the conclusion of the war and what great teams he would have then.

Players who attended this dinner report that President O'Donnell never congratulated the 1944 team on its season or mentioned the current team in any way. Needless to say, this did not sit well with the players or their coach.

After the banquet, McKeever invited Kelly and Szymanski to his home. He was particularly close to these two and wanted them with him so he could vent his emotions about the banquet. McKeever told Kelly and Szymanski how angry he was at Father O'Donnell for not mentioning his team. According to Kelly, "This infuriated McKeever, not because O'Donnell didn't talk about him, but that Father O'Donnell did not give any credit to the 1944 team and their accomplishments— he never mentioned the team once during his talk."

It was not too long afterward that McKeever got an offer from Cornell to be head coach and accepted it. "The reason McKeever left, more than anything," said Kelly, "was because of what happened that night with Father O'Donnell, the president of Notre Dame."

Chapter Seven

THE 1945 SEASON

With Frank Leahy still in the Navy and Ed McKeever off to assume his new head coach duties at Cornell, Hughie Devore was named the acting head football coach and athletic director for the 1945 football season.

Devore's staff included holdovers Wally Ziemba and Jake Kline. As his new backfield coach, Devore hired his former Notre Dame teammate, Joe Sheeketski. In addition, Devore secured the services of Ken Stilley and Harry Jacunski to assist with the line.

Devore had a wealth of coaching experience to draw upon as he assumed his new duties. He had been the freshmen coach under Elmer Layden before leaving Notre Dame in 1935 to serve as end coach for Jim Crowley at Fordham. After three years at Fordham he served as head coach at Providence from 1938 to 1941, after which he left to become the assistant head coach at Holy Cross in 1942. In 1943 Frank Leahy asked him to return to his alma mater to coach the ends. He stayed in this job for two seasons.

In addition to his experience as a coach, Devore had something extra in his favor—he had the complete respect, which would later grow into love, of every player who had previously played for him. He was more than qualified to assume his duties as head coach.

Although the war had ended, most of the servicemen had not yet returned to Notre Dame. There were, however, some notable exceptions. One was freshman Phil Colella, a Navy veteran of several Pacific battles, who was slated to start at left halfback. Another was Stanley Krivik, one of the famed Eighth Air Force's most distinguished B-24 pilots, scheduled to play fullback and be the extra-point kicker.

Like McKeever before him, Devore faced the problem of molding a team composed of mainly inexperienced young players, many of them freshmen.

In the line, only Bob Skoglund at end, Pete Berezney at tackle, and John Mastrangelo and Fred Rovai at guard had won monograms in 1944.

The backfield prospects were a little brighter because the two top quarterbacks from the previous season, Frank Dancewicz and Joe Gasparella, were returning for the 1945 season. Elmer Angsman, the starting fullback from the previous year's team, was also on hand. Devore knew what Angsman could do as a running back, so he switched him to right halfback where his quick start and punishing running could be better utilized.

As the team prepared for its opening game against a favored Illinois team, Devore settled on his starting lineup. At the end position were two Chicago area players, Bob Skoglund from Loyola Academy and Dick Cronin from Fenwick High School. Skoglund had started some games the previous year and had gained considerable game time. He was considered one of the veterans on the team. Cronin, on the other hand, had no game experience. A senior pre-med student, he had never even been on the team before that fall. Cronin was starting in place of Bill "Hopie" Leonard, an 18-year-old freshman, who suffered a leg injury a week before the opening game.

Slated to start at left tackle was another Chicago player from Tilden Tech, Ed Mieszkowski. Mieszkowski, like another Tilden player, Lou Rymkus from the 1942 team, had been a champion wrestler in high school and, like Rymkus, was an excellent blocker and a hard-nosed defensive player. Mieszkowski had experience as a member of the 1943 National Championship team. At right tackle was Berezney, who played his high school football at Dickinson High in Jersey City, New Jersey. Berezney also played on the 1943 National Championship team and saw considerable action as a tackle on the 1944 team. He was the type of player the coaches could always depend on to do his job both on offense and defense.

The guards were John Mastrangelo from Vandergrift, Pennsylvania, and Fred Rovai from Hammond, Indiana, both veterans from the previous year and both outstanding blockers and tough on defense. These two would prove to be as good a pair of guards as any in the country. Mastrangelo was big and strong, but very quiet and unassuming. Once he put his football uniform on and went on the field, he would become a fierce competitor. Indeed, Mastrangelo would make All-America that year.

The starting center was Bill Walsh, a 17-year-old freshman from Phillipsburg High School in Phillipsburg, New Jersey. Walsh adapted quickly to college ball and became a mainstay in the line at the difficult center job, as did his understudy, Walter Grothaus, a freshman from Cincinnati.

"Boley" Dancewicz, at quarterback, was one of the most experienced players on the team. He had played on the 1943 team and had been the starting quarterback the previous year. He was an excellent field general, a very good passer, and an outstanding defensive player. As a mark of his leadership, he was elected captain of the team. Playing behind Dancewicz were three solid quarterbacks, Joe Gasparella, George Ratterman, and Frank Tripucka.

At halfback were Colella and Angsman, another Chicago product from Mt. Carmel High School. Angsman, like Dancewicz, had played on the 1943 team and was a starter the previous season at fullback. Angsman had a quick start which Devore would take advantage of by designing some quick traps up the middle that were suited for his type of running.

The fullback was Frank "Rooge" Ruggerio from Orange High School in Orange, New Jersey. Ruggerio played at Holy Cross in 1942 and at Notre Dame in 1943 and 1944. Ruggerio's previous experience, plus his tough brand of running and blocking, would prove to be a big asset in the coming season.

One of the newcomers on the team who would delight Notre Dame fans for the next four years was Terry Brennan. Another freshman who reported that fall for the 1945 season, who would make his mark as one of Notre Dame's top quarterbacks, was Frank Tripucka.

Frank Tripucka

Tripucka was All-State in both football and baseball while at Bloomfield High School in Bloomfield, New Jersey. His big decision was whether to pursue a football or baseball career. As a catcher/first baseman in baseball, he had a couple of tryouts with the New York Yankees and with the Newark Bears. He made the decision that he wanted to attend college and specifically Notre Dame.

Tripucka's high school backfield coach was George Melinkovich, who was the starting fullback at Notre Dame in 1931 and 1932 and a teammate of Hughie Devore and Moose Krause. As Tripucka recalls,

"Once he heard that I had my eyes and ears and heart ready for Notre Dame, he was thrilled. At the end of the 1944 football season he contacted Hughie Devore, who had taken over for Ed McKeever as head coach. Hughie Devore came into town around Christmastime in 1944. He took me to Madison Square Garden and I saw that game where George Ratterman, playing for Notre Dame, scored about 25 or 30 points against NYU. I told Hughie I definitely wanted to go to Notre Dame and he said as long as my grades were comfortable he was offering me a full scholarship.

"There were two other players they were recruiting from New Jersey, John Panelli and Bill Walsh. Panelli had been at Cheshire Academy in Connecticut at prep school, so he was a year ahead of Bill and me. I had never met Pep [Panelli] or Bill until we were ready to go to Notre Dame. It was during the war, so Notre Dame was on tri-semesters. Hughie wanted us at Notre Dame on July 5th of 1945. We met under the clock in Grand Central Station. We got on the Pacemaker and went to South Bend. We got to the train station about six o'clock in the morning and didn't know where to go. We caught a cab and went to the athletic offices at Zahm Hall. We sat on the curb until this big guy came along—it was Wally Ziemba, the center coach. He told us to go to the Administration Building and get registered.

"That afternoon we drew our equipment and started knocking heads the first day. I'll never forget it as long as I live. The first scrimmage I got into —here I am a hotshot from New Jersey. I thought I was pretty good. The players in that scrimmage were bigger, faster and they hit harder than I had ever been hit in my life. And I'm wondering, did I make the right choice in coming here?

"Then a few days later I visited the Rockne Memorial to see what it looked like. I went in one of the apparatus rooms and there, hanging from some rings, is this short baldheaded guy, with hair all over his chest and body. Someone said he's one of the guards on the football team. I thought, 'Oh, my God, I've made the wrong choice; how can I play against someone like that?' It was Vince Scott. He was a great guy and a terrific player. We played against each other for years in Canada.

"In the long run things turned out very well for me. Hughie Devore was the guy that decided I should be a quarterback. He knew I was a halfback in high school, not that great a runner, but I could throw the ball."

Bill Fischer, a tackle, was also an incoming 17-year-old freshman. He would go on to have a sensational four-year career as one of Notre Dame's all-time great linemen.

Bill "Moose" Fischer

Fischer attended Lane Tech, one of the powerhouse football teams in the Chicago Public League, a school with an enrollment of more than 7,000 boys. In Fischer's senior year, Lane played in the Public League championship game, but lost to Fenger High School. With that kind of exposure, Fischer and many of his teammates made All-City, and Bill was named All-State as well.

In those days the Illinois All-State team was invited to Champaign, Illinois, to be honored by the University of Illinois. Ray Eliot, the coach of the Illini, had the weekend to recruit, and he made a strong bid to have Fischer attend his school. Bill had pretty much made up his mind to go there, but Hughie Devore had other thoughts about Bill's future.

Gene Ronzani, the former Chicago Bear quarterback and then an assistant under Devore, was assigned to recruit Fischer. As Fischer tells it, "Devore, being a smart recruiter in those days before we had letters of intent, told Ronzani to pick me up at my house and take me to Notre Dame three days before everyone was scheduled to leave for the college of their choice. Ronzani came to my house and asked me to come with him to Notre Dame. I didn't know how to say no, so I told him I had to go shopping for some clothes. In the meantime, he put his arms around my mother and said, 'Don't worry, we'll take good care of your son.' My mother looked at me and said, 'Billy, I think you should go with him.'

"I didn't know how to say no, so I went with Ronzani. When we got to South Bend, he took me to Gilbert's men's store to shop. I didn't know what to buy. I only had one pair of shoes and needed some badly, but instead I bought socks, underwear, and tee shirts. I bought a satin men's robe; why I did it I'll never know—I never wore it. So, for less than $100, Ronzani got off the hook on his commitment to take me shopping.

"I enrolled at Notre Dame but didn't unpack my bags for three weeks—I was that certain I would leave and head for Champaign. Dottie Sheridan, the wife of Benny Sheridan, the great back in the late

'30s, was Hugh Devore's secretary. She apparently recognized some homesickness and had several of the players and me over to dinner. I became good friends with Benny, and, with football in progress, I soon forgot my homesickness and unpacked my bags to stay. Thank God I did.

"Every time I would see Gene Ronzani I would say, 'Thank you for picking me up and taking me to Notre Dame.'

"Playing football at Notre Dame in 1945 when I was 17 years old and traveling around the country was awesome. Playing for Hughie Devore was a wonderful experience. He was a tough hard-nosed coach, yet off the field he was a warm, kindhearted person. I was in the tackle corps under Lou Rymkus, who had a significant effect on my outlook and approach to pass blocking."

Fischer played on the second team in 1945 behind Ed Mieszkowski. Like Terry Brennan, Bill Walsh, and the other freshmen that year, he gained invaluable experience that served him well in his four-year career. He became a two-time All-American, an Outland Trophy winner, and, in 1983, was selected for induction into the National Football Foundation and Hall of Fame.

Illinois

On September 29th, the 1945 Notre Dame football team showed the opening day home crowd of 45,000 the spirited football it planned to play that year by defeating a favored Illinois team, 7-0.

Skoglund fumbled the short kickoff, but it was recovered by Ruggerio on Notre Dame's 24-yard line. On the first play from scrimmage, Dancewicz called for Colella to go around the right end. As soon as he made the corner, Colella cut back to pick up five or six teammates who blocked all the defenders in sight. Colella raced 76 yards for a touchdown. It was a textbook-type play as Colella ran perfectly and all 10 players involved executed their jobs as they are drawn on the chalkboard. Krivik drop-kicked the extra point to put Notre Dame ahead, 7-0, with only 45 seconds of the game clock used.

For the remainder of the game the Irish would be tested over and over again as they tried to keep the Illinois offense in check. Once they held for downs only a foot from their goal line and another time on the three-yard line. Just prior to halftime they held on their five-yard line.

The Notre Dame team put together a couple of drives but fumbled seven times and lost the ball on six of them. The Irish made many mistakes, typical of an inexperienced team, but what they lacked in execution they more than made up for by their aggressive play.

Skoglund's play at defensive end, as well as Dancewicz's defensive play in the secondary, earned the plaudits of the sportswriters covering the game. Mastrangelo and Rovai, helped by Tom Potter, Vince Scott, and Fallon at guard, repeatedly stopped the Illini attack, as did Mieszkowski, Berezney, and Bill Fischer at tackle. Cronin, playing in place of the injured Leonard, so impressed Coach Devore that he was named to the starting lineup for the next game against Georgia Tech.

Georgia Tech

Hugh Devore took 35 players to Atlanta, Georgia, to play against the Yellow Jackets and used them all as Notre Dame defeated the home team by a score of 40-7.

After spotting Tech the first touchdown in the middle of the first quarter, the Irish roared back to score four minutes later when Dancewicz threw a 39-yard touchdown pass to Colella. Early in the second period, Angsman shot through tackle, reversed his field, and scored unimpeded for the go-ahead touchdown. Before halftime, Gasparella uncorked a long 50-yard touchdown pass to Bill Zehler, playing right halfback. This made the score 21-7 after Krivik dropkicked his third straight extra-point try.

In the second half, Angsman scored again after a 32-yard drive. This prompted Devore to put in the reserves for some game experience. The backfield of Ratterman, John Agnone, Emil Slovak, and Joe Yonto played like the first team as they scored two more times on runs by Agnone and Slovak.

Dartmouth

The third game of the year was at home against Dartmouth, which had lost its first two games to Holy Cross and Pennsylvania. Slated to start at quarterback for Dartmouth was an amazing young man named Meryll "Jack" Frost. Frost had been a fighter pilot in the

Eighth Air Force. One day in battle over the western front his plane was shot up and caught fire. Before he could bail out, his clothing caught fire and, as he parachuted to the ground, the onrushing air fanned the flames thus causing him to be horribly burned by the time he hit the ground. Plastic surgery was required to restore the damaged portion of his ears, but his burns left him badly disfigured about the face and body. He was never expected to play football again, but after receiving his doctors' permission, he not only overcame his injuries and made the team, but battled his way to the number one back on the Dartmouth team.

On game day, Devore gave an example of why he is universally loved by all his former players. With his players gathered around him in the locker room, Coach Devore told them about the war experience of "Jack" Frost, in particular about the damage that was done to his face. Devore instructed his players to play hard football, but to be especially careful when tackling or blocking Frost so as not to go near his face. He told them that this courageous former pilot had suffered enough from his war injuries. The concern for an opposing player that Devore expressed that day has never been forgotten by the players of that 1945 team.

Notre Dame easily whipped Dartmouth, 34-0. From the opening whistle the game was no contest. On the first play from scrimmage, Dancewicz hurled a 64-yard touchdown pass to the fleet Colella who had outraced the Dartmouth secondary to get in the clear before he caught the ball for an easy score.

Skoglund made a leaping catch of a Dancewicz pass to score the second touchdown. With the score 13-0 at the end of the first quarter, Devore replaced his first unit. They would not see any further action that game as Devore went to the limit to keep the score within reason. He used 50 of the 53 players dressed for the game; he did not use either the first or second team in the second half; he did not allow his team to throw a pass in the second half; he confined the plays to simple, no-tricks kind of plays. Despite these precautions, Notre Dame did score three more touchdowns. Zehler, Krivik, and Yonto each scored once.

The standout player for Dartmouth was the badly scarred co-captain, Meryll "Jack" Frost, who was all over the field making tackles the first half. Dartmouth's coach, Tuss McLaughry, wisely did not let Frost play in the second half because he did not want to risk injury to the courageous player in a lost cause.

Pittsburgh

Going into their fourth game of the season, against Pitt, the young Irish were ranked third nationally behind Navy and Army.

Although Notre Dame beat Pitt at Pittsburgh, 39-9, Devore was not happy that Pitt controlled the ball for so much of the game. Ruggerio opened the scoring by plunging over after Dancewicz tossed a 21-yard pass to Colella, who was brought down on the one-yard line. Pitt controlled the ball for 25 out of 26 plays, making five first downs despite being repeatedly penalized for delay of game caused by Pitt coach Clark Shaughnessy and his interminable substitutions. The one play Pitt did not have the ball, it scored a safety when a block was missed and Terry Brennan was tackled in the end zone.

Notre Dame finally got untracked and scored five more touchdowns. Bill Leonard, John Panelli, and Ernie Virok each scored one, and Angsman went over the goal line twice. Walsh, Skoglund, Panelli, Virok, Cronin, and Dancewicz were praised for their alert defensive play.

Iowa

Although there were still five more games to be played, the Iowa game would be the final home game of the season. Iowa was in last place in the Big Ten and presented no real threat. Ordinarily a coach would have a difficult time getting his players "up" for this type of game. However, Devore had no such problem with his team. The Notre Dame team knew that it could be the first ever to beat an Iowa team and this had them excited and eager for the kickoff.

As it turned out, the game was a complete mismatch as the Irish easily romped to a 56-0 win. Devore used 55 of the 56 players he dressed for the game—fullback John Panelli was being kept out of action because of a leg injury. The regulars had played only 11 minutes when they were excused for the day, leaving with a 21-0 lead.

The second team did not play much longer before Devore put in the third, fourth, and fifth teams. To keep the score within bounds, Notre Dame threw only one pass all game and confined the running game to just three basic plays once the first half ended with the score 41-0.

Meanwhile, Lt. Comdr. Frank Leahy was assigned to St. Mary's

Pre-Flight while he was waiting for his orders to be discharged. Anxious to get back to Notre Dame and get back to coaching, he went to the commanding officer and asked, "Can you tell me when I am going to be discharged?"

The Navy captain replied, "I can tell you exactly when you are going to be discharged. As soon as Navy plays Notre Dame and not one minute before."

Navy

The next game against Navy promised to be one of the highlights of the college football season. Navy and Notre Dame were undefeated, and they were ranked numbers two and three nationally.

The game, played in Cleveland before 82,000 fans, was not decided until the final whistle with Notre Dame on Navy's one-foot line. Navy had managed to salvage a 6-6 tie by twice halting Notre Dame drives into the line from a foot away.

As the final whistle sounded, referee Bill Blake was still unpiling the players to see if Dancewicz had scored on the second of his two quarterback sneaks. After the officials consulted for what seemed like five minutes, they decided there was no touchdown.

It was a bitter disappointment for the team and the Notre Dame fans who thought the game had been won two plays earlier. Colella caught a pass from Dancewicz for what seemed to the Notre Dame fans to be the winning touchdown, but the officials ruled that Tony Minisi's tackle had driven him out of bounds at the one-foot line. Notre Dame fans were irritated because the referee had mistakenly signaled a touchdown, thus adding to the confusion and letdown. As Frank Tripucka recalls, "If the defensive back had hit him low he would have fallen across the goal line. Instead, he was hit high and it seemed like every part of Colella was over the goal except his arms and the ball. Devore was ready to kill the official, but later, when we reviewed the movies, it was the right call."

Notre Dame did have the consolation of knowing it had outplayed the powerful Navy team. The Irish outgained Navy in total yardage, with 295 yards to Navy's 115.

The second time Notre Dame had possession of the ball, and still in the first period, the Irish started a drive on Navy's 34. With Angsman, Ruggerio, and Colella hitting repeatedly between the tackles, Ruggerio bulled his way into the end zone for what proved to be Notre Dame's only score. Navy scored its lone touchdown with seven minutes left to play when Clyde "Smackover" Scott raced 60 yards with an intercepted pass. As did Notre Dame, Navy missed the extra-point try.

It was a very physical game as Elmer Angsman could attest. In the middle of the first quarter, Navy's Dick Scott, a linebacker, caught Angsman with a forearm in the mouth, knocking out his four upper front teeth and causing his four lower front teeth to be jammed into his gums. He ran to the sidelines where he was met by Devore, who was shocked by the severity of Angsman's injury. Devore said, "Elmer, you better go to the locker room."

Through a mouth that was spurting blood, Angsman replied, "No, I don't want to. I want to go back in." The Notre Dame trainer stopped the flow of blood the best he could, applied some pain medication, and with gauze packing in his mouth, Angsman went back in the game. He played 54 minutes that day despite his injury. No one ever doubted his toughness or his devotion to the team, and with his display of courage that day, Angsman assured his place in the folklore of Notre Dame football.

Army

It was an ailing Notre Dame team that began preparations for the battle with Army, the number one-ranked team in the country. Panelli, the number two fullback, was declared out for the season with a shoulder separation incurred early in the Navy game. Leonard, the number two right end, who was already suffering from a thigh injury, hurt his knee when tackled after going 52 yards on a Ratterman pass late in the game. Angsman, the starting right halfback, lost eight teeth and suffered a severely lacerated mouth which required 26 stitches. Ruggerio, the number one fullback, lost two teeth and suffered a gash on his jaw which required 13 stitches to close. Hughie Burns' training room looked like a battlefield hospital.

As if the injuries were not enough, the Notre Dame team had to face a powerful Army team that had in its lineup such great players as: John Green, Dewitt "Tex" Coulter, Dan Foldberg, Arnold Tucker and the touchdown twins—"Mr. Inside and Mr. Outside"—Felix "Doc" Blanchard and Glenn Davis. To add to Devore's concerns, Army's coach, Col. Earl "Red" Blaik, announced that all his players were in top condition for the game to be played on November 10th at Yankee Stadium.

Angsman, because of the injury to his mouth, looked like he was a candidate for a part in a horror film. Pieces of stitches were sticking out of his puffed lips as he worked out before the game. Since he was not expected to play, he was not wearing his shoulder pads under his football jersey. While the team was still on the field going through its pre-game warm-up, Devore came up to Angsman and asked, "How are you feeling, Elmer?"

"Not too bad," replied Angsman.

"Do you think you could play a few minutes? We're really short-handed with all the injuries," explained Devore.

Angsman, always a team player responded, "Sure, Coach, just get me a face mask and I'll play."

Before the game, the trainer attached a face mask to Angsman's helmet that allowed him to play. Angsman not only played, but played 55 minutes in one of the toughest games of the year.

Fischer was the kickoff specialist for the team. Before the game he was practicing his kickoffs. His style was to take about 10 giant steps backwards and then run as fast as he could to the ball to kick it as hard as he could. He was doing quite well, kicking the ball to the five and sometimes into the end zone. The Army squad came on the field. Blanchard, who was the Cadets' kicker, came to where Fischer was practicing and put his tee down next to Fischer's. As Fischer described the scene, "He took two-and-a-half steps back and drilled it through the uprights on the fly. I watched him again and he barely missed the uprights, but put the ball into the stands, which was about an 80-yard kick. On his third attempt, he put it right through the pipes again. I said to our manager, 'I've had enough. I'm all warmed up.' After watching Blanchard with his two-and-a-half-step approach, I wouldn't dare run up to the ball and kick it with all my might and maybe put it five yards into the end zone, when this guy was putting it out of the park."

Davis scored on a 27-yard run just 66 seconds into the game to begin a dismal day for the Irish as Army rolled to a 48-0 win. The statistics tell the story of the game. Army netted 414 yards on offense, compared with 184 for Notre Dame. Davis ended up with three touchdowns and Blanchard two. The score might have been larger if it were not for Dancewicz, who was sensational on defense. He repeatedly saved potential scores by tackling Davis, Blanchard, and the other Army backs.

Fischer recently recalled the game and how he received a quick introduction to big-time football. "Jack Fallon and I were freshman tackles. Ed Mieszkowski was the first-string tackle and I was his substitute. After we were down about 21 points, Devore told Fallon and me to warm up and get ready to go in. As we're about to go in the game, Fallon turned to me and said, 'We may not win, but let's go in and kick the hell out of them.'

"The Army had the ball. The quarterback went back to pass. I was trying to get around my guy, I was hitting him in the face [no face masks] and everything else I could possibly do. The guy grabbed me and almost picked me off my feet and said, 'Listen fat boy, if you don't behave you're going to get killed.' I looked up at him and replied, 'Okay, Tex.' The player was Dewitt Tex Coulter, the All-American Army tackle who was about 6-feet-6, weighed about 260, and was the heavyweight boxing champion of both military academies.

"After that incident, I said to Fallon on the sidelines, 'You get me in more damn trouble.' It sure got me introduced in a hurry to the big leagues. From that time on, I always approached an opponent with a great deal of respect."

The Monday after the game, Devore praised his team for carrying on despite injuries and the power of Army. He praised Angsman and Ruggerio for playing all-out even though they both had suffered severe injuries in the Navy game. He also had high praise for Terry Brennan and Mastrangelo for their spirited play despite the odds the Cadets threw against them. Devore said, "Nobody showed any signs of quitting against Army. Our kids knew they were up against too many big guns, but they fought back all the way."

Northwestern

As Notre Dame prepared for its next game against Northwestern, Devore summed up the situation when he said, "We have just come through two bruising games against the Navy and Army, and our players are pretty badly injured and tired out. Northwestern has definitely proved that it is a very serious threat to any team in the Middle West, and we'll have to regain our old edge if we're to stay in this game."

108

After being stunned by several Northwestern drives early in the game, Notre Dame got its offense going and managed to defeat a young, but tough Wildcat team, 34-7, before 49,500 fans, the largest crowd ever to see a football game in Dyche Stadium.

Angsman was sensational at halfback, gaining 118 yards in 12 carries and scoring one of the five Notre Dame touchdowns. Angsman had another one nullified when the officials ruled that Leonard, after a pass from Ratterman, had made a forward pass, not a lateral. Floyd Simmons, a new fullback who had recently been discharged from the Navy, also had a great day and scored one of the touchdowns. Bill Gompers, the speedy halfback, scored two touchdowns, one on an intercepted pass and his second on a beautifully thrown pass from Ratterman. Jim McGurk, playing for the injured Ruggerio at fullback, scored on a plunge from the two-yard line early in the second quarter.

It was a satisfying victory for the team and coaches, particularly after the two physical games against Navy and Army. One of the spectators who was very pleased with Notre Dame's performance was Lt. Comdr. Frank Leahy. He had arrived in time to see the game from the pressbox where Joe Sheeketski, Notre Dame's backfield coach, was manning the phones to the bench.

When questioned about the printed reports that he would act in an advisory capacity to Devore for the remainder of the year Leahy said, "This is Devore's team and he and his assistants have done a great job. I'll just be a fan for the rest of the season."

Tulane

Notre Dame beat Tulane in the next game, 32-6, but only after being stunned in the first half by Tulane's play. The first time the Green Wave got the ball, they marched 68 yards to score, sending most of the 63,000 spectators, the largest crowd ever to see a regularly scheduled football game in the South, into ecstasy. The Tulane fans were hopeful their team could hold down the score on the heavily favored Irish, and here they were leading their highly touted opponent.

Notre Dame seemed to come to life at the start of the second half. Brennan, starting at left halfback, ran 30 yards to the Tulane 47. On the next play Brennan went wide around right end and went all the way with the help of Mastrangelo, Ruggerio, and Berezney, all of whom threw key downfield blocks. When Krivik kicked the extra point, Notre Dame took the lead and went on to dominate the game.

Before the third quarter ended, Notre Dame put together a 35-yard drive that resulted in a touchdown when Angsman cracked into the end zone from the three. In the last period, the Irish scored three times, two of the touchdowns through the air. Ratterman hit Brennan for his second touchdown, and after an 84-yard drive with Brennan and Angsman gaining most of the yardage, Panelli boomed over from the three-yard line. Notre Dame's final touchdown came as a result of a Frank Tripucka pass to John Agnone.

Tripucka recalled his touchdown pass in the Tulane game that led to his first meeting with Frank Leahy, a meeting that would give a valuable insight to Leahy's obsession with avenging the lopsided defeats by Army. "I'll never forget getting into the Tulane game. With about five minutes left to play, Devore put me in and said, just run the regular offense. John Agnone was playing halfback. John said in the huddle, 'I can run by this guy on a go pattern.' Well, that was right up my alley. I threw to him for a touchdown, my first collegiate touchdown.

"After the game in the locker room I see this man all dressed up in a Navy uniform. He walked up to me and shakes my hand and said, 'I'm Frank Leahy.' Let me tell you, it was like meeting God. Leahy said, 'I'd like to ride back with you to the hotel in the bus.' I couldn't believe it—he's asking me for permission to ride with me. Fifty years later I still can't get over it.

"He got on the bus and he sat next to me. He proceeded to tell me that we have to prepare and get ready to play Army next year. We talked for a while, and when I told him I was from Bloomfield, New Jersey, he said, 'I was the line coach at Fordham and I saw them play a game for the championship against New Brunswick. They won, 42-0. Francis, we would have taken that whole team to Fordham.' [He did take six of the players to Fordham.]

"Back at the hotel Leahy asked, 'What are you doing over Christmas vacation?' I told him I was going home, that I hadn't been home since July. He said, 'I'd like very much for you to stay so we can get ready for Army.' I told him I just had to go home, that I was homesick. He said, 'Okay, but the very day you get back to the campus, we have to get ready.'

"He didn't forget, because as soon as I returned to the campus

110

after the holidays we started right in doing all those quarterback maneuvers, or 'corkscrewing' with all those reverse pivots, as Leahy would say."

Notre Dame had played four games in a row on the road and it was beginning to wear on the players. In commenting on the situation, Devore said, "We've been on the road since we played Iowa here on October 26th and this constant weekend travel for the last month has taken its toll. Two or three times, because of our trips, we haven't been able to practice between Thursday and the next Tuesday..."

Great Lakes

The final game of the season was to be played against Great Lakes at the Naval Training Center not too far from Chicago. The game would be the last for Devore as head coach. Leahy had already returned to the Notre Dame campus from his service in the Navy and was ready to resume his former duties as soon as the season ended.

The game would also mark the end of the collegiate careers of Dancewicz (quarterback), Berezney (right tackle), Angsman (right halfback) and Ruggerio (fullback).

As in the previous year's match-up against Great Lakes, the Notre Dame players would see some familiar faces across the line. Zeke O'Connor at left end, George Terlep at quarterback, and Marty Wendell at center and linebacker were all in the starting 11 for Great Lakes. In addition to facing these former Notre Dame players, they would have to face Frank Aschenbrenner, the former Marquette star halfback, and fullback Marion Motley from the University of Nevada (who would later gain fame as the bruising fullback for the Cleveland Browns). Great Lakes also had an 18-year-old starting at right end by the name of Bud Grant, who would later become the head coach of the Minnesota Vikings and lead them to many championships. The head coach of the Blue Jackets was Paul Brown, one of the greatest coaches in the history of professional football. There is no question, Great Lakes had a very good football team.

Great Lakes scored first in the opening period when Aschenbrenner returned the kickoff to the Notre Dame 19. After the sailors worked the ball down to the one-yard line, Terlep sneaked over for the touchdown.

111

Notre Dame took a 7-6 lead in the second quarter when Ruggerio scored four plays after he had recovered a Great Lakes fumble on the Blue Jackets' 24-yard line.

Great Lakes came back after the kickoff with a 63-yard drive to score. This put the Navy team in the lead to stay. After a scoreless third period, Great Lakes scored four times in the last quarter to make the final score 39-7. Its final touchdown was scored by O'Connor on a pass from Terlep.

For Devore, it was a sad end to the season. He had done such a brilliant job with inexperienced material. The Sailors were just too much for the young Notre Dame team as the Irish were outplayed in every facet of the game despite some great individual performances from Notre Dame players.

The players, too, felt bad about the loss. They very much wanted to win as a farewell gift for Devore, who had their respect and admiration. But it was not to be. The team ended the season with a record of 7-2-1.

Even one of the opposing players felt bad about Notre Dame's loss. O'Connor (the starting left end on the 1944 Notre Dame team), who was the starting left end for Great Lakes that day and caught a touchdown pass, confesses to having mixed feelings about the game. He recently told me, "My only bad feeling about the Great Lakes-Notre Dame game was that Hughie Devore was the coach. Of all the people coaching that I have ever met, even where I have a strong tie—like to my original high school coach—Hughie Devore was something special. Many of the coaches care, many of the coaches say a lot, help people a lot, but as to a real caring guy, not just for you, but for football and people in general, Hughie was the best."

When the All-America teams were announced, John Mastrangelo at right guard and Frank Dancewicz at quarterback had been selected. Mastrangelo, who seemed to improve with every game, had an outstanding year both on offense and defense. Dancewicz, too, was outstanding as a two-way player. He led the team in passing, punt returns, and interceptions.

Angsman led the team in rushing, gaining 616 yards on 87 carries for an amazing seven-yard-plus average. He also led the team in scoring with seven touchdowns for a total of 42 points. During the course of the season Angsman had three long touchdown runs totaling almost 200 yards nullified because of penalties. Had those plays not been called back, Angsman would have had a nine-yards-per-carry rushing average, topping George Gipp's record of 8.1 yards per carry set in 1920. (Gipp's per-carry record would have held as the official record because Angsman's total carries would have been 10 carries short of the required 100 minimum.)

Frank Tripucka recalled Angsman's year this way: "Elmer was about six feet tall and weighed about 195 pounds. We were playing a game in about the middle of the season. Up to then, Angsman was an average halfback. In that particular game, he took the ball on a quick opener and lowered his shoulder on the linebacker. He popped that linebacker, bowled him right over, and kept on running for a touchdown. From that point on, it was like opening up a door, he just felt he could do this to everybody. He became one great halfback, and one of the nicest guys you ever want to meet. Of course, he eventually went on with the Chicago Cardinals as part of their 'Dream Backfield.' "

As a testament to the team's accomplishments it was ranked ninth in the national post-season polls. Every man on the squad could be very proud to have been a member of a team that was known for its fighting spirit and never-quit type of play. Because it was a young team and partly because of injuries, Devore had no hesitation about substituting freely, which meant a host of players on the squad made significant contributions to the success of the team.

In addition to the usual starting line of Skoglund and Cronin, Mieszkowski and Berezney, Mastrangelo and Rovai and Walsh, players such as Bill Flynn, Bruno Opela, Oswald Clark, Al Burnett, Bill Fischer, Bill Russell, Vince Scott, Steve Oracko, Ed Fay, Walt Grothaus, Ernie Virok, Tom Potter, Jack Fallon, Jack Vanisi, John Glaab, Bill Leonard, Phil O'Connor, and Roy Bush all made important contributions to the team.

The same held true in the backfield. At one time or another Dancewicz, Colella, Brennan, Angsman, Gompers, Ruggerio, and Panelli started for the Irish. Others making their presence felt were: George Ratterman, Joe Gasparella, Frank Tripucka, John Agnone, Bill Zehler, Emil Slovak, Jim McGurk, Stan Krivik, and Joe Yonto.

With Leahy back on campus to resume the head coach role, it was time for Devore to move on. He accepted the head coaching position at St. Bonaventure.

Very few, if any, of these players will ever forget the privilege each of them had of playing under one of the best coaches and finest men ever to coach college football, Hughie Devore.

Chapter Eight

THE POST-WAR YEARS

The year 1946 marked the beginning of a post-war era that would see the number of students on the Notre Dame campus grow as many GI's returned to Notre Dame to continue their education and thousands more enrolled as freshmen to take advantage of the GI Bill. In addressing this challenge, one of the first acts of the Congregation of Holy Cross fathers was the selection of Fr. John J. Cavanaugh, CSC, as the 14th president of Notre Dame. It would prove to be an inspired choice as this legendary Holy Cross priest led the university into a new period of prosperity and growth.

In the early months of 1946, hundreds of thousands of servicemen from every state in the Union were discharged and sent home, eagerly awaiting the start of the fall semester when they would either resume or begin their college educations. Among those returning were an unprecedented number of experienced football players. These athletes with prior football education would fill college football rosters for the next several years and result in a new age of college football.

The 1920s is called the "Golden Era of Sports," and rightly so. This decade saw the emergence of sports legends who endure to this day. Great individual stars such as Babe Ruth in baseball, Jack Dempsey in boxing, Bobby Jones in golf, Bill Tilden in tennis, Red Grange in football, and Johnny Weissmuller in swimming captured the hearts of the public as never before. The times, a post-war period and a depression, seemed to make the public yearn for heroes who could take its mind off the problems of the day. These immortals obliged by giving unbelievable performances.

Team sports also blossomed in that era, particularly in college football, and Notre Dame was the very best, winning four National

114

Championships during the 1920s under the coaching of the legendary Knute Rockne.

After World War II, team sports again flourished and college football was at its finest. Never in collegiate history was there such an array of football talent on the college campuses as in the immediate post-war years of 1946 and 1947. Of all the great players and all the outstanding teams of that time, the Notre Dame teams were the best. Reflecting this, the four years, 1946-49, have been dubbed "The Golden Era of Notre Dame Football."

The stories of three players on the 1946 team illustrate the depth of football talent at Notre Dame that season.

George "Cud" Tobin had played guard on the 1942 pre-war team and earned his monogram. After that season he entered the Navy to play first-string guard on the great 1943 Iowa Pre-Flight team that lost only one game—to Notre Dame, 14-13.

After the war, Tobin returned to Notre Dame, one of many returning lettermen at the guard position. Despite his ability, Tobin did not get much playing time during the 1946 season because of the number of outstanding guards.

Before the 1947 season, Tobin asked Coach Leahy for his advice about the future. Tobin had been offered $5,000 (a good sum of money in those days) to play for the New York Giants of the National Football League for the 1947 season. He asked Leahy if he should consider the offer or return to Notre Dame for his last year of eligibility. Leahy suggested he take the Giants' offer because he would probably play on the first team with the Giants and Leahy could not promise he would play much at Notre Dame. Tobin signed with the Giants and did play on the first team. He later returned to Notre Dame to graduate.

Art Statuto was a reserve center behind Herb Coleman (All-American) and Frank Szymanski on the 1943 National Championship team and, although he saw action in seven games, he did not have enough playing time to earn his monogram (a player had to have a minimum of 60 minutes). Statuto played on the 1944 team, was on the traveling squad, and had a lot of playing time before he was called to active duty in the Navy, but again he fell short of the time required to earn his monogram. He returned to Notre Dame in the spring of 1946 and was the first-team center in spring practice.

By summer practice all the players were back from service and

115

Statuto, despite his ability, found himself playing behind George Strohmeyer (All-American), Marty Wendell (All-American), and Bill Walsh (first string 1945, 1947, 1948). Thus, again in 1946, Statuto did not have sufficient playing time to earn his monogram. In recognition of Statuto's proficiency as a player he was selected for the College All-Star team and was drafted by the Buffalo Bills. He went on to play as first-team center for several years with Buffalo before signing with the Los Angeles Rams where he again not only started at center, but was named to the All-Pro team.

In short, though Statuto never won his letter at Notre Dame, he played first string on two different pro teams and was named All-Pro. (Years later Statuto was awarded an honorary monogram by the Notre Dame Monogram Club in recognition of his contribution to the teams on which he played.)

The third player is William "Zeke" O'Connor. At 6-feet-4, 220 pounds, O'Connor was the starting left end on the 1944 Notre Dame team. The following year, while in the Navy, he was the starting left end for the Great Lakes team that defeated Notre Dame. In 1946, O'Connor was out of the service and back at Notre Dame.

He had stiff competition at the end position from Paul Limont and Jack Zilly (players from the 1943 team), Jim Martin (who became an All-American), Frank Kosikowski (who was All-Service with Fleet City), Leon Hart (a three-time All-American and Heisman winner), and several other seasoned players. O'Connor made the coveted traveling squad for the opener against Illinois and played in that game, but subsequently was injured, forcing him to miss a week of practice. He could not make the traveling squad after that, nor did he play in any varsity game the remainder of the season.

O'Connor was back in 1947 and was switched to tackle, but did not have an opportunity to play because of the competition. He did not get a monogram in either 1946 or 1947.

Even though he did not see any game action in 1947, he was selected to be on the 1948 College All-Star team. He played in the All-Star Game and received an offer from the Buffalo Bills, which he accepted. O'Connor became the starting left end for Buffalo and later played with the Cleveland Browns and the New York Yankees before going to the Canadian League where he starred for the Toronto Argonauts.

These three, Tobin, Statuto, and O'Connor, could not play a sufficient amount of time at Notre Dame in those years (1946-47) to win a monogram, yet each of the three played on first teams in the National Football League. The three are not isolated cases; they are examples of what many other players on those teams experienced.

From 1946 through 1949, the Notre Dame teams were undefeated in 38 games and won three National Championships. These teams produced two Heisman Award winners, John Lujack and Leon Hart; two Outland Trophy winners, George Connor and Bill Fischer; eight future Hall-of-Famers, John Lujack, Leon Hart, George Connor, Bill Fischer, Red Sitko, Ziggie Czarobski, Bob Williams, and Jerry Groom; and 12 All-Americans—the eight Hall-of-Famers plus John Mastrangelo, George Strohmeyer, Marty Wendell, and Jim Martin.

Frank Leahy, who returned to Notre Dame in late 1945 to resume his job as the head football coach and athletic director, began to assemble his coaching staff. He knew this staff would have to be the best in the business to handle the task of molding the vast amount of talent available for the coming season into a cohesive football team. He wanted as many of his former assistants as possible on his post-war staff.

Leahy contacted former assistant coaches John Druze, Moose Krause, Joe McArdle, and Wally Ziemba, and was assured by each of them that he would return to coach for the 1946 season. With Ed McKeever now coaching at Cornell, he needed a top-flight backfield coach as well as a new freshmen coach to replace Jake Kline, who was confining his coaching to baseball.

The man Leahy had in mind for the varsity backfield job was Bernie Crimmins, the converted fullback who made All-American as a guard on the 1941 team.

Crimmins' release from the Navy in 1945 came in time for him to play several games with the Green Bay Packers as a guard. As the season neared its end, Crimmins received a call from Leahy concerning a coaching position. They met and Crimmins signed on as a member of Leahy's staff for the coming season.

By early January 1946, Druze, McArdle, and Krause had returned to the Notre Dame campus to join Ziemba, Crimmins, and Leahy who were already there. In recalling that time, Crimmins said, "Leahy had never told me what position I was going to coach. So after all these coaches got back here, I finally went to the office one day and said:

" 'Coach, I'd like to talk to you. I was just wondering what position I'm going to coach.'

117

" 'I forgot to tell you,' he said, 'you're going to be my quarterback coach and in charge of my offense.'

"That was amazing," said Crimmins.

It was amazing. Leahy was again demonstrating his uncanny ability to pick the right person for the right job. Crimmins had been a halfback his sophomore year at Notre Dame, a fullback his junior year, and a guard his senior year. On the face of it, Crimmins' credentials would hardly seem to make him an ideal candidate for the position of quarterback coach.

But Leahy knew his man better than anyone. Crimmins, it turned out, was the perfect choice for this important job. He would go on to become nationally recognized as one of the best offensive coaches in the country.

Another addition to the coaching staff was Bill Earley, a halfback from the 1942 team, who was hired as an assistant backfield coach. As with all Leahy's assistants, Earley had been his kind of player. He was tough and played with reckless abandon. The story is told of how, in a game in 1942 while playing defense, he charged so hard from his defensive halfback position that he crossed the line of scrimmage in time to be trapped by the opposing guard. It may have been the only time a back was ever the victim of a trap block behind the line of scrimmage.

To assist with the backfield Leahy also hired Marty Brill, a teammate from the 1930 Notre Dame team. Completion of the coaching staff was accomplished by the hiring of Jack Barry, another Leahy-type player, as the B-team coach. Barry had played end on the undefeated 1941 team. At 5 feet, 9 inches, he looked nothing like an end, but when he was seen crashing into opposing players from his right end position, he might just as well have been 6-feet-3.

Barry was back at Notre Dame attending law school, so there was no problem in acquiring his services. With his addition to the coaching staff, Leahy's staff was complete and ready to get on with preparations for the 1946 season.

The 1946 Notre Dame Team

The 1946 Notre Dame football team was different from previous Frank Leahy-coached teams primarily for two reasons. The first, obviously, was because of World War II.

Before the war, college players, with few exceptions, came directly from high school, at ages 17, 18, or 19, and stayed in school until they were graduated four years later. The war, however, had interrupted the football careers of most of the undergraduate players from 1941 through 1945.

Many of the returnees were now in their early to mid-20s. They had been in combat, some even prisoners of war, and some had been decorated as war heroes. In short, they were not only older chronologically, but old beyond their years because of their war experience. Others had spent much of their military service playing football on the various Army, Navy, and Marine Corps teams of that day. The majority who had played at Notre Dame before being called to military service returned after the hostilities to be a part of the first post-war team.

These players were joined on the '46 team by the usual high school influx, the outstanding players from the service that Coach Leahy had so aggressively recruited during the war, and the returning squad members of the 1945 team. This gathering of so many players from so many teams, and from so many teams over so many years, resulted in what has been called the greatest assemblage of talent ever seen on a college football field.

Not only was there such an unbelievable amount of football talent in the immediate post-war era, but the character of the players had changed. Most of them had seen too much of life to be easily affected by the customary schemes or oratory of the coaches. As a result, the behavior of these players was unlike that of any prior Notre Dame team and certainly different than any Coach Leahy had experienced. Leahy was known as a strict disciplinarian who allowed no joking or other nonsense on the practice field. But this team had a group of players unlike any of the previous years, and, as a result, the coach was in for some antics that even he, with all his meticulous planning, could not have foreseen.

The second reason this team was so different was that a more mature, older, and wiser Ziggie Czarobski was back from the service to play football again.

Ziggie Czarobski

Ziggie, as most people called him, was also known to some of his teammates as Zig, number "76" (his playing number), and Pierre (his

119

middle name). Born on Chicago's southeast side, he was christened Zigismund, but later became known as Zygmont Pierre Czarobski. The name Ziggie captures his personality and it would not seem proper to refer to him in any other way.

Ziggie enrolled at Mt. Carmel High School on Chicago's south side in 1937. He was the starting left tackle on the 1938, 1939, and 1940 teams, earning All-Catholic recognition all three years, and was an All-City and All-State selection his senior year. The 1938 and 1939 Mt. Carmel teams, as Chicago Catholic League champions, played for the city championship against Fenger High School, the Public League champions, in the Mayor Kelly Bowl at Soldier Field before 85,000 fans in 1938, and before over 100,000 in 1939. Mt. Carmel lost to Fenger, 12-0, in 1938 and tied Fenger, 12-12, in 1939.

Ziggie was popular with his teammates and classmates at Mt. Carmel. He was elected class secretary as a junior, was president of the Monogram Club as a senior, and was an active participant in school activities.

In those days, Ziggie was not only a thinner version of his later self, he was also a little more serious than later at Notre Dame. However, he did display some signs of the later Ziggie. He wore the big wide-brimmed hat that he would later become known for, and he was known to lead the cheers at the basketball games and take over as emcee on any occasion, particularly at the pep rallies.

One of Ziggie's teammates at Carmel, Bob Batchelor, recalls: "Ziggie would sing at the drop of a hat…Being a member of the cast of *The Mikado* as a sophomore made, I think, a lasting impression on him. His vocalizing in the shower room after a rough practice was always welcome. I do believe that until the day he died, Ziggie would have loved to have been a professional entertainer."

Ziggie enrolled at Notre Dame in the fall of 1941. He played on the freshman team that year, on the 1942 and 1943 varsity teams before being called into the service, and as a returning Marine veteran on the 1946 and 1947 post-war teams. He was the starting right tackle on three National Championship teams (1943, 1946, and 1947). He made the All-America team in 1947 and was selected by the National Football Foundation and Hall of Fame for enshrinement in 1977.

Ziggie was one of the funniest, most talented, loveable players in all of Notre Dame's history. As a player he was not the leader on the field in a football sense, but he was the one who relieved the tension on the practice field by some antic or quip; he was the leader in the locker room, on the trips, at the noon meetings, and any extracurricular activity off the campus. He entertained the players and challenged the coaches with his humor, quick wit, and uncanny ability to always do or say the unpredictable. He was a hero to his teammates and a joy to the assistant coaches. In a way, he drove Coach Leahy crazy, but secretly Leahy had to love him as we did, for Ziggie was not only a great ballplayer, but Leahy never had to worry about the team being uptight with Ziggie around.

As Jim Mello, his teammate and longtime close friend, once said, "Thank God for Ziggie. He had that special ability to mobilize the whole gang of us through humor, laughter, jokes, songs, and, yes, even prayers. Who can forget Ziggie yelling in the midst of a football game when things were not going right—'For chrissake, let's get back in the huddle and say a Hail Mary!' "

Johnny Lujack, Ziggie's teammate on the three National Championship teams and the Heisman winner in 1947, when remembering Ziggie, said, "He was the most popular player ever to play for Notre Dame. No matter where he went or what he did, you could always be assured of getting a belly laugh. You never wanted not to be around him, because he was an entertainer."

Jim Martin, the starting left end, said, "Ziggie brought us together and kept us happy. Without Ziggie and Johnny Druze, my end coach, I would have never made it at Notre Dame. They settled me down. If it wasn't for the laughter, I don't know what I would have done. Ziggie was so funny. I remember him so well. Just thinking about him can start me laughing.

"I have been asked, 'How good a ballplayer was Ziggie?' Let me tell you, that guy was an excellent tackle. He could knock your head off. But the main thing, he was clever—he was heady. He never went out of his way for trouble, but you couldn't get by him either."

How do you describe this Ziggie Czarobski, who charmed and delighted teammates, friends, audiences, and people of all kinds for over four decades?

When I think of Ziggie, words come to mind like incomparable, irrepressible, unique, funny, spontaneous, compassionate, sentimental, loving, intensely loyal, and so many others. All of them are accurate, but none quite adequate to describe this man of so many talents with so much love that he could evoke a laugh or touch the hearts of the most hardened of people. Anyone who truly knew him would say he was the most entertaining and loveable person they had ever encountered.

Ziggie had a marvelous sense of humor. He never made anyone else the butt of his stories, rather, he reserved that role for himself. One of his stories was about being invited to a pot party. When he arrived, he found that he was the only one to bring Tupperware. He used to say he was the only student to graduate from Notre Dame taking English as a foreign language.

As Ziggie poked fun at himself, he left himself open for his teammates, particularly Johnny Lujack, Creighton Miller, and George Connor, to do likewise. At speaking engagements where one of these players was on the program with Ziggie, they liked to relate to the audience Ziggie's comment about football players' academic grades. "You show me a teammate with a straight-A average and I'll show you a guy that's letting his team down." Or, the story about the time Ziggie was filling out an application and when he came to the question—*Church preference*, Ziggie wrote, "Red brick."

We will be hearing a lot more of Ziggie later.

There were several new faces on the 1946 squad that began summer practice in mid-August. Some, though never having played at Notre Dame before, were not coming in as kids out of high school. Notable among this group was George Connor, my brother, who would quickly make his mark as one of the greatest Notre Dame football players.

George Connor

George was an All-State tackle in his senior year at De La Salle Institute in Chicago. His coach, Joe Gleason, himself a star halfback on the 1935-36 Notre Dame teams, describes George as "big, smart, fast, very mobile, and the toughest player in the Catholic League." He says that George hit so hard in practice that he often held him out of contact drills and scrimmages for fear he would hurt his teammates.

George was recruited by almost every major college team in the country. He was recruited particularly by Notre Dame. Our dad, Dr. Charles H. Connor, had a brother, Msgr. George S.L. Connor who was president of the Alumni Association at Holy Cross College in

Worcester, Massachusetts, in 1942. Father George, as he was called, asked his brother to intercede with George and influence him to come to Holy Cross.

Being the youngest of the four Connor children, I can recall how we were indoctrinated from childhood with the traditions of both Holy Cross and Notre Dame. Although George was no stranger to the benefits of going to Holy Cross, his heart was set on going to Notre Dame. Our dad had not said anything about his conversations with Father George regarding Holy Cross, yet George was aware of the pressures put on Dad and he knew that the matter had to be brought into the open and discussed.

One evening, George asked Dad if they could talk. After he was seated near his father, George said, "Dad, I would like to go to Notre Dame, but I know Father George has requested that I go to Holy Cross. How do you feel about it?"

Our dad, never at a loss for an opinion, said, "George, I know you would like to go to Notre Dame, but you would have to play on the freshman team. Freshmen are eligible for the varsity at Holy Cross, so if you went there for one year, you could play some ball. That would take care of any family responsibilities and then you could switch to Notre Dame." (The rule requiring transfer students to sit out a year before becoming eligible was not in effect at that time.)

George said, "Dad, if that's what you want, that's what I'll do."

George joined a Holy Cross team coached by Ank Scanlon in August for the summer practice before the 1942 season. In his letters home, George did not comment much about his progress on the football field, but just prior to the team's first game, the family received a clipping from the *Worcester Telegram*, the local newspaper, from George. It was a picture of George in his football gear with a caption that read, "Freshman may play Saturday." George had crossed out "May play" and wrote in, "Will start."

And not only did he start the first game as a 17-year-old freshman, but he earned All-Eastern honors that season. The team lost its first four games that year, but after the Crusaders beat Manhattan College in their fifth game, they improved with each subsequent contest. The final game was against their archrival, Boston College. The BC team was undefeated, ranked number one in the country, and was supposed to play in the Sugar Bowl. From their respective records, and from any perspective, it looked like the mismatch of the year. No football expert gave Holy Cross any chance at all of giving the great Boston College team any kind of game, let alone of winning.

The morning of the game, George saw his uncle, Father George. During the course of the conversation, the monsignor inquired, "George, do you think the Holy Cross team can give BC any kind of game?"

Without hesitation George replied, "Father George, we are going to beat them today."

Stunned by George's reply, the monsignor tried to ease what he thought would be a terrible disappointment for George. "You must realize they have the most devastating team in the country, so I hope you do not get your hopes too high."

"I know they have a great team," replied George, "but so do we and we're going to win today."

The monsignor walked away, no doubt wondering what type of lunacy had befallen his nephew.

On the cover of the program that day was a picture of the Boston College co-captains, Fred Naumetz and Mike Holovak, wearing their football jerseys with the numbers 55 and 12. As fate would have it, that was the final score of the historic game played at Fenway Park—with Holy Cross the winner. The game stunned sports fans throughout the nation. In 1950 a panel of sportswriters voted this game as the upset of the half-century. Many of today's football historians and sportswriters still call it the greatest upset ever.

From the opening kickoff, Holy Cross dominated the game. The Crusaders did everything right and Boston College could never seem to get its vaunted offense and defense going. George became a star that day by his continual trapping of BC's All-American tackle, Gil Bouley. In the third quarter, Bouley made his first tackle of the game and the Cross fans in the stands began a cheer, "Bouley made a tackle, Bouley made a tackle." The Holy Cross backfield of Ray "Cookie" Ball, John Grigas, Tom Sullivan, and Johnny Bezemes kept the BC team off balance the whole game with dazzling runs, sharp passes, and doing the unexpected.

The Cross linemen, Captain Ed Murphy, George Connor, John DiGangi, George Titus, Tom Albergini, Ted Strojny, and Bill Swiacki devastated the Eagles in blocking for their explosive backfield. On defense, they completely dominated the BC line, which was considered the best in the country. Holy Cross not only beat the Eagles that day—the Crusaders totally destroyed and embarrassed them.

The game, aside from the football aspect, will long be remembered by many people in the Boston area. As the projected easy winner of the game, the Boston College team was invited to attend a celebration party at the Cocoanut Grove, a landmark Boston nightclub. When Boston College lost the game, the players declined to attend. That night there was a fire that consumed the Cocoanut Grove, killing hundreds of people in the worst nightclub disaster in the nation's history. Because there was just one exit, a revolving door that jammed, it took only 12 minutes for 492 of the 1,100 people gathered there that fateful November 28th to lose their lives and for 200 more to suffer extensive injuries.

The disaster left its imprint on history as new safety laws were initiated throughout the country to prevent any such tragedy from ever happening again. As a consequence of the Holy Cross victory that day, the Boston College team did not meet the same fate as those who were at the Cocoanut Grove that night. Although BC lost the game, the team and their families can be forever grateful that losing a game proved to be the stroke of luck that spared the BC team from being caught in that dreadful fire.

George did not transfer to Notre Dame after his freshman year, as originally planned, but he did have the opportunity to do so. In his words this is what happened:

"I was an 18-year-old V-12 student at Holy Cross College in early 1943. Most of the players from our 1942 team were in either the Army reserves or the Marine reserves. After the season, the Army guys were all called to regular duty and the Marine reservists were transferred to other schools. This left only about nine or 10 players available for the 1943 season.

"One day, I was ordered to see the senior military officer on campus, Capt. Robert Davis, USN. My first thought was, what did I do wrong? The only thing I could think of was I had been late getting on campus a few nights before, yet it didn't make sense that such an offense would call for a meeting before the captain.

"When I entered the office, Captain Davis said, 'Mr. Connor, have a seat.'

125

"I said, 'I prefer to stand, sir,' figuring I would take my punishment standing up.

"Captain Davis got right to the point: 'I have orders on my desk for you to report to the University of Notre Dame to continue your studies for your sophomore year [1943 season].'

"I said, 'Captain, I only have one question. Will Holy Cross field a team next year?'

" 'Absolutely,' answered the captain.

" 'Then I would like to play for Holy Cross, so as far as those orders are concerned, you can tear them up.'

"Captain Davis smiled and said, 'It will be a pleasure to cancel these orders. Consider the matter closed, and good luck next season.'

"I never did find out who used their influence to secure those orders for me to report to Notre Dame in 1943."

George stayed on at Holy Cross to play the 1943 season. As a sophomore, he was elected captain of the team. He had a great year, making several All-America teams, and was voted the George Bulger Lowe Award as the outstanding player in New England.

Early in 1944, George's V-12 unit was called to active duty. He was commissioned an ensign and assigned to a subchaser in the Pacific, which eventually docked at Pearl Harbor. A command car pulled up to the dock and a Navy sailor approached the ship and asked where he could find Ensign Connor. Connor, who was the one he asked, said, "I am Ensign Connor." The sailor said, "Sir, I have been sent here by Commander Leahy, who requests that you meet him at Navy headquarters right away."

Connor went below, changed uniforms, and was driven to headquarters. He explains what happened. "I met with Coach Leahy, who was very cordial and inquired as to my well-being as well as my family. Then he said, 'George, I wanted you to come to Notre Dame when you graduated from high school and I want you to come to Notre Dame after the war. If you come there, I can promise you two things: we will win the National Championship and you will be an All-American. I want to be fair and tell you that, as a transfer student, our publicity department will not give you much publicity—they don't like to do that, so you'll have to do it on your own.' Leahy could be very direct and forceful when he wanted to be."

When George's tour of duty was over and after he was discharged from the Navy, he did transfer to Notre Dame. Our father

126

was ill at the time and unable to work. George, despite his strong feelings of affection for Holy Cross, decided it was best to be close to
home. He entered Notre Dame for summer school before the 1946
season to join our brother Chuck, who had also transferred to Notre
Dame earlier in the year and was playing guard on the football team
during spring practice.

George vividly recalls his first day as a Notre Dame player. "My
first day of practice at Notre Dame was in the summer of 1946. I was
amazed at the number of players that were out for practice. There
were some 110 ballplayers on the field. We went through calisthenics,
blocking and tackling drills, and then at the end of the two-and-one-half
hour workout, Coach Leahy called the team up to huddle around him.
There were a lot of veteran players from other years on the squad. I
only knew a few, like Ziggie Czarobski from Chicago, John Lujack,
whom I knew from the Navy, and a few others. Leahy appointed 11
players to choose sides of 10 men on a team to have a relay race. He
said the team that won would not have to run 10 laps after practice, and
it had been a long, hot day, so I wanted to win that race.

"I was picked sixth on my team. The last player to be picked for
our team was a big heavy guy who seemed to have bigger feet than
my size 14s, and my immediate reaction was, 'Damn, there goes our
chance of winning.' Each participant had to carry a football and run
the length of the field, go around one of the assistant coaches, and
then back to the starting point. When it came to our last man, this
chubby guy with the big feet, we were in about fourth place. This guy
took off and passed all of them—ends, fullbacks, halfbacks—and
when the race was over, our team didn't have to run the laps. I went
up to him and said, 'I don't know you and I'm not going to tell you
what I said about you, but my name is George Connor and I want to
be on your side.'

"He said, 'My name is Bill Fischer,' and we did play on the same
side, right next to each other, for the next two years, and he was the
greatest."

At the first scrimmage of the summer football session, Coach
Leahy did not pick George for either the first or second team. As the
two teams were going at it, Leahy noticed that George was very rest-
less on the sidelines watching the scrimmage. He looked over at
George and said, "George Connor, do you think you could do a better
job if I put you in the scrimmage?"

"Just let me play." George shot back.

"Get in there at tackle on the defense and let's see what you can do."

Leahy liked to test his players, so he had the first team run a play directly at George. George drove through the guy opposite him and made a devastating hit on the back an instant after he received the handoff, driving him farther into the backfield. After a few more plays that were almost a repeat of the first one, Leahy said,

"George Connor, I think you better get over here on the first team before you kill somebody."

George was consensus All-American that year and was voted by the Philadelphia sportswriters as the nation's Lineman of the Year. That same year he was named the first-ever recipient of the Outland Award as the best interior lineman in the country.

Unlimited Talent

Other first-time Notre Dame players who had spent time in the military before coming to Notre Dame included: Jim Martin, Gus Cifelli, George Strohmeyer, Bob Walsh, Frank Kosikowski, Ernie Zalejski, and Emil Sitko (who spent his freshman year, 1942, at ND). Of this group, Martin, Strohmeyer, and Sitko would become starters as freshmen. Martin and Sitko would start for four straight years and all three would make All-American.

The players from previous Notre Dame teams who reported back to play in 1946 were from teams dating back to 1941 and from all the years in-between. Bob McBride and Russell "Pete" Ashbaugh played on the 1941 team as well as the 1942 team. George Tobin, Bill Vangen, William "Bucky" O'Connor, Luke Higgins, Marty Brutz, Bob Livingstone, Corwin Clatt, and Gerry Cowhig were back from the 1942 team. Bernie "Bud" Meter, Ziggie Czarobski, Paul Limont, and Jim Mello, who played on both the 1942 and 1943 teams before being called to military service, reported back to play. Jim Flanagan, Gasper Urban, Art Statuto, George Sullivan, Joe Signaigo, Jack Zilly, John Lujack, Fred Earley, Bob Kelly, and Bob Hanlon had all played on the 1943 team.

Other players from the 1944 and 1945 teams who returned were: Zeke O'Connor, Frank Tripucka, Bob Skoglund, John Mastrangelo,

Fred Rovai, Jack Fallon, Joe Gasparella, Jim Brennan, Terry Brennan, Marty Wendell, John Glaab, Vince Scott, Bill Fischer, Bill Russell, Bill Walsh, Tom Potter, George Ratterman, John Agnone, Emil Slovak, Bill Gompers, John Panelli, Jim McGurk, Al Lesko, Joe Yonto, Coy McGee, and Floyd Simmons.

There were 46 players returning who had won a monogram on one of the pre-1946 teams, with more than a dozen of them winning two or more football monograms.

In addition to all these players were the regular freshman players who came straight from high school. Some of the more prominent ones were: Leon Hart, Mike Swistowicz, Larry Coutre, Bill Wightkin, and Ralph McGehee. Each of these men had enjoyed outstanding high school careers and each would go on to make his mark as a Notre Dame football player.

Leon Hart

Hart was born in Pittsburgh and moved to Wilkens Township near Turtle Creek, Pennsylvania, in 1940. He attended Turtle Creek High School where he earned 10 varsity letters in basketball, baseball, football, and track.

At 17 years old, 6 feet, 5 inches and 220 pounds (he weighed 252 by 1949), Hart was heavily recruited by Pitt and many of the schools in the area as well as in the South. Fritz Wilson, a Notre Dame alumnus from Pittsburgh, had heard about Hart's exploits on the gridiron in nearby Turtle Creek. Hart explained what happened: "Through my uncle, Michael Jansen, he [Wilson] lined up a meeting with Frank Leahy in Pittsburgh. When we met, Leahy told me of the advantages of going to Notre Dame and then looked me right in the eye and said, 'You are coming to Notre Dame this fall, aren't you, Leon?'

"I said, 'Gee, Coach, I don't know. I have never seen the place.'

"Maybe it was a step he didn't think he had to take. I was being romanced by a lot of schools and I know I always wanted to go to Notre Dame, but I wanted to see it. Leahy turned to Wilson and said, 'We can arrange a visit, can't we, Fritz?' Wilson acknowledged that such a visit could be arranged.

"The one-way train fare to South Bend in those days was $11. Wilson gave me $20 to make the trip. I went to South Bend after spring practice was over. I arrived at the New York Central station in

South Bend about 12:30 A.M. I was 17 years old and hadn't preplanned anything. Here I am in the station at that hour and I didn't know where to go. I was trying to remember whom I had received a letter from. The name Krause came to mind, so I went to the phone book to look up his name in the directory. I found the number and called.

"His wife, Elise, answered the phone. I identified myself and asked for Mr. Krause. She told me he had a bad cold bordering on pneumonia and she didn't think he could help me. I asked her if she would mind asking him what I should do. Then I heard this loud noise like someone falling down the stairs and Moose got on the phone with a voice that was barely a whisper. 'Leon, stay where you are. I'll be right down.'

"About a half hour later Moose came in the train station with his big hat on, wearing slippers and an overcoat. He drove me out to the stadium locker room, and took me to the training room, which had about eight beds around the room. I later found out that this is where they housed some of the players who stayed at school for the summer and worked in South Bend. Moose said, 'You sleep here tonight.' "

Hart went to bed, but his unusual night was not over. After he had fallen asleep, he felt someone shaking him and a rough voice said, "Get the hell out of my bed."

Hart looked around and saw every other bed empty, so he said, "All the others are open."

"I know they're empty, but this is my bed," replied Theodore "Bull" Budynkiewicz, an ex-Marine who was an aspiring tackle on the football team.

Hart, recalling the incident, chuckled and said, "Bull was a rough, tough guy and I'm a 17-year-old kid and he scared the hell out of me, so I gave him the bed. Later when I got my guns [became an established player], I got even with him."

Hart was obviously not expected, or there was some mix-up because there was no coach available to visit with him. He did get a tour of the campus with a student delegated for the job by the secretary in the athletic office. He was barely on the campus for one day when he took the train back to Pittsburgh and then the 13-mile streetcar ride to Turtle Creek. It had not been an inspiring visit to the Notre Dame campus, but Hart was impressed by the devotion of Moose Krause, who got out of his sick bed to meet him at the train station. Hart never forgot Moose's kindness.

Hart visited several other schools where he was treated very well, but none of them sparked his interest. Around the end of July he was invited to visit Auburn. Hart was sent a one-way ticket which did not sit too well with him. He made up his mind to go to Notre Dame. When this was conveyed to Fritz Wilson by Hart's Uncle Mike, Wilson said, "We didn't think he was interested in going, we thought he was going someplace else." Arrangements were made for Hart to report to Notre Dame in early August.

Drawing football equipment the first day at Notre Dame was always a shocking experience and it proved no different for Leon Hart. He had to face John MacAllister, the infamous equipment manager who every player since Rockne had faced from his first until last day of practice. The way Mac, as he was known to the players, operated in his equipment room, he wasn't the manager—he was God. He ran it his way and you had better toe the line or else.

When it came Hart's turn to get his equipment, he told Mac the size he wore for each piece of equipment including that he wore a size-14 shoe. Mac doled out the gear and Hart went to his locker to dress. When he got to his shoes, he discovered they were size 13. He went back to Mac and said, "I wear a size-14 shoe and you gave me 13s."

Mac said, "Nobody that wore size 14s were ever any good—so you're wearing 13s."

Hart knew it was useless to argue with Mac so he wore size 13s his entire four-year football career at Notre Dame. Later when Hart played with the Detroit Lions, his football shoes were custom made by the Riddell Company. His feet were carefully measured and they were size 14. Recalling those times, Hart said, "I wore a size 14 while playing professional football, but I had them put size 13 on the tongue of the shoe. I guess I was afraid that Mac would get mad at me if he knew I was wearing 14s."

Hart and Wightkin would compete for a spot on the roster at right end. Despite this personal competition, they became close friends, entered the Engineering School together and became roommates. Hart recalls, "Bill and I used to wonder if we could get a spot on the roster with 21 ends—11 of them returning monogram winners. I knew we were in for a rough time when at one of the first noon meetings we heard Leahy say, 'There are only two excuses for missing practice: the death of one of your parents, or your own death.'"

Hart was right, the practices were rough. In recalling those days,

Hart said, "When my son, Lee, complained about two-a-day practices, I reminded him that in 1946 we had three-a-day practices starting in the first part of August. We were there to make a movie and we did make a movie, but Leahy managed to get in some scrimmages too. [There was a documentary about Notre Dame football made in early August of 1946.] We got up at six in the morning, had some orange juice, got in our sweatsuits, and met Hughie Burns [the team trainer] to run the lakes before breakfast. Coach Leahy had a thing about the returning vets—that they had weak legs from riding in jeeps during the war. Making the team run the lakes [five miles] was his way of making sure everyone's legs would be in shape.

"We would come back and shower, have breakfast, have a little time before we reported for the morning movie session. We were supposed to be making a movie instead of practicing, but Leahy always found a way to get some practice time in.

"Leahy would appear on the practice field during the time the movie was being made. He would don a helmet so he would look like one of the players since the coaches were not supposed to be on the field. I'll never forget the time we were all huddled around a blackboard that he had on the field. He started to draw plays on the blackboard but stopped when a Piper Cub flew over the field. Leahy watched the plane with his head tilted until the plane was away from the field and then he took the helmet off. We couldn't believe it—he actually thought there were spies in the plane that would report him for being on the field during movie time. These so-called movie sessions were so rough that George Connor broke his hand in one of the scrimmages. I remember thinking, if actual moviemaking is so hard, I never want to be a movie star."

It was an amazing collection of football players that gathered at Notre Dame to begin summer practice in August 1946. In addition to the varsity squad, there was another group of football players who added another 40 or so to the number of players on Cartier Field. The B squad, as it was called, had players that had not yet been invited to be on the varsity team. Freshmen were eligible to play varsity football, but only those freshmen who had been there for spring practice, played service ball, or had outstanding reputations, like Leon Hart, Jim Martin, and Larry Coutre, were on the varsity team. All others were on the B team.

With the unbelievable amount of talent available, playing on the 1946 football team was a unique experience no matter how much prior football training a player had. To participate in the practice sessions right out of high school—as I was fortunate enough to do—was something that none of us will ever forget. My experience that first year is typical, I am sure, of my fellow freshman teammates. Here is an account of what it was like for me:

In late August of 1946 I arrived on the Notre Dame campus from my home on the south side of Chicago. I was nervous and excited to be starting college, particularly at Notre Dame, which I had heard about all my life. I was especially apprehensive about the thought of reporting for my first day of football practice the next morning.

On Cartier Field that day there seemed to be football players as far as the eye could see. Footballs were flying all around the monstrous tower set in the middle of the many practice fields. I was later to learn that it was from this tower that Coach Frank Leahy, and only Leahy, could oversee several scrimmages going on at the same time.

We B-team players were clad in our coarse and itchy green jerseys and stationed at one end of the vast practice area, while the varsity squad dressed in their smooth and much cooler white jerseys were at the other end. No doubt Coach Leahy was already giving us an incentive to try to make the varsity squad so we could wear those nice smooth white jerseys.

After some calisthenics, the backs and linemen were separated into two groups and, being a halfback, I was with the backs. I happened to be standing next to Coach Earley when we heard Coach Leahy's voice on the loudspeaker from his tower at midfield, "Coach Earley, send me six of your toughest and hardest-running, green-shirt backs."

Bill Earley, having seen us for less than an hour, had no idea who was the best of our group, so he did the expedient thing. He pointed to the ones nearest to him and said, "Report to Coach Leahy at the tower."

I was the nearest, so I started to run to the tower area, which was about 100 yards away, at what I thought was a pretty good pace. I had run only about 25 yards when Bernie Crimmins, the backfield coach, hollered in a loud voice that needed no amplification, "Don't jog here, let's see you sprint." So I sprinted the rest of the way and arrived just beneath Leahy's tower somewhat out of breath and very excited to be so close to the famous coach.

The moment I saw the way all the varsity linemen were being arranged, I knew that I was to be the victim of a dreaded backs' drill called "murderers' row."

"Murderers' row" is a drill that is probably as old as the game of football. No doubt it was invented by some fiendish coach who, under the pretense of seeing how the linemen tackled, secretly was attempting to punish and run a gut check on the backs. The drill is really very simple. The linemen are arranged in single-file rows with about five yards between each man. The back, who has the ball under his arm, starts running at the first man from a dead start about seven yards away, with the objective of evading the lineman's tackle. To add to the one-sided nature of the drill, the back can only use a yard or two on either side of the would-be tackler as his path.

Coach Crimmins handed me the ball and said, "Take this line." It was all 14 varsity guards lined up in a row that stretched for about 60 yards. It's a good thing I didn't recognize any of the players, or know about their backgrounds, otherwise I might have quit the team right then and there.

As I was later to learn, 11 of the guards had lettered on previous Notre Dame teams and six of them had each earned two monograms.

Oblivious to all this, I was going to show Coach Leahy that I was a good, hard-nosed back who had a bright future at Notre Dame. I grabbed the ball tightly and ran with all the speed I could muster directly at the first man, Bill Fischer, and when almost at the point of impact, gave him what I thought was a dazzling move, veering to my right with my left arm as a stiff arm when suddenly there seemed to be an explosion. I found myself hurtling backward for what seemed like several seconds and then the back of my head bounced a couple of times on the ground as my body was slammed to the turf.

I am sure I was hit as hard many times during my four years at Notre Dame, but up to that point I had never experienced anything like that hit. I guess my reaction was a combination of training, fear of disgrace, and a bit of shock because I bounced immediately to my feet without even thinking and began running full speed to the second man, Mastrangelo, who had been All-American the previous year. I tried a similar maneuver on him, only this time to the left side, with exactly the same result.

Since that maneuver didn't work, I decided I would try to deceive the third man by giving him a head fake and then trying to run right through him. Signaigo, who had a lot of playing time on the '43 team, was not about to be fooled and hit me with the same force as the previous two. The rest of the line was more of the same as I was slammed to the ground by each of them, but somehow I managed to survive and get to the end.

As I got to my feet and started to jog the same 70 yards back to the starting point, the soon-to-be familiar voice of Coach Crimmins again yelled at me, "Throw the ball back!" Having done some of the passing for our high school team, I could always throw for pretty good distance. So while about 50 yards away, I cocked my arm back to throw what I hoped would be a perfect spiral to Coach Crimmins and show Coach Leahy how versatile I was. To my complete amazement and embarrassment, the ball fluttered in the air and fell limply to the ground about 25 yards short of Crimmins. He just laughed, knowing what I did not then realize, that my arms and shoulders were so bruised and sore that there was no way I could have thrown a decent pass.

I was so relieved to have that ordeal over that I happily started to run back to the B-team area. To my surprise, Coach Krause, the tackle coach, hollered to me, "Hey, get back here, you're not through yet; you're next in line for the tackles." The tackles also had 14 men lined up in their row. Six of them had earned their monograms in previous years, and four of them had more than one. Of the six that had not been previous letter winners, three were to become first-team players during their careers, and one of them, George Connor, my brother, was to make the All-America team in 1946 and captain and All-American in 1947.

As I waited for my turn, I saw that my brother George was the first of the tackles I would have to face. Since I was here straight from high school and George had played two years at Holy Cross College prior to his years in the Navy, this was the first time we had been on a football field at the same time as players. If I entertained any thoughts that because he was my brother he might somehow go easy on me, they were quickly dispelled. He hit me even harder than had Bill Fischer. The only difference was the pain was less because by now my body was becoming numb from getting hit so many times. So much for brotherly love!

I somehow managed to get through the whole line. As I returned to the starting point I was not the least surprised to learn, by the way

135

the day was going, that I would also have to take my turn through the lines composed of the centers and ends.

These two lines were much the same as the guards and tackles as to caliber of players and returning lettermen. Four of them would later become All-Americans, and one, Leon Hart, would win the Heisman Trophy and be selected to the College Hall of Fame.

What seemed like hours of running through the Notre Dame varsity linemen, over 50 in total, mercifully came to an end. I was told I could report back to Coach Earley at the B-team area. As I was trotting away, Joe McArdle, the varsity guard coach, who had a reputation as a tough, no-nonsense type of coach, said in a low voice as I went by him, "Nice going, kid."

At the time I did not know what he meant, but when I reflected on this later, I know he did not mean that I actually did a good job, having been clobbered by each man I ran against, but rather it must have been his way of congratulating me for not only surviving the drill, but also for not committing a back's cardinal sin—fumbling the football.

Since I was the first of the B-team backs to be selected for the drill, I was the first to return to our designated practice area. Our coach, Bill Earley, was waiting for me and casually asked, "How was it?"

I said, "Coach, I have never been hit that way in my life. Is it always like this?"

His face broke out in a wide grin and with a chuckle he replied, "Welcome to Notre Dame football. This is only your first day, it gets worse when we get in full swing."

My only thought was, "It gets worse? How will I be able to survive?" I think the only thing that saved me from being killed was that at 5 feet, 11 inches, 188 pounds, and 18 years old, I was in superb physical shape. The rest of my first day was a blur.

In some ways it did get worse because getting hit hard was not a one-time experience, it was an all-the-time experience. But, in another sense, it did get better. Within a few days the hard hitting, which was constant and experienced by everyone who played on Cartier Field, became something you got used to. It actually became enjoyable as you learned to hit harder yourself and feel the exhilaration of a good hard tackle or block. Thank God for youth as the body amazingly adjusts to the punishment that goes with playing with and against such talented players.

Noon Meetings

At 12:30 P.M. each practice day we had our team meeting in the auditorium of the Law Building. During the warm-weather months the players would arrive early and lounge on the grass next to the building.

This informal gathering was a great opportunity for the younger players to mix with the veterans. I don't know of any young player that was not made to feel a part of the team. The older players, many of whom had won two or three monograms in previous seasons, always treated the new ones as accepted members of the team. This played an important role in making the 1946 team a cohesive unit.

These gatherings were also a time for some lighthearted banter, a few stories, and always many laughs. One day a group of freshman players were sitting on the lawn discussing Coach Leahy's speech mannerisms and quaint sayings, all of which were new to us. One of his sayings that we were discussing was about "the Old Harry." Whenever Leahy wanted to emphasize how well a back could run, he would say, "He ran like the Old Harry."

As we were discussing this, one of the vets, Russell (Pete) Ashbaugh, came strolling down the walk from the chow hall. Ashbaugh was a legend to us, and also one of our favorites. He played on the 1942 and '43 teams as a backup halfback. Ashbaugh was not as big as some of the other backs, but it seemed he could do everything on a football field. He handled the ball well, could throw the ball about 80 yards, was a good runner, and was dynamite on defense. Off the field, he was an easygoing, friendly guy with a great sense of humor.

Ashbaugh walked directly to our group and very seriously said, "Fellas, I heard you talking about the 'Old Harry.' I think you have been here long enough to be let in on the big secret." He then looked over both shoulders as if to see who might be eavesdropping and very dramatically confided to us, "I am the Old Harry the coach speaks about."

A favorite pastime of the older players was imitating the way Leahy talked. Leahy had a habit, when he would meet a player on the campus, of asking questions—always the same questions—and not paying the slightest attention to the answers.

One day at one of these lawn gatherings we were entertained by

Jim Mello and Pete Ashbaugh. Ashbaugh played the part of Coach Leahy encountering Mello on the campus. The meeting went like this:

Mello: "Good morning, Coach."

Ashbaugh: "Oh, James, how are you feeling?"

Mello: "Not so good, Coach. I went to see the doctor last night and he thinks I might have a serious disease."

Ashbaugh: "That's fine, James, and how much do you weigh?"

Mello: "Because of the illness I have dropped 20 pounds."

Ashbaugh: "That's fine, lad, and how are your studies coming?"

Mello: "Not good at all, Coach. I think I may be flunking all my courses."

Ashbaugh: "That's fine, James, and how are your folks?"

Mello: "Not very good. My mother passed away yesterday and my dad is seriously ill."

Ashbaugh: "Oh, that's fine, James. I'll see you on the practice field at 3:30."

Ashbaugh could do Leahy so well that if you closed your eyes it was Leahy speaking. Since all of us had one of these encounters on campus with the coach, we knew the accuracy of Leahy's side of the dialogue. Some of the players, such as John Lujack, Jim Mello, Pete Ashbaugh, and Bob Livingstone, all of whom played under Leahy before the war, could do Leahy to perfection. By the end of the season every player on the team could do a passable imitation of Leahy.

All of the players were required to bring a large notebook to the noon meetings. Each day, beginning with the first day of summer practice, Coach Leahy would diagram a play or two which the players would copy in their notebooks. This practice of installing new plays continued throughout the season right up to the last game of the year. Although the basic offense was in place by the first game, new plays were added each week that were specially designed for our opponent that particular Saturday. By the end of the season each player's notebook would be bulging with plays. There were special plays for every type of defense we faced all year.

Every Monday during game week the team would hear a scouting report from Leahy or one of his assistant coaches about the team we were playing that Saturday. The coaches, and especially Leahy, would make the opposing team sound like the greatest team we

Above Photo: Rev. J. Hugh O'Donnell, CSC, president of Notre Dame, looks on as Frank Leahy signs a contract to become head football coach and athletic director of the university in 1941. (*Courtesy of the University of Notre Dame Archives*)

Photo at Left: Leahy (on the left) with assistant coach, Edward "Moose" Krause. (*Courtesy of the University of Notre Dame Sports Information Department*)

Former Leahy "lad" and monogram winner, Wally Ziemba, joined the Leahy coaching staff in 1946. (*Courtesy of the University of Notre Dame Sports Information Department*)

The 1941 Team

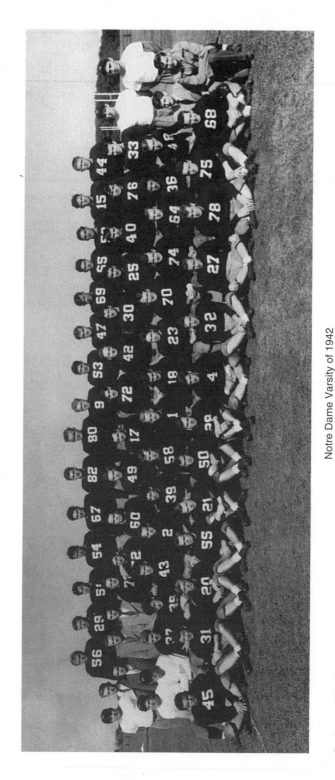

Notre Dame Varsity of 1942

Back row: Zilly, Cusick, Dwyer, Huber, Halay, Yonakor, Adams, J. Creevey, Cowhig, McBride, Clatt, Mello, Brutz, O'Connor and Coleman. Third Row: Coach Snyder, Mgrs. Jennings, Keating, Murray, Wiggins; White, Filley, Webb, Meter, Tobin, Sullivan, Dove, Limont, Piccone, Livingstone, Czarobski; Krupa, Coach Krause, R. Miller. Second Row: Coach McKeever, Head Coach Leahy, C. Miller, McGinnis, R. Creevy, T. Creevy, David, T. Miller, Earley, Capt. Murphy, Evans, Rymkus, Ziemba, Naff, Peasewell, Bertelli, Mgrs. Amato, Boss. Front Row: Szymanski, Frawley, Kudlacz, Ashbaugh, Lanahan, Walsh, O'Hara, Wright, Warner, Kelly, King, Higgins, Brock.

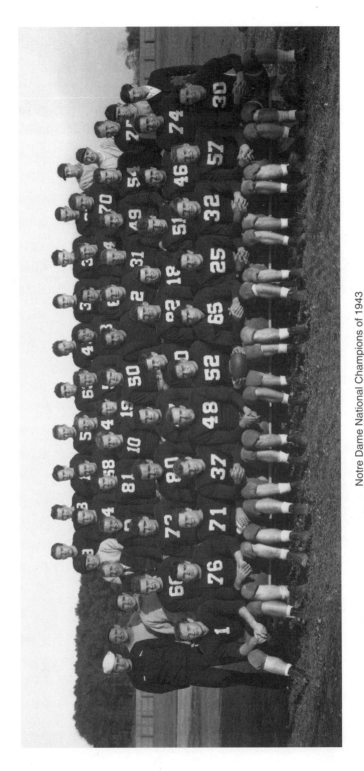

Notre Dame National Champions of 1943

Front row: Earley, Czarobski, White, Miller, Bertelli, Filley, Mello, Nemeth, Lujack, Perko, Limont. Second row: Boss, Ziemba, McKeever, Kuffel, Curley, Adams, Berezney, Rykovich, Yonakor, Flanagan, Hanlon, Palladino, Signaigo, Krause, Amato. Third row: Young, Skat, Yacobi, McGuire, Atkin, Gainey, Paulian, Terlep, Davis, Meter, Sullivan, Urban. Fourth row: Kline, Cannon, Rellas, Dancewicz, Cibula, Lopez, Angone, Coleman, Tharp, Devore. Fifth row: Waldron, Quail, Skinner, Miezkowski, Ruggerio, Syzmanski, Snyder, Lyden, Statuto, Leahy.

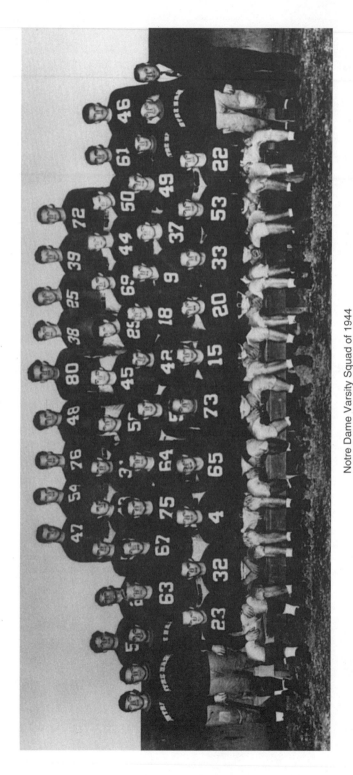

Notre Dame Varsity Squad of 1944

First Row: Kelly, Marino, Dancewicz, Szymanski, Mergenthal, Angsman, Nemeth, Toczylowski, Lanigan, Lebrou. Second Row: Coach Walsh, Coach Brewbaker, Coach Devore, Martz, Bernhardt, Mastrangelo, Glaab, Capt. Filley, Roval, Skoglund, Dee, Brennan, Westenkirchner, Coach McKeever, Coach Kline, Trainer Young. Third Row: Archer, Slovak, Fitzgerald, Endress, McGurk, Wendell, Chandler, Dailer, Ducato. Waybright, Ganey, Stewart, Eilers. Fourth Row: Berezney, Sullivan, Schreiber, Gasparella, Adams, Guthrie, O'Connor, Benigni, Schuster.

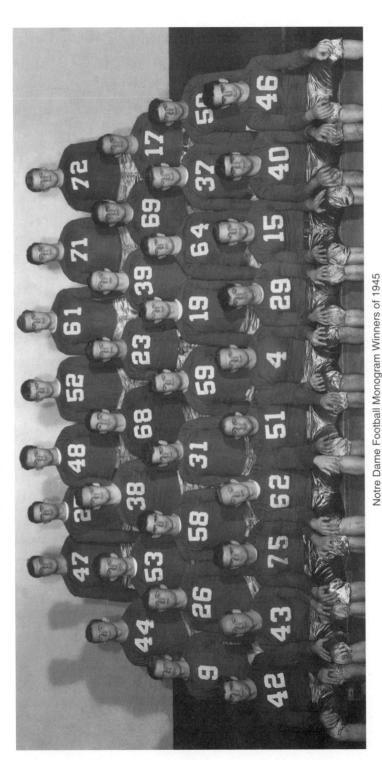

Notre Dame Football Monogram Winners of 1945

Top Row: Berezney, O'Connor, Gasparella, Grothaus, Russell, Vainisi, Fischer. Third Row: Leonard, Virok, Cronin, Fallon, Gompers, Oracko, Van Summern, Agnone. Second Row: Ratterman, Clark, Burnett, McGurk, Fay, Zehler, Glaab, Brennan, Krivik. First Row: Rovai, Potter, Mastrangelo, Mieszkowski, Scott, Dancewicz, Colelia, Angsman, Ruggerio, Walsh.

36

Notre Dame Squad of 1946

Front row: Martin, Kosikowski, Czarobski, Signaigo, Strohmeyer, Vangen, Lujack, Mello, Livingstone, Creevey. Second row: Caroll, Kronburger, Earley, Meter, Potter, Limont, Mastrangelo, Sitko, Iannuccillo, O'Connor. Third row: Ashbaugh, Wendell, Fallon, Wm. Walsh, Daugherty, Dickson, Chas. Connor, McGehee, Cowhig, Frampton, Gompers. Fourth row: J. Brennan, Coutre, Foristieri, Slovak, Cifelli, McGurk, Statuto, Ratterman, G. Bagley, D. Bagley, Russell, Wm. L. Smith. Fifth row: Mgr. Boss, Espenan, Sullivan, Hanlon, Higgins, Burtz, Schuster, Wightkin, Tripucka, Fischer, Agnone, McBride, Mgr. Earls. Sixth row: Mgr. Kelly, Gortiser, Flanagan, Zilly, R. Walsh, Clatt, Gasperella, Rovai, Panelli, Scott, Skaglund, G. Connor, Heywood, and Mgr. Flaherty.

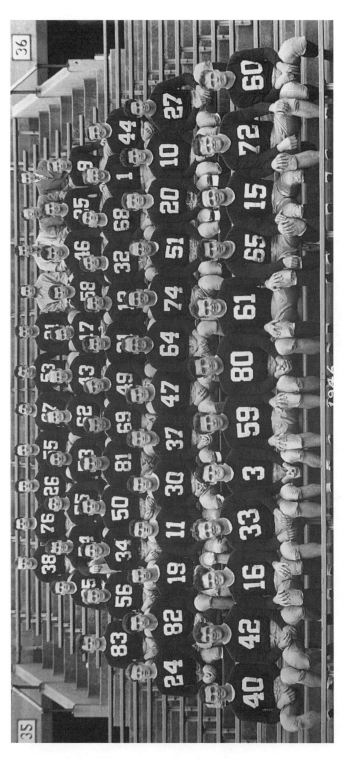

Notre Dame National Champions of 1946

First row: Livingstone, Rovai, Skogland, Kosikowski, Brown, Zmijewski, Cifelli, Russell, Mello, Angnone, Fischer, and Strohmeyer. Second row: Coutre, Hart, McGee, J. Brennan, Gompers, T. Brennan, McBride, Urban, Signaigo, Scott, Smith, Heywood, and Espenan. Third row: Wightkin, Zilly, Limont, Wm.Walsh, Connor, Clatt, Meter, McGurk, Ashbaugh, Lujack, Fallon, Earley, LeCluyse. Fourth row: Zalejski, Sullivan, Mastrangelo, Brutz, Simmons, Potter, Tobin, Wendell, R. Walsh, O'Connor, and Ratterman. Fifth row: Martin, Czarobski, McGehee, Swistowicz, Panelli, Cowhig, Statuto, and Mgrs. Boss, Flaherty, Earls, and Kelly.

Notre Dame Varsity Football Squad of 1947

First row: McGee, Sitko, Strohmeyer, Panelli, G. Connor (Capt.), Lujack, Brown, J. Brennan, Begley, Zmijewski. Second row: Ashbaugh, Martin, Tripucka, Sullivan, O'Connor (Zeke), Wendell, Grothaus, Schuster, Lally, Czarobski, Frampton, Leous. Third row: Urban, Michaels, Ramsberger, Coutre, Spaniel, Jeffers, Traney, Oracko, Compers, Dalier, Wilke, Sinkovitz, Budynkiewicz. Fourth row: Johnson, Lesko, Joe Helwig, Kosikowski, Skall, Couch, Livingstone, McGehee, Hart, Earley, Wightkin, Carter, Fischer, Simmons. Fifth row: T. Brennan, Waybright, Signaigo, Saggau, Joe Fallon, O'Connor (Bucky), Gaul, LeCluyse, Espenan, Flanagan, Walsh, Hudak, John Helwig, Cifelli, Jack Connor. Sixth row: Mgrs. Ryan, Brown, and Costello.

Notre Dame All-Americans of 1947: Standing left to right: John Lujack, Ziggie Czarobski, and George Connor. (*Courtesy of Doris Czarobski*)

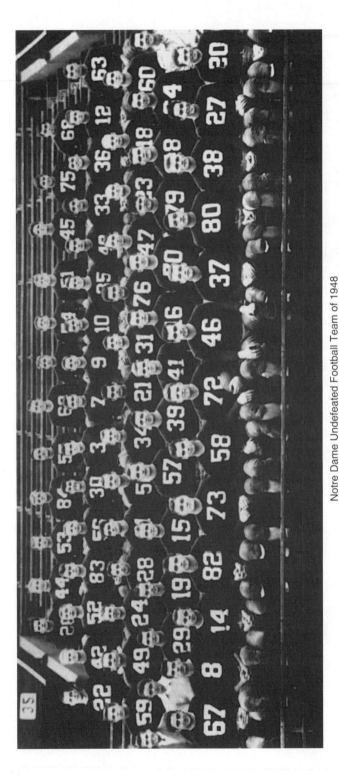

Notre Dame Undefeated Football Team of 1948

Front row: Panelli, Tripucka, Sitko, Hart, Gaul, Wendell, Fischer (Capt.), Walsh, Brennan, Cifelli, Martin, Espenan, L. Smith. Second row: Michaud (Mgr.), Madden (Mgr.), Dailer, McGee, E. Smith, Lally, Oracko, Flynn, Lesko, Mahoney, Schwartz, Wallner, Brickson, Nolan (Mgr.) Third row: Zmijewski, Hudak, Coutre, Spaniel, Higgins, Jeffers, Saggau, Connor, Joseph Fallon, Ste. Marie, Helwig, Dickson, Johnson, Groom. Fourth row: Gay, Waybright, Grothaus, Wightkin, Yanoschik, Landry, Soisson, Begley, Williams, Whiteside, Pearson, McKillip, Jonardi, Frampton, Zalejski, Budynkiewicz. Fifth row: McGehee, Holmes, Feigl, Ciechanowicz, Swistowicz, Huber, Carter, Cantwell, Cotter, Murphy, Palmisano, and Fallon.

Notre Dame National Champions of 1949

Front row: Steve Oracko, George Dickson, Ed Hudak, Frank Johnson, Gus Cifelli, Co-Capt. Jim Martin and Leon Hart, Ray Espenan, Gerry Begley, Ralph McGehee, Bob Lally, Bill Wightkin. Second row: Bill Kramer, Larry Coutre, Frank Spaniel, Bill Gay, Mike Swistowicz, Paul Burns, Don Huml, Bill Barrett, Gerry Groom, John Helwig, Jim Mutscheller, Chet Ostrowski, Joe Caprara, Jack Landry. Third row: Marty Kiousis, Jim Bartlett, Jim Hamby, Frank Johnston, Tom Huber, Bill Flynn, John O'Neil, Jack Nusskern, Ernie Zalejski, Jim Mahoney, Ernie Knapik, Doug Waybright, Jack Connor, Fred Wallner. Fourth row: Jim Funari (Mgr.), Ed Smith, John Zancha, Bob Dolmetsch, Bryon Boji, Bob Toneff, Bill Whiteside, Dan Modak, Art Perry, Jack Bush, Bill Higgins, Emil Sitko, Dick Cotter, Jim Dailer, Al Zmijewski. Fifth row: Don Lueck (Mgr.), John O'Hara, John Mazur, Bob Williams, Gene Smith, Robert Kapish, Bill Hovey, John Petitbon, Del Gander, Walt Grothaus, Tony Zambroski, Dave Koch, Jack Daut, Jack Finnegan (Mgr.), Leo McKillip.

En route to Iowa City for a date with the Hawkeyes in October 1946, Notre Dame players stop briefly in Chicago and are pictured here talking technique with train engineer, John Cristoph. The Irish lineup from left to right: Fullback Jim Mello; tackles George Connor and Ziggie Czarobski; and halfback Jerry Cowhig. (*Courtesy of the University of Notre Dame Sports Information Department*)

On the sidelines at Notre Dame Stadium, 1948. Left to right: Freddie Miller, Larry Coutre, Ralph McGehee, Coach Frank Leahy, Lank Smith, Mike Swistowitz, Gus Cefelli, Bill Walsh, Frank Tripucka, Coy McGee, Emil "Red" Sitko, Moose Krause, Jerry Groom, Bob Williams, and Leon Hart. (*Courtesy of the University of Notre Dame Archives*)

In 1949, Coach Leahy surrounded by some of his standouts: Kneeling left to right: Emil "Red" Sitko and Leon Hart; Standing left to right: Bob Williams, Leahy, and Jim Martin. (*Courtesy of the University of Notre Dame Archives*)

Out of uniform—Frank Leahy (center) is reunited with two of his "lads," Creighton Miller (left) and John Lujack (right) in 1963. (*Courtesy of the University of Notre Dame Sports Information Department*)

Here is the photo Ziggie Czarobski sent to Mrs. Connor with the inscription: "Your Polish son Ziggie, one of your four boys." Mother Connor's favorite photograph, taken at a Rockne Dinner in Chicago in the early 1970s, pictures from left to right: George, Ziggy, Chuck, and Jack. "Ziggy was part of our family," writes Jack Connor.

would ever play. If the other team had a particularly big lineman, they would exaggerate his size and weight. Most of the time it was serious business, but occasionally there was a light moment.

Such a moment happened the day Leahy was talking about a big tackle that would line up opposite Czarobski that coming Saturday. "He is 6-feet-6, weights 260 pounds, is mean, and is a Phi Beta Kappa." Looking directly at Czarobski sitting in one of the front rows, Leahy asked, "Zygmont, how are you going to handle him?"

"No problem, Coach," Czarobski shot back, "I'll just hit him a couple of times and he'll be as dumb as I am."

Leahy gave us more than just the plays at these noon meetings. He used these occasions to expound on his philosophy of football and life. More often than not, he would begin the meeting by asking a question about his topic of the day. For example, if the topic was playing the end position, he would ask, "What are the prerequisites to be a good end?" The answer was always the same and each player could have automatically answered, "The burning desire to be a good end." Whatever the topic, the answer always began with, "The burning desire to…" "What are the prerequisites for catching a pass?" "The burning desire to catch the pass."

Leahy use to tell us at the noon meetings that we were going to be the best-conditioned team in football—that when we played a tough opponent we would eventually win because in the 58th or 59th minute when the other team was tired, we would still have something left and would be able to win. No matter how hard you worked, or what the circumstances, be it in practice or a game, to be tired was never an excuse on a Leahy-coached team.

He used these sessions to get across to the players some of his pet theories. One that we heard repeatedly was how to behave when you meet someone. He would stress that you should always look the person in the eye, shake the hand firmly, and always end by saying, "It was nice to meet you, Mr. Smith." One sure way to get demoted was to look at the ground or to the side when talking to Leahy. No matter what he was saying when talking to you, you had better look him right in the eye, or you might as well have missed four tackles in a row.

At almost every noon meeting Bill Fischer would fall asleep because of his narcolepsy (a chronic ailment consisting of recurrent attacks of drowsiness and sleep). Leahy, mindful of Fischer's condition, never bothered him. On the contrary, he made it a rule that the players who sat on either side of Bill had the assignment of making sure he did not fall out of his seat and injure himself.

Periodically he would remind the team that if he dressed you down or corrected some fault on the practice field, you should not be discouraged. He pointed out to us that the time to be concerned is when he never said anything to you.

Leahy told the players, particularly the seniors, that they should learn how to speak in public since many would be invited to speak at various sports functions. He reminded them that wherever they would go, they would be representing the university; therefore they should be prepared to stand before a crowd and speak intelligently.

One day he announced that for the remainder of the season he would devote the final five minutes of the meeting to listening to one of the players speak. He called on a player at random, who then got up on the stage and gave a three-minute extemporaneous talk. Most of the players did a fairly good job when called upon. However, these practice speaking sessions came to a complete halt the day Joe Signaigo was asked to speak.

Signaigo, a great ballplayer and every inch a gentleman, related a story about a Marine Corps sergeant inspecting a group of trainees. Signaigo's delivery, with his Tennessee drawl, was flawless until he came to the punch line. The surprise off-color ending had the entire team, plus the assistant coaches, practically falling out of their seats with laughter. Coach Leahy immediately exited the meeting. We never knew if he left because he did not want the team to see him laughing, or because he did not like the story. Whatever the case, it was the last time he ever called on a player to tell a story.

Leahy, as he always did, evaluated each player daily. At each evening coaching session, Leahy asked his assistant coaches to discuss each player's strengths and weaknesses. He put great faith in the opinion of his assistants, but, naturally, would add his own opinion. From the input Leahy received from these discussions, he made his judgment as to who among the players was the best at playing his brand of football, regardless of position.

As he had done in other years, Leahy shifted the positions of several of the players. Jim Martin, who had been a center, was switched to end. Bill Fischer, who was a backup tackle on the 1945 team as a freshman, was shifted to guard. Gerry Cowhig, who had played full-back on the 1942 team, became a halfback.

Summer practice continued with two sessions a day. A typical day would be breakfast followed by the morning practice session on Cartier Field from 9 to 11 A.M. After lunch we had a team meeting at 12:30 P.M. in the Law Auditorium for about 30 to 45 minutes. The team stayed in Sorin Hall until school started, then the players would move into their regular halls for the school year. You could find most of the players lounging on the lawn in front of Sorin until the afternoon practice started at 3 P.M. as it was too hot during the day to stay in their rooms. During the school year the practices would begin at 3:30 to accommodate those who had a 2:15 P.M. class.

Everyone welcomed that break between sessions when you could stretch out on the lawn and maybe even doze a little if the aches would permit. I will never forget the day when a group of us were on the lawn relishing just doing nothing when someone in the group said, "Do you see what I see?" It was Terry and Jim Brennan with their golf clubs slung over their shoulders on the way to the Notre Dame golf course to get in a fast nine holes before the afternoon practice started. We could not believe they had the energy to voluntarily play golf when they could have rested between the brutal sessions. Yet, there was no mistake. It was Jim and Terry, and they were headed for the golf course. One of the linemen quipped, "Those backs must not be doing what we're doing. I think I'll ask to be switched to the backfield."

It was a particularly brutal summer practice. There were so many good players on the field that Leahy made the practices like a camp for the survival of the fittest. He had told the team that he was going to play the 11 best players. He seemed determined to find out who they were, even if he killed everyone in the process.

Practice sessions on Cartier Field were loud. Inside the green fence that surrounded the field, the players could be seen grouped in various units depending on what drills were going on at the time. You could hear the assistant coaches barking out orders to their charges and the sound of pad hitting against pad—always the hitting.

When Leahy was in his tower instead of roaming the field with that eagle eye of his, you could hear his voice over the speaker system as he called out, "Who made that block? Who missed that tackle?

141

Keep those feet churning on your block. Blockers, blockers, blockers," in the event of an interception during a scrimmage.

These sounds were normal at any college practice. One of the sounds that was different and always amazed visitors was the sound of grunts and growls—I don't know how else to describe it. Leahy was enamored with sound—the sound of a good tackle or block, the sound of the center snapping the ball to the quarterback—any football sound that signified to him success. A good block in the middle of the line could not be differentiated from all the other sounds. Leahy once said, "I'm going to play the 11 most savage ballplayers." Someone in the huddle started to growl—it caught on. From then on growling and grunting became a standard sound heard on Cartier Field. Linemen started to grunt when they applied a block to demonstrate to the coaches, and particularly Leahy, how hard they were working. The other players quickly caught on. From then on a good block without a grunt was passable, but a good block coupled with a loud grunt often merited commendation from Leahy. To a visitor, it sounded weird. One visitor, after hearing grunts all over the field commented, "I thought I was at a zoo with all the animals grunting and growling."

The other sound that was different was that of "bugle calls" and cheers. As far as can be determined, it was Ziggie (who else?) who started the practice of giving a cheer to a former player, coach, or school official who was visiting that day. A typical instance would have one of the players spot Bert Metzger (the "watch charm" guard of Rockne's 1930 National Championship team) on the sidelines. Ziggie, imitating a bugle, would sound an introduction, then all the players would chant, "He's a man, who's a man, he's a Notre Dame man, Bert Metzger! Bert Metzger!" This was followed by a round of applause and waves to Metzger on the sidelines. I know this was appreciated by those that received such recognition, and it was good for the players too. It was a way of introducing the new players to the legends of the past and forming a link with these former greats. It made all of us feel a part of the tradition of Notre Dame football. I am not sure when the practice of cheering former players ceased, but it's too bad it did.

One of the favorite stories of the players is about registration day in 1946. At the noon meeting on the last day of summer practice, Coach Leahy reminded the players that the next day was registration day for the start of the school year. He advised the team that he had

142

made special arrangements with the registrar to have the team registered as a group, providing they all reported to the Administration Building at eight o'clock. He warned the team to be on time.

The players, mindful of Leahy's warning, were all in a line in front of the registrar's office when, at eight o'clock sharp, the registrar's door opened. Seated behind a desk was Stella Novokowski, the registrar's assistant. There was a large sign on the desk that read, "State your full name, and the name and location of your high school."

The first man walked up to the desk and said, "Michael P. Swistowicz, Tilden High School, Chicago, Illinois."

Stella handed him a form and said, "Fine, Michael, go to the next desk."

The next man in line announced himself, "Theodore J. Budynkiewicz, Chicopee High, Chicopee, Massachusetts."

"Thanks, Ted, you can go on," replied Stella.

The third man reported to the table, "Zygmont Pierre Czarobski, Mt. Carmel High School, South Chicago, Illinois."

"Here is your card, Zig, go right in."

The fourth player stepped up to the desk and said, "George Connor" and, before he could get the rest out, Stella interrupted him and asked, "How do you spell it?"

Who named them "The Fighting *Irish?*"

With classes starting, practices were limited to once a day. Thankfully the two-a-day practices were over, but the practice sessions continued to be hard and long. With the opening game only two weeks away, Leahy still was not sure who his starting 11 would be. Leahy, realizing he had so much depth, still scrimmaged the team constantly in an attempt to find the best player at each position. Some of the players, like Livingstone, McBride, Cowhig, and Limont, had not played any football for three or four years and had some problems getting their legs in pre-war shape. However, no one dared rest for a day or two because, with the depth at each position, it meant a player could lose his well-earned place on the team.

It was the same for anyone who was injured. With few exceptions, if a player missed a few days of practice because of an injury, that player might find upon his return that he had to start at the bottom and work his way back up the roster.

In order to get a better handle on just who were the players to be in the starting lineup, Leahy called for a scrimmage to be played under game conditions in the stadium two weeks before the opening game. It pitted the first team against the second team with Leahy up in the press booth to get a better view of the proceedings.

It was a savage game as both squads really went at each other. When the final whistle blew, the so-called second team had defeated the so-called first team, 19-7. As a result of their play that day, Jack Zilly and Fred Rovai were moved to the first team.

As part of the preparation for the first game of the 1946 season against Illinois, Coach Leahy decided the B team was to play the part of the Illini in scrimmages against the varsity and assigned the B-team men the task of learning the Illinois plays. To make it as realistic as possible, the B team was to wear orange and blue jerseys, the colors of Illinois, and each one of the 11 was to wear the exact number of his Illinois counterpart. In this way, each varsity man would become familiar with the Illinois player assigned to block him, as well as who was to carry the ball.

On the Monday before the opening game, the B team was gathered about Coach Earley as he was about to pick his 11 "Illinois" men for the much-awaited scrimmage. As he called out names, he handed the player his specific number and sent the player sprinting to the tower area. Earley had called out 10 names, all but the right halfback position, which belonged to Illinois' best ball carrier, Claude "Buddy" Young, number 66. Young, a short, stocky, baby-faced, black athlete had been a high school sprint champion. He was also the star halfback from Chicago's Wendell Phillips High, and in the 1944 Notre Dame-Illinois game, he had sprinted 74 yards for a touchdown.

Coach Earley looked at the backs crowded around him and after a pause, tossed jersey number 66 to me and said, "You're the darkest; put this on and get up there."

After the B team, alias Illinois, was assembled, we huddled for the start of the scrimmage about 20 yards from Leahy's tower. We all knew that the coach would be watching every play with that eagle eye of his. This was our chance to shine against the first-team varsity and we all knew it. My adrenaline was pumping so fast that I felt like I could run as fast as Buddy Young if given the chance.

I did not have to wait long. After a few plays, Coach Earley called "Buddy Special right on two," and then proceeded to explain in our huddle what he wanted us to do. The play called for the ball to be snapped between the legs of Dick Leous, our quarterback, wearing

144

Perry Moss' number, directly to me playing the right halfback role of Buddy Young. The other two backs, Jerry Ramsberger and Paul Owens, were to fake to their left, while Leous and Buddy Romano playing guard, trapped the opposing left tackle, George Connor. I was to fake a counter before going wide to my right and then hit off tackle. Upon hearing the play explained, Dick Leous said to Coach Earley, "You want me to trap George Connor?"

"Yes," replied Earley.

Everyone in the huddle laughed. (The thought of an inexperienced quarterback trapping Connor sounded like an insane idea.) We broke the huddle and came up to the line of scrimmage. Leous barked the signals and I received the direct snap and started to run to my right, parallel to the line of scrimmage. After about three steps I planted my foot to cut off tackle. Leous and Romano came crashing into me so hard the three of us landed on our backs another three yards further back. As we looked up, there was George smiling down at us. (It was the only time I ever saw George smile with a football helmet on.) I know for a fact that Dick, Buddy, and I were not smiling. Dick later explained that as he went to make his trap block, George picked him up and threw him into Romano and me.

The rest of the scrimmage was not as disastrous as that play as we did manage to gain some yardage. We scrimmaged for about 45 minutes, and, when we did pick up a few yards, Leahy would have us run the same play over and keep repeating it until they stopped us for no gain. We scrimmaged like that for the next three days against the first-, second-, and third-string varsity teams.

By the end of the week we might not have managed to impress Coach Leahy with our talent, but we did have the satisfaction of knowing we made a contribution to the first win of the year. The real Illinois team was repeatedly stopped as it tried to run the same plays we had practiced running against the varsity that week.

Leahy had settled the issue of who would play on the first team about a week prior to the opening game. Martin and Zilly—ends, Connor and Czarobski—tackles, Fischer and Rovai—guards, and Strohmeyer or Wendell at center. Lujack at quarterback, Mello at fullback, Sitko at right halfback, and Livingstone at left halfback.

By Wednesday the second team was set. The big question was who would make the third team. This may not seem like a big issue to some, but I can assure you that it meant a great deal to the players.

145

For one thing, Leahy only took three teams and a few extra players on trips. Since the Illinois game was an away game, it meant the difference of making the traveling squad or staying home. Secondly, there were so many experienced players who had won monograms on previous teams, that no matter how you worked the numbers, there were going to be quite a few lettermen, which included first-string players from previous years, who were not going to make the traveling team. It became a matter of pride to all the players to make this trip.

In most cases, the difference in ability between players at almost every position on the third, fourth, and fifth teams was negligible. At the noon meeting on Thursday prior to Saturday's game, Leahy announced that he would have a scrimmage that afternoon to determine the final spots on the roster.

That day at practice the team had its usual calisthenics after which Leahy called the squad together. He called out the names of the first two teams, who were then sent to another part of the practice field to work on the plays in a dummy scrimmage (no live contact). The rest of the team assembled in Leahy's favorite spot on the practice field for the all-important scrimmage.

You could feel the excitement in the air. Men who ordinarily stood still were fidgeting, while some others were pacing, if only for a foot or two.

Leahy called out the offensive team and then the defensive team. Already there were disappointed looks on some faces as a result of not being included in the first part of the scrimmage, even though they knew eventually they would get an opportunity to play. From the very first snap of the ball, the hitting was ferocious. Early in the scrimmage, Art Statuto, who was playing offensive center, came back to the huddle slightly bent over. Wally Ziemba, the center coach, asked Statuto if he was all right. Statuto snapped back that he was fine. We later learned that Art had severely bruised his ribs, but there was no way he was coming out of that scrimmage. That seemed to be every player's attitude as I cannot recall anyone coming out because of an injury, and, believe me, there were many who were hurting that day.

At one point, Jim Brennan ran around end and then cut back sharply to go all the way for the first touchdown of the scrimmage. Jim was one of the best cutback runners on the team, a talent that those who saw him play in 1944 remembered well. He did that several more times in the scrimmage that day.

No one can remember the details of a scrimmage played that long ago, but there is one thing that almost every player present remembers, that it was one of the toughest, most hard-fought scrimmages that anyone has ever seen or participated in.

When the scrimmage ended, about the only conclusions that could be reached were that there was a war going on at Cartier that day, that everyone played their hearts out and had acquitted themselves well, and that Jim Brennan seemed a cinch to make the traveling team. Shortly after the team filed into the locker room, the list was posted on the board. Jim Brennan's name was not on the 36-man list.

No one could ever explain why Jim Brennan did not make the trip, particularly after his performance that day. As a matter of fact, he never could seem to get in Leahy's good graces. It was not because of a lack of talent because Jim could run, block, and catch with the best of them. As Jim puts it, "I started on the 1944 team for a few games and never got on track when Frank Leahy became coach."

As it turned out, of the 46 monogram men that came out for summer practice, just 25 made the 36-man traveling squad.

The competition on the practice field was very intense as the players battled for places on the first unit, or second, or a spot on the traveling team. Each player had great respect for the talents of the other players he faced daily in practice. Off the field, the players were getting reacquainted or, in some cases, getting to know each other for the first time, thanks to Ziggie.

Since there were so many returning players from the earlier years, plus the new guys, Ziggie thought it would be a good idea if they met often off the field to get to know each other better. Seeing each other on the practice field and occasionally on the campus was one thing, but Ziggie, in his wise ways, knew that for the players to really get to know each other, they had to meet in a more relaxed atmosphere. Besides, Ziggie liked a party.

One of Ziggie's favorite haunts was Flytraps Bar in Elkhart, Indiana, not too far from the campus. Ziggie got a group of the "old-timers"—including Marty Brutz, Paul Limont, Jack Zilly, Joe Signaigo, Corny Clatt, Bob Livingstone, and others who had played on the teams before their military service—and started a club. Ziggie called it "The Muggers Club." They would meet once a week at Flytraps for some light refreshments, a lot of stories, and good clean fun with all serious subjects off-limits.

The cadre of old-timers would then invite some of the "new guys" to be part of the group. George and Chuck Connor were invited, as were Zeke O'Connor, Marty Wendell, Bill Fischer, Bill Walsh, and many of the guys who had come more recently to Notre Dame. Ziggie invented an initiation for each guy, even the old-timers, that he would dictate. For instance, John Lujack was asked to remove his false teeth and sing some crazy song, after which he had to chug-a-lug several beers.

It became a mark of distinction to be selected to join the Muggers Club. Yet, it was not an elitist group in that it was not just the lettermen or top players who were invited. It was more the older guys, regardless of where on the squad they played. Ziggie was leery about inviting some new guy, who might be only 18 or 19.

Ziggie would send a postcard to the members reminding them of their weekly meeting. Ziggie would sign the card, "KYBO." He did this so the school authorities could never connect him with instigating such a meeting should they ever get wise to the club. When some new member asked, "Who the hell is KYBO?" everyone would laugh because it meant, "Keep your bowels open."

The members met once a week and from reports, they had a great time. Being only 18, my freshman pals and I were not invited and we understood. As the season progressed the team jelled not only on the field, but in our friendship with each other off the field. We were becoming a family, probably without realizing it. This did not mean that we did not block and tackle each other with all we had during practice—Leahy demanded no less and the players demanded no less of ourselves.

Ziggie would ask each new member for five dollars for the cost of a mug that would have his own name on it. Marty Wendell tells the story of giving Ziggie five dollars for a mug, but he never received it. About 10 years after both were out of school, Wendell and Ziggie were together in Chicago having a beer and Marty said, "You know Zig, I gave you five dollars for a mug 10 years ago and never got it."

Ziggie immediately shot back, "You know these things have gone up in price." You could never get the best of Ziggie in a verbal exchange.

We learned years later that Leahy was well aware of the Muggers Club and the beer-drinking sessions. As Bernie Crimmins recalls those years, "The assistant coaches knew what was going on and Leahy did too. The attitude was that we couldn't treat them like high school seniors. They were fellows who had been in the war. They had been used to a certain style of life during the last couple of years and you couldn't change everything.

"Later on, in talking to various coaches on other college staffs, a lot of them ran into a tremendous amount of trouble. They tried to have everybody follow a straight line and found out it didn't work because of the type of life those guys had the previous years in the service. So Frank knew they were going out and having a few beers once in a while. He didn't stress it at meetings, but occasionally he would say, 'Do you think this lad here is overindulging? Is he putting out as much as he should?' But, overall he didn't get too rough with anybody. I think it worked out real well."

Because of Leahy's sensitive handling of what could have been a difficult problem, there was probably less drinking by the 1946-47 football players than at a lot of other schools. Everyone had to be in by the 10 P.M. bed check, and all the players knew how tough the next day's practice would be, so there was no flagrant abuse of Leahy's "let them live" philosophy. From the records these teams compiled, it would seem that Leahy's way of dealing with these veteran players worked.

Chapter Nine

THE 1946 SEASON—LEAHY'S SECOND NATIONAL CHAMPIONSHIP

Illinois

Notre Dame opened the 1946 season against Illinois in Champaign on September 28th before 75,000 fans. Leahy, of course, was coaching his first game since 1943. He knew he was facing a very good Illini team which included the fastest back in all of football, Claude "Buddy" Young. Teamed with Young in the backfield were Perry Moss at quarterback, big Ruck Steger at fullback, and Julie Rykovich, who had started for Notre Dame on the 1943 National Championship team, at the other halfback. The Illinois line, led by Alex Agase, was equally talented. It promised to be a hard-fought game between two teams loaded with veteran players ready to resume their football careers.

This season would see a first at Notre Dame—the team would be without a regular captain. Leahy opted instead to name a captain or captains for each game. One can only surmise that given so many returning players from so many of the past teams, he thought it would be very difficult, if not detrimental, to have an election to pick a full-season captain. He chose John Lujack to be captain for the opening game.

George Connor's hand, broken in early August during the "movie session," was almost healed. However, he still needed some added protection to prevent further injury. Hughie Burns, the team trainer, and one of the doctors in town devised a plastic guard that would fit over the top of the hand. They put a two-inch-thick sponge rubber pad over the plastic and then taped the hand so it resembled a boxer's hand taped for a fight.

In order to conceal which hand had the injury, they taped the other hand in identical fashion. This taping of the whole hand was the beginning of a new trend in college football. Until then, linemen, and some backs, taped their wrists, but not the whole hand. By mid-season, all Notre Dame interior linemen taped their hands in a similar way, less the plastic guard and the sponge rubber. The trend caught on and spread to other colleges.

Connor, playing his first game for Notre Dame, was to kickoff for the Irish. Connor's kickoffs in practice that week had been traveling well into the end zone. With his adrenaline pumping in anticipation of his first appearance in a Notre Dame uniform, there was no reason to think he would not again boom one deep into the end zone.

Instead, Connor's kickoff turned out to be a line drive about five feet off the ground. It went through the first row of linemen and started bouncing at Illinois' 30-yard line. Steger, playing as the short man on the kickoff, finally scooped up the ball, but took just two steps before Connor, running full tilt, hit him with a vicious tackle that echoed over the stadium. As Knute Rockne once said, "You don't have to see a good tackle, you can hear it." Connor's hit on that first play fully illustrated Rockne's contention.

Ironically, Connor's poor kickoff was probably the best thing that could have happened. He was so embarrassed and mad at himself for the kick that he was determined to do something to redeem himself. His tackle of Steger set the tone for how the whole team would hit that day.

After a scoreless first period, Tom Gallagher of Illinois got off a beautiful punt that Pete Ashbaugh fielded on Notre Dame's two and could only return to the five-yard line. Livingstone and Mello drove to the 15 for a first down, the first of the day. On the very next play, Lujack, on a reverse pivot, faked the ball on a dive to Livingstone playing left halfback and pitched to Red Sitko who was sweeping left end. Sitko got around the defensive right end and, with some excellent downfield blocking plus some great cuts on his part, ran 83 yards to the Illini two-yard line where he was knocked out of bounds. Livingstone scored on the following play. Fred Earley's kick was wide, giving Notre Dame a 6-0 lead with six minutes to play in the half.

With two minutes left in the half and the ball on the Irish 33, Sitko and Mello made big yardage on three running plays to get the ball to Illinois' four-yard line. Mello circled right end for the touchdown. Earley converted making the score, 13-0, at intermission.

151

The second half was all Notre Dame as the Irish repeatedly stopped the Illini attack, keeping them back in their own territory for most of the two periods.

In the fourth quarter, with Notre Dame on the Illini 39-yard line, Lujack hit Ashbaugh with a perfect pass that Ashbaugh took to the eight. Three plays later, Terry Brennan drove over right tackle for the score. Later in the period, Frank Tripucka, now playing quarterback, tossed a pass from Notre Dame's 30 to Mike Swistowicz, who fumbled the ball in the air only to have it batted by a defender allowing Swistowicz to grab it before it hit the ground. The play netted 18 yards. Swistowicz gained four and, from the eight-yard line, Corwin Clatt drove into the end zone for Notre Dame's final touchdown.

On the first play after the second-half kickoff, Illinois averted a shutout when Julie Rykovich, on a halfback option pass, threw to Bill Heiss, who had gotten behind the Notre Dame safety man, for Illinois' lone touchdown. The final score was 26-6.

Notre Dame beat a very good Illinois team, a team that would go on to become the Big Ten Champion and play in the Rose Bowl. The Irish held the elusive Buddy Young to an average of 3.6 yards on 11 carries. The Notre Dame coaches knew that most of Young's runs were to his left, so when Notre Dame was on defense, Connor and Ziggie Czarobski changed sides. The coaches, aware that Connor was a penetrating-type defensive player, reasoned that his style would cause Young to make his cut earlier and give the linebackers time to hit him before he got in the open. The strategy worked to perfection as Mello, George Strohmeyer, Marty Wendell, and John Panelli continually stopped Young for short yardage. The strategy was further helped by Notre Dame's use of a 5-3-2-1 defense. To get Wendell in the game as a linebacker, Leahy removed the right guard, either Fred Rovai or John Mastrangelo.

Lujack, playing defensive halfback, was in on so many of the tackles near the line of scrimmage that Young must have thought John was also playing linebacker. On one of the plays in which Lujack was in on the tackle, Young, as he was lying on the ground, looked at Lujack and exclaimed, "John, not you again?"

Although Buddy Young was held in check by the Notre Dame defenders, he showed why he was considered one of the finest sportsman the Irish would ever meet. When the game was over, he went up to Czarobski and said, "Congratulations, Ziggie. The better team won—I hope you guys go on and win all your games." Young was not only one of the best runners ever to play football, but, as many of us who had the privilege to know him later in life can attest, he was a true gentleman who always conducted himself with class.

Sitko led the runners with 116 yards in eight attempts and was followed by Mello who got 68 yards in nine tries. Both had exceptionally good defensive games. Lujack, playing nearly 60 minutes, was flawless in directing the team on offense and his defensive play was sensational. Notre Dame showed considerable depth as Leahy had 10 different backs carry the ball.

This Irish victory marked the beginning of a 39-game winning streak that lasted until the second game of the 1950 season. It was also the beginning of an era (1946 to 1949) that would be called "The Golden Years of Notre Dame Football."

Every player on the Notre Dame team who played in that game played well. Mello, the starting fullback who also started on the 1943 team, had a very good game. He made several long runs, blocked well, and scored one of the touchdowns. But evidently Leahy must have thought Mello could have done an even better job. Mello recalls what happened:

"I was married at the time and living in South Bend. Leahy was never too keen about married men playing on the team. After the Illinois game, at our usual noon meeting the following Monday, Leahy reviewed the film of the game for the team. After the meeting as I was walking out of the room, Leahy pulled me aside. He said, 'James Mello, you're not blocking and tackling like you did in 1943,' and he pulled me a little closer and said, 'Are you doing things at home that you shouldn't?'

"I said, 'No, Coach, I'm just fulfilling my marital obligation.' "

Leahy was always an innovator when it came to making a play or some technique better. For example, one day at practice the first team was in a scrimmage when the play to be run called for Lujack to fake a flip to Mello, the fullback, who was running wide, then pivot and hand the ball to the halfback, who would go up the middle on a trap. Lujack made his fake of the flip, but when he pivoted to hand the ball to the halfback, the back was already by him. Lujack alertly spun back and pitched the ball with an underhanded lateral to Mello, who was just standing there. No one knew where the ball was. Mello had an open field and could have trotted into the end zone. The play had completely fooled the defense and the coaches.

Leahy, never having seen the play, asked the backfield coach, "What on earth was that?" They explained what happened and Leahy drew up the play, gave it a name, and incorporated it into the repertoire of plays. In recalling that day, Lujack said, "That play alone gained over 100 yards against Army in 1947 and countless yards against other opponents the rest of the season. That was Leahy at his best. There was an error either by me or by the back, but as a result this play came out of it, and it became part of Notre Dame's T-formation and other teams' formations for years to come. So that was recognition of something terrific out of a mistake."

Another example concerns Chuck, my oldest brother. Chuck was an excellent guard on his high school team and later at the University of Wisconsin and at Iowa Pre-Flight during the 1943 season. Chuck, who had transferred to Notre Dame after the war, arrived in time to play in the spring practice of 1946. He did well in practice, but at the beginning of summer practice he sustained a head injury that ended his football career.

Leahy liked Chuck and the aggressive way he played. Leahy also knew that Chuck was smart and knew football well. So he designed a special job for him that proved to be very interesting for Chuck and very helpful to the coaching staff.

At the scrimmages during the week, Chuck would note on his clipboard what play was called in the huddle. Then he noted who carried the ball, how much yardage the play gained, and what defensive position made the tackle. He would further note any pertinent comments Leahy made about the play. He did this throughout the scrimmage and for every scrimmage involving the first two teams.

Every evening of a major scrimmage, Chuck would tabulate his findings and present them to Leahy before the next day's practice. He might say, for example, that the 43 play gained an average of five yards when Sitko carried the ball and averaged 3.5 yards when any other back was the ball carrier. He might note that the left linebacker made the majority of the tackles no matter who carried the ball. Chuck's data gave Leahy precise information as to which backs consistently gained the most yardage and, in addition, it told him who was making the tackle. Armed with this information, Leahy would experiment with different blocking assignments until the play consistently gained additional yardage.

There was one play, a counterplay, in which both guards pulled out with the lead guard assigned to block the defensive end, and the offside guard to lead the play inside the end and block the first man he encountered. Chuck's findings showed that the middle linebacker was stopping, after only a few yards, what should have been a big-yardage play. Leahy pondered the problem and came up with the solution.

The linebacker in question had an unobstructed view of what was happening in the offensive backfield, so despite the faking that was going on by the backs, the linebacker could see the handoff. This allowed him time to meet the ball carrier at the line of scrimmage. Leahy, now knowing the problem, instructed the strong side guard to lift up when pulling out, contrary to the way the guard would normally begin his pulling-out maneuver.

In the scrimmage the following day, the play was run with the guard performing as instructed. As Leahy had anticipated, the linebacker's view was obstructed for a split second, long enough to cause him to hesitate until he could see what direction the play was going. That maneuver on the part of the guard was all that was needed to make the play a big gainer. That play, with the new way of running it, became one of the bread-and-butter plays that year.

In today's world, with the ability to videotape each practice session, a job such as Chuck's would not be needed. In those days, such attention to small details was one aspect of Frank Leahy's style that distinguished him from other coaches.

Pittsburgh

The second game of the season was at home against Pittsburgh. Pitt had lost its opening game to Illinois, but bounced back to defeat West Virginia, 33-7. By merit of its decisive win over Illinois, the Irish were the overwhelming favorites. Jack Zilly, the tall right end who had played so well in 1943, was named by Leahy as Notre Dame's game captain. Leahy announced that he would start Gerry Cowhig, the converted fullback from the 1942 team, in place of Livingstone.

Six of the players to start against Pitt had been stars on previous Notre Dame teams before they went into service: Wendell (who alternated with Strohmeyer), Czarobski, Lujack, Cowhig, Mello, and Zilly. Four of the starters were making their first home appearance in Notre Dame uniforms: Jim Martin, Sitko, Connor, and Strohmeyer. Two holdovers from the previous year's team were starting: Bill Fischer and Fred Rovai.

The young Panthers of Pitt surprised the Irish by holding them scoreless in the first period of play. But in the second quarter, Notre Dame got untracked when Lujack hit Livingstone on a 24-yard pass play to score the first points of the game. Notre Dame had little problem with Pitt after that. Terry Brennan scored twice, first on a two-yard run and then on a 25-yard run after a key block by Bob Skoglund. Mello also scored twice, once on a pass from Lujack and then on a plunge from inside the five-yard line. Notre Dame won handily, 33-0.

Notre Dame, despite the win, did not look as sharp on offense as it had against Illinois. Some sportswriters blamed the warm weather, and some attributed the below standard performance to Sitko being taken out of the game in the first quarter with a broken blood vessel in his left leg. However, Leahy's opinion was all that mattered and he was not happy with the way the team had played. With Leahy in that frame of mind, nobody looked forward to the review of the game films that following Monday or, for that matter, to the practice sessions that week.

When the regular season was under way, the daily practice sessions followed a regular format. Practice started promptly at 3:30 P.M., but most players were on the field by 3:15. As a player entered the gate to Cartier Field his name was noted by a student manager who was guarding the entrance. After picking up his helmet, or his "bonnet" as Coach McArdle liked to call them, he would report to the area to where his particular position was assigned.

Before Coach Leahy arrived on the field, which was promptly at 3:30, each of the assistant coaches had his players work on the basic fundamentals of stance, lunges, handoffs, and other things crucial to their positions. Shortly after he arrived, Leahy blew his whistle, which was the signal for all players to report to the center of the field for a snappy 10 minutes of calisthenics.

After this drill, Leahy would gather the whole team around him and he would assign players to the various drills he had planned for the day. This was a good time for the coaching staff to gauge the team's feelings about the upcoming game. If they were quiet, it was a bad sign. If the team had a lot of chatter and had some cheer, it was a good sign.

At Tuesday's practice, anticipating Leahy's foul mood after the Pitt game, Ziggie started a cheer as soon as the team was gathered around Leahy. He started clapping his hands and yelled, "Beat

Purdue! Beat Purdue!" As soon as Ziggie started, the whole squad fell to repeating the chant which lasted several minutes. At first Leahy scowled, but it went on so long that you could see a faint hint of a smile around his mouth. I am sure it did not change his plans to work the hell out of the team, but maybe it lifted his bad mood just a little.

Leahy did work the team extra hard that day and also extra long. The hour the team would usually be dismissed from practice was long past when Ziggie started another cheer. Leahy was with a second group about 30 yards away from Ziggie's group observing a scrimmage when Ziggie, supported by his group who were also scrimmaging, started to yell, "We want to eat! We want to eat!" Leahy heard the cheer and almost had apoplexy. He spun around to face Ziggie's group and demanded, "What did you say?"

Without missing a beat, Ziggie started to yell, "We want to eat...Purdue! We want to eat...Purdue!" By the look on his face, it was clear Leahy did not know what to think. But he did send the team to the showers five minutes later.

Purdue

With Sitko sidelined with his leg injury, Panelli, usually the backup fullback, was scheduled to start at right halfback. Playing at home before a capacity crowd of 55,452, Notre Dame was ranked third nationally as it went up against the always-tough Boilermakers.

As it turned out, Notre Dame had little trouble defeating Purdue, 49-6, for its third straight victory. The Irish scored 35 points before Purdue could manage a touchdown on the first play of the fourth quarter. Johnny Galvin dazzled the fans with a brilliant 55-yard run from scrimmage. He scored standing up, but Purdue failed the try for the extra point.

Notre Dame got off to a slow start, taking 10 minutes before managing a first down. With the ball on the Irish 34, Mello, acting captain for the game, sprinted around right end for 33 yards aided by some crisp downfield blocking. Panelli got 17 and then 10 before Mello took it over for the touchdown. Earley's conversion made it, 7-0.

In the second quarter after Brennan got 31 yards in two carries, Clatt went over from the two. Two minutes later, Cowhig, aided by some great downfield blocking, took a Purdue punt and returned it 51 yards, to the Purdue 29. Three plays later, Lujack threw a perfect pass to Terry Brennan for the score. With Earley's third straight conversion, Notre Dame led, 21-0, as the first half ended.

After Martin recovered a fumble minutes into the second half, Panelli raced around left end from Purdue's 19-yard line to score. Earley made it, 28-0.

Late in the third quarter, Notre Dame got the ball on its own 30 following a Purdue punt. Panelli got 14 yards and then made a great run through most of the Purdue team to take the ball to the Boilermaker 14 where he was caught from behind. After a couple of plays, Lujack hit Zilly in the end zone for Notre Dame's fifth touchdown. The Irish scored twice more after that, once on a midair recovery of a fumble by Skoglund after Hart had creamed the quarterback when he was attempting to pass, and once on a 21-yard scamper by Gompers.

There were some great runs in the game and some devastating blocking by the Notre Dame line. The downfield blocking was a coach's delight. There were three or four blockers downfield on almost every play clearing the way for Mello, Panelli, Brennan, and the other backs.

On one play, Panelli, playing right halfback for the injured Sitko, ran around left end. Connor, playing left tackle, blocked the opposing tackle until Panelli was around the corner then he released to go downfield. About 30 yards downfield, Connor, who was now ahead of Panelli, threw a body block on one of the defenders, knocking him down and causing him to crash into a second defender, who also went down, nearly tripping a third defender and at least causing him to be out of the play.

On other plays, Mastrangelo, Strohmeyer, Zilly, Martin, and the other linemen could be seen knocking someone down in the secondary.

One of the highlights for South Bend residents attending the game was the appearance of Ernie Zalejski, whom many considered the greatest high school football player ever produced in South Bend. Zalejski had been in school only two days after his discharge from the Army. With just seconds to go in the first half, Leahy put the former Washington High School star into the game for one play on which he gained two yards. With 45 seconds remaining in the game, Leahy put him back in. He hit off the right side of the line for nine yards, but the play was called back because of a penalty. On the next play, Zalejski went through tackle, cut back, eluded some would-be tacklers, and appeared to be on the way to a 49-yard touchdown run when he slipped and fell, avoiding the last Purdue man between him and the goal line. He got the ball again and fought for eight yards up the middle as the game ended.

The wealth of running backs on the Notre Dame team became more obvious after the Purdue game. Panelli, normally a fullback, was the running star at right halfback, gaining 123 yards in nine attempts. Simmons, injured all season, got in the game in the fourth period and gained 52 yards in four carries. Add Panelli, Simmons, and Zalejski to the other ball carriers, Mello, Livingstone, Sitko, Clatt, Brennan, Cowhig, Gompers, and Swistowicz, and you have as great an array of ball carriers as ever played at one time at Notre Dame.

Two players were injured: Livingstone, who injured his knee early in the game after fielding a punt; and Fischer, who sustained a broken nose. Fischer tells about his injury:

"I came out of the game with a bloody nose and face. As I came out, Coach Leahy met me at the sidelines and said, 'Bill Fischer, if you don't do a better job of blocking, I'll put you back in there and let that Purdue lineman kill you.' The lineman he was referring to was Purdue's All-American guard, Dick Barwegan.

"The team doctor quickly determined that I had a broken nose, which he immediately set back in place and asked, 'How do you feel?'

" 'Not so good,' I replied.

"I was taken to St. Joe's Hospital after the game because the nose started to bleed again. After I was treated, the doctor said, 'For the next two days at least, no pads—just some light stretching.'

"I asked him, 'Will you tell the coach?'

"He said, 'You tell the coach.'

"That Monday before practice, I told Hughie Burns, the team trainer, about the doctor's instructions. Burns said, 'Put on your sweatpants and do what the doctor ordered.'

"I put on my sweatsuit and went out to the practice field with a big smile on my face as I watched the rest of the team getting ready for the day's drills. Leahy spotted me and called over, 'Oh my God, Bill Fischer, where are your pads?'

"I couldn't believe he was asking me that, so I said, 'Coach, if you recall in the game Saturday, I broke my nose. After the game it started bleeding again and I had to go to the hospital for more treatment. The doctor told me that, in addition to the broken nose, I had a concussion and a hemorrhage, and that I should go very easy for a few days.'

"Leahy said, 'Well, you know nowadays doctors are inclined to be old-fashioned—after all, your nose has been broken and you have had those other problems, so what more can happen?'

"I went back to the locker room and put on my pads. I broke my nose twice more that week—once when I pulled out the wrong way and collided with Marty Wendell and once when I caught an elbow from Bill Walsh."

Fischer had one consolation to that bad week—he received permission to have a nose guard put on his helmet.

While the varsity was defeating Purdue, Notre Dame's B team was annihilating the Great Lakes varsity team in a game at the Great Lakes Naval Training Center just outside of Chicago. The morning of the game I was approached by a very large Navy seaman. He inquired if I was on the Notre Dame team that was going to play Great Lakes that day. I told him I was. He proceeded to tell me that he was the captain of their team and he had a message he wanted me to deliver to my teammates.

In a very gentlemanly way and in a calm voice, he said, "Last year our team beat your varsity and the very next year we are playing Notre Dame's B team. We are very upset about this. We know it's not your team's fault about this scheduling, but we are going to whip you good. Tell your team there is nothing personal in this."

In an equally civil way, I replied, "I wouldn't count on beating us. I think you should know that we have on our team every varsity player that did not make the varsity trip for their game. We have some great players on our team."

He just smiled and said, "I'm glad to hear that. I won't feel so bad when we pour it on."

I did not want to appear to be a wise guy, so I just said, "I will pass along what you said and good luck today. I'll see you on the field."

He smiled and said, "You can count on it."

When we were boarding the bus to take us to the field, I spotted Luke Higgins, a big, strong veteran player who played guard. Higgins had played on the '42 team and easily won his letter. He was a tremendous player but was in Leahy's doghouse, so he was playing with the B team. I thought Luke was the ideal one to give the message to because he was not too pleased to be there.

I repeated to Higgins what the Navy man had said. Higgins inquired as to what position the guy played. When I told him he was a tackle, Higgins just smiled and said, "This ought to be interesting."

And interesting it was! Our line, led by Luke Higgins, completely manhandled the Great Lakes line, including the big tackle I had spoken to earlier that day. Our backs ran wild to the point that when the score reached 40-0, Coach Earley had some of us switch positions just to have some fun and not run up the score any more than we already had. It is no exaggeration to say the score could have been 100-0 if Coach Earley had wanted to pour it on. It was another example of the unbelievable amount of football talent at Notre Dame in 1946.

Iowa

The next varsity game was to be played in Iowa City against a strong Iowa team coached by Dr. Eddie Anderson. Anderson was a starter at right end for four straight years under Rockne and played on the 1919 and 1920 National Championship teams that featured George Gipp. Anderson, who captained the 1921 Notre Dame team, always fielded a capable 11 and this season was no exception. His team was 4-1 going into the game and was ranked 17th in the national polls.

No Notre Dame football team had ever defeated Iowa in Iowa City. Leahy, well aware of the significance of the game, worked his team extra hard during the week to prepare for the Iowa attack, particularly for the running of the highly acclaimed Iowa fullback, Dick Hoerner. Leahy designated George Connor captain for the game.

As part of the preparation to stop the running of Hoerner, Leahy had the B team repeatedly run fullback plays against the varsity during the week prior to the game. During one of the scrimmages, Joe Yonto, our burly fullback playing the part of Hoerner, ran an off-tackle play to his right and was hit at the line by Connor, Martin, and Wendell. When the players unpiled, Yonto was on the ground with the most badly broken leg any of us had ever seen. Yonto's foot was at a 90-degree angle from where it should have been. When Joe was carried off the field on a stretcher, no one thought he would ever walk again, let alone play football.

For some weeks, the doctors treating Yonto shared our layman's opinion. Fortunately, after many surgeries and some painful therapy, Yonto did walk again. The injury ended his playing days, but as Notre Dame fans know, he went on to a long and brilliant coaching career at Notre Dame as a premier defensive coach.

As it turned out, the 1946 Notre Dame team broke the 25-year jinx and crushed the Hawkeyes, 41-6.

During the first quarter, there was a brief communication between Leahy and Ratterman, the second-team quarterback. Coach Leahy turned to Ratterman and said, "If Panelli picks up the first down—we'll go on to victory."

Panelli made the first down on the next play. Ratterman, who was never at a loss for words, responded immediately, "Coach, Panelli just picked up the first down, we've just won—so when are you going to put me in the game?"

Needless to say, Ratterman did not get in until Leahy decided it was the right time.

With the game only three minutes old, Lujack recovered a Hoerner fumble on Iowa's 34-yard line. Lujack then threw a perfect pass to Brennan, who had slipped behind the Iowa secondary. Brennan caught it on the two and stepped into the end zone for the first score of the game. Earley made the score, 7-0.

As the second quarter got under way, Notre Dame had the ball on its own 38. Cowhig got eight and Hart, subbing for the injured Zilly at right end, made a brilliant catch of a Lujack pass for a 43-yard gain that took the ball to the Iowa 11. After two plays, Panelli drove over for the score.

Later in the same period, Notre Dame started a drive from its own 20. Lujack hit Hart and then Swistowicz as part of the drive that took the ball to the 48. On the next play there was a fumble in the Notre Dame backfield. Lujack, ever alert to where the action was, scooped up the ball, ran to his left down the sideline, and eluded several defenders on the way to a touchdown. Earley, making the second of his three first-half extra-point tries, made the score, 20-0.

With less than a minute to play in the half, Iowa's Em Tunnell threw a long pass to Jack Dittmer, who fell down about 10 feet from where the ball landed. The officials gave Iowa a gift when they ruled that Ashbaugh, who was defending on the play, had interfered with

Dittmer, giving Iowa a first down on Notre Dame's 10-yard line. Hoerner, the Iowa fullback, scored the lone Hawkeye touchdown on a one-yard sweep of the end. As with every opponent that year, Iowa failed to make the extra point, as the half ended with the score 20-6.

Using Coy McGee (a sophomore playing for the first time), Mello, and Sitko, Lujack engineered a drive from midfield that culminated in the fourth Irish touchdown when Sitko drove over from the three. When Sitko scored again, Leahy sent in the reserves. Bill Gompers scored the sixth touchdown with a 25-yard run around left end. On the play, Frank Tripucka, subbing for Lujack, made a great fake to Coutre going through the line, made his spin, and then tossed out to Gompers going to his left. Ralph McGehee pulled out from his left tackle position to cut down the Iowa linebacker, allowing Gompers to score before most of the Iowa team realized who had the ball. After the game, Lujack called it, "The best-executed play of the game." In recalling the play, Tripucka said, "One of the referees came up to me after the game and said, 'That was one of the greatest jobs of faking I have ever seen. I couldn't follow the ball.'" (Years later, Leahy called that play the best-executed play *he* had ever seen.)

Strohmeyer, the number one center, and Swistowicz, Sitko's backup at right halfback, suffered injuries that prevented them from seeing action against Navy, Notre Dame's next opponent. This news was balanced by the good news that Livingstone and Zilly, who missed the Iowa game because of injuries, were scheduled to be back for the Navy game.

Navy

Going into the Navy game, Notre Dame was ranked as the number two team in the country with four straight one-sided victories. Navy, on the other hand, had lost four in a row after barely winning its opener against Villanova, 7-0. Despite this, Leahy was more worried than usual about the upcoming game. During the week he said, "We are in a perfect spot to be knocked off by Navy. Those Middies are due to explode one of these days…they can redeem themselves in one afternoon and, unless we get this idea over to our players, this might be the week they do redeem themselves."

In that frame of mind, Leahy worked the team hard during the week's practice sessions. He seemed to want perfection on every play.

An example of this is Leahy's comments to Livingstone during a scrimmage that week. Livingstone, who was a sensational runner, took a handoff from Lujack at quarterback and slashed through the line away from two tacklers. Finding himself temporarily in the clear, he cut sharply to his left to head for the sideline. As he was running down the sideline, the defensive safety man angled towards him, so Livingstone cut sharply to his right making the would-be tackler completely miss him. He then outran the rest of his pursuers to finish off a brilliant 80-yard touchdown run.

No sooner had Livingstone crossed the goal line than Coach Leahy came up to him and scolded, "Robert, when you ran through the line you were much too high. You should bend your knees more to be lower and not make such a big target—you could have been hurt if someone had hit you. When you cut to the sideline, you should have switched the ball to your other hand so you could use your right arm as a stiff arm. Then as you were further upfield, you cut back without waiting for your blockers—you had three fast linemen coming up to block for you and you didn't use them."

Livingstone, who had taken the dressing down in silence, looked Leahy in the eye and asked, "Coach, how was it for distance?"

Mastrangelo at right guard, who had been named Lineman of the Week by the Associated Press in the previous year's Navy game and had been improving each week during this season, was recognized by Leahy for his contributions by being named game captain for the Navy game.

I particularly recall one incident concerning Mastrangelo. One day at practice, Coach Leahy wanted to see the first-team line pass block. The B team, as usual, was the cannon fodder on defense. I was to play guard against Mastrangelo, who was as tough a player as his All-American honors suggested.

I was relieved to see that there were about three teams of B-squad linemen who would participate in the line scrimmage. This was Coach Leahy's idea. In this way we could alternate every third play or so in order to be fresh and give the first team a better contest.

I was at left defensive guard opposite Mastrangelo. As the team came to the line of scrimmage, Mastrangelo whispered to me, "Let's take it easy. This could be a long afternoon."

I just nodded my head very slightly. I knew what Mastrangelo was saying—that we should conserve our strength for the all-out scrimmage that was sure to follow. The unwritten rule for such an occasion meant that I could charge straight forward as hard as I wanted, which was no problem for Mastrangelo, but under no circumstances was I to do the unexpected.

I performed my role according to the unwritten script. To anyone watching it looked as though we were really going at it, but compared to what it could have been if Mastrangelo were really extending himself, it was a piece of cake for both of us. As I finished my stint, my great pal, Buddy Romano from Chicago's Fenwick High School, took his turn. I watched and saw Mastrangelo say a few words to Romano and I knew he was getting the same words that I had received. Romano charged straight into Mastrangelo, grunting and groaning as we all did to show how hard we were working. Romano also "performed" and survived without incident and, when his turn was over, he was replaced by a player I will call Bill.

Before the next play started, Romano, who was now standing next to me, said, "I hope Bill isn't his usual cocky self and decides to try something goofy—Mastrangelo will eat him alive."

Romano and I watched intently as the first-team line broke the huddle and took their positions at the line of scrimmage. Mastrangelo could be seen saying something to Bill, who gave no hint of a response. When the ball was snapped, Bill, who was very quick, submarined Mastrangelo, got to his feet almost in one motion, and dumped the unprotected John Lujack on his back.

The way Leahy laced into him, you would think Mastrangelo had just committed treason.

"John Mastrangelo, you let some freshman guard get by you and he hit our quarterback. If this were a regular game, the quarterback could have been killed. Don't you want to be a part of this team and block like all the others? We are going to run this play again, and I want to see if you really want to play football at Notre Dame."

Romano leaned over to me and said, "Now Bill is going to get it. I almost hate to watch."

Just the look on Mastrangelo's face as he approached the line of scrimmage for the next play told the story. At that moment I completely understood that age-old expression, "If looks could kill." As the ball was snapped, instead of assuming the pass-blocking stance, Mastrangelo fired out like a man possessed and hit Bill so hard that he reeled over backwards while Mastrangelo drove him relentlessly to the ground. The hit was so hard and the results so devastating that no one said a word as Bill lay prostrate, out cold on the ground some seven yards behind where he had begun.

That play ended the drill and Bill's football career at Notre Dame. Bill never again appeared on the Notre Dame practice field and he switched schools at the end of the semester. I understand that he did play football at another major college, so at least his injury was not permanent, but I will bet he was never hit that hard the rest of his football career.

In the 20th annual battle between the two schools, Notre Dame blanked Navy, 28-0, in Baltimore before 65,000 fans, which included Red Blaik, Army's head coach, and some of Blaik's assistants who were scouting the Irish in preparation for the Notre Dame-Army game the following week.

Notre Dame gained a total of 414 yards compared with Navy's 139 and made 27 first downs to Navy's eight. By the statistics it would appear that the Irish should have scored more than 28 points, but a rash of fumbles (seven times, losing four) ended many of the drives that the Notre Dame offense mounted.

After 10 minutes of play, Leahy sent in Cowhig and Gompers. This move seemed to spark the team as the two backs gained some good yardage. Cowhig, after recovering a Navy fumble, took a pitch from Lujack, shot through the right side of the line, and with some shifty running sprinted to a 30-yard touchdown for the first score of the game.

Early in the second quarter, Simmons, who played an excellent game, gained substantial yardage on several runs before he ploughed through the line from the four to score the second touchdown. Earley made it 14-0. About eight minutes later, Simmons recovered a Navy fumble on Notre Dame's 48. Notre Dame marched down the field to score on a short plunge by Simmons after runs by Simmons and Livingstone, and a Ratterman-to-Livingstone pass took the ball to the one-yard line. Score: Notre Dame 21, Navy 0.

The Middies came charging out for the second half. Starting from their own 31, they marched down the field to the Notre Dame one where the Irish held on downs. While still deep in Navy territory,

Lujack, who liked to do the unexpected, threw a 29-yard pass to the right end, Zilly. The march soon ended when Sitko fumbled, but Notre Dame got the ball back minutes later on a Navy fumble.

Leahy changed his backfield to start the fourth quarter. Cowhig, now playing left halfback, took a shovel pass from Ratterman, who had replaced Lujack, and sprinted 83 yards for a touchdown. However, a call on Notre Dame for clipping nullified the play. The Irish regrouped and put together a 68-yard drive only to lose the ball on their seventh fumble of the game.

Leahy again changed his backfield—putting in Tripucka, Zalejski, Gompers, and Simmons. This unit quickly marched 56 yards in six plays, with Gompers going in from the two with only 40 seconds left to play. On the drive, Zalejski accounted for 33 of the 56 yards. Tripucka had 19. Gompers had the rest, including the touchdown.

Hart, the freshman right end, celebrated his 18th birthday by creaming a Navy back for a 15-yard loss as the game ended.

There were injuries to some key players resulting from the Navy game. Czarobski, who had played on the 1942 and 1943 teams that defeated Army, hurt his hip muscle; Simmons, who had looked very good in the last two games, reinjured the leg that had kept him out of action for the first three games; Strohmeyer and McBride sustained ankle injuries; and Terry Brennan pulled a muscle in his leg. Burns, the team trainer, thought that, of the five, only Czarobski and Simmons would be unable to play against Army.

Army

On November 9, 1946, the long-awaited Army-Notre Dame game was played before 74,000 fans in New York City's Yankee Stadium. It was billed as the game of the year.

The Irish, under Coach Leahy, fielded one of the most powerful football teams ever assembled at the University of Notre Dame, and possibly in all football history. Before their college careers would end, 10 of the players on that Notre Dame team would become All-Americans, two would be Heisman Award winners, two would be Outland Trophy winners, and six of them would one day be selected for the College Football Hall of Fame.

The Irish had demolished their first five opponents by a combined score of 177-12. Only Illinois and Iowa had managed to score a touchdown against Notre Dame's powerful defense. Neither team could convert the extra point.

Col. Earl H. "Red" Blaik's Army team was equally impressive. The Black Knights had just won consecutive National Championships with one of the finest backfields ever assembled, including the famous Doc Blanchard and Glenn Davis, who were known as "Mr. Inside" and "Mr. Outside." This great duo was supported by a group of veterans who had gone undefeated in 1944 and 1945 and had won seven games in 1946—a streak of 25 straight victories.

This game was more than two great teams playing each other. It was the 33rd renewal of an intense rivalry that dated back to 1913 when Knute Rockne caught passes from Gus Dorais to defeat the favored Army team, 35-13. It became the most celebrated intersectional rivalry in college football and was further fueled by Army's 59-0 victory in 1944, the worst defeat ever suffered by Notre Dame. In addition, in 1945, Army had trounced a previously undefeated Notre Dame team, 48-0. Notre Dame had a couple of scores to settle.

On the other side of the ledger, Army had not been able to score a point against the Leahy-coached teams of 1941, 1942, and 1943. These three games produced a 0-0 tie and two Notre Dame victories, 13-0 and 26-0. Army, too, had extra reasons for wanting to win.

Blaik, who became the winningest coach in Army's illustrious history, and Leahy respected each other as coaches, but on a personal level there was no love lost between the two. Perhaps they were too much alike; both stern disciplinarians, both intensely dedicated to the game, both with a talent for instilling in their players a fierce competitive spirit, and both were winners.

As the teams prepared, sportswriters filled the sports pages with daily hype. Seats for the game had been sold out since July and the asking price for tickets was $200. The New York City restaurants and hotels loved the Army-Notre Dame game because the week's income surrounding this event was reportedly larger than almost any other event held in New York. Only the New Year's Eve celebration generated more revenue.

As Notre Dame began its practice sessions, the cheer of the week was "Fifty-nine and forty-eight, this is the year we retaliate."

On the Notre Dame campus, the students too were caught up in the spirit of avenging the previous losses. The campus was flooded with coat lapel tags bearing the letters "SPATNC," which stood for "Society for the Prevention of Army's Third National Championship." Students were making plans for the New York Central train trip to New York, while Frank Leahy and his coaching staff were busy in meetings and on the practice field preparing the team for the historic battle.

On the Tuesday before the game, Leahy had the "Hamburgers" (the name the B team called themselves) running Army's plays against the first-team varsity. Gerry Ramsburger, our big fullback who was about the same size as Blanchard of Army, was running Blanchard's favorite plays. After one off-tackle play, Ramsburger returned to the huddle and said with a groan to his pal, Dick Cordasco, who was playing halfback with the Hamburgers, "Boy, George Connor hit me with a shot in the jaw and it's killing me." Cordasco told him, "Shake it off—it'll be okay."

After the next play, Ramsburger was obviously in great pain, so Cordasco motioned to Hughie Burns, the team trainer, that Ramsburger needed attention. Burns examined his jaw and said, "It's broken, Gerry." Leahy, who was watching, said, "Take Gerald right to St. Joe Hospital and have them wire the jaw and bring him back; he's a fine lad." (Ramsburger did have his jaw wired, but was never able to play again. He was a good one and would have played a lot of football for Notre Dame had circumstances been different.)

Leahy, wearing his usual pessimistic pre-game face for the press, predicted that if Notre Dame played at its very best, Army would win by "only about 27-14." Leahy did concede that if his team stayed close to Army until the last quarter, it was possible for the Irish to score on a tired Army team and win out.

In his discussions with the sportswriters, Red Blaik predicted that it would be a high-scoring game. He thought it was possible that Notre Dame might "run us into the ground." However, he suspected that Army would win.

Leahy's biggest concern was Lujack, who had sprained his ankle during practice that week and had to spend two nights in the infirmary.

Prior to the game Lujack's ankle was heavily taped. In the pre-game warm-up Leahy watched Lujack carefully as he worked out. Leahy had him test the ankle with a few punts. His performance seemed to satisfy Leahy that he was fit to play. Leahy named Lujack and Cowhig, the big halfback who played such a great game against Navy, as co-captains.

Both squads were fully prepared and confident they could win. Army went into the game as the number one ranked team in the country. Notre Dame was ranked number two.

The result completely frustrated and disappointed the players, coaches, and fans of both teams as the game ended in a 0-0 tie. Not even a statistical edge could be claimed by either side, as the final statistics were uncannily similar.

It was a classic defensive game with both squads playing defense as it was meant to be played. On offense, neither team could get its much-heralded attack going. In the second quarter, Notre Dame did put together a drive and managed to get to Army's four-yard line, but could not score. On fourth down, with only a few yards to go, Lujack tried a quarterback sneak that failed to gain. Bill Fischer vividly recalls the play, "When we were on the two- or three-yard line and Lujack tried the quarterback sneak, Strohmeyer was stuffed by the guy on his head. If John had just been able to take one step to the left and follow George Connor and me, he would have scored because George and I had knocked our guys into the end zone."

Lujack, who played 60 minutes that day, observed that he did not like his play-calling on the series of downs near the goal line. If he had it to do over, Lujack recalls, he would have run left on first down to give the Irish more open field on the right where Notre Dame had been successful running a sweep with its big back, Cowhig.

For Army's part, Blanchard and Davis were repeatedly stopped near the line of scrimmage. Army's one big chance to score came late in the game when Blanchard, after a counter fake to his right, took the handoff going to his left and broke into the clear with only Lujack, the Notre Dame safety, as an obstacle to the goal line. The Cadets and Army fans went wild as Blanchard, running in the clear, angled for the sideline. After Blanchard ran about 25 yards, Lujack hit him with a tackle below the knees and the big fullback went down. The Army fans groaned. They had never seen the powerful Blanchard stopped once he was in the open field.

On the other side, the Notre Dame fans had never seen Lujack miss a tackle anywhere on the field, regardless of who was the ballcarrier. Lujack not only did not miss this time, but made a textbook tackle by driving his shoulder into Blanchard with his arms firmly wrapped around the fullback's legs. This hit left little doubt that the potential touchdown run was over. There were no more scoring threats by either team.

In recalling that day, assistant coach Bernie Crimmins, who was assigned to the booth upstairs, said, "I'll never forget sitting up there with Moose and Jack Lavalle [Notre Dame scout for the game]. Normally, after the game was over, people would leave in droves, but this day hardly anyone moved for at least a half hour. It was as if they expected another half, or come on, let's play some overtime. They just sat there and talked about the game.

"Leahy, McArdle, and I replayed the game in a little office off of the dressing room. We must have replayed it 100 times, and when we finally did leave, it was around nine o'clock. All the cars were gone so we found a policeman who flagged a cab to take us back downtown."

Some of the Notre Dame fans second-guessed Leahy after the game, saying he should have kicked a field goal when Notre Dame was at Army's four-yard line. Others said Leahy should have put in Ratterman, who had the quarterbacking ability to open up a game with his bold play. No doubt some Army fans had their own list of "should haves." The fact remains that both teams fielded their best players and neither could score. As frustrating as the tie was for everyone, perhaps that was the way it was meant to be.

Most of the publicity after the game centered around the tackle Lujack made on Blanchard to save a touchdown. Lujack could never understand what all the fuss was about. In recalling the event he said, "It could have been Blanchard, Davis, or Jones. As a defensive man you're back there to make the tackle. He was aiming towards the sideline and I cut him off and made the tackle. There were other people who made tackles that day, so I saw no particular greatness in that play."

Lujack was right; there were other tackles that day. On two straight plays the charging Notre Dame linemen led by Sullivan at tackle (who played a great game substituting for the injured Czarobski) dropped Davis for losses totaling 17 yards. On another play, Blanchard caught a pass and was headed for the goal line when Swistowicz, playing defensive halfback, literally wrestled Blanchard to the ground.

Notre Dame's defense did something no other team had ever done—it held the famous "Touchdown Twins," Blanchard and Davis, to a total of 79 yards.

On the offensive side, Skoglund and Terry Brennan made terrific catches of Lujack-thrown passes, and Cowhig, Brennan, Gompers, and Lujack made some excellent gains running the ball. Yet, despite it all, Notre Dame could not score against the very tough Army defense.

171

Those who saw this game witnessed what could be a once-in-sports-history event. They saw four Heisman winners on the same field. Doc Blanchard of Army won it in 1945 and his teammate, Glenn Davis, was the winner in 1946. From Notre Dame, John Lujack won the Heisman in 1947 and Leon Hart in 1949.

Both Leahy and Blaik called the game "a terrific battle of defenses." As an indication of how the defense of both teams dominated, seven linemen in that game were nominated for Lineman of the Week honors in the weekly Associated Press poll. Joe Steffy, an Army guard, won the honor, closely followed in the balloting by George Sullivan and Jim Martin of Notre Dame. Also nominated were Barney Poole of Army, and Jack Zilly, John Mastrangelo, and George Connor from Notre Dame.

As with many serious events, there is also a lighter side of things. Immediately following the game, Leahy wanted to talk to the squad in private and did not want any visitors for about 20 minutes. Armed with these instructions from Leahy, Clarence Kozak, the perennial door-keeper warmly known to Notre Dame players as "Kozy," went to answer a knock on the locker room door just as the team meeting was getting underway. Kozy told the visitor no one was allowed in the locker room until he got the OK from Leahy. The visitor said, "Perhaps you don't know who I am. I'm Dan Topping and I own this stadium."

Kozy shot back, "I'm Clarence Kozak from Notre Dame and we have rented this stadium for today, and when we say no visitors, we mean no visitors." He closed the door on a surprised Topping. (Topping was admitted a short time later when Moose Krause informed Kozy he was cleared for admittance.)

There is another incident concerning this game that took place years later. Oddly, Blanchard and Lujack did not cross paths after the famous game in 1946 until a few years ago when they were both attending a Heisman Award function. They greeted each other warmly, as do most former adversaries when they meet away from the field. After they exchanged pleasantries, Blanchard said, "Remember that tackle you made on me in the '46 game? You scared the hell out of me."

Lujack knew he had hit Blanchard hard, but was surprised at this comment from the indestructible Army ace. He could only reply, "Really?"

"Yes," said Blanchard, "I thought I had killed you."

Leahy did not have to worry about a letdown after the tie with Army. The players were not happy with the tie—they thought they should have beaten Army. But it was the kind of game you did not rehash. Rather, you dismissed and looked ahead to the next one.

Northwestern

Notre Dame was favored to beat Northwestern in a home contest, but listening to Leahy describe the Wildcat team, one could get the impression that it was the other way around. "Northwestern has the best average in the entire Western Conference when it comes to rushing the ball...They have averaged 5.2 yards every time they snapped the ball against conference opponents. I don't know why anybody takes any of Waldorf's teams lightly; most surely, I don't."

With the exception of Strohmeyer and Simmons, all the players who had been injured, including Lujack with his bad ankle, were ready to play. Livingstone, starting at left halfback, and Connor, at left tackle, were named co-captains for the game.

Notre Dame defeated Northwestern, 27-0, but it took the Irish until the fourth quarter to put away the stubborn Wildcat team. It appeared to the 56,000 rain-soaked fans that they would see a rout as the Irish marched 63 yards for a touchdown on their first possession of the game. Sitko, who was the game's leading rusher with 107 yards in 15 carries, started the drive with a beautiful 34-yard run that put the ball on Northwestern's 25. Livingstone, Mello, and Sitko each contributed in bringing the ball to the one-foot line where Sitko drove over for the touchdown. Earley added the extra point to make the score 7-0, with the game only five and a half minutes old.

For the next two and a half quarters, Notre Dame compiled some impressive statistics but could not get the ball across the goal line. Finally, after about four minutes of the fourth period had passed, Ratterman, with Cowhig, Panelli, and Gompers running the ball, covered 41 yards to the two in seven plays. Panelli dove over for Notre Dame's second touchdown.

A few minutes later, with McGee added to the backfield in place of Cowhig, the team marched 59 yards in 12 plays and, again, Panelli bulled over from short yardage. With a little over four minutes to play, Notre Dame led, 20-0. After a recovered fumble, Slovak scored the last touchdown on an 18-yard run.

Tulane

Jim Martin, Notre Dame's starting left end, suffered a leg injury in the Northwestern game that would keep him out of action for the upcoming Tulane game. Coming back from injuries and expected to play against Tulane were Strohmeyer and Simmons.

Paul Limont, who was the starting left end on the 1943 National Championship team, had difficulty getting his legs in pre-war shape and, as a result, had not accumulated much playing time. However, he was slated to start in the Tulane game and, along with Joe Signaigo, a guard, was named co-captain for the game. How this came about illustrates the type of player Limont was.

While the varsity was playing Iowa in Iowa City on October 26th, the B team was playing the third game of its schedule against the Purdue B team in East Lafayette, Indiana. In order to give Limont more game time, Leahy assigned him to the B team. Although Limont did not say anything about his feelings, it was obvious from the look on his face prior to the game that he was not at all happy about playing with the B team. Bill Earley, the B-team coach, named Limont team captain for the game. I am sure Earley meant it as a compliment, but it only seemed to make Limont angrier.

From the opening kickoff, Limont played like a man possessed. He was all over the field making tackles, catching everything the quarterback could throw, knocking someone down with his blocking. He was clearly the outstanding player on the field.

When the coaches met that Sunday to review the two games (Varsity—Iowa, B team—Purdue), Coach Earley gave a full report to Leahy regarding the B game and particularly about the individual performance of the players. The following Monday Limont was back playing with the varsity. He played so well during practice for the next three weeks that Leahy rewarded his efforts with a starting call and naming him as co-captain for the Tulane game.

It was a great lesson for all of us. You never give up, and always play your best no matter what the circumstances.

Some 70,000 spectators, the largest number ever to see a regular-season game in the South, breaking the record set the year before, watched Notre Dame take the opening kickoff 77 yards to a touchdown in 11 plays. Mello plunged over from the four, but Earley missed the extra point to leave the score 6-0. The next time the Irish got the ball, they went 88 yards to another score in eight plays. Earley made it 13-0. Before the day was over, Notre Dame gained a total of 552 yards, 422 of them on running plays, as the Irish trounced Tulane, 41-0.

Lujack completed eight of nine passes for 101 yards. When Sitko was injured in the first quarter, Gompers, his replacement, had his best day gaining 103 yards in 10 carries. He also had runs of 35 and 17 yards called back because of penalties. Brennan, Mello, Zalejski, and Swistowicz also had great days running the football. The line play was superb as Limont, Connor, Signaigo, Strohmeyer, Mastrangelo, Czarobski, and Zilly repeatedly opened huge holes for the backs and then devastated the Tulane secondary with their downfield blocking. Connor was named the Lineman of the Week by the Associated Press.

After the game, the Tulane coach, Henry Frnka, said, "They made us look like high school kids at times, but it wasn't because we are so bad; it was because they are so good. This Notre Dame team is one of the best I have ever seen, and if they rank them as National Champions, it's all right with me and everybody else around here."

During the train ride back to South Bend, Jim Costin, the fine sportswriter for the *South Bend Tribune*, asked Czarobski which was the best line Notre Dame had faced that season. Ziggie's answer echos the sentiments of all the players from that team when asked that question.

"The best line we faced all year was the one we had to go against most of the season when we scrimmaged out there on Cartier Field. I'd rather play on Saturday afternoons than scrimmage against fellows like Bob Walsh, Zeke O'Connor, Bill Russell, Ted Budynkiewicz, Vince Scott, and Tom Potter, to name a few. Give me a ballgame anytime rather than a scrimmage against those guys."

Southern California

At this point in the season, Leahy had become ill with the flu and a case of laryngitis aggravated by a recurrence of his spinal arthritis condition (the one that had caused him to enter the Mayo Clinic during the 1942 season). On doctor's orders, he was confined to bed at his Long Beach home on the Monday before the final game of the 1946 season against Southern California. Moose

Krause, the tackle coach, was designated to be the acting head coach in Leahy's absence.

The atmosphere at practice with Krause in charge was much more relaxed than it would have been had Leahy been present. It was not that Krause was not a tough taskmaster when the occasion called for it, but rather that he recognized that at this stage of the season, the team was in top form and did not need any extra prodding to get the job done.

Because it was late November, darkness came early, usually before the practice session was over. On Thursday of that week as darkness was settling on the field, the first team was running plays in dummy scrimmage (no contact) against some of the reserves, with Krause overseeing the drill. Some distance away, the second offensive team was doing the same under the direction of McArdle and Ziemba. Just as the first team was breaking from its huddle, Connor said, "Look at that, look at them."

The second team, led by Bill Walsh and his pal Wendell, was running backwards like a movie film going in reverse. The second team was mimicking the rewinding of the film as it was done at the noon meetings.

At our Monday noon meetings, Leahy always showed the films of the previous game. If there was a particular play he did not like, or if some player really goofed, Leahy would call out, "Run that play over again." The team dreaded hearing those five words—"Run that play over again"—because it meant someone was about to be chewed out as only Leahy with his sarcastic comments could do. The projectionist would reverse the film showing the players going backward until they were back in their original positions at the line of scrimmage.

Krause, and all the players who were in his group, stopped their scrimmage and watched as the second team, playing against some reserves, went to the line and ran a play. At just the right moment, Krause, now in the spirit of the fun, hollered, "Run that play over again." It was the most comical thing any player had ever seen on Cartier Field as Walsh, Wendell, Fallon, Ratterman, and the rest of that squad halted their movements and immediately went in reverse, zigzagging as they ran backwards to their original positions. In the semidarkness, it looked exactly like the game films we watched. Krause and all the players and coaches were laughing so hard they could hardly speak, but Krause did manage to say, "Marvelous, marvelous."

There was no question that the team was loose going into the final game of the year.

Army and Notre Dame were the number one- and two-rated teams in the country. The National Championship hinged on how each fared in its final game. A victory for Notre Dame would give the Irish their first undefeated team since 1941 and their second since 1930.

Two seniors, Bob Skoglund, slated to start at left end in place of the injured Jim Martin, and Fred Rovai, who had started several games at right guard, were named co-captains.

One of the great motivational speeches the players like to recall took place in the Notre Dame locker room before the game that Saturday. The Irish had completed their pre-game drills and were gathered in the locker room ready to go out and play. The game official came and said to Krause, "Coach Krause, five minutes to the kickoff."

Krause didn't say a word.

A short time later, Freddie Miller, who was a former player and teammate of Leahy's, said, "Three minutes to go Moose." Still there was silence.

Then Miller said, "Two minutes, Moose."

Coach Krause stopped his pacing, turned to the assembled team, and said, "I left your coach this morning down in Michigan City. He's very sick and hasn't even shaved in days, he looks terrible."

With that, Livingstone, one of Notre Dame's great halfbacks and a veteran player, piped up, "Let's chip in and buy him some razor blades."

Undaunted, Krause continued in his effort to get the team fired up and said, "OK, let's get out there now and kick the hell out of these guys."

John Lujack spoke up, "Who's starting, Coach?"

Krause replied, "We'll all start."

Everyone just looked at each other, until someone said, "All right, we'll all start."

With that, the team filed out of the locker room, took the field and did kick the hell out of USC by the score of 26-6.

After a scoreless first quarter, the fans were treated to two sensational plays just minutes apart in the second quarter. First, Verl Lillywhite, the Trojan quarterback, surprised the Irish with a quick kick. The line of scrimmage was the USC 17, and Lillywhite's kick rolled over the Notre Dame goal line—83 yards away. With the ball on the Notre Dame 20 and with Ratterman, McGee, Panelli, and Simmons now in the backfield for Notre Dame, Simmons got three yards. Then McGee, who had earlier run 49 yards, took a shovel pass from Ratterman and went around right end behind a couple of blockers for a sensational 77-yard touchdown run. During the run, McGee evaded five or six Trojans, using his blockers to perfection as he cut, faked, and sidestepped would-be tacklers. At the 20, he broke into the clear to score standing up on one of the finest runs ever seen in Notre Dame Stadium.

Hart scored the second touchdown after receiving a pass from Ratterman. McGee, who gained a total of 146 yards on only six carries for a remarkable 24-yard average, scored again on an 18-yard jaunt that had the Trojans wondering who had the ball because of Ratterman's superb faking. Cowhig scored the fourth touchdown on a 13-yard run.

With this final victory and some assistance from Navy, Notre Dame was declared the National Champion. The Middies had lost seven straight games before playing Army in their finale. Army was an overwhelming favorite, but won only 21-18 and Navy had the ball on the Cadets' four-yard line when the game ended.

Notre Dame finished the season with a total offense of 3,972 yards for an average of 441 per game, the highest in the nation. On defense the Irish wound up yielding only an average 142 yards, the lowest in the nation. They led all college teams with 3,061 rushing yards, for an average of 340 yards per game.

One of the most astonishing accomplishments of the 1946 team is that it allowed its opponents only 24 points. It was the least points allowed since 1917 and still stands as a modern record. No one scored more than one touchdown, and no one scored an extra point or field goal. Of the four touchdowns that were scored against the Irish, only one (USC) was scored against the first team.

The team statistics for the year showed that Sitko led the team in rushing, Lujack in passing, Terry Brennan in receiving, and Terry Brennan and Mello tied for the scoring lead.

As the All-America teams were announced, John Mastrangelo (right guard), George Strohmeyer (center), George Connor (left tackle), and John Lujack (quarterback) were named to almost all of the teams.

Connor was given the honor of being selected by the Football Writers' Association of America as the first recipient of the Outland Award honoring the outstanding interior lineman in the country. In addition, he was named by the Philadelphia Sportswriters as the Lineman of the Year.

Lujack had a fantastic year, both on offense and defense. He called all the plays on offense, mixing the pass and the run so effectively he prompted Leahy to say, "Having Lujack direct the team was like having a coach on the field." When the occasion called for it, Lujack could run the ball as well as any back on the team. On defense, he was outstanding, particularly in the Illinois and Army games. He placed third in the Heisman voting behind Army's Blanchard and Davis. Strohmeyer was an excellent blocker on offense and was particularly adept in blocking downfield. He backed up the line on defense and, along with Marty Wendell, gave Notre Dame two of the best linebackers in college football.

Mastrangelo saw extensive action in the first few games even though he did not start. He simply got better each week and was considered one of the best blocking linemen in the country.

In assessing the success of the 1946 team, many of the major sportswriters gave much of the credit to the Notre Dame line. It seemed to be the consensus opinion that other Notre Dame lines—particularly the 1929 and 1943 lines—may have been the equal of the starting line, but no college team ever equaled the depth of outstanding lineman on the 1946 team. As one writer put it, "They [Notre Dame] have the best two lines in the country."

Bill Fischer, in recalling the season, said, "The 1946 season was an interesting one for me as a sophomore starting most of the games. I can remember on several occasions, on a Friday night before a game, being with Ziggie, George Connor, Jack Zilly, Bob Livingstone and a bunch of the guys who had been in service. We would find a nice quite saloon and go in the back room to be unnoticed. We would have a beer and Ziggie would say, 'I suppose those silly coaches are having a meeting and worrying about that game tomorrow. But we're going to kick the hell out of them tomorrow, aren't we?' Everyone there would yell, 'Hell yes!' Ziggie would call the waiter over and say, 'Bring us another round of beers.'

"As a result of being in the company of guys that were older, us younger guys, Bill Walsh, Terry Brennan, Bill Gompers, John Panelli, and the others that started in 1945, grew up and matured much faster."

Fischer went on to give his account of why the team was so successful. "One day about 15 years ago I told Moose Krause they failed to give Leahy an award I think he should have received. Since Leahy had received so many awards, Moose was shocked. 'What did they forget?' Moose asked. I think they should have awarded Leahy, 'The Salesman of the Century Award,' because every week, week after week during the season, I was convinced that we were playing the toughest team in the country.

"The other reason for the award, and the most important reason, is what he did when he was in the Navy. It was the sales job he did that brought all the players back from service instead of signing pro contracts. When Leahy was in the Navy he traveled all over the world, wherever his lads were serving in the military. He would seek them out and have lunch or dinner with them. A good example of how he operated is his meeting with Lujack. Leahy told Lujack, 'Oh, John, I just left Jim Mello and the last thing he said was, 'Tell Lujack we're counting on him and he better be back.'"

"A week later he had dinner with Jim Mello and told him, 'I just had dinner with John Lujack and he wanted me to be sure to remind you, Jim Mello, that we're counting on you to come back and win the National Championship and not to disappoint us.'

"He was so convincing in sending that message to all the previous players. That was his great wisdom in convincing these players to come back to win a National Championship. He had guys that came back with a purpose—to be the best team in the country and to be the best team in the history of football. As a result, we had these mature guys who came back with a oneness of purpose and goal."

It was a remarkable and satisfying season for the players and the coaches. With only Mello, Zilly, and Mastrangelo on the first team, and very few on the second and third teams scheduled to graduate, the prospects for the 1947 season were indeed bright. When asked about the future of the team, even Coach Leahy could not suppress a smile as he thought of the many outstanding players he would have returning.

The All-Star Game

For the 1947 All-Star Game, seven Notre Dame players were selected from the 1946 National Championship team to play for the College All-Star team: Bob McBride, Jim Mello, Jack Zilly, Jerry Cowhig, John Mastrangelo, Bob Skoglund, and George Ratterman.

In addition to the Notre Dame players, others selected were Doc Blanchard, Glenn Davis, and Arnold Tucker from Army; Buddy Young and Alex Agase from Illinois' Rose Bowl team; Charlie Trippi from Georgia; Weldon Humble from Rice; Vic Schwall from Northwestern; and a host of other stars from that season.

Frank Leahy was named to coach the All-Stars. He picked as his assistants Bob Voights of Northwestern, Moose Krause from Notre Dame, Wally Butts of Georgia, and Leahy's former teammate from their Notre Dame days, Marchy Schwartz.

Ratterman, Mastrangelo, and Skoglund were in the starting lineup. Cowhig and McBride acquitted themselves well in their playing time as did Mello and Zilly, who scored the only touchdowns, as the All-Stars defeated the Chicago Bears, 16-0, before 80,000 paying fans at Soldier Field in Chicago.

During the 1946 season, Notre Dame had a play called "37-H" that was used successfully on short-yardage situations. On this play, the quarterback faked to the right halfback on a dive straight ahead and then gave the ball to the fullback who hit off tackle. Leahy included this play in the game plan against the Bears. Jim Mello recently related what happened when that play was called against Chicago:

"During the game, we [All-Stars] had the ball at midfield with second down and two yards to go. Leahy called for the 37-H. Doc Blanchard, playing fullback, took the handoff and went off tackle as designed, but the Bears had anticipated the play. Bulldog Turner, the Bears' All-Pro center and linebacker, hit Blanchard so hard it appeared as though he decapitated him. Leahy got all excited and called me over. 'James Mello, you get in there and show Blanchard how to run the 37-H.' I thought, 'I'm going to show Doc Blanchard how to run a play against Bulldog Turner? You've got to be out of your mind.'

"When I got in the game the quarterback called 37-H. There was no way I was going to run at Turner, so I improvised and followed the halfback through the hole and found myself 10 yards in the secondary before I was tackled. Blanchard came back in at fullback and the team marched down inside the five-yard line when 37-H was called and, again, Turner smashed into Blanchard for no gain. Leahy sent me in again with instructions to run 37-H. I followed the halfback again and scored a touchdown."

Mello said it was probably the only time in his career he ran that play contrary to the way Leahy always instructed the fullback to run, but he was very happy he did.

The day after the All-Star Game, Leahy returned to the Notre Dame campus to continue preparations for the 1947 football season.

Chapter Ten

The 1947 Season—Leahy's Third National Championship

George, Ziggie, and Weight

Lake Delevan, Wisconsin, was definitely the place to be during the summer of 1947.

If Zygmont Pierre Czarobski, the star right tackle on the Notre Dame football team, and George Connor, the All-American left tackle and captain-elect, thought it was a good place to spend their summer, then it must have been good. Ziggie and George always seemed to know the right place to be.

Lake Delevan is one of Wisconsin's medium-sized lakes located about 10 miles from the more famous Lake Geneva, and about 90 miles from Chicago. At that time, it had everything a young college lad would want: good restaurants, picturesque surroundings, beautiful girls, many watering holes, friendly people, a nice town nearby, and a close proximity to other resorts where there were more beautiful girls and more watering holes.

Ziggie was employed as a bouncer for one of the local night spots called the Dutch Mill. Ziggie did not fit the stereotype of a bouncer— during the entire summer he never forcibly evicted anyone. Not that there were no troublemakers. When Ziggie was alerted to a problem situation, he would ease up to the guy most likely to start something and, with his massive frame directly in front of the guy, he would extend those big paws at the end of his huge arms and say, "Hi, my name is Ziggie Czarobski. What's yours?" The guy was either so scared at the sight of Ziggie, or he was so surprised at Ziggie's friendly manner that he, too, would extend his hand and give his name. Ziggie would gently steer him away from the problem area, and before the guy realized what was happening, Ziggie was turning on the charm and holding the guy in deep conversation. In very quick order, trouble was avoided. The result of this approach was either the guy stayed and caused no more commotion or he left of his own volition.

George was hired for the summer by Ray Morrissey, who had attended Notre Dame and was partial to Notre Dame players, to do construction work on Morrissey's private lake near Lake Delevan. Because he worked directly for Morrissey and not the construction foreman, George was allowed some extra liberties. There was an additional bonus in working for Morrissey—he owned a tavern in the town of Delevan.

The word was that George worked very hard in the mornings pouring concrete, but would mysteriously disappear in the afternoons, much to the chagrin of the construction foreman. If the foreman had searched for George on one of Lake Delevan's beaches where the vacationing girls were often found, he would have spied him sipping a few cold ones with Ziggie. Nobody ever accused Moose Krause's tackles of being dumb.

And so for Ziggie and George the summer of 1947 flowed very nicely.

But early in August, the reality of the upcoming football season hit Ziggie head-on. He made a frantic phone call to George.

"George, I got a telegram from Coach Leahy," sputtered Ziggie, unable to mask his anxiety.

"I know," said George. "He sent me one too, and a copy of yours."

"He sent you a telegram too? What does it say?" Ziggie asked.

"It says: 'As Captain of the 1947 Notre Dame team you should know that I have sent a telegram to your teammate Zygmont Czarobski. I want you to know and to tell Zygmont that I mean every word of it. Frank Leahy.'"

George went on. "The copy I received is addressed to you and it reads: 'Mr. Zygmont Czarobski: Understand you weigh 275 pounds. You could make All-American next season if you were in proper condition. You must report for summer practice at 225 pounds or you will not play for The University of Notre Dame this fall. I do not want any funny fat men on my team. Frank Leahy.'"

"My God," blurted Ziggie, "he sent you one too? You're not kidding me, are you?"

184

"Honest '76,' I'm telling you the truth."

"Do you suppose the old man is serious?" asked Ziggie.

"You know the coach," responded George, "when he gets his mind set on something, that's final."

"Yeah," groaned Ziggie, "I sure do."

Ziggie and George met the next day. Ziggie had obviously given the matter some serious thought since their phone call the previous night. He told George he was going on a diet immediately and wanted George to start working out with him in the evenings.

Three weeks later, when they reported to summer football practice, despite Ziggie's crash diet and evening workouts, he was still 25 pounds overweight.

The day the team reported for summer sessions, Ziggie sought out his pal George.

"What do you think I should do about my weight?" Ziggie asked.

George answered, "You're going to have to face Leahy sometime. Why not go directly to him and ask for more time."

Ziggie did not particularly like the suggestion, but he figured he had no other choice. Before the first practice started, Ziggie went to Leahy's office and asked to see the coach. The moment Ziggie entered the office and saw the look on Leahy's face, he knew Leahy indeed meant what he said about the weight.

Seizing the initiative, Ziggie spoke up and said, "Coach, I know I am still a little overweight, so I would like an extension on your deadline."

Leahy was no fool and knew he needed Ziggie if he wanted to repeat as National Champion. Ziggie was never just a funny fat man—he was an exceptional football player. So after a moment's hesitation, Leahy replied, "Zygmont, I will give you two weeks to make your weight and not one moment more."

"You won't regret this, Coach. I'll do it."

"See that you do, Zygmont," Leahy solemnly responded.

As Ziggie left the office, beads of perspiration ran down his face. It wasn't just the 95-degree heat. He knew he was facing two weeks of sheer agony, and he was not looking forward to it—at all.

Temperatures climbed a few degrees and hovered around the 100-degree mark for most of those two grueling weeks. There were double sessions every day. Before each session, Ziggie put on a rubber suit under the rest of his football paraphernalia. After completing practice, he would take his laps around the field and then head for the training room where he would strip down and soak in the hot tub. After leaving the locker room, he would walk—very slowly—to the dining hall to drink gallons of liquids and stoically go light on the food.

As the days wore on, the pounds dropped off Ziggie. But the once boisterous, fun-loving Ziggie now went about his business in a quiet, subdued manner. The players and the assistant coaches observed this in silence and with a great deal of sympathy and admiration for the beloved Ziggie.

When it seemed he could take no more, weigh-in day arrived. All Ziggie's work had paid off. He looked like an ad for Charles Atlas (the macho image of that day). He looked fantastic.

There was only one problem. He was still seven pounds overweight. But there was no way Ziggie was going to squander all his hard work, only to be thrown off the team for a mere seven pounds. He pondered the problem and came up with the perfect, Ziggie-type solution.

He met with Joe Dierickx, who was the caretaker of the stadium where the team dressed for practice, and slipped Dierickx 10 bucks to rig the locker room scale light by eight pounds. Ziggie was now all set.

There was an air of excitement in the locker room as the team dressed for the day's practice. Every member knew—this was "76's" crucial weigh-in day, and a few knew about the unbalanced scale.

With the whole team watching, Ziggie confidently walked to the coaches' room and knocked. Joe McArdle, the guard coach, opened the door and asked, "What do you want, Zig?"

"I want to see Coach Leahy," replied Ziggie.

A few seconds later, Leahy appeared.

"Hmmmm, Zygmont, what do you want?"

"Do you know what day this is?" asked Ziggie.

"Yes, Zygmont," replied Leahy. "Today is Tuesday."

"No," said Ziggie, "this is my weigh-in day."

"Oh yes, Zygmont, so it is, and how much do you weigh, lad?"

"I weigh 224 pounds," Ziggie said proudly.

"That's wonderful, Zygmont," said Leahy approvingly. "Congratulations! You will help us win the National Championship."

"But Coach, aren't you going to weigh me?"

"No, Zygmont," replied Leahy. "I'll take your word for it."

It was later said that Leahy had no idea Ziggie had rigged the scales, but that he was not about to make Ziggie weigh in and risk having to cut him from the squad. The coach had already accomplished what he wanted, which was to have Ziggie in the best shape of his life. Ziggie was thrilled to have passed the test, but let down because he was deprived of his weigh-in show. He decided to have his show anyway.

To the delight of his teammates, Ziggie stepped onto the scale fully clothed. The scale showed he was over the weight limit. As Ziggie put on a sad face, a loud groan went up from the team. But with his unique stage presence, Ziggie began to strip, much to the delight and cheers of his teammates.

When he was down to only his jockstrap, he dramatically got on the scale again. It registered 224 pounds. Ziggie's face broke out in a big smile, and a great roar went out from the team as Ziggie held his arms high in a victory salute.

From the reaction, you would think Ziggie had just been elected mayor, and in a way he had. Their pal was back. He was his jovial self once again, with smiling face, holding court as only he could do.

As predicted by Leahy, Ziggie did go on to make All-American that year, and the Irish did repeat as National Champions.

However, there was one odd twist. Each player had to get on the scale each day and record his weight. When Leahy reviewed the team weight records at the end of Ziggie's big day, he was shocked to see that his players had lost 640 pounds since the day before.

The 1947 Team

As the team practiced in preparation for the coming season, there was great enthusiasm among both the players and the coaching staff. With good reason. In 1946, Notre Dame had been undefeated and won the National Championship. The 1947 team had almost the entire first and second teams returning. In the first-team backfield, John Lujack, Red Sitko, and either Bob Livingstone or Terry Brennan were all returning, so the only change was that John Panelli would be the fullback instead of Jim Mello.

In the line, Leon Hart took the place of Jack Zilly (who had graduated) at right end. Both tackles, George Connor and Ziggie Czarobski were back, as were Bill Fischer, the left guard, Jim Martin, the left end, and George Strohmeyer, the center. Marty Wendell and Joe Signaigo replaced John Mastrangelo at right guard. Bill Walsh would eventually win the starting assignment at center from Strohmeyer, who had made the All-American team the previous year. With this array, there was every reason to believe Notre Dame could repeat as National Champions. Evidently, Coach Leahy believed this too.

After many weeks of practice, the veteran players began to notice a difference in Leahy's coaching style from previous seasons, most particularly from the previous year. There seemed to be less emphasis on fundamentals and more concentration on scrimmaging without the attention to the techniques of blocking and tackling that Leahy had always emphasized.

Warren Brown, one of the premier sportswriters of the day and a confidant of Coach Leahy, traveled from Chicago to watch the team. At the conclusion of practice, he was troubled by what he had witnessed. In the locker room immediately after practice, he sought out Connor, the team captain, and asked him: "George, tell me the truth. What is going on here? This isn't the same team I saw last year. You should be better than before with so many returning players, but you look ragged. What is wrong?"

Connor had tremendous respect for Warren Brown and knew he had to level with him. He told Brown exactly what bothered not only him, but several other veteran players.

"Mr. Brown, you're right. We have the makings of an even better team than last year, but we are not going in the right direction. I have talked to a few of the guys and we all feel the same way. In our opinion, Coach Leahy has forgotten what made us great—fundamentals. We were always in better condition and could block and tackle better than any team we faced. We don't concentrate on fundamentals anymore and we are starting to play sloppy football. The coach thinks he can just work on timing without regard to the basics of the game. At this rate, we could end up just another football team."

Brown thanked George for his honesty and left the locker room. As the players were leaving, Brown and Leahy could be seen walking around the outside of Cartier Field, deeply engrossed in conversation.

The following day at our usual noon meeting, Leahy astounded the team by beginning with an apology. He said, "Lads, I owe you an apology. I seemed to have forgotten what has made Notre Dame great—attention to fundamentals." As he continued, most of the team sat wondering at his change of heart. Most of the players at the meeting will never forget that day, not only because it marked a turning point in the team's performance, but also because of the famous remark made by the incomparable Ziggie Czarobski.

After his apology, Leahy announced, "We are going back to fundamentals starting right now." He put his hand in the shelf under the top of the dias and pulled out a football. He held the football over his head and said, "Lads, this is a football."

Ziggie, sitting in the front row, immediately called out, "Coach, wait a minute, I'm trying to take notes—you're going too fast."

George Strohmeyer

Bill Walsh, who was the starting center on the 1945 team, but had played behind Strohmeyer on the previous year's team, beat out Strohmeyer for the starting center job despite the fact that Strohmeyer was an All-American the year before.

Strohmeyer was from McAllen, Texas, a town located in the southern part of the state near the Mexican border. Unlike the movie stereotype of a Texan—the tall rangy cowboy—Strohmeyer was about 5 feet, 9 inches and 190 pounds, but every ounce seemed to be muscle. During his high school athletic career, he accomplished what few athletes ever did—he earned six letters, all four years, for a total of 24 letters. He was the city boxing champion, the city wrestling champion, and All-State in football, basketball, baseball, and track.

Leahy, while he was in the Navy in 1944, heard of this amazing athlete, who was then playing football for one of the Pre-Flight schools, and recruited him to attend Notre Dame.

Strohmeyer entered Notre Dame in 1946 as a freshman. He joined the team in mid-August for summer practice preceding the regular-season play. Strohmeyer made himself known as soon as he arrived on campus by proclaiming to all who would listen that he would be the first-string center on Notre Dame's team for the coming year. This kind of comment was not typical for a Notre Dame player, especially from an incoming freshman on a team that already had six centers who had previously established their credentials. Among them were Marty Wendell, who was a fullback/linebacker from the 1944 team, now a center; Walsh, who was the first team center on the 1945 squad; Art Statuto, who played on the 1943, '44, and '45 teams and had been first-string center in the preceding spring practice; and

189

Jim Martin, who would be switched to end and be first string for the next four years. Whether Strohmeyer knew about this array of talent is not known, but as one got to know Strohmeyer, one had the feeling he would have made the comment anyway.

As soon as the practice sessions began, Strohmeyer made his presence felt on the practice field, both by his play and with his mouth. He would announce what he intended to do, and, to the delight of the coaches, but the dismay of the players, he would do exactly what he said he would do. He never seemed to miss a block on offense and, on defense, he was all over the place, not only making tackles, but bone-crushing ones.

A typical Strohmeyer scenario occurred one day in a scrimmage when he was backing up the line on defense against a very good offensive team. While the offense huddled, Strohmeyer declared to all, "You just run a play Old Stroh's way and I'll put that ball carrier right on his back."

There were two reactions from the players. The first was disbelief that anyone would have the nerve to brag like that on a Notre Dame practice field. The second reaction came primarily from the players on the offensive team. They could not wait to run the next play Strohmeyer's way and ram the ball down his throat. Naturally, the quarterback called for a play that went right at Strohmeyer. But Strohmeyer shed his blocker, moved into the hole at the line, and hit the ball carrier with a fierce tackle that put him on his back. Leahy called out, "That-a-way-to-hit, George Strohmeyer."

Strohmeyer responded, "I told you what happens when you run Old Stroh's way."

He told the quarterbacks one day that he could snap the ball so hard he could draw blood from their hand. They just looked at him with an "Are you nuts?" look. One of them took him up on the challenge. The player put his hand under the center to take the snap and, on the agreed upon count, Strohmeyer snapped the ball. As soon as the ball was snapped, Strohmeyer turned to look at the quarterback, who had a big smile on his face until he looked down at his hand. The smile changed to a look of amazement when he saw blood trickling from his hand along one of the crease lines. Strohmeyer, in his Texas drawl, said, "I told you old Strohmeyer could draw blood." He had backed up his bragging again.

It didn't take long for Strohmeyer to earn the starting center job.

Not only was he the first-string center and linebacker that season, but he made almost everyone's All-America team.

Despite his play on the football field, he was not liked by his teammates, who acknowledged his ability as a player, but had little use for his attitude.

Despite Strohmeyer's utterances and peculiar ways, it never affected the team during games. Off the field, the players did not choose to associate with Old Stroh.

At the start of summer practice for the 1947 season, all of us were astounded to see how Strohmeyer looked when he reported. The once trim, heavily muscled man was now about 35 pounds overweight. At 5 feet, 9 inches he looked rotund.

From the very start of practice sessions, it was obvious Strohmeyer could not perform as he had the previous year when he was in top physical shape. He was slower off the ball, could not react as quickly as before, and, for the first time, was being pushed around by players with lesser abilities, but were in better shape. Strohmeyer then made a mistake in judgment that would haunt him for a long time. He made the comment to someone off campus that the coaches at Notre Dame did not work the players very hard. Somehow the remark got back to Leahy.

The following day, Leahy passed on the remark to Wally Ziemba, the center coach. Leahy told Ziemba to give Strohmeyer a workout he would long remember. I am not sure how long Strohmeyer remembered it, but the players on that team still remember it as the day Ziemba almost killed Strohmeyer.

Before the official practice began at 3:30 P.M., Ziemba had Strohmeyer off in one corner of Cartier Field for a little one-on-one blocking, with Strohmeyer doing the blocking. To understand what happened, you have to understand the size and ability of Ziemba who was the first-string center on the Leahy-coached teams of 1941 and 1942. Ziemba was about 6 feet, 4 inches, weighed around 250 pounds, and was still in great shape (as were all of Leahy's assistant coaches). And, he was mad. Every time Strohmeyer snapped the ball, Ziemba would hit him with a forearm right in the face with all his power. Within 10 minutes, Strohmeyer was a bloody mess and totally exhausted from trying to defend himself against the irate Ziemba.

When the official practice started, Strohmeyer's hell continued. Weakened by his battle with Coach Ziemba, let alone being out of shape, he was ripe for retribution by some of the players who'd had to take his mouthing off, oftentimes coupled with a physical beating, the previous year. In the drills and scrimmage that followed, several players took delight in slamming into Strohmeyer and beating him in the one-on-one contest that was a part of most drills and scrimmages.

When the practice ended, Ziemba again called Strohmeyer off to a corner of the field. They repeated the drill they had gone through earlier. Ziemba pounded Strohmeyer until he could hardly stand. The next anyone saw of him, he staggered into the locker room and fell to the floor, unable to get up.

It was not long before Walsh became the first-string center for the 1947 Irish team. Walsh was a devastating blocker and Strohmeyer's opposite in personality. Walsh was very humble, fun-loving, and one of the best-liked guys on the team. The players, as a whole, rejoiced that Walsh had the starting role.

To Strohmeyer's credit, he never complained about the beating he took that day, nor did he ever miss practice or play with any less intensity. He saw a lot of playing time as the second-string center that year, but never fully reached the level of play of the previous year. Although he had two more years of eligibility after the 1947 season, he opted to sign on with Brooklyn of the old All-American Football Conference.

In a practice scrimmage a few weeks before the first game of the season against Pittsburgh, George Connor incurred an ankle injury. He was rushed by ambulance to St. Joseph's Hospital in South Bend to have X-rays taken and be treated. Fortunately, the ankle was not broken, but it was severely sprained.

Connor insisted he be returned to his room in Alumni Hall rather than stay in the hospital or the student infirmary on campus. As George's roommate and brother, I helped him to get situated in his bed and saw to it that he had something to eat.

When I was satisfied that George was resting as well as he could, I left the room to walk the short distance to the cafeteria to call our parents. (There were no phones in student rooms in those days.) Our father, Dr. Charles H. Connor, was a physician and surgeon, and our mother, Esther, was a nurse. Moreover, having raised three boys who had participated in sports since the early days of grammar school, both of them were very familiar with the treatment of football injuries. I wanted some advice on what I could do to help George.

After talking to my mother, my father got on the line and questioned me about George's injury. I described everything in detail and answered his many questions as best I could. My dad then began to give me precise instructions about what I should do and when I should do it. His instructions were so complete and exact that I had to take notes.

One part of his instructions was how I should prepare George for the night ahead, which my dad knew would be a painful one. Dad instructed me to get several pillows, some ace bandages, and a heating pad. At about 10:15 P.M., I was to prepare George for the night by cradling his bad foot in the pillows, which held the heating pad. Then I was to wrap the ace bandage around the outside of the pillows to secure the heating pad, ankle, and foot in place.

Armed with Dad's instructions, I returned to our room with the needed supplies which I had scrounged along the way. When the appointed time came, I began my medical role getting George set for the night. At first everything went well, as I gently placed George's leg in the pillows, making sure the heating pad was in the proper place. I was almost finished when George said, "Oh no, the angle isn't right—that hurts, you better start over."

So I started over, and again partway through George said, "I don't think that's going to work that way, it's throbbing too much." (Older brothers can be a problem.)

Again I retraced the steps of the procedure. After several more times of George telling me to change something or other about the pillow arrangement, he was finally satisfied and I was about out of patience. By now it was about five minutes to 11. I was exhausted from the long day at practice and from playing nurse, and very ready to get to my bed to get what I hoped would be a good night's sleep. I undressed, turned the light out and gratefully crawled in bed.

About two bliss-filled minutes passed before I was startled from my half-asleep state to hear laughter coming from my brother across the room. He was laughing so hard I couldn't imagine what was wrong. "What's wrong?" I shouted as I stumbled out of bed in the darkness.

Gasping for breath between his peals of laughter, he finally blurted out, "We have to be the dumbest guys in the world—all that work for nothing. The electricity is off."

He was right. In our effort to get Dad's instructions right about the heating pad, we completely forgot that the main current to all the student rooms was automatically cut off at 11 P.M. every night. All that work of getting the heating pad set for the night had been for nothing. I crawled back into bed and must have laughed myself to sleep. I never did ask George how he slept that night.

Because of the injury, George missed the opening game against Pittsburgh. As the Notre Dame team prepared for Pittsburgh, the sportswriters across the country were predicting greatness for the Irish 11. As one sportswriter said, "Notre Dame is the machine most likely to go through undefeated and untied. It is doubtful any team ever went into a normal season, as distinguished from a wartime season, recognized so universally as a team without a weakness. Barring something like an injury to Lujack, Notre Dame has an excellent opportunity to establish itself not only as champion but as the greatest team in football history."

Leahy, in response to statements like this, said, "With so many outstanding players returning from last year's squad, we have the makings of an excellent team, even a great one. However, I have never known a football team that has won any games without going out on the field and earning the victory. I think we should wait until the season unfolds before making any judgment about how good we are."

Pittsburgh

The Notre Dame traveling team boarded the train to Pittsburgh on Thursday evening for the Pitt game to be played on Saturday, October 4th. When the players checked into a downtown hotel on Friday morning, they were told to meet in one of the conference rooms for breakfast. As the team was walking through the corridor to the breakfast room, George, who was walking with his pal Ziggie, and several other players, happened to notice that in one of the other rooms a big press conference was just ending. The conference was to promote the new Paramount Studio movie *Unconquered,* starring Gary Cooper and Paulette Goddard, and directed by the famous Cecil B. DeMille. Goddard was not there, but Liz Scott, another Hollywood beauty, was at the conference. Columnist Hedda Hopper and many members of the cast were present to help promote the new show. Connor, Ziggie, and the others went into the room. Connor relates what happened:

"I asked who the public relations guy was for the group. I introduced myself to him—told him who we were and that we were on our way to have breakfast down the hall. Of course, that was a PR man's dream. We were introduced to the group as they were breaking up. Zig took Liz Scott by the arm and said, 'Why don't you walk with me? These teammates of mine are a bunch of wolves.'

"Zygmont escorted Liz Scott down the hall to the breakfast room, where all the teammates were seated for breakfast. The whole entourage came with us—the team didn't know what was going on. The PR guy gets ready to do the introductions—Ziggie sat him at a table and said, 'I'll handle this,' and gave the guy a bowl of oatmeal.

"Ziggie said, 'We're blessed this morning. We have a Hollywood group here that wants to meet the Notre Dame team. One of the premier producers and directors in Hollywood, who used to buy his meat at Ziggie's Meat Market in South Chicago—Cese [Cecil] DeMille.' Then he said, 'A lady who used to shop for hats with my mother—Hada [Hedda] Hopper. Now an old girlfriend of mine—I think we might be going steady after this meeting—Liz Scott.'

"The Hollywood group had to move on, but this was the start of something. Ziggie started to write to Liz Scott at Paramount Studio. Ziggie wrote to Liz and they were corresponding back and forth the remainder of the season. Zig said he would be out there and did she need any tickets. Zig didn't know it, but Miss Scott's secretary was working him for all kinds of tickets. Zig didn't know that he is corresponding with the secretary—Liz Scott probably knows what's going on. Zig asks 'Liz' if she will throw a party for him and his teammates. She [or the secretary writing in her stead] agreed. This led to a great time after the final game of season against Southern California."

Against Pittsburgh Brennan scored first for the Irish from the three after a 34-yard pass to Martin. Doug Waybright, playing left end, scored the second touchdown on an across-the-middle pass from Lujack. In the third quarter, Lujack found Martin with a 65-yard touchdown pass and later hit Hart for the fourth Notre Dame tally. After Ziggie had sacked the passer and recovered his fumble, McGee went through the middle of the line for a score. After Swistowicz intercepted a Panther pass on Pitt's 30-yard line and returned it to the 10, Lank Smith went off tackle for the final score as the Irish cruised, 40-6.

Hughie Burns, Notre Dame's trainer, who was considered one of the best college trainers in the country, had personally been in charge of Connor's recovery since the ankle injury two weeks before. He used all the tools available to him plus his own vast knowledge of athletic injuries to have Connor ready to play against Purdue.

During practice that week, Leahy noticed that Connor was somewhat tentative in his drills, as if not trusting that the ankle was ready for all-out play. Leahy was a master psychologist in dealing with his players. He sensed that he had to do something to convince Connor that his ankle would not prevent him from playing with his usual reckless abandon. Leahy hit upon an idea that he put into practice the Thursday before the game. He had the second-team backfield, and only the right side of the line including the center, in a live scrimmage with George as the sole defensive player. They ran off tackle plays, traps, up-the-middle plays, quick openers, all at George. They did this for a half hour and the offensive team never gained more than a yard or two. At the end of the drill, Connor was convinced that his ankle was fine and he demonstrated his renewed confidence in his play the remainder of the season.

Years later, Frank Leahy told his nephew, Jack Leahy, about that day on the practice field in 1947. Jack Leahy recently passed on to me his recollection of the conversation. He said, "Frank was reminiscing one day about the 1946 and 1947 teams and he told me about the day when he had George play against a half a line. He said, 'Jack, in all my years of playing and coaching football, it was the greatest exhibition of defensive tackle play I have ever seen.'"

The Pep Rallies

During the 1940s, the pep rallies preceding a football game were held at the old fieldhouse on Friday nights, or earlier in the week if it was an away game. The football players would sit in the balcony above the main floor where they could be seen by the students below. They were seated with the director of athletics, one of the priests representing the hierarchy of the school, the coaching staff, and any visiting dignitaries. At each rally, some representative of the school would act as emcee for the evening.

196

With the band standing below the balcony, and the ground level jammed to capacity with hyped-up students, it is an understatement to say it was a very noisy place. After the band played the Notre Dame Victory March and the students went wild with cheering, the emcee would ask for quiet to start the evening's program.

The emcee would introduce the visiting dignitaries, then call on the school representative and Coach Leahy to say a few words. Both were usually very brief in their remarks. Now it was the time in the program that the students really came to hear—the talks by the players. The routine was the same at each rally. The emcee called on the captain of the team to lead off with his remarks and, when he finished, he would ask the students from whom they wanted to hear. The shouting of various names went on for several minutes until either one name dominated or, failing that, the captain would select one of the names he had heard.

At the very first pep rally of the 1947 season, it became obvious that the Notre Dame pep rallies that year would be something special.

Connor was introduced as the captain of that year's team. He then introduced the individual players as was the custom at the first pep rally of the season. He made his brief remarks and, following tradition, asked the mass of students gathered below from whom they would like to hear. There was no doubt as to who the favorite was, when, almost in one voice, they shouted, "Ziggie!" Connor turned to face the players and spotted Ziggie sitting in the fourth row at the end of the aisle. He turned back to the microphone and said, "It is my pleasure to introduce my teammate, Zygmont Pierre Czarobski."

The crowd went wild with applause and catcalls in anticipation of hearing Ziggie. With that, Ziggie, playing the crowd as always, rose slowly from his seat and waved, but did not make a move to go to the microphone. Now all eyes were on Ziggie. In a slow, deliberate way he took a wad of chewing gum from his mouth and, with great care, placed the wad of gum under his seat. The crowd howled. Ziggie walked slowly down the stairs from his fourth-row seat, waving to the crowd, all the way to the center of the balcony where the microphone was situated. As he stood before the crowd waiting to speak, the students cheered and whistled as Ziggie, with that big smile of his, stood patiently at the mike, soaking it all in.

As the noise level subsided, Ziggie still had not uttered a word. It slowly dawned on the students that he was not going to speak until there was absolute silence. They finally obliged him by becoming very quiet.

Ziggie began, "Reverend Fathers, distinguished members of the coaching staff, fellow teammates, my dear ladies of the chow hall."

By this time the audience is starting to break up with laughter as Ziggie continued, "Honored guests, Mishawaka Ruthie, and friends."

After the laughter died down, Ziggie continued, "It behooves me greatly."

Those four words set the crowd off as they went wild again with their cheering and whistling. No one can remember what Ziggie said after that, except to recall that he had them laughing for about 20 minutes. By now it was past the allotted time, so the rally ended with no other player getting an opportunity to speak.

The following Monday on campus, all anyone was talking about was Ziggie at the pep rally and the victory over Pittsburgh. An enterprising editor of the student weekly publication featured a new column that week entitled, "It Behooves Me Greatly," written by the man himself—Zygmont Pierre Czarobski, or so the byline indicated. Ziggie could be very secretive when he wanted to. He did not talk much about writing the column, but the grapevine had it that Ziggie worked with a ghostwriter from the English department who helped him deliberately fracture the language to make the column more comical. The column became an instant success.

The following week, before the Purdue game, the pep rally had such a big crowd that the students were out the doors and surrounding the fieldhouse. Most of the new ones came to hear Ziggie. The word had spread. When Connor, as captain, finished his very brief remarks, he somewhat jokingly asked the crowd from whom they wanted to hear. The shout was deafening as the students shouted, "Ziggie!" You could hardly hear Connor as he introduced the man of the hour, Zygmont Pierre.

After one of his crazy stories, Ziggie waited until the laughter subsided, then turned around and looked directly at Freddie Miller sitting in the first row. Miller was the president and owner of Miller Brewing Company of Milwaukee. He was also a former Notre Dame All-American tackle and one of the university's biggest benefactors.

Without saying a word Ziggie turned back to the crowd. He then said, "Looking around reminds me of two brothers that owned a brewery in Milwaukee, Wisconsin. One day they received a letter from the United States Bureau of Standards in Washington wanting to know the alcoholic content of their beer. The brothers packaged a bottle of their beer and sent it off to Washington to be tested. In a few days the brothers received a telegram from the Bureau of Standards that said, 'Dear Sirs: Please rest this horse for six weeks.' "

Pandemonium broke out as the students laughed, hooted, and yelled. Miller turned five shades of red and Leahy almost dove under his seat. From that point on, the pep rally was in such chaos one had to wonder if the old fieldhouse walls would hold up.

That Monday after the Purdue game, Father Kehoe, the prefect of discipline for the university, sought out Connor. Father Kehoe opened the discussion, "George, I don't want you to call on Ziggie anymore at the pep rallies; his carrying on is really getting out of hand."

"I couldn't do that, Father, everyone expects him to speak," replied George.

"You're going to have to," said Father Kehoe. "He insulted one of the university's biggest supporters and his antics have the students getting too wild. I'm afraid he just can't speak at future rallies."

"Father," said George, "I just couldn't do that to Ziggie. We all love Ziggie and wouldn't want to hurt him for the world. I know I speak for the rest of the team when I tell you that if Ziggie doesn't speak, there is no team, and if there is no team, there is no pep rally."

Father Kehoe thought that over for a moment and replied, "Well, at minimum, he has to submit his talk to me in writing before he speaks."

Connor started to chuckle, "Father, that wouldn't work. Ziggie never puts anything in writing. Besides I don't think he knows what he is going to say until he says it."

Father Kehoe sighed, got a resigned look on his face, and said, "It's nice talking to you, George," and walked away.

The pep rallies continued the rest of the season, as they began, with Ziggie the main attraction. Ziggie also continued to write his article, "It Behooves Me Greatly." I would venture to say that the pep rallies on through the years have never had the hilarity as the ones in 1947.

Purdue

Notre Dame defeated a very tough Purdue team, 22-7, in the second game of the season. Panelli got things going for the Irish when he recovered a fumble in midair on the Boilermaker 25-yard line. After flanking out wide on a play, Brennan made a great over-the-shoulder reception deep in the end zone to give the Irish the lead.

Purdue came right back and scored on a Bob DeMoss-to-Harry Szulborski pass, good for eight yards and a touchdown. Purdue's successful extra point was the first one made against Notre Dame in 11 games (going back to the Great Lakes game in 1945).

By far the most electrifying play of the game was a pass from Lujack to Larry Coutre, the sophomore speedster, who, a step ahead of the defenders, caught the perfectly thrown ball on Purdue's 40 and then outsprinted them to the end zone. Unfortunately, a penalty nullified the play. Later Lujack hit Coutre again and he took the ball to the Boilermaker 21. On the next play Lujack faded to pass, but seeing everyone covered, ran to his left for a score aided by a crushing downfield block by Martin, who eliminated the last defender on the five-yard line.

Coy McGee returned a punt 44 yards with classic punt-return blocking as Sitko hit the first defender and Ashbaugh the second, while McGee ran behind the wall of Panelli, Martin, and Walsh before being forced out of bounds. When Purdue held, Steve Oracko kicked an 18-yard field goal. With the reserves in the game, McGee made another of his dazzling punt returns, allowing Simmons to score from the three for the final touchdown of the day.

When the Associated Press weekly poll announced the Monday after the Purdue game that Fritz Crisler's Michigan team was the nation's number one team, it was the first time in more than three years that a college team other than Army, Notre Dame, or Texas was given the top rating. Notre Dame, which held the number one position in the final poll of 1946 and was installed in the top slot after the season's opener, just ahead of Michigan, slipped into second place despite its second straight victory.

At the Chicago Quarterback Luncheon, Leahy reacted in an uncharacteristic manner when somebody asked, "What's the matter with Notre Dame?" "How bad do you think Michigan could whip Notre Dame?" Leahy immediately shot back, "I just wish we had the opportunity to beat Michigan. We'd be happy to play them anywhere, any Saturday, any fall." (His statement referred to the fact that Notre Dame had experienced difficulty in recent years years booking games with Michigan, Minnesota, Ohio State, and Illinois.) Leahy went on to say, "Publicity has jeopardized our chances early in the season. I want to say that our boys have been subjected to more of that than any team I can remember. It is bound to have an effect on young lads like ours. I can promise you one thing: We'll be a little better every week—you can count on that."

Leahy, no doubt making good on his promise to have the Irish improve, continued to work the team hard in practice. The demands from Leahy and the extra-hard work seemed to affect all the players, but the tackles a little less than the others.

The tackles, because of Ziggie and his pal, George, were the envy of all the players on the field, particularly the guards. For the first part of practice, the team was separated by positions to work on the fundamentals of their particular position. The guards, under the watchful eye of the guard coach, McArdle, would be killing each other with live one-on-one, two-on-one, and other blocking and defensive drills Leahy ordered, while the tackles would be standing in a circle talking to Moose Krause and Freddie Miller. This prompted Bill Fischer, the starting left guard, to comment, "Here we are pounding each other half to death and those guys look like they're having a tea party."

Miller (the same one from the pep rally) was a former teammate of Leahy's. They both played on the 1928 Notre Dame team coached by Knute Rockne. Miller flew his own plane, a sleek two-engine one, that was small enough to land on the field next to Cartier Field. Miller usually landed his plane in time for practice at least once, sometimes twice a week. He would wear the coaches' garb and go with the tackles as one of the coaches.

Miller was a great advocate of the "forearm shiver," a defensive ploy to ward off the opposing blocker. He designed a sled that he used to demonstrate the use of his pet technique. On the days Miller was at practice, Ziggie would ask him a question as soon as the tackles were assembled for their group drills. A typical question would be, "Coach Miller, when you put your arms out, do you have your thumbs pointing out or do you bend them?"

Miller would then take about 10 minutes to describe the proper technique while the tackles stood around and listened. This drove Leahy crazy, but he couldn't say or do anything to offend his longtime friend and business benefactor. No sooner would Miller be through with Ziggie's question when George would pipe up, "Coach, what do you do if the opposing player dips his body as he starts his block?"

Miller would really warm to the subject and take another 10 minutes to describe the appropriate application of the forearm shiver in such a case. All this time the guards would be working their tails off. Each week Ziggie and George would vary the questions, but they never failed to get Miller talking.

Ziggie, always alert to ways of saving his energy on the practice field, started the same questioning routine with Moose Krause the tackle coach. On Mondays following a game, Ziggie always had a question to start the group sessions. When the tackles would be lined up to begin one-on-one or two-on-one drills, Ziggie would inquire, "Coach, in Saturday's game the tackle was playing on my outside shoulder and I wanted to take him in. Should I have put my head on the opposite side I wanted to take him?"

Krause would then explain the proper technique which included a time-consuming demonstration that Ziggie always requested. When the tackles were only a few minutes into their drills, Ziggie's accomplice, George, would come up with another question that required an answer and demonstration. More time to stand around and rest.

One day Krause had had enough of Ziggie and George and their endless questions, so he announced that the two could no longer ask any questions. Not to be defeated, before practice Ziggie and George fed questions to the other tackles to ask Krause during the tackle drills. This ploy was shortlived however, as these players did not have the flair for pulling off the delaying tactic like George and Ziggie.

When former players gathered with Moose Krause, who was universally loved and respected by all of them, guards loved to kid Krause about how hard they worked under Captain Bligh (Joe McArdle, the guard coach) while the tackles stood around and talked. At the 1991 Monogram Club dinner, Krause spotted me on crutches from a recent hip replacement and inquired as to what was wrong. I told him I had recently had hip surgery and that it was his fault. I told him if he were really a friend, he would have switched me from my guard position where I got the hell kicked out of me to tackle where I could have enjoyed the leisurely life of "tea parties." As usual Moose got the last word and responded, "You weren't smart enough to play tackle."

Nebraska

Notre Dame blanked the Nebraska Cornhuskers, 31-0, in the first home game of the season. As part of a long drive, Coutre ran around left end, aided by a good block from Panelli, to gain 17 yards. On the next play, Coutre returned the favor by blocking the linebacker, allowing Panelli to go seven yards off-tackle for a touchdown.

In the second quarter, Tripucka hit Brennan for a 22-yard pass completion. Swistowicz, playing fullback, carried twice to the three where, on the next play, he banged straight ahead to score the second Irish touchdown. In the third period, McGee, who had a habit of thrilling the Notre Dame fans with his brilliant runs with punts, did it again, as he returned a punt 30 yards (helped by a well-executed block by Wendell). Lujack passed to Swistowicz for 35 yards and McGee took it the remaining 15 to score on a burst up the middle. Tripucka threw a 15-yard touchdown pass to Waybright and Sitko scored the final touchdown on a 10-yard sweep around end.

During the week following the Nebraska game, McArdle took on each guard in a one-on-one drill as all the coaches did periodically. Just as it was Signaigo's turn, Leahy walked by to observe the drill. As usual, McArdle cheated on the count and got the best of Signaigo. This prompted Leahy to comment, "Oh, Joseph Signaigo, you have to be more aggressive when you block and keep your legs churning."

"Let me try it again," hissed Signaigo between clenched teeth.

McArdle did not like that idea at all—a player usually had only one attempt. "No, you've had your turn. Get back to the end of the line," ordered McArdle.

"Oh, Coach McArdle," said Leahy, "let's see Joseph try one more time."

They lined up again, Signaigo the blocker facing McArdle the defensive man. McArdle said, "On two" (meaning they both would start on the snap count of two). McArdle began the signals—"Ready, set, down," and Signaigo, not waiting for the count to even reach one let alone two, slammed into McArdle with a vicious block. He caught McArdle completely by surprise and drove him back about seven yards before he knocked him to the ground. For good measure he threw a well-placed forearm to McArdle's face as they hit the ground.

"That's the way to block an opponent, Joseph," shouted Leahy. Turning to a prostrate McArdle still dazed by Signaigo's block and well-aimed forearm, he said, "Oh, Coach McArdle, you better get in better shape to fight off those guards of yours."

Signaigo was definitely the hero of the day as far as his fellow guards were concerned. He did what every guard dreamed of—cheating on the count and putting McArdle on his back.

Iowa

Going into its fourth game of the season against Iowa at home, Notre Dame was still ranked number two in the country behind an undefeated Michigan team. Dr. Eddie Anderson, the former Notre Dame great and then the head coach of Iowa, was always a formidable opponent. Notre Dame beat the Hawkeyes, 21-0, but as Leahy suspected in preparing his team for the game, the Iowans were no pushovers. They played their hearts out, only to be worn down by a relentless Irish attack.

After a Lujack-to-Martin pass over the middle, Brennan scored from the three-yard line. He scored again from the seven as the second quarter got underway. Iowa had its best chance to score in the third quarter when Em Tunnell, who would later go on to be an All-Pro defensive back with the New York Giants, ran 65 yards on an off-tackle play before Lujack and Brennan knocked him out of bounds at the Notre Dame 10-yard line. It was the first time Lujack was in on defense that season and the Notre Dame fans were glad he was. Notre Dame held and Iowa never threatened to score again.

Sitko took a pitch-out from Lujack and circled his left end to break in the open as Martin cut down a defensive back with a perfect block. With Fischer and Walsh leading the downfield blockers, Sitko gained 40 yards before being knocked out of bounds. The 98-yard drive ended with Coutre going in for the touchdown from the two-yard line. Later, Tripucka threw a beautiful touchdown pass to Wightkin that was nullified because of an Irish infraction.

Navy

With the Irish having scored a one-sided victory over Iowa and Michigan having been held to a single-touchdown win over Minnesota the same day, Notre Dame was again rated the number one team in the country going into the Navy game. Before a crowd of 84,000 in Cleveland's Municipal Stadium, the Irish sank the Navy, 27-0, for their third straight shutout.

Lujack got things going with a short pass to Hart, who tossed a lateral to Sitko for a 14-yard gain. Lujack then threw a beautifully arched ball that Brennan caught over his shoulder just a yard before going out of the end zone for a 29-yard touchdown completion. In the second quarter, with the ball on Notre Dame's six-yard line, Lujack, on a gutsy call, faded into his own end zone and when he saw the huge open space created by Martin and Connor as they drove their men apart, he took off on a 70-yard run. Unfortunately, he fumbled as he was hit and the ball was recovered by Navy. It was the first time anyone could recall seeing Lujack fumble in his three years of varsity football.

When Notre Dame got the ball back, Tripucka hit Hart with a 32-yard touchdown pass. After Hart recovered a Navy fumble, Lujack passed to Martin on a play that took the ball to the one-yard line, where Brennan smashed over the center for the score. Livingstone, playing defensive left halfback, intercepted a Navy pass and took it to pay dirt standing up for the final Irish touchdown.

Army

The game against Army would mark the end of one of the most intense rivalries in college sports. It was to be the last scheduled game between these two schools, a rivalry that dated back to 1913 when the little-known South Bend school upset the heavily favored Army team.

The desperation of both coaches and teams to win the final game of the series prompted newspaper stories stating that Blaik and Leahy were bitter enemies. Leahy spoke out about his relationship with Blaik and said, "We do not know each other too well, but I have the utmost admiration for him, both as a superlative coach and as a leader."

And I am sure he did, but, nevertheless, Leahy wanted to beat Army and he wanted to beat Blaik.

There was an upbeat air in the practice sessions that week as the team prepared for the game. The players did not have to be told this was the last game in the fabled series, nor did they have to be reminded that last year's game had ended in a tie—they knew and practiced accordingly. One could sense the confidence of the players as they went about the daily preparations for the game. There had not been a point scored against them in the last three games, and offensively, the team was getting better with every game. Notre Dame was ready to play the Army Cadets.

One day at practice that week, Krause, the tackle and head line coach, was conducting a pass-blocking drill with the first-string line on offense and some reserves on the defense. As with all the assistant coaches, Krause liked to have a spirited drill, which was oftentimes accomplished by pitting one player against another. This particular day, Krause wanted to make sure that Ziggie got a good workout.

Playing opposite Ziggie that day was Dean Thomas, a 6-foot-4 tackle from Leo High School in Chicago, who was a transfer student from Northwestern. The prior year, Thomas (then a freshman) had played first string for the Northwestern Wildcats. He was known as a guy who played with great intensity and was a real handful to block when aroused.

Knowing this, and after a few plays were run, Krause leaned into the offensive huddle as if listening to what was being said. He straightened up and looked directly at Thomas, who stood facing the offensive group in his three-point defensive stance, and said, "Dean Thomas, do you know what Ziggie just said about you? He said that you weren't any competition at all—that he can block you left or right and that there is no way you can get by him."

Thomas got so excited he could not reply. His eyes got glassy, he started to snort and dig his feet into the ground to get ready for the next play.

Sensing this—and never one to work any harder in practice than he had to—Ziggie turned around from his position in the offensive huddle, looked right at Thomas, and said, "Dean, I never said anything of the kind. What I *did* say is that you are one of the best players ever to come to Notre Dame—that you have a great future—and you are a fine Christian gentleman."

With that, Thomas calmed down and maybe even smiled. Ziggie avoided trouble once again, much to the chagrin of Coach Krause.

Leahy, as usual, was always the pessimist before a game. He planned so meticulously for every game that he was always devising ways he would play against his own teams. He was always afraid that another coach might pick out some flaw and exploit it. More than that, he always feared the unpredictable — the weather, a crucial fumble, an injury, or some psychological aspect. He remembered too well the story of Rockne scouting Army when his own team was playing Carnegie Tech, a supposed pushover, only to hear that Carnegie Tech had defeated a favored Notre Dame team, 19-0, to ruin an undefeated season. He also recalled his own prediction before a Florida-

Boston College game that his BC team was going to beat Florida. Florida won, 7-0.

He told us at the noon meetings, "If you hear that I told the press that we will lose on Saturday, don't believe I really think that. I might say that so the press can never blame the players for not winning a game even their own coach said they should win. If we happen to lose, I will take the blame."

Leahy's pessimism was so well known that Fr. John Cavanaugh, president of Notre Dame and a very good friend of Leahy's, liked to tease him about it. One day at practice after watching the team scrimmage, Father Cavanaugh said to Leahy, "I know why you expect to lose three or four games. Those fellows don't know how to block or tackle." Leahy blew his top before he realized he was being ribbed by a smiling Father Cavanaugh.

He was so used to being pessimistic before a game that his conversation with one of his former standouts, Angelo Bertelli, was typical. Bertelli tells what happened. "I remember going back to school to see the Army game in 1947—the one that Terry Brennan ran the kickoff back for a touchdown. I was standing in the end zone, at the ramp where the players come on the field. I watched the Army team run out and then the Notre Dame team run out and behind the team comes Leahy. I said, 'Good luck today, Coach.'

"He said, 'Oh, Angelo, oh, Angelo, have you seen the size of those Cadet lads? They're big and powerful.'

"And, I'm thinking, didn't I just see George Connor go by and Bill Fischer and all those other monsters? So, I said, 'You have some huge lads yourself, Coach.'

"He said, 'Oh no, we will be fortunate to survive by just one point.'"

Leahy's pessimism aside, Notre Dame scored on the opening kickoff and was never threatened as the Irish rolled to a 27-7 victory over a formidable Army team.

It was a very cold and windy day. Army won the toss and elected to defend the goal that would give them the wind—Notre Dame elected to receive. The opening kick went out of bounds, necessitating a second kickoff by Army. Terry Brennan, playing deep for the Irish on the kickoff, at first misjudged the line-drive kick. He was forced to make an over-the-head catch of the long kick at the three-yard line. He turned and headed straight upfield to keep the Army defenders spread out across the field. By design, at about the 15-yard line he gave ground to his left to allow time for his blockers to set up their targets.

Connor, playing left tackle and one of the players responsible for opening a hole between the defenders, had an unusual thing happen. "I was so eager to get to my assignment that I tripped. While falling, I fell into an Army man, who went down tripping another Army defender, opening a nice hole."

Fischer made his block and that was all Brennan needed. With that one crack of daylight, and with the defenders spread across the field, he ran down the sidelines for 97 yards, untouched, for the touchdown. The capacity crowd of 59,171 roared its approval.

Ironically, Brennan's father, Martin Brennan, missed Terry's long run because he was delayed in the parking lot. As he was starting up the ramp to his seat in the stadium, he heard a tremendous roar. When he got to the top of the ramp and could see the field, he asked an usher what had happened. "Terry Brennan just ran the kickoff all the way for a touchdown," he was told.

Later in the first quarter, Lujack hit Hart on a run-action pass play that netted 25 yards. Sitko, after bobbling the handoff, picked up another 12 yards going wide around left end. Martin gained 16 on an end-around. With the ball on the three-yard line, Hart and Ziggie collapsed their side of the line and Wendell, pulling from his guard position, knocked the defensive end down to allow Brennan to go through the huge hole for the second Irish touchdown.

In the first minutes of the third quarter, Swistowicz went off tackle for 15 yards to set up Livingstone's six-yard touchdown run. Although Livingstone's run was only six yards, it demonstrated his elusiveness. He took the handoff from Lujack on what was to be a slant off tackle but when the hole was jammed, he started outside, leaving the Army linebacker all alone against him. Livingstone, in one of his typical moves, "gave him a leg and took it away" as the football saying goes, leaving the linebacker grabbing air, as he easily ran into the end zone for the touchdown.

In the fourth quarter, Rip Rowen of Army scored on a short plunge for the Cadets' only touchdown. It was the first touchdown scored by a Blaik-coached Army team against a Leahy-coached team in the five meetings between these two schools (1941, 0-0; 1942, 13-0;

208

1943, 26-0; 1946, 0-0). Later in the period, Coutre scored for the Irish on an 11-yard run, aided by a great block by Hart.

Leahy in his post-game comments said, "Being sentimental and Irish, we like to think that maybe dreams can come true. Certainly, one came true for us when the Irish beat Army, 27-7. A dream that began on a tropic island in the Pacific during war years [where Leahy listened by radio to the Notre Dame defeat by Army, 59-0] and ended in a flurry of snow in Notre Dame Stadium. Terry Brennan had a lot to do with making our dream a reality. In running back the opening Army kickoff 97 yards for a touchdown, Terry not only showed canny running ability, he showed courage in gambling and taking the high-flying kick over his shoulder and running, instead of permitting it to fall in the end zone for a touchback, the usual procedure. If we had to single out individuals, we should mention the left side of our line—Martin, Connor, and Fischer—as a unit…Army, in ending the series that began in 1913, as usual was high-spirited and well-coached. We are indeed sorry to see the series end."

That following week, Leahy had more matters to worry about than preparing for the next opponent. Joe Williams, of the *New York World Telegram*, and H.G. Salsinger, of the *Detroit News*, both wrote that Leahy had offered to resign as head coach at Notre Dame. Salsinger wrote, "Frank Leahy may retire as head football coach after the current season. There is a well-founded rumor in South Bend that he has already tendered his verbal resignation."

The article went on to say that Leahy was deeply hurt by criticism directed at him when he was accused of being responsible for Army and several other colleges, namely, Michigan, Ohio State, Illinois, and Minnesota terminating football relations with Notre Dame and reducing the schedule to that of a secondary school. The article concluded with these words, "If Leahy substitutes a written resignation for the oral one he delivered [to the Notre Dame Administration] early in November, he will become the first coach in football history who quit because he was too good."

To quiet the press, which was hounding him about his future plans, Leahy issued a statement through the Notre Dame publicity office that he would, "consider it an honor and privilege to remain at Notre Dame for as long a period of time as the University's officials believe I can be an asset to this institution." Leahy made himself unavailable to answer any more questions on the matter as he became engrossed in preparations for the Northwestern game.

Fr. John H. Murphy, a university vice president and chairman of the faculty board in control of athletics, issued a statement on behalf of the university denying that Leahy had ever submitted an "oral" resignation. Privately he was heard to say, "Some people certainly love to pick on a winner."

The team, meanwhile, went about its business as usual—going to classes and going to practice. It was not that the players were oblivious to the publicity surrounding Leahy's supposed "retirement," but they treated the matter as just something that sportswriters like to write about and paid no attention to it.

Northwestern

On a rain-drenched field at Dyche Stadium in Evanston, Illinois, the Wildcats put up a brave battle against the favored Irish only to lose, 26-19.

Panelli got Notre Dame going in the first quarter on a 20-yard run through center and a sweep of the end for another 11 yards to the Wildcat 17. Brennan, on two tries, took it to the five where Panelli again ran left end for six points. After recovering a fumble on the ensuing kickoff at the Northwestern 18, the Irish were temporarily stalled, but on fourth down, Lujack passed to Brennan for the second Irish touchdown. Earley converted to put the Irish ahead, 13-0. Later in the period, Alex Sarkisian intercepted a Lujack pass and ran it to the Irish 21-yard line where he was caught from behind by Connor. On Northwestern's first play, the Wildcats fumbled and Connor recovered for Notre Dame. However, the Irish gave the ball right back when Art Murakowski intercepted a Lujack pass and, as the second quarter got underway, Northwestern scored from the one-yard line.

The second half opened with Notre Dame leading, 20-6. The Wildcats mounted an impressive 82-yard drive, scoring from the Irish eight-yard line on a Don Burson pass to make the score, 20-12. In the fourth quarter, Brennan returned a kick to the Wildcat 37. From the seven-yard line, Lujack passed to Hart for the final Notre Dame touchdown. After the ball changed hands several times, Tripucka, from his own eight-yard line, had his pass intercepted by PeeWee Day, who ran into the end zone for a touchdown. Final score, ND 26, NU 19.

Tulane

With the win over Northwestern, the Irish were untied and unde-feated with only two games remaining on their 1947 schedule. Two more victories and this team would be the first Notre Dame team since the 1930 Rockne team to have a perfect season. Two games remained—Tulane and Southern Cal. Leahy was not worried about Tulane, but he was nervous about Jeff Cravath's Southern California Trojans.

In practice that week as the team prepared for the Tulane game, there was a noticeable air of confidence on the part of the older players on the team. It was not cockiness, but a mature confidence one sees with people who are comfortable with themselves and what they are doing. This team had matured. The rough edges were off—the team was in superb physical condition, the plays and the execution were by now second nature to all the players—even down to the fourth and fifth teams. The 1947 team was now like a well-oiled machine that could perform its tasks repeatedly without any glitches. One had the feeling that if told they had to play the number one team in the pro ranks, they would have just shrugged their shoulders and gone about their busi-ness without any apprehension as to the outcome.

Leahy, perhaps mindful of the team's confidence, and no doubt equally mindful of the time when Rockne scouted Army when his own team was playing Carnegie Tech, nevertheless opted to put Krause in charge of the team for the Tulane game. In so doing, he could personally scout the feared Southern California team in its game against UCLA.

With Leahy on the West Coast scouting the Trojans, Notre Dame got off to a fast start against Tulane. The score at the end of the first quarter was Notre Dame 32 and Tulane 0 as the Irish romped to a 59-6 victory before the hometown fans. Krause, who was in charge of the team for the final game of the 1946 season when Notre Dame de-feated Southern Cal, kept his undefeated record intact. (Former play-ers loved to kid Krause that with a record of 2-0, he is the only unde-feated head coach in Notre Dame history.)

After Brennan intercepted a Tulane pass on the Green Wave 42-yard line, he ran it back to the three where he was knocked out of bounds. Sitko bulled over to score the first of nine Notre Dame touchdowns. On the ensuing kickoff, Martin recovered a fumble on the Tulane 20. Lujack passed to Sitko, who made a great over-the-shoulder catch deep in the end zone for a touchdown. Later, Sitko skirted end for 25 yards, getting a big assist from Fischer who executed a perfect downfield block, knocking down two Tulane defenders. Brennan, on a trap up the middle, sprinted 20 yards for the third Irish touchdown.

Not letting up on the shellshocked Tulane team for a minute, Hart recovered a fumble on the kickoff following the Brennan score and, on the first play from scrimmage, Gompers, on an off-tackle play, ran 35 yards to score. A little later Ziggie recovered a Tulane fumble on the Notre Dame 41. The Irish quickly marched to the Tulane five-yard line where Lujack passed to Brennan for the fifth Irish touchdown, making the score 32-0 as the first quarter ended. It had been six minutes between touchdowns, prompting Bill Walsh, the offensive center, to say to the eager reserves gathered on the sideline, "Sorry for taking so long to score—it won't happen again."

Tulane scored its only touchdown in the second quarter on a short plunge. Notre Dame continued its scoring spree as Gompers, Panelli, Clatt, and Jim Brennan each scored before the game ended.

Those who witnessed the Tulane game were treated to one of the finest exhibitions of downfield blocking that anyone had ever seen on any football field. Time after time there were three, four, or five players downfield knocking down Tulane defenders. One of the things that made the running attack of this team so potent was the ability of every player on the team, lineman or back, first string and all the others, to pick out a player wearing an opponent's jersey and apply a well-executed and well-timed block. Another factor was the speed of the linemen. Often, on a long run, one would see Martin, Connor, Fischer, Walsh, Wendell, Signaigo, Hart, and others matching a back who was running with the ball stride for stride before applying a block on the appropriate defensive man.

Southern California

Notre Dame had a week off after the Tulane game which gave Leahy plenty of time to prepare for the final game of the year. The team was loose, confident, and eager to play the Trojans of Southern California. The Irish knew that a win over the number three-ranked, undefeated Trojans would mean a perfect season. It also would mean a second straight National Championship.

Ziggie had some ideas about playing against Southern Cal's highly regarded tackle, John Ferraro, who had been at Notre Dame before the war. Ferraro was not only big, but was a hard-charging player who had had a terrific season that earned him recognition as an All-American candidate. Being a left tackle, he would be opposing right tackle Ziggie across the line.

Ziggie, always quick to spot ways of making life easier on himself, had a plan for playing opposite Ferraro. To initiate his plan, Ziggie wrote to Ferraro several weeks before the game to renew an acquaintance from his freshman year. He reminded Ferraro they were at Notre Dame together, told him how happy he was that Ferraro had such a great season, and that he was one of Ferraro's biggest fans. He ended the letter by saying that he was looking forward to seeing him again. Ziggie signed the letter, "Your Pal, Zig."

Several days later, Ziggie heard back from Ferraro, who was equally warm in his remarks to Ziggie. He congratulated Ziggie on his fine season and said that he, too, was looking forward to their meeting on the West Coast. Ziggie then accelerated his "wooing" of Ferraro by writing another letter telling Ferraro he was anxious to meet his family and how nice his parents must be to produce such a wonderful son. When the team was on the train going to Los Angeles, Ziggie sent Ferraro a telegram at every stop, always reminding him to line up some girls. Ziggie, in all his communications with Ferraro, made it sound like seeing his "pal John" was the biggest thing in his life.

Leahy was adamant on his rule that no player on his team could talk to an opposing player before the game. Ziggie spotted Ferraro, but couldn't do anything about it. Ferraro, by now, with the letters and telegrams from Ziggie, couldn't wait to greet his "dear friend." As the Notre Dame team was doing its pre-game calisthenics, Ferraro came over to the Notre Dame team area, found Ziggie, and gave him a big hug. Ziggie, of course, hugged him in return and told him how good it was to see him.

When the team got back in the locker room, Ziggie cornered Lujack and said, "Call the first play over my side, I think I've got Ferraro's number." The Irish gained 25 yards the first play and Ziggie had no problems the rest of the day with the feared Ferraro. (Ferraro was a great player and made several All-America teams that year, but what player would not be taken by Ziggie's charm?)

In practice before the team departed for the West Coast, it was evident that Terry Brennan's knee was so bad that there was no way he could play that coming Saturday. (Terry suffered the knee injury while making a downfield block in the Tulane game.) The day the list of the traveling squad was to be posted, George Connor was walking across the campus when he encountered the football team's student manager. The manager confided in George that he had seen a copy of the list of the squad members who would make the trip to California. He told George that Brennan's name was not on the list.

George was upset to hear this because he thought Brennan should make the trip even though he could not play. Brennan, who was well liked by his teammates, had had a great year and was a key player in the team's success. The more George thought about Brennan not being on the list, the more he knew that something had to be done about the situation. The USC game was the last game of the season and, if Notre Dame won, it would be the National Champion for the second straight year. The team could then relax and celebrate. Brennan should be a part of that, George reasoned.

George's mind was made up; he would see Leahy about it right away. He marched over to Leahy's office and asked to see him. When he was ushered into the office, Leahy said, "Oh, George, what is it, lad? Do you need some tickets for the game Saturday?"

"I could use some tickets, but there is something else I want to talk to you about."

The smile left Leahy's face as sensed a problem coming. He asked, "What is it, George?"

"Coach, I hear Terry Brennan's name is not listed on the traveling team."

Leahy gave George that one-sided smile of his and said, "That's right, George, maybe you forgot, Terry Brennan has a very bad knee and will be unable to play this Saturday."

George looked the coach in the eye and said in as serious a tone as he could, "I know he's injured, and so does the rest of the team. I want to tell you that if Terry doesn't make the trip, none of us makes the trip."

Leahy just looked at George and said nothing. There was an awkward silence as neither of them spoke. George turned around and left Leahy's office without another word between them.

It was only a short time later when the same student manager who George had talked to earlier came to George's room. He said, "I'm glad you're here. I just wanted to tell you that I've seen a new traveling list and Terry Brennan's name is on it." (Brennan never knew about this until years later when George told him the true story of how he made the trip.)

The game, played before 104,943 fans—the largest crowd to see a college football game that season—was dominated by the Irish as they defeated a valiant, but outmatched Trojan team, 38-7. Early in the first quarter, Connor recovered a Trojan fumble that led to Earley's field goal to put the Irish ahead, 3-0. Livingstone then started the Notre Dame team on an 87-yard drive by running 18 yards to the Notre Dame 31. A Lujack-to-Livingstone pass was lateralled to Sitko who picked up another 21 yards. Then Lujack, playing left halfback, took a direct snap from center and skirted left end on a beautiful 45-yard run before he was knocked out of bounds at the Trojan three. Sitko ran it in for the score.

In the second quarter, Southern Cal's best, the Trojans temporarily got back in the game when Kirby ran seven yards around end to score. Ashbaugh later stopped another Trojan drive by intercepting a pass.

In the third period with the ball on the Notre Dame 24-yard line, Sitko took a handoff from Lujack, burst through the middle of the line to daylight, and followed a bevy of blockers down the right sideline. With Connor ahead of him, Sitko made a move to the center of the field at about the Trojan 30, giving Connor the angle to cut down the one remaining Trojan defender, allowing Sitko to complete a 76-yard touchdown run. Later in the same period, Lujack intercepted a pass and returned it 41 yards. Panelli scored from the five on a plunge off-tackle.

In the last quarter, Southern Cal had a potential scoring opportunity halted by Lujack, who batted down a fourth-down pass on the goal line. With possession of the ball on their own eight-yard line, Lujack handed off to Livingstone, who ran through a big hole on his left side, faked the linebacker with one of his patented moves, and raced 92 yards for Notre Dame's third touchdown. Livingstone's 92-yard run set an all-time Notre Dame record for a run from scrimmage. That record, set over 45 years ago, stands today.

With the reserves in the game for Notre Dame, Al (Adam) Zmijewski, a tackle, intercepted a lateral on the Trojan 35-yard line and ran it in for Notre Dame's fifth and final touchdown. Earley kicked the extra point for the last point of the game and the season.

In the Trojan dressing room, Coach Jeff Cravath told newsmen, "That's one of the greatest, if not the greatest team I've ever seen. Our boys tried all the way, but the Irish just had a little too much of everything."

With this victory over number three-ranked Southern Cal, the Irish were awarded their second consecutive National Championship. It was the third National Championship in a row for Leahy-coached teams (1943, 1946, and 1947). The season record of 9-0 marked the first time a Notre Dame team had been unbeaten and untied since the legendary Rockne's 1930 team. The job was over, it was time to celebrate.

Back at the hotel where the players were getting dressed to go out for a good time, Leahy had asked his assistant coaches to join him in his room. Krause, Druze, Crimmins, Ziemba, and Earley gathered in what they hoped would be a short meeting as they all had plans to go out with friends and celebrate. At one of our "Ziggie" reunions, Ziemba recalled what happened.

"We [the assistant coaches] were looking forward to a night of relaxation without having to think football. It had been a long season for everyone. Leahy had invited all the coaches to his room in the hotel, so we went there to pay our respects before we left for the party. We congratulated Leahy on a great season. He then produced a bottle and poured each of us a drink. After we had our drink and were ready to leave, Leahy pulled out a pad and pen and said, 'Now, let's start planning for next year.' We looked at each other in disbelief. Here we had just finished the last game of a long season with a great victory that meant we had won back-to-back National Championships, and Coach Leahy wanted to get to work on next year—unbelievable. Somehow we managed some excuses and did go out and celebrate."

Looking back at the season, the 1947 team had a great year. As with the 1946 team, there was so much depth at each position, and, with all the units, first, second, and third teams functioning to perfection, it is not an exaggeration to say that any one of the units could have gone to a bowl game and won.

On an individual basis, all the players on these units, as well as other reserves, contributed to the success of the team. Red Sitko led the team in rushing for the second straight year. Terry Brennan was the team leader in receiving for the second year in a row, as well as the leader in points scored—66. Coy McGee led in punt return average, and John Lujack was the passing leader. Lujack and George Connor were consensus All-Americans for the second straight season. Their teammates, Bill Fischer, Ziggie, and Leon Hart, were named to an All-America team for the first time.

Lujack received an overwhelming number of votes in winning the Heisman Trophy as the outstanding player in the nation. He became the second Notre Dame player to win that award. (Bertelli won it in 1943.) He also earned the Associated Press Male Athlete of the Year Award.

Lujack was one of the greatest signal callers in college football history. In addition, he may have been the greatest defensive back ever to play college football. He was an amazing athlete. At 6 feet and 190 pounds, he had everything a coach could want: speed, power, a great throwing arm, toughness, an uncanny ability to be around the ball, great running instincts, durability, and, above all, a fierce competitive spirit. He was the kind of player who could have been an All-American at any position. When I recently said this to Lujack, he said, "Duffy Daugherty, the former coach at Michigan State whom I got to know pretty well, once said to me, 'John, I really wish I had been able to coach you. You would have made a helluva guard.' I said, 'Thanks, but no thanks.'"

Lujack was an all-around athlete who excelled in every sport he tried. He was also deceptively fast. He had a long stride when he ran that gave the illusion of someone with average speed. This was not the case. Lank Smith, who played on the 1946, 1947, and 1948 teams, and was on the starting unit on defense in 1947 and 1948, was the school's 60-yard dash champion. He lost only one race at Notre Dame—to Lujack. Lujack recently recalled what happened.

"I came out of the locker room onto the indoor track and I saw a group, including Lank Smith, lining up for a 60-yard dash. I noticed there were a couple of spots in the lineup where there were openings, so I kiddingly said to the track coach, 'Do you want me to run in this thing?' Keep in mind that I just came out of the locker room and was not warmed up. He said, 'Yeah, get in there.'

"I was always a fast starter off the blocks. I got a jump on Lank and beat him, and he's never forgotten—he sent me an affidavit that it's true. That was the semifinals, as I found out. Well, by the time I crossed the finish line, my legs had tied up because I wasn't warmed up. I think I came in third in the finals."

Lujack's career at Notre Dame could be called "The Ultimate Success Story." In his three years of varsity football, he starred on three National Championship teams (1943, 1946, and 1947). He led the team in passing all three years; he played the most minutes of any player on the team as a sophomore; he was called the best defensive player in football; he was a consensus All-American two years; he came in third in the Heisman balloting as a junior, and was the winner as a senior. He was elected to the College Hall of Fame in 1960. All that for a modest young man from Connellsville, Pennsylvania, who was not sure he was good enough to play at Notre Dame.

George Connor, the captain of the '47 team, missed the opening game against Pittsburgh because of an ankle injury, but he played outstanding football the remaining eight games. He capped a great college football career by being named to the All-American team for the second straight year. At 6-feet-$3\frac{1}{2}$, 235 pounds, he was strong, aggressive, football smart, and one of the fastest linemen on the team. He was a devastating blocker on offense and was called the best defensive tackle in football.

Including his two years at Holy Cross (1942, 1943), he was named to the All-Eastern team in 1942 and won national acclaim for his play against Boston College in that famous 55-12 upset as a 17-year-old freshman; he was captain of the Holy Cross team and was named an All-American in 1943; he received the George Bolger Lowe Award as the outstanding player in New England in 1943; he was voted the first recipient of the Outland Trophy in 1946 as the best interior lineman in the nation; he was named the Lineman of the Year in 1946. He was inducted into the College Hall of Fame in 1963.

Jim Martin, the great left end who played next to Connor for two years, recently commented about that experience.

"When they ask me who was the best, I don't even hesitate— George Connor. He was so good, I just loved playing next to him because I knew he would bust the play for me, or I would do it for him. We were so confident and played so well side-by-side, never a problem. At the beginning of some of the games, I would get tired before I got my second wind. I would be gasping for air and look at

218

George, who wasn't breathing hard at all. I looked up to him so much I wouldn't dare ask for a time-out. Then I'd get my breath and be back humming again for the rest of the game."

Ziggie Czarobski finished four years of varsity football (1942-43, 1946-47) with his best year. He was recognized as an All-American for his consistently excellent play on both offense and defense. He was the first-string right tackle on three National Championship teams (1943, 1946, and 1947). Frank Tripucka explained the reason for the recognition of Ziggie's outstanding play in the 1947 season: "George Connor received a great deal of publicity in 1946 and rightly so. He was one of the greatest tackles I've ever seen. In the '47 season the opposing teams were scared to death to run against him. He was like a man playing against a bunch of boys, so big, so fast, so strong—he just completely destroyed them. Consequently, in '47 they seemed to say, 'Let's go the other way, let's stay away from Connor.' If you're a coach or a quarterback, that's the way you would do it. That's when Ziggie came through. They ran at him and he was destroying people. Now they had no place to go. That's why Ziggie ended up being everyone's All-American."

As Tripucka, Connor, Lujack, Martin, and all Ziggie's teammates knew, for all his zaniness off the field, Ziggie was an excellent football player. Ziggie was inducted into the College Hall of Fame in 1977.

Bill "Moose" Fischer, a junior playing his second straight year as the starting left guard, had an exceptional year both on offense and defense. At 6 feet, 2 inches and 255 pounds, Fischer was deceptively fast and would often be seen leading the ball carriers on off-tackle plays or wide sweeps after pulling out from his guard position. On defense he anchored the center of the line where opponents gained very little yardage.

Leon Hart, at 6-feet-5 and 245 pounds, also had an exceptional year. Hart was a tremendous blocker both on the line and downfield. With his size and strength, he would often cave in the left side of the defensive line on plays directed his way. On plays going to the other side, he utilized his speed to go downfield to lead the ball carriers on long gainers. He became a real threat as a pass receiver. He was as good on defense as he was on offense. This all-around expertise would eventually earn him a Heisman Award.

When the roster for the 1948 College All-Star team was announced later in the year, 14 players from the 1947 Notre Dame team were on it. Five backs were named: John Lujack, Bob Livingstone, Bill Gompers, Pete Ashbaugh, and Floyd Simmons. The nine linemen included: George Connor, Ziggie Czarobski, Joe Signaigo, Art Statuto, Zeke O'Connor, Gasper Urban, George Sullivan, George Strohmeyer, and Bucky O'Connor. Frank Leahy was named to coach the All-Stars for the second straight year.

With the exception of Bucky O'Connor, all of the players named above went on to play professional football. In addition to those named, Corwin Clatt and Frank Kosikowski from the 1947 squad also joined the professional ranks.

As the number one coach in the country, Leahy was inundated with requests to speak at athletic banquets, coaches' clinics, and civic gatherings across the country. He tried to honor as many of the requests as possible. But, as on the night of the final game of the season, his thoughts were mainly on the preparation for the 1948 season.

Chapter Eleven

ZIGGIE AND FUN AFTER THE SEASON

The East-West Game

John Lujack, George Connor, and Ziggie Czarobski were selected to represent Notre Dame on the East squad in the annual East-West Shrine All-Star football game to be played in San Francisco's Kezar Stadium on New Year's Day.

As Lujack and Connor tell the story, Howie O'Dell of Yale was the head coach, but, in reality, Bernie Bierman of the University of Minnesota was in charge. Assisting O'Dell and Bierman was Andy Kerr, the retired coach of Colgate, who had been a member of the East coaching staff for all 31 East-West games.

It was Bierman who addressed the 26-man East squad (composed of star players from various schools in the Midwest and East) when they first assembled at the practice facility at Santa Clara University. He told them that there was very little time to prepare for the game, so he wanted each player to give his very best. He emphasized that conditioning would be a key factor. Little did Bierman know what was in store for him with Ziggie Czarobski on the squad.

Ziggie immediately commandeered the players and escorted them to the many bars he alone seemed able to find. He told stories, sang songs, and constantly entertained. Other than Lujack and Connor, the players had never encountered anyone like Ziggie. They loved him. A few days after their arrival, they held a team meeting to elect a team captain. It was the first time in the history of the East-West Game that a captain was elected unanimously. Ziggie voted for himself and the team loved it.

At practice, he led the team in cheers and, in general, drove the coaches, particularly Bierman, crazy. When practice was over, Ziggie always had some new bar or party to take his teammates to.

221

One night Bierman conducted a bed-check and of the 26-man squad only George Savitsky of Pennsylvania and George Connor were in their rooms, and they only because they both had the flu. At the next day's meeting, Bierman gave the team hell for being out so late and missing bed-check. Ziggie interrupted his tirade and said, "Coach, I'm sorry to tell you, but the joke is on you. We knew you were going to have a bed-check, so we were all on the floor above having a pillow fight."

Bierman just muttered something to himself and stormed out of the room.

A few days before the game, Connor was interviewed by a local radio station for background information on the upcoming contest. The announcer asked George, "You were Ziggie's captain at Notre Dame and he's the captain of this team. How does it feel to have him as your captain?"

George said, "Very truthfully, Ziggie deserves to be captain of this team because he is our leader, and I want to tell you very sincerely that everything Ziggie ever accomplished in his life, he owes to one thing," and then George paused.

The announcer pressed, "What?"

George replied, "Clean living."

The announcer could hardly finish the broadcast he was laughing so hard.

On the day of the game, Bierman gave the team his final tongue lashing.

"Of all the football teams I have ever been associated with, this is the worst and most poorly conditioned. In a minor league baseball league that I was connected to, there was a sign in one of the locker rooms that read, 'You can't bat around all night and bat .300.' That goes for this team. I know there is no way you can win this game, so I just hope you don't get killed and that they don't beat you too badly."

Andy Kerr rose to say a few words. "I have been in football a long time, and I have never seen any group of players have so much fun. If somehow you could manage to win by one point in addition to the fun you've had, it would be the greatest team ever to play in the East-West Shriners' Game. Good luck!"

Ziggie's East kicked off to the West team, which returned the ball to the 30-yard line. The West team then quickly marched 70 yards down the field for a touchdown. Lujack says that, after the extra point, Ziggie hollered to his teammates, "Everyone assemble on the 50-yard line."

Lujack assumed that, as captain of the team, Ziggie was going to chew them out for what was, admittedly, a terrible exhibition of defensive football. Ziggie gathered them together and said to his teammates:

"Wasn't that a magnificent drive the West team just had? We ought to give them a cheer!"

The fans, and particularly Bierman, couldn't believe what they were witnessing when the 11-man East squad huddled at midfield and shouted with loud voices:

"Who's a Team, They're a Team, They're a Great Team, The West Team, the West Team, the West Team."

The East team, comprised of some wonderfully talented football players, then settled down. Their natural talent and years of training were evident as they methodically ripped the West team apart. To the surprise of most of the fans and to the utter amazement of Bierman, the East team went on to soundly defeat an excellent West squad, 40-9. To that date, it was the most points scored by one team in the history of the East-West Game.

As a footnote to this game, players who later played under Bierman at Minnesota say he was never quite the same after coaching the East team. From their own perspective, the East players will always remember this game too, not just because of their victory, but mainly because of the experience of playing with the most fun-loving player they had ever encountered—their captain, Ziggie Czarobski.

The Old-Timers' Game

During the 1940s and for a few years beyond, there was an Old-Timers' Game each year at the close of Notre Dame's spring practice. (Today there is an intrasquad game called the Blue-Gold Game which concludes spring practice.) In former years, the graduating seniors and a few players who had graduated earlier would play the current varsity team under game conditions in Notre Dame Stadium. To augment the roster of the Old-Timers' team, Leahy would assign some reserve varsity players to play on the Old-Timers' squad.

The Old-Timers' Game played at the end of the 1948 spring practice promised to be an exciting one. The graduating seniors who would play for the Old-Timers included: John Lujack, George Connor, Ziggie Czarobski, Gasper Urban, Joe Signaigo, George Sullivan, Bob Livingstone, Cornie Clatt, and other seniors who had made a major impact on the fortunes of Notre Dame football during their time there. The 1948 squad—with returning veterans such as Red Sitko, Frank Tripucka, Bill Fischer, Marty Wendell, Bill Walsh, Bob Lally, Gus Cifelli, Ralph McGehee, Mike Swistowitz, Bill Gay, Larry Coutre, Jim Martin, Leon Hart, and so many more—was definitely a team to be reckoned with. Nobody doubted it would be a terrific game.

What added an extra bit of anticipation was the fact that Ziggie would be on the Old-Timers' team and, for the first time, be out from under the restraining hand of Leahy. It was a given that Ziggie would pull some crazy stunt. The question was: What would Ziggie try? The students, the regular fans, and Leahy would find out soon enough.

The visiting team locker room where the Old-Timers dressed the day of the game resembled a scene from some slapstick comedy movie. The players were clowning around, throwing things at each other, and having a great time.

When the Old-Timers returned to the locker room after the pre-game warm-up, the atmosphere was a little more subdued, but still very loose. Bill Earley, one of the varsity assistant coaches, was the coach in charge of the team that day. A few minutes before game time he called the team together in the traditional way to give the starting lineup and some last minute remarks. In a very business-like manner he announced the starting lineup and then said, "Since this is such a special team, I wanted you to have a special pep talk, so I asked an old friend if he would come here today and say a few words."

With that he nodded his head slightly to an assistant manager who was in the doorway leading to the coaches' room. The voice everyone heard was that of Knute Rockne. The student manager, according to plan, had put on a portable turntable a record of Rockne (who died in 1931) giving one of his famous halftime pep talks. As soon as the team heard the voice they knew exactly what and who it was. They immediately broke into hilarious laughter. In that mood and with smiles on their faces, they filed out of the locker room to begin the short journey up the ramp at the end of the stadium. But, instead of all of them running onto the field, the starting 11 stopped at the ramp entrance.

By pre-arrangement, they waited at the top of the ramp until a hearse, which had the insides gutted, entered the stadium and was driven to the top of the ramp. While this was going on, Leahy, who had the varsity squad on the field for about 10 minutes, was fuming and asking the officials to get the Old-Timers out there. The officials ran up to Bill Earley and ordered him to get his team on the field.

The Old-Timers' starting team (including Ziggie, Connor, Lujack, Urban, Signaigo, Livingstone, Clatt, and Pete Asbaugh) piled into the hearse. With the siren they had installed blaring as loudly as possible, the hearse was driven up the center of the field. At about the 30-yard line it stopped, the doors opened, and the Old-Timers scrambled out. Naturally, the last man out of the hearse was number "76," Zygmont Pierre Czarobski, who paused and raised his arms to acknowledge the cheers of the fans before he joined the team which had spread across the field in anticipation of the kickoff.

Ziggie took himself out of the game immediately after the kickoff. He was a "little" overweight and wanted to be rested for the Old-Timers' party later that evening. He, as well as his teammates, knew it was at the party that number "76" would be the star performer.

The varsity team ready to receive the kickoff was, however, not fooled for a moment into thinking that the Old-Timers were there just for laughs. They knew these players too well—having played with most of them on last year's team and, in many cases, for several years. The Old-Timers played all out that day. Maybe some of the fans who had watched the pre-game fun were surprised at the intensity of the game they witnessed, and even the outcome, but it was no surprise to those who knew these men. The Old-Timers defeated the varsity by a score of 20-14.

Ziggie's days as a Notre Dame football player were over, but his days of clowning and causing mischief were not. Notre Dame's 1948 senior prom was made to order for him.

The Senior Prom

The events before the prom will long be remembered by South Bend residents who witnessed the arrival of Ziggie Czarobski, George

Connor, Marty Brutz, and their dates at the entrance of the Palais Royale Ballroom on prom night.

Ziggie, George, and Marty borrowed a 1930 Packard hearse that had been refurbished by the proprietor of Flytraps, one of the football team's favorite watering holes, as their means of transportation to the prom (Ziggie and George had this thing about hearses). The three enlisted the services of Benny Sheridan, a local businessman and once the elusive halfback from the 1938 and 1939 Notre Dame teams, to serve as the chauffeur. Kevin O'Shea, Notre Dame's All-American basketball player, was recruited as the footman. Both Sheridan and O'Shea wore top hats and white waist-length coats borrowed from bartenders at Sweeney's Shamrock Tavern in South Bend. They also wore heavy white gloves borrowed from a construction worker they knew from Flytraps. The evening was well planned.

Word of the plan spread through the student body on campus. Joe Boland, the local sports announcer, made mention on his 6 P.M. sportscast of the fact that Ziggie had elaborate plans for the prom. No doubt this broadcast accounted for the large crowd which greeted the boys when they arrived by hearse for the prom. Even Father Kehoe, the Notre Dame prefect of discipline, intended to be among those who greeted the boys and their dates. Father Kehoe was well aware of Ziggie's reputation for having a good time, so he wanted to make sure Ziggie's group did not sneak the forbidden bottle of booze into the dance or try some other equally unauthorized escapade.

It was amazing to see the crowd, students and townspeople, gathered on the sidewalk under the bright lights of the ballroom entrance, waiting for the arrival of Ziggie and his pals. The crowd started to stir when they heard a siren in the distance. As the noise got louder, someone in the crowd shouted, "Here they come!"

Sure enough, the hearse was coming down the street and it headed towards the entrance to the ballroom. As the hearse approached and slowed as if to park, Sheridan (the driver), probably at the instigation of Ziggie, sped up again to go around the block and add a little more anticipation to their arrival.

As the hearse came around the corner after circling the block, the crowd, now fully into the spirit of evening, cheered loudly like movie star fans at a Hollywood premiere. When the hearse came to a halt at the well-lit entrance, Sheridan and O'Shea hurried from their places in the front seat to the rear of the hearse carrying a rolled-up red carpet.

Before they opened the door, they laid the carpet gently down on the pavement and rolled it slowly to its end, as if they were expecting no less than a king and his queen to step out.

With a dignity befitting the circumstances, Sheridan and O'Shea walked to the door of the hearse and opened it, while bowing as if to royalty. Out of the door stepped the man of the hour dressed in his tuxedo—Zygmont Pierre Czarobski. Ziggie bowed to the crowd as they cheered him. He graciously helped his date out of the hearse and stepped aside to let George, Brutz, and their dates exit.

The crowd gathered around them. From the edge of the crowd you couldn't hear what Ziggie was saying, but, judging from the laughter coming from the mass of people, he was obviously entertaining the throng with one of his stories or rapid-fire one-liners.

The last sighting of Ziggie and his group for the evening was when they entered the ballroom with big smiles on their faces. No doubt the smiles were largely a result of the fun they were having, but a little bit of their merriment could be attributed to the fact that they knew that such a big crowd had prevented Father Kehoe from checking their dates' purses—where the forbidden elixir for the night had been hidden. Ziggie really did know how to prepare for all contingencies.

With the graduation of Connor, Czarobski, Lujack, Clatt, Livingstone, Signaigo, and the rest of the seniors came the end of an era—the immediate post-war years. The Notre Dame teams in the next two years would continue the undefeated streak and win a National Championship (1949), but somehow, for those of us who had been part of the 1946 and 1947 teams, it would never be the same. Granted, their leaving presented greater opportunities for us to play, yet, the fun would be missing. And, how could it be otherwise with no Ziggie?

Chapter Twelve

THE 1948 SEASON

The squad that assembled on Cartier Field for summer practice in preparation for the coming season was in many ways a veteran team, but with some important differences from the previous year's team. This team would be the first post-war team that did not have monogram winners from the 1942 or 1943 teams on the squad. It was also the first post-war team that had more starters who were non-service veterans rather than veterans. Jim Martin and Red Sitko were now the "old men" of the team.

The squad was still loaded with players of exceptional ability and a cadre of seasoned players who blended well with the new faces. The big difference, in pure football terms, between the 1948 team and the previous post-war teams (1946-1947) was in the depth of experienced players at each position.

As Leahy put it, "A new era in Notre Dame football will begin with the opening of the 1948 season. It makes sense that a team does not lose three All-Americans, one of whom was the key operative in the intricate T-formation and a total of five starters from the final game of the year before without having to start anew. We thought we had made some progress in spring practice, but this was dispelled after the Old-Timers, with only one day of practice, trounced the varsity, 20-14."

At the all-important quarterback position, Leahy had Frank Tripucka, a veteran of the 1945, '46, and '47 teams, directing the team. Tripucka was a clever ball handler, an outstanding passer, and a smart signal caller. Like Lujack before him, he also was an outstanding punter, a task he performed with distinction throughout the season. Tripucka had seen a lot of action the past two years and was more than prepared to assume the starting role. He was not an all-around player like Lujack (who was?), but on offense he was outstanding. Leahy, expressed concern to the press as to whether Tripucka could do the job, but I will wager that in truth he had no real worries.

Backing up Tripucka at quarterback was Bob Williams, who had impressed everyone by his play on the freshman team and his excellent performance during spring practice (Williams would later become All-American and be inducted into the Hall of Fame). Also available for duty was the dependable Gerry Begley.

Leahy had many experienced runners returning in the backfield. Red Sitko, the team's leading rusher the past two years, was back at right halfback and John Panelli, the punishing runner, was back at fullback. Terry Brennan, playing his fourth season, returned at left halfback, but the knee he had injured the previous year caused him to miss spring practice. It remained a concern to the coaches. Typical of Brennan, he would responded with another great year.

Ernie Zalejski, a South Bend product who had electrified the crowd with some dazzling runs during the 1946 season, was back, but, like Brennan, was having difficulties with his knee. Lank Smith, who had replaced Lujack on defense the previous season, was returning for his final year.

Larry Coutre, the former sprint champion and star runner from St. George High School in Evanston, Illinois, was back, as were Bill Gay and Mike Swistowicz from Tilden Tech in Chicago, the elusive Coy McGee, and Frank Spaniel. These backs were joined by newcomers Jack Landry, Leo McKillip, Fred Wallner, and Dick Cotter.

The end position was solid with Jim Martin and Leon Hart returning as starters and backed up by Bill Wightkin, Bill Leonard, Doug Waybright, Ray Espenan, and Bill Flynn.

Ralph McGehee, the junior from Tilden Tech in Chicago who had earned his monogram the two previous seasons, took over the left tackle spot vacated by George Connor. Jack Fallon, a veteran of the 1944, 1945, and 1946 teams, who had sat out the 1947 season because of injuries, returned to take over the right tackle spot. Three experienced players, Gus Cifelli, Ted Budynkiewicz, and Frank Gaul were backups.

The guard position was well manned with both Bill Fischer, the captain, and Marty Wendell back as starters. Both were in their fourth year with already brilliant careers. In reserve were returning monogram winners Bob Lally, John Frampton, Jim Dailer, and

Steve Oracko plus Frank "Rodney" Johnson, Bill Higgins, John Helwig, and me.

Bill Walsh, the starting center from the previous season, was back, assisted by the veteran Walter Grothaus. Jerry Groom, just up from the freshman team, had already made his mark in spring practice and was slated to start as a linebacker.

Because of the loss of Pete Ashbaugh and the abundance of good running backs, Swistowicz, now a junior, was named a starter on defense.

During the 1947 season, the rule making freshmen ineligible to play varsity football was reinstated. As a consequence, the 1948 squad was the first since 1942 to be filled with players that were moving up to the varsity after a year of freshman ball. One of the best was Jerry Groom.

Jerry "Boomer" Groom

Groom attended Dowling High School in Des Moines, Iowa. He was a starter as a center and linebacker all four years, 1943-46, earning All-State honors his junior and senior years. At 6 feet, 3 inches and 255 pounds, he was sought after by many of the colleges in the Midwest, particularly by the University of Iowa.

At his high school banquet his senior year, Groom and his dad spent some time with Frank Leahy, the guest speaker for the evening. During the course of the conversation, Leahy said, "Jerry, I would certainly love for you to visit Notre Dame. I know there are a lot of schools interested in recruiting you, but would you promise me one thing? Before you make a definite decision, would you come visit the Notre Dame campus?" Groom promised he would do so.

Groom had also promised Dr. Eddie Anderson, the coach of Iowa, that he would call him before he made any final decision as to his college choice. Groom visited Notre Dame that spring and liked everything he saw. His mind was made up—Notre Dame was the place for him.

True to his word, Groom called Dr. Anderson, who hastily arranged a meeting to discuss the matter. At the meeting Anderson informed Groom that he was to be the first recipient of the Nile Kinnick Scholarship Award (named after Iowa's great halfback who was killed during WWII). Groom told Anderson how honored he was to receive such an offer, but that he had made up his mind to attend Notre Dame. In recalling that meeting, Groom said, "I'll never forget Anderson's words. He said, 'Jerry, if you decide not to come to Iowa, the next school I would like to see you go to is Notre Dame. I have mixed emotions about the whole thing. I'd love to have you at Iowa, but you won't make a mistake by going to Notre Dame.' That made me feel real good."

As an incoming freshman in 1947, Groom arrived on campus before the other freshmen reported. In a taping session with him for this book, he said, "Let me tell you a story about your brother George. I was the only freshman there and worked out in sweat clothes. I remember it was raining cats and dogs and nobody wanted to go out for practice. Finally, one of the coaches hollered at the players to get out on the practice field. There was one player already out there, and that was George. He was smart, he knew they were going to practice rain or sleet. So, after three hours of practice, Leahy says in that voice of his, 'Okay, lads, start running laps—with the exception of the captain. Connor, you can go in because you were smart enough to come out early.'

"I remember the day of my first scrimmage. We had been practicing for a couple of weeks when all of a sudden Leahy said, 'Coach Brutz [Marty Brutz, a guard from the 1946 team], send the boys over.' The first thing they did was put us in a box for tackling practice—they would just run halfbacks one after another. [A drill consisting of putting a defensive player in a fixed area with the purpose of having that player tackle a back who would run at him full speed with about a seven-yard start. The back had to run within the fixed area—about three yards wide.]

"It was like horses coming at you. The first one I tried to hit was Sitko. Red was about 190 and had a lot of speed; he was at top speed in two steps. I was low and I caught him low and it was a helluva thump. Leahy, of course, is watching all this from his tower. The next one that came through was John Panelli and there was another loud pop. I thought to myself, 'How long is this going to go on?' The next guy is Billy Gompers—and the first thing I know, a leg is here and a leg is there and I'm just grabbing air. Then it was Coy McGee and Bob Livingstone and I'm grabbing for air again as all the backs are now laughing. That lasted for about 15 minutes.

231

"Then we had a line scrimmage and I'm playing against guys like George Connor, George Strohmeyer, Marty Wendell, Joe Signaigo, George Sullivan, and the rest of those guys. Now they decide we'll have a little scrimmage. I don't think they really wanted to put the freshmen in there so fast, but Leahy couldn't resist—he wanted to see what we had. The scrimmage lasted an hour and a half. If a freshman would crack one of the varsity, Leahy would say, 'This is just a freshman, what are you going to do when you meet Purdue in the opening game?'

"As time went on I can remember having some terrific battles, particularly with the guards. Leahy would love it when a freshman would make a good play against the varsity. I can remember going at it on the line of scrimmage for hours, even under the lights. [When the time changed in the fall, Leahy would turn the lights on so he could keep the team on the field.]

"The great thing about Notre Dame is that on the field you were a freshman, but there was no harassing or hazing or any of that type of stuff. When I went over to the dining hall, it was great—I'd sit with George Connor, Bill Walsh, other freshmen, or a Heisman Trophy winner; it didn't matter and everybody treated you the same.

"The 1947 team was a tremendous team. George Strohmeyer was second string and he made All-American the year before. Bill Wightkin had tremendous speed. At 6-foot-3 and about 220 he was the greatest end I've seen—and he was second string. As freshmen we scrimmaged them constantly. I tell people it was the greatest football education possible. When my freshman year was over, I had the equivalent of five years' experience."

Groom was one of the mainstays on defense for the next three years. He was captain of the 1950 team and was named to most All-America teams that year. He is scheduled to be inducted into the College Hall of Fame at its annual awards dinner in New York on December 6, 1994.

The week before the opening game against Purdue, Leahy held his usual pre-season scrimmage in the stadium. During the course of the scrimmage, Groom had his two front teeth knocked out and two more pushed back in his mouth. Later, at the dentist's office, Groom had the four roots extracted after the dentist had pulled the loose ones out with his fingers.

That Monday at practice, Leahy came over to Groom and explained that he did not want him to scrimmage, to just run the plays

232

without any contact. Then he said, "Let me tell you a little story. We had a great halfback here by the name of Elmer Angsman in 1945. I was in the service and not coaching, but I am told when Notre Dame played Navy in Baltimore, this great halfback got hit in the mouth and had 16 teeth knocked out [the actual count was eight]. They tell me it was like popcorn all over the ground. You know, they just put some mouthwash in his mouth and he went right back in and finished the game. I just thought I would tell you about that."

As Groom recalls, "I got the message—I only had four, he had 16."

The Friday before the game, Groom's parents, who had come in from Iowa to visit their son, watched Friday's practice. Groom described what happened. "They were outside the locker room after practice talking to Leahy when I came out. I went up and said, 'Hi,' and I thought my mother would faint when she saw me because she didn't know about my teeth. Leahy said, 'Now, Mrs. Groom, don't worry. Jerry's going to get a new bridge and it will be better than the teeth he originally had.' "

Purdue

Notre Dame opened the 1948 football season against the Boilermakers of Purdue on September 25th at Notre Dame Stadium in a thriller that kept the fans cheering from start to finish. The luck o' the Irish was evident in the game as the home team edged the tough Purdue squad by a score of 28-27.

The Boilermakers battled Notre Dame the entire game and had a 13-12 lead in the third period. It was the first time Notre Dame had trailed anyone since the defeat by Great Lakes 19 games ago. It took a 70-yard return of a punt by John Panelli, a 23-yard field goal, and an extra point by Steve Oracko (who had missed three earlier attempts), and a seven-yard return of a tipped ball by reserve tackle Al Zmijewski for Notre Dame to bring its total to 28 points.

Notre Dame opened the scoring when Red Sitko scored from the two-yard line after Tripucka hit Brennan for 10 and Martin for 25 yards. A short while later, Panelli went wide around right end for 33 yards, setting up another two-yard score for Sitko. This gave the Irish an early 12-0 lead. But Purdue fought back, scored, and made it 12-7 at halftime.

At the start of the second half, Purdue stormed back again with a

74-yard march to score, but failed to make the extra point. This gave the Boilermakers a one-point lead, 13-12.

With Purdue held on downs, Martin, from his left-end position, blocked a punt that Panelli fielded in a crowd at the Notre Dame 30-yard line. In the first five yards of Panelli's runback, three Purdue players hit him, but he escaped their grasp. Aided by Fischer, who blocked two Purdue players, Panelli broke into the clear and picked up a convoy of four blockers who helped him to go all the way for the go-ahead touchdown.

What happened after that is best described by Dave Condon of the *Chicago Tribune* in a column written weeks later. Here is what he wrote after reminiscing with Leahy:

> Oracko was Notre Dame's place-kicking specialist, but was nothing special thru his first three extra point attempts, the third when Notre Dame had forged back in front, 18-13.
>
> " And as I recall," said Leahy, "Oracko also missed some early field goal attempts from inside the 15. Anyhow, as the fourth quarter opened and with Purdue getting tougher every moment, it seemed that those extra points we missed might be Notre Dame's downfall. We had an inspired foe.
>
> "Then Bob DeMoss passed from behind Purdue's goal line. Mike Swistowicz intercepted for us on the Purdue 20. They held like demons, so by fourth down we were no closer than the 16—and any field goal attempt would have to be from an angle.
>
> "I looked around the bench for Oracko. I figured by the law of averages he finally should be able to kick one thru the crossbars."
>
> Leahy recalled that he put his arms around Oracko and ordered the field goal attempt. As Oracko sprinted out on the turf, Leahy remembered, Notre Dame's president—the Rev. John J. Cavanaugh — arose in the University's official box and shouted: "No, Frank, no! Good Heavens, Frank. No!"
>
> Leahy pretended not to hear, fortunately. Oracko kicked the 26-yard field goal that made up for the three missed extra points. This, coupled with a successful conversion following a fourth touchdown, was the key to Notre Dame's slender victory. Oracko had been the man of the moment, and it was to be recorded as quite a moment:

A hush had settled over Notre Dame Stadium when Oracko swung his foot against the ball on that crucial field goal kick. By the time the ball bull's-eyed thru the crossbars, it was so quiet one could have heard the brush of angel wings. It turned out that thousands did hear Joe McArdle.

McArdle, Leahy's chief aide, always observed the game from inside the scoreboard high in the end zone. His duty was to spot the opposition's line spacing. So McArdle was a perspiring observer from his peephole perch when Oracko made the kick.

The instant the kick was good, McArdle flung open the door to the scoreboard and, from on high, shouted into the silence: "God bless you, Steve Oracko!"

By the time thousands had turned toward the sound of this booming praise, McArdle had slammed the door and was hidden inside the scoreboard. That night, there was a celebration in Leahy's home. An old priest took Leahy aside and confided that at the moment of the decisive kick, thousands sitting with him in the end zone had heard Knute Rockne thunder from the heavens: "God bless you, Steve Oracko!"

One of the highlights of the game was the performance of Tripucka, who put on a great exhibition of quarterbacking and passing. Panelli was outstanding as a linebacker and, as a runner, quickly dispelled any thoughts that early summer surgery on his knee had hampered his playing ability. Although Notre Dame kept its 19-game undefeated streak intact, it was too close a game for the team to feel cocky about the future.

On Tuesday following the Purdue game, the university announced that Edward "Moose" Krause was retiring as first assistant to Leahy. The demands of his duties as assistant athletic director, a position he had been named to the previous spring, were too great. No immediate successor for the football role vacated by Krause was named. (The position was later filled by Bob McBride, who played on the 1942 and 1946 teams.)

There was no question that Moose would be missed by the team as an assistant coach. He was not only a top-flight football coach, but he had a rapport with the players, a calming influence, and a delightful sense of humor that added balance to the often tedious practice sessions.

Pittsburgh

In their next game the Irish trounced a spunky Pittsburgh team by a score of 40-0 before 63,000 fans in Pitt Stadium. After seven minutes of play, Spaniel intercepted a Pitt pass and took the ball to the Pitt nine. Tripucka hit Hart for the score. A little later Sitko broke loose on a 60-yard run. By halftime, the Irish had a 28-0 lead. From then on, Leahy used his reserves as Landry and McKillip scored from in close. The highlight of the second half was an 85-yard punt return by Lank Smith, who went to his right, then cut left to midfield, and from there he outsprinted the defenders to the end zone. Trying to keep the score down, Leahy did not permit a pass to be thrown in the final 44 minutes of the game.

Michigan State

Michigan State, the next opponent, was back on the schedule after a 27-year hiatus. Clarence "Biggie" Munn, the Spartan coach, always fielded a team well schooled in the fundamentals of football and armed with a diversified offensive attack. State wanted very much to knock off Notre Dame and end its undefeated string.

With the game only seven minutes old, Michigan State scored. An intercepted Tripucka pass put the ball on the Notre Dame 20, where the Spartans scored in four plays, adding the extra point for a 7-0 lead. Notre Dame came right back with a 71-yard drive which ended with a Tripucka-to-Hart pass for the touchdown. Still trailing 7-6 in the second period, Notre Dame, after holding State on downs on the four-yard line, marched 96 yards, climaxed by a 12-yard Swistowicz run to put Notre Dame ahead for good. Brennan and Sitko scored on short runs before the game ended with Notre Dame the victor, 26-7.

Leahy liked to get his reserves in the game but, out of respect, for the Spartan attack, kept the regulars in most of the way. Sitko was the workhorse in the backfield, gaining 186 yards on 24 carries. Fischer, captain and left guard, suffered a dislocated elbow, and Swistowicz, fullback and premier defensive back, had to be carried from the field on a stretcher due to a back sprain. Both were expected to miss the Nebraska game.

Nebraska

The Cornhuskers were decided underdogs when the Irish traveled to Lincoln, Nebraska, for the first time in 23 years. Notre Dame would be without the services of Coy McGee, the elusive left halfback, who had suffered fractures of the left leg and foot at practice the day before the team was scheduled to leave for Omaha. As with any player with McGee's running ability and potential to break a game wide open, he would be missed. Fortunately, Bill Gay was on hand to take over the punt-return duties.

The battle began before the two teams took the field for the kickoff. Bill Fischer decribed what happened. "After the pre-game warmup as we were leaving the field, some people in the stands began hollering obscenities about the school, our religion, and how they were going to kick our butts. Bill Vangen [a reserve center and former Naval officer] went up in the stands in his uniform and was about to hit one of the guys when the police stopped him. They escorted Vangen back to the locker room. Leahy said, 'Did you hear what they said about Our Blessed Mother? And did you hear what they said about our school? God bless you, William Vangen, for defending Our Mother and you're not even a Catholic. I want to tell you lads what we're going to do today. We are going to trounce this team like they have never been beaten before.' "

Frank Tripucka also recalled that day. "The only team I ever saw that Leahy wanted to run up a score on was Nebraska. They taunted us about our religion and the statue on the Dome, all unheard of stuff to me. I never heard anyone talk that way before. That was the last time we ever played Nebraska in Nebraska, he wouldn't go back there again. We beat them that day and he kept the starters in the game. Any other team he would put in the reserves when we got four touchdowns ahead. He never wanted to embarrass a team, but that game was different."

Notre Dame had no trouble with Nebraska—battering the Huskers, 44-13. Early in the first quarter, the Irish put together an 80-yard drive, which was helped by some excellent Brennan runs. Sitko skirted left end for a 10-yard touchdown run. When Notre Dame gained possession of the ball again, Tripucka made an excellent fake to Sitko through the middle before pitching to Panelli, who took it 73 yards for Notre Dame's second touchdown. Later in the first period, Spaniel, playing fullback for the injured Swistowicz, gained 30 yards on a well-executed trap play up the middle. He gained 16 more on another trap play, setting up a Tripucka-to-Wightkin play-action pass for Notre Dame's third touchdown.

After Groom intercepted a pass, Coutre picked up 14 yards before Landry burst up the middle for seven yards and the fourth Irish touchdown to give them a 25-7 halftime lead.

In the second half, Sitko scored his second touchdown of the day on a two-yard plunge and Gay returned a punt 67 yards, setting up a Tripucka-to-Martin pass for a touchdown. Coutre scored the final Irish tally on a 13-yard sprint up the middle. Nebraska scored its second touchdown on the last play of the game.

Iowa

Playing its second straight road game, Notre Dame scored in the first minute and went on to defeat a stubborn Iowa team, 27-12. Iowa fumbled the opening kickoff. Panelli recovered it. Tripucka, after a beautiful fake into the line, tossed out to Panelli, who scampered 35 yards for a quick touchdown to make the score, 6-0. Iowa retaliated when Al DiMarco's passes carried to the eight-yard line. Two plays later, Iowa scored to tie it at 6-6.

Sitko took the ensuing kickoff from his own 10-yard line to the Iowa 10 on some great blocks by Walsh, Coutre, and Hart. After the ball exchanged hands, Gay, from the Iowa five-yard line, skirted right end for a touchdown, giving ND a 13-6 halftime lead.

In the third quarter, with the ball on Iowa's 45, Landry got five before Panelli, on the same well-executed toss play, and ran the end for a 40-yard touchdown aided by a great block by Fischer. In the fourth quarter, Coutre went up the middle on a 35-yard run for Notre Dame's fourth and final touchdown. Iowa got its second score after an interception with five and a half minutes left to play.

Navy

Notre Dame had no trouble with Navy in their Baltimore matchup; the Irish defeated the Middies, 41-7, as Sitko, Panelli, Gay, Lank Smith, Spaniel, and Landry scored in succession. Using few passes and many substitutions, Leahy showed a powerful offensive attack as the Irish scored in every quarter and were never in trouble.

Tripucka was five-for-five in passing with Bob Williams, his backup, completing four of six. Sitko had a great day, gaining 172 yards in 17 carries. Bob Lally, getting a lot of playing time at guard, lost three front teeth during the game when, as Jim Costin of the *South Bend Tribune* put it, "he swung his mouth against a Navy lineman's elbow."

Notre Dame led Navy, 26-0, at halftime. Leahy never wanted his teams to take anything for granted or assume because they were ahead in a game that it was won until the final whistle blew. Accordingly, he severely lectured the players about the mistakes they had made in the first half. Then, as the team was leaving the locker room, he pulled Tripucka, the quarterback, aside and said, "Oh, Francis, we don't want to embarrass the great Naval Academy team, so no passes and just run the straight dive plays."

Indiana

Showing a balanced and well-executed passing and running attack, the Irish defeated the Hoosiers, 42-6. Tripucka hit Wightkin and Gay with long arching aerials as he continued to demonstrate his excellent passing skills. Spaniel, Dick Cotter, Landry, and Leo McKillip teamed with Panelli and Gay to help Notre Dame to an easy victory.

With guards Fischer, Wendell, Lally, and Frampton banged up, Bill Higgins from Fenwick High School in Oak Park, Illinois, and I practiced during the week with the first team. At game time, Leahy decided to start Wendell on offense despite his bad knee. He lasted five minutes before Leahy sent Higgins in to play opposite Gordon Goldsberry, who was playing nose guard and was mentioned as an All-Big Ten candidate. In the huddle, Bill Walsh, the center, said to Higgins, "Don't worry about him," nodding toward Goldsberry, "Marty and I softened him up a bit." Higgins had a great game as he continually blocked Goldsberry and opened up big holes for the Irish backs. Unfortunately, near the end of the game, he suffered a knee injury and joined the ranks of the other wounded, which included Sitko with bruised ribs and Wendell with a bad shoulder.

Northwestern

On a dreary, cloudy day in South Bend, Notre Dame came from behind to defeat a stubborn Wildcat 11, 12-7. The Irish got off to a good start in the first quarter by marching 91 yards to score on a Panelli plunge. Brennan and Panelli, with some excellent running, combined to take the ball to the Wildcat 17. On a great fake by Tripucka, Hart took the ball on an end-around to the one, where Panelli made it 6-0.

After a scoreless second quarter, Notre Dame had an excellent chance to score in the third period with the ball on Northwestern's nine-yard line. Art Murakowski, the Wildcat linebacker, intercepted a Tripucka flat pass and ran it all the way for a touchdown. With a successful conversion Northwestern led, 7-6. In the fourth quarter, with the ball at midfield, Landry, on successive quick dives over the middle, took the ball to the Wildcat nine. In two plays, Gay scored the go-ahead touchdown to cinch the victory for the Irish.

Washington

Lancaster (Lank) Smith, the starting defensive safety on the 1947-48 teams, passed on to me a story he heard from a member of the 1948 Washington University team. It concerns the scouting report the Washington Huskies received before the 1948 game with Notre Dame. According to Smith, the Husky player told him:

"They had scouted every game that year and said Notre Dame was an overrated team and that 'Moose' Fischer was an overrated player, a gutless nose guard in the Notre Dame wide tackle 5-4 defense. He didn't have it here [pointing to his heart]. All week our center smashed his elbow into a stand-up dummy with Fischer's face on it.

"The first play after the kickoff, the center smashed Fischer in the face. Fischer just blinked. The next play Fischer stuck his face in the face of the center, spit out some blood, and said, 'Fella, if that's the way you want it, that's the way it's going to be.' Our chicken center stood up and yelled, 'Time out,' and limped off the field.

"From then on our second-string center snapped and stuck his head in the ground. Fischer would step over him into our backfield. It seemed like he made one hundred tackles and quarterback sacks that day.

"You guys won something like 46-0—even punting on third down while using every player on the bench."

Converting four Huskie fumbles into quick first period scores was all the Irish needed to subdue an inept Washington squad by a score of 46-0.

The Irish added one tally in each of the three remaining periods. Leahy kept the passing attack under wraps, but Tripucka made the best of his limited opportunities, completing three of five for touchdowns.

Leahy, no doubt thinking ahead to the 1949 season, got the idea of switching Hart to tackle. Without any practice at the position and with Notre Dame comfortably ahead, he put Hart in the game at defensive tackle. Hart said, "I would go across the line and instinctively start to paddle out [the maneuver where the end wards off the blocker and drifts to the sideline to protect against end sweeps]. I would take myself right out of the play, so I wasn't too good at playing tackle." That ended the experiment.

Southern California

The final game of the year against Southern California marked the end of the collegiate careers of 11 seniors: Bill Fischer, Marty Wendell, Frank Tripucka, Bill Walsh, John Frampton, Frank Gaul, Al Lesko, John Panelli, Terry Brennan, Lank Smith, and Ted Budynkiewicz.

These seniors, indeed the entire team, had a lot riding on the outcome of this game. Notre Dame was ranked number two in the country behind Michigan and the team's 27-game streak without a defeat was on the line. They did not need a pep talk to get them up for the final game.

However, it took an electrifying 87-yard kickoff return by Gay with only two minutes remaining and a crucial extra point by Oracko for Notre Dame to escape with a 14-14 tie. After a scoreless first period, Hart made a shoestring catch of a Tripucka short pass. Nearly falling down, Hart got his balance on the USC 40-yard line, ran through two defenders, cut back to evade two more, and trampled a fifth on his way to the first touchdown of the game. Oracko converted, making the score 7-0. On the last play of the first half, Tripucka was caught in a pileup and cracked a vertebra in his back. Bob Williams directed the team the remainder of the game.

Bill Martin of Southern California scored twice in the fourth quarter on short plunges to set the stage for the final heroics of Gay and Oracko. With Notre Dame behind, 14-7, Gay was the deep man for Notre Dame as the Irish prepared to receive the Trojan kickoff.

Gay went to the nearest official and asked, "Mr. Official, how much time is left?"

The official said, "Two minutes."

Gay responded, "That's just long enough."

He was right, it was long enough. He returned the kickoff 87 yards on a beautiful run before he was knocked out of bounds on the Trojan 10-yard line. After a penalty, Sitko, on a plunge from the one, scored to set up Oracko's crucial extra-point try with about a minute remaining. Oracko made the kick to tie the score at 14.

The Irish had a chance to win when they got the ball back, but time ran out. If they'd had a time-out left, they might have been able to score, but Leahy himself squandered Notre Dame's last chance to stop the clock.

Leahy had a thing against time-outs. He never wanted his team to call a time-out in the early part of the game, no matter what the circumstances, and he so instructed his captain. It was his feeling that a time-out was a precious commodity to be saved until the end of the game. He knew games were won and lost in the final minutes, and the team with time-outs remaining had an advantage. In this instance, the final time-out was not saved for when it was needed. Leahy himself was to blame.

After Oracko tied the score with his second conversion, he recovered his own short kickoff on the USC 43-yard line. Leahy, confused in the excitement, thought the Irish were ahead and sent Sitko in the game with instructions to run out the clock. Sitko repeated the order in the huddle and added, "If you do, I'll never play with any of you guys again."

The players were completely in agreement with Sitko's position that they go all-out to win, but, confused by Leahy's instructions, they called a time-out. On the Irish sideline, when Leahy was informed the game was tied, that Notre Dame was not ahead as he thought, he exclaimed, "Oh, my God, go out and win the game!"

Notre Dame began to move the ball and completed a pass to the Trojans' 32-yard line. Under the rules of 1948, when a player went down with an injury, the clock was stopped and a time-out was charged to the officials. All teams were prepared to fake an injury when an extra time-out was needed, and Gus Cifelli had been chosen to be the injured player. At the appropriate time, Cifelli forgot to fake. The other 10 Notre Dame players desperately took it upon themselves to play injured and fell to the ground. Hart said, "It looked as though someone gunned us down with a machine gun—Cifelli was the only one left standing." The officials, witnessing the bizarre event, blew the whistle to signal the end of the game as time ran out.

The Irish ended the season with their undefeated streak intact (28 games). With a season record of nine wins, no losses, and one tie, they were ranked number two in the nation behind Michigan. By any standards, it was a excellent showing, especially considering Leahy's pessimism at the outset of the season about the team's chances of going undefeated.

Tripucka recently gave a good assessment of the team: "In 1948, freshmen were not eligible. Guys like Bob Toneff, Jim Mutscheller, Paul Burns, and Billy Barrett were all freshmen. If we had that group playing for us in '48, we would have won the National Championship. I remember one day Leahy said, 'Bring the freshmen up here.' In the scrimmage that followed, we ran against the one side of the line with Toneff, Burns, and Mutscheller. We ran there once or twice and got nothing. Leahy called me over and said, 'Oh Francis, let's stay away from that side, let's run the other side.' That's how good they were. In '48 we didn't have those players. We had a good team, enough to go undefeated, but we didn't have the depth like in 1946 and '47. That was the difference."

Individually, there were some great performers during the course of the season. Red Sitko led the team in rushing for the third consecutive year, tying a Notre Dame record held jointly by George Gipp (1918-20) and Christie Flanagan (1925-27). With nine touchdowns, Sitko also led the team in scoring. Leon Hart, who had a fantastic year playing both ways, led the team in receiving. Lank Smith led the team in punt return average with a phenomenal 31.4 average.

Frank Tripucka had an outstanding year in several respects: directing the team, ball handling, punting, and leading the team in passing. All of Leahy's quarterbacks during the 1940s were excellent ball handlers, proficient in spins, reverse spins, and the art of deception. Tripucka was the best—he was like a magician. Leahy used to proclaim that Tripucka was the best ball-handling, faking quarterback he ever had. There were times when he faked a pitchout so superbly that one would swear he saw the ball in flight, only to find Tripucka had faked it and had handed the ball to a back going through the line.

Tripucka's skill at handling the football oftentimes caused the defenders to "freeze" until they could determine who had the ball. This ability of his was of immense importance to the success of the team's offense.

When the All-America teams were announced, Bill Fischer and Leon Hart were named for the second straight year. For the first time, Red Sitko and Marty Wendell were named to most All-America teams.

Fischer ended his four years at Notre Dame by also being selected as the recipient of the Outland Trophy. Fischer had a phenomenal four-year career. As a 17-year-old freshman out of Lane Tech in Chicago, he was the understudy to Ed Mieszkowski at tackle in 1945. For the next three years, he was the starting left guard on teams that were undefeated and which won two National Championships. For a big man he had speed, agility, and quickness. He put these assets to good use in becoming one of the nation's premier blocking guards, and on defense he was unmovable. In 1983, Fischer was inducted into the Collegiate Hall of Fame.

Marty Wendell, teamed with Fischer, gave Notre Dame the best pair of guards in the country. Wendell, like Fischer, had an outstanding four-year career. As a freshman fullback in 1944, he became a starter as a defensive linebacker. After playing under Paul Brown at Great Lakes in 1945, he returned to Notre Dame in 1946 as a center to again be a starter as a linebacker. In 1947, he was switched to guard where he played on the first team on both offense and defense for two straight years. Wendell was known for his bone-crushing tackles. Any player who was ever tackled by him will attest to the fact that he hit as hard as anybody in college football. He has the distinction, which very few have, of winning four monograms while playing three different positions.

Although he was not named to the All-America team, an oversight as far as his teammates were concerned, Bill Walsh had another outstanding year. He was, without a doubt, the best blocking center in college football. He was the first team center in 1945, backed up the All-American George Strohmeyer in 1946, then beat out Strohmeyer in 1947 to become first string. Walsh, in addition to his blocking skills, was the best long snapper in football. He could snap it 17 yards and the ball would never get a foot off the ground. When he knew where the punter liked to have the ball snapped, the only question was,

"Laces up or down?" All of his teammates are in agreement with me when I say he was the finest pure snapper I have ever seen.

Leahy was again the subject of numerous newspaper articles about moving to the professional ranks. He gave the matter more thought than usual, but before any of the offers turned into negotiations, he made his decision to stay at Notre Dame.

Chapter Thirteen

THE 1949 SEASON—LEAHY'S
FOURTH NATIONAL CHAMPIONSHIP

Frank Leahy opened his campaign with the press as he did each year, by playing down the team's chances for an undefeated season. He told the press that the team may be as good as last year's, but won't win as many games because the other teams will be "loaded to the hilt."

He admitted that Bob Williams at quarterback "is going to be mighty handy to have around"—but lamented the losses in the line. "We won't be able to make those drives of 50 and 60 yards at a clip," he commented. "We'll have to give up the ball more than I like, and that's where it will hurt."

It was true that Leahy had losses in the line with Jack Fallon, Bill Fischer, Bill Walsh, and Marty Wendell having graduated, but what he failed to mention is that he had 27 monogram winners returning that would make any coach drool. They included Leon Hart, Jim Martin, Red Sitko, Ralph McGehee, Walt Grothaus, Larry Coutre, Frank Spaniel, and Jerry Groom. There was no question, Leahy had the makings of an outstanding team—they turned out to be just that.

During the last days of summer practice, he held a special meeting for just the seniors and he revealed his true feelings about the coming season. "We can go all the way, but the critical game will be against Tulane. They have one of the greatest teams in the country and if we could somehow beat them in the last few minutes, we can have an undefeated season." As in past years, he instructed us not to pay attention to what he told the press about the team. "I will never build you up too high. In the event something goes wrong, I never want the team to get the blame."

During the 1949 season, the Notre Dame team would be led by co-captains for the first time since the 1933 season. Leading the team

246

were Jim Martin and Leon Hart. Both Hart and Martin had won three straight monograms and both were ends. Following his usual pattern of trying to get the best 11 men on the field, Leahy switched Martin from left end, where he had been a starter for three years, to tackle. Bill Wightkin, Hart's roommate, had been the backup right end behind Hart. Wightkin was too good not to be in the starting lineup, so he was switched to left end. This was good news for Wightkin who would now be in the starting lineup, but for Martin, it was not easy to accept the switch. Being the unselfish player he always was, and for the good of the team, Martin went along with Leahy's request. Martin, at his new tackle position, had a great year, making the All-America team. Wightkin was outstanding, and Hart was so good he won the Heisman Trophy.

The 1949 season ushered in the two-platoon system. As one watched the Notre Dame team play, it was not so obvious because so many of the players still played both ways. Leahy believed that a good player was a complete football player, proficient in going both ways. Leahy's best players were so good at playing both ways that he had them on the first team on both offense and defense.

Jim Martin, who was switched to offensive left tackle, continued to play part-time at left end on defense and the remainder of the time at defensive right tackle. Hart continued to play both ways at right end and, as the season progressed, he also played fullback. Ralph McGehee, going for his fourth consecutive monogram and the starter at left tackle from the previous season, was switched to right tackle on offense, while sophomore Bob Toneff started as defensive left tackle.

Other linemen started on either offense or defense but continued to play the opposite way as backups. Bill Wightkin replaced Martin as the starting offensive left end, but also backed up Martin on defense. Bob Lally, a two-year monogram winner, played both ways behind Fred Wallner, who started at both offensive guard and at linebacker. Paul Burns, a sophomore, started at middle guard on defense and was the backup to Frank "Rodney" Johnson at offensive left guard. As it turned out, Johnson at guard and Walter Grothaus at center were the only starters on the offensive line who played one way almost exclusively.

The Irish began their official practice for the coming season on August 20th. Jim Martin had already played three seasons as a starter and felt like an old pro. He stopped off on the way to South Bend for summer practice to visit a friend and stayed too long—he was several days late in reporting. To his dismay, he found that the team had already had four scrimmages and he was way behind in his conditioning and training.

When Martin came on the practice field, the coaches put him in every conceivable drill to make up for the lost time. It was extremely hot and the next thing Jim knew he was being carried into the locker room as a result of heat prostration. He looked up from the stretcher and could make out the coaches looking down on him. Then he heard Leahy's unmistakable voice, "Who is this? Is this our captain? He must be out of shape from doing bad things."

The trainer iced down Martin in the training room until he recovered. With Leahy's remarks about his conditioning in his mind, Martin got off the training table, put his equipment back on, and returned to the practice field.

In recalling the incident, Martin said, "At the end of practice Leahy ordered one lap around the inside fence of Cartier Field [about a quarter of a mile]. I was so embarrassed by being carried off the field and being in Leahy's doghouse that I made up my mind that I would be the first one to finish. I ran and ran and finally did finish first." It was that kind of determination and toughness that made Martin one of the best players of the 1940s. Because of his friendly, easy going manner off the field, he was one of the best-liked players on the team.

Despite finishing first in the laps, Leahy demoted Martin to the fourth team. Gradually, through hard work, Martin worked his way back to the second team. It seemed as though he would never get out of Leahy's doghouse. Then, the Wednesday before the opening game, there was a scrimmage with Martin playing on defense. Fidel Gander, a big, fast fullback, carried the ball and Martin hit him so hard Gander was knocked out cold. Leahy hollered, "Who made that tackle?"

One of the assistant coaches yelled, "Jim Martin."

There was silence. "All right, James Martin," Leahy finally said, "You can come back to your starting position now, you earned it."

As with all summer practices, Leahy worked the team hard. One of the first casualties was Rodney Johnson, slated to replace Fischer as the starting left guard. On September 1st, in a seven-on-seven pass drill, Johnson suffered torn ligaments in his knee. The knee ballooned to a huge size and stayed that way for 13 days. Johnson's knee was finally casted from upper thigh to the ankle. Johnson hobbled onto Cartier Field to see Coach Leahy. Seeing Johnson approaching him, Leahy said, "Oh, Rodney, what seems to be the problem?"

In reply, Johnson said, "Coach, I have had a problem with my knee for 17 days. The doctor said it needed a cast."

"Oh Rodney," Leahy said, "those doctors are alarmists. They would put a cast on a wart."

The next day Johnson took the cast off himself. He missed the opening game against Indiana, but made the trip to Washington. At halftime, the team was struggling, so Leahy said to Johnson, "Rodney, are you ready?" Johnson played the rest of the game and kept playing the remainder of the season.

Leahy knew he had a winner in Bob Williams, his junior quarterback. Williams had been the understudy to Frank Tripucka during the 1948 season and, with a spring practice under his belt, he was ready to fill the role of his predecessors, Bertelli, Dancewicz, Lujack, and Tripucka.

Bob Williams

Williams, born in Cumberland, Maryland, attended Loyola High School in Towson, Maryland, where he was an all-around athlete earning All-State honors in baseball, basketball, and football. He made the prep All-America team in football his senior year.

Bob had his heart set on Notre Dame from the age of eight when he visited the campus with his brother Harold. Harold, a student at Notre Dame at the time, introduced the future star quarterback to Coach Elmer Layden during Bob's visit there. From then on Bob's dream was to play quarterback for the Irish. Despite Bob's committment to Notre Dame and his impressive credentials, Notre Dame did not aggressively recruit him. As Williams recalls, "I was lucky. I wanted to go to Notre Dame, but they didn't chase me. The first I heard of my acceptance was in June of my senior year. Charlie Callahan, the publicity director, told me that they were trying for some other player who went elsewhere and they called me to fill the slot."

Williams was lucky, but, indeed, Notre Dame was even luckier because Williams went on to have a brilliant career. That year he set a Notre Dame passing record, made the All-America team, and, in 1988, was elected to the College Hall of Fame.

The second casualty of summer practice was Leon Hart. Toward the end of the sessions on a particularly hot day, Leahy worked the squad exceptionally hard, no doubt on the lookout for those that wanted "to pay the price." As Hart started off the field, he became lightheaded and barely made it to the locker room where he collapsed. The next thing he knew, he was in a hospital room with Leahy looking down at him. He could barely hear what Leahy was saying. He finally heard Leahy say, "Leon, did you take your salt pills?" Leon replied, "Where do you get salt pills?"

We had never had salt pills available, but from that day forward there was a container with salt pills next to the drinking fountain in the locker room. Hart, as it turned out, had a 104-degree fever and a severe case of heat prostration. Despite being so sick, Hart was out for practice the following day.

The Irish planned to open the season with a new look. Instead of the usual huddle where the team circles the quarterback to get their signals, Leahy installed what became known as the "open huddle." The three running backs and ends lined up in a straight line with the tackles, guards, and center in front of them. The maneuver was designed to permit the team to look over their opponents while getting the next play, and enable them to run more plays per game. "The team that controls the ball usually wins the game," Leahy said.

Indiana

The Irish opened their season at home with an impressive display of offense in whipping Indiana, 49-6. Sitko, playing fullback for the first time in a regular game, opened the scoring on a beautifully executed counter-trap play over right tackle for a 17-yard touchdown run. Bob Toneff blocked an Indiana punt for a safety. The Hoosiers came back and scored on Milan Sellers' 17-yard end run for their only score.

In the second quarter, Bill Gay made a sensational over-the-shoulder catch of Williams' 28-yard pass to score, and it was all Notre Dame from then on. Sitko scored again on the same counter-trap play that he ran in the first quarter. Larry Coutre bulled his way to score on short yardage after Gay's 50-yard punt return. Sitko scored on a short plunge for his third touchdown and Bill Wightkin, with a Williams' pass, ended the Notre Dame scoring spree.

Leahy evaluated the players as he always did. He came to the conclusion that there was a back on the squad who would be more valuable to the team as a guard. With rare exceptions, a back did not look forward to switching to guard. It meant giving up forever the chance to carry the ball. It also entailed learning a new position under the toughest coach on the field, Joe McArdle, otherwise known as "Captain Bligh." More often than not, it also meant starting at the bottom.

A good example of this occurred during the week after the Indiana game. We were having our usual drills in which we were grouped by position. I was with the guards, who were some distance from the backs, when I happened to see a fellow Chicago teammate, Frank "Blackie" Johnston, running over to our area. Blackie, who was an All-State back from Leo High School in Chicago and had done well on the freshman team the year before, was running alone toward the area of the guards with his head down. He did not look too happy. I knew immediately what had happened to him and how he must feel, because I too had been switched from a back to guard several years before.

At the risk of incurring Coach McArdle's wrath, I broke ranks from the guards to meet Blackie part way. I hoped to make him feel welcome at his new position.

As we met, I put out my hand and said, "Welcome to the guards, Blackie."

Wearing a very sad face and in a sarcastic tone, he shot back, "Sure, the 15th right guard."

I said, "No, Blackie, congratulations, you lucked out—a guard just got hurt, you're now the 14th right guard."

Not too long ago I received a letter from Johnston who now resides in Toronto and he signed the letter, "Blackie, the 14th right guard." Some things you never forget. (Blackie was anything but the 14th right guard as he worked his way up the roster and earned his monogram the following year.)

Washington

Notre Dame was shocked early in its first away game when Washington's Don Heinrich found Roland Kirkby behind the Irish defenders and lofted a 55-yard touchdown pass to give the Huskies the early lead.

As the second quarter got under way with the Huskies still leading, Leahy knew he had to get some spark in the team to get momentum going his way. Hart, who did not start the game because of a severely sprained knee, was called to Leahy's side. "Leon," he said, "the chemistry of this game isn't right. I'm going to send you in the game and I want you to do something big to jolt the team. I'll get you out of the game as soon as I can."

Not long after Hart entered the game with the ball on Washington's 20, Williams sent him on a crossing pattern from his right-end position. As he was about to catch Williams' pass on about the five-yard line, he saw an official who was directly in his path. The official ducked and Hart caught the ball, arched his back over the bent-over official, and, with an acrobatic move, scored the needed touchdown. Leahy got his wish, a dramatic play that brought the Irish to life.

Leahy did take Hart out of the game. When Hart got to the sideline, Leahy said, "Well, Leon, you certainly follow instructions." (A few minutes later, Hart was put back in and played the remainder of the game.)

Despite their renewed enthusiasm, the Irish offense was stalled on several occasions, not by the Huskies' defense, but by the West Coast officials who repeatedly flagged Notre Dame for holding. An irate Leahy could do nothing about it other than to complain from the sideline.

In the third period, Hart scored again from Washington's six on an end-around play, dragging several defenders into the end zone. Coutre scored on a 30-yard burst up the middle. After Hart got to the Husky five on another end-around, Landry plunged over from the two on the first play of the fourth period to complete the scoring in Notre Dame's 30th consecutive game without a loss. The final score, ND 27, Washington 7.

Purdue

The Irish showed a great ground attack as they defeated Purdue, 35-12. Early in the game, with the ball on the Notre Dame four-yard line, Frank Spaniel skirted right end for 56 yards. Sitko, on the counter-trap play that was becoming one of Notre Dame's most productive plays, went off right guard for a 40-yard touchdown run.

Later, Coutre set up Sitko's second touchdown with a 39-yard run, allowing Sitko to bull into the end zone from the nine. Sitko scored his third touchdown of the day after taking a toss from Williams from the newly installed option play, and racing around end to score from the eight. Purdue took to the air, but to no avail as Gay intercepted a pass and sprinted 61 yards to score. John Helwig, playing linebacker, intercepted a Purdue pass to set up Barrett's six-yard touchdown run. Purdue scored two touchdowns in the fourth quarter after the Irish had scored all their points.

With Hart playing outstanding football, the sportswriters were writing about him almost on a daily basis. Leahy, aware that the publicity might start to affect him, went on a campaign to make sure he kept his accomplishments in perspective.

Hart did not know why, but Leahy started to pick on him at every little mistake and at times when there wasn't a mistake. One day in practice, Wightkin dropped a pass and Leahy said, "William Wightkin, take 10 laps." A short while later Hart dropped a pass only to hear Leahy say, "Leon, you follow William around the field."

A few days later Hart was leaving the field after a grueling practice when Leahy stopped him and asked, "Leon, how do you feel?"

"That was a tough practice, Coach, I'm a little tired."

"Oh, Leon, you must not be in proper shape, take 10 laps."

The following day Leahy was again waiting for Hart as he was leaving the practice field. "Leon, how do you feel?"

Not to be fooled again, Hart replied, "I feel great, Coach."

"Oh, Leon," Leahy said, "If you feel so good, you must not have had enough of a workout. Take 10 laps."

For the third day in a row Leahy was waiting for Hart at the end of practice. "How do you feel, Leon?"

Hart now searching for the right answer replied, "How do you want me to feel, Coach?"

That made even Leahy smile as he said, "You can go in, Leon."

Hart had a few days respite from Leahy's taunting ways before Leahy again started picking on him. One day he said to Druze, the end coach, "Coach Druze, I'm going to send Bob McBride [the tackle coach that replaced Moose Krause] to work on Leon. You're too easy on your players."

McBride and Hart lined up for their one-on-one blocking drill. McBride cheated on the count and hit Hart before he was out of his

253

three-point stance. Being hit this way hurt Hart's back because of the odd position he was in. They wrestled around and McBride ripped Hart's headgear off. As Hart leaned over to pick up his headgear, McBride hit him with his elbow and dislocated Hart's jaw.

Hart says, "I saw red. In an instant I remembered what happened to Zeke O'Connor in a one-on-one drill with Moose Krause several years before, and I wasn't going to let that happen to me. [Krause beat the hell out of O'Connor.] The next time I didn't wait for the signals and hit him just as he was about to begin the count. He fell down on all fours and I kept pounding him—I was going to kill him. He's hollering, 'You can't do this! You can't do this!' Leahy came running across the field, 'Leon, that's enough, that's enough! Coach Druze, stop them, separate them. Leon, you get back over and join the rest of the squad.'"

Hart was finally seperated from McBride, but you could still see the intense anger on his face. As Hart joined his fellow ends who had been intently watching the clash between coach and player, the rest of the squad went about their tasks, oblivious to the fight that had just taken place. Before the day was over, every player on the squad had received a blow-by-blow description of Hart's encounter with McBride from one of the eyewitness ends. The episode that day of a player nearly killing a coach ended Leahy's fixation with finding fault with Hart.

Tulane

Rockne would have been proud of his pupil as Leahy used all his skills of motivation in preparing the team for the invasion of the Green Wave from Tulane. The psychological ploys started with the scouting report given at the noon meeting on the Monday prior to the game. Assistants Bob McBride and John Druze had scouted Tulane, but it was Leahy who made most of the comments. "That tackle is so big and mean he is known to beat up on all the ends he has faced this year. Leon Hart, he makes you look small. I hear that he claims he'll have you out of the game in the first five minutes." And so went the report. According to Leahy, each Tulane player was the biggest, fastest player the team had ever faced. The Tulane team was reported to be the best team to come out of the South in 10 years.

During the practice sessions, Leahy kept up the barrage of warnings about how tough the Tulane players were with such comments as, "Rodney Johnson, if you block that way in the game Saturday, that Tulane player opposite you will kill our backs." In my four years at Notre Dame (1946-49), I never heard Leahy build up an opposing team more that he did that week. By game time Saturday he had the team at such an emotional level, you could almost feel the vibrations in the locker room as Leahy gave his last pitch to the players.

"Lads, this is the game we have been waiting and preparing for. This Tulane team thinks they can come to our field and shame us— don't let them do it. From the opening kickoff you must..." By the time Leahy finished his pre-game talk, the players were so fired up they could have run through the walls of the locker room.

Eight plays after the opening kickoff Notre Dame scored its first touchdown. The much-heralded Tulane Green Wave never was in the game, as the Irish won handily, 47-6.

A few years later when I was in the Marine Corps, I was stationed with one of the Tulane players. He described what it was like to play opposite Notre Dame in that game. "When you guys kicked off, we heard this eerie scream as your team came running down the field— it was scary. [What the player heard was an unplanned yell that came out of each ND player as he released the pent-up emotion.] I spotted my man to block and hit him as well as I have ever hit anyone one and I just bounced off. The guy ran right through me as if I wasn't there—I never experienced that before. After you had caused us to fumble twice and had scored both times, I looked around in the huddle and saw our backs with their heads down, as if to say, 'Don't call my play.' The game was only minutes old, but I knew we were a beaten team."

Notre Dame not only won the game, 47-6, but it crushed the spirit of the Tulane players. By the middle of the first quarter, the Irish had scored four touchdowns on Coutre runs of 14 and 81 yards plus a plunge of two yards and a Williams-to-Wightkin pass.

Billy Barrett, the short chunky sophomore, ended the scoring for the Irish on a 59-yard run. Notre Dame so outplayed Tulane that the visitors had a minus 23 yards rushing.

Leahy was quoted several days later as saying, "Maintaining the peak performance reached last Saturday will be close to an impossibility, but after witnessing the determination with which the team went about Saturday's assignment, I feel that the team that defeats Notre

Dame will have to play their best brand of football for 60 minutes, not 59. I can truthfully state that it was the greatest team victory with which we have ever been associated."

Navy

Notre Dame had a week off before playing Navy, which prompted various opinions to be expressed on what future opponent Leahy would personally scout. With such teams as Iowa, Southern Methodist, Michigan State, and Southern California yet to play, it was assumed that Leahy would scout one of these teams rather than Navy, which had been easily defeated by Wisconsin and Southern California. True to his statement, "We regard one game on our schedule as of equal importance with another," Leahy scouted the Navy game.

Notre Dame easily went through its 33rd consecutive game without a defeat by crushing an outclassed Navy team, 40-0. Williams, playing before his hometown fans in Baltimore, showed them why he was at the helm for the Irish when he threw a 49-yard touchdown pass to Ernie Zalejski early in the game. Before halftime, Notre Dame scored three more touchdowns: once on a brilliant 91-yard run by Coutre (only one yard short of Bob Livingstone's record 92-yard run in 1947); a 16-yard run by Sitko; and another Williams-to-Zalejski pass. Leahy played most of the reserves the second half and limited the play selection to basics plays. Despite playing conservative football, the Irish scored two more touchdowns on a 16-yard run by Landry and a 76-yard sprint by Zalejski.

Michigan State

The Spartans opened the game by marching down the field on some beautifully executed plays. Michigan State's unbalanced line and single-wing formation seemed to have the Irish baffled at the outset, but they quickly settled down and played tough defense. Fortunately for the Irish, they recovered a Michigan State fumble on their own four-yard line. After exchanging punts, Williams hit Zaleski with a 20-yard touchdown pass to put the Irish in the lead. A short time later, Williams fumbled on his five to allow the Spartans to score. Notre Dame mounted a drive that saw Coutre plunging over from the two for a 14-7 halftime lead.

Williams, executing the option play perfectly, found an opening to scamper 40 yards for a touchdown. Later, Sitko went in from the six and Williams found Hart in the end zone for the final Notre Dame tally. Michigan State fought back and scored twice, but it was not enough to prevent a Notre Dame victory, 34-21.

North Carolina

It took Notre Dame until the third quarter to pull ahead and finally win, 42-6, over a stubborn North Carolina team. The first time Williams punted for Notre Dame it was blocked and North Carolina went on to score to take a 6-0 lead. The Tar Heels scored on a "student body" left-type of play through Hart's position at right end. Hart, in recalling the play, said, " Their touchdown was scored over me and I really felt bad about that. Their guard put the best block on me I ever had put on me—he got to my midsection and drove me right out. Years later, the guy came up to me and said, 'I'm the guard who blocked you when we [North Carolina] scored on you. Do you remember?'

"I told him it was the best block anyone ever put on me. He smiled and was so happy to hear it that I was glad I said it."

Later in the game, the Irish had the ball deep in their own territory on the 24, where it was fourth down and three. Williams, who had iron nerves when it came to play selection, called for a pass. There was an audible gasp from the players in the huddle who were well aware that, if the play failed, Leahy's wrath would hold no bounds. Added to their concern was the fact that the pass was a swing pass to Larry Coutre, who could not see well without his glasses.

The concern was obviously also on Williams' mind. After he called the play, he said, "Larry, if you don't catch my pass, just keep running because I'm going to run the other way out of the stadium—Leahy will be after both of us."

Fortunately, Williams threw a perfect pass to Coutre, who caught the ball and picked up the first down with plenty to spare. The Irish scored on a 78-yard Spaniel run to tie the score at 6-6, where it remained until the third quarter. A Williams-to-Hart 10-yard hook pass and lateral to Barrett covered 45 yards and broke the tie. Oddly, the play was not a designed play. In the huddle before the play, Hart told Barrett to follow him for a lateral, which is exactly what happened. A couple of minutes later, the Irish ran the same play with similar results. Needless to say, the play was put in the play book for the remainder of the season. The Irish dominated the game from that point on.

One of the highlights of the game was an interception by Mike Swistowicz, who, with some outstanding blocking from Lally, Toneff, Jim Mutscheller, and the rest of the squad, returned the ball 85 yards for a touchdown. In commenting about that play after the game, Leahy said, "A friend told me he saw 22 Notre Dame blocks on that play. Each player got his man and then did it over again."

At one point, the ball was on the one-foot line and the Irish were ready to punch over the goal line. One of the North Carolina linemen said, "Start saying your Hail Marys." The Irish scored. As the teams were lining up for the extra-point try, one of the Notre Dame linemen, rubbing in the fact that they had scored, started to say the Hail Mary in a loud voice. In the meantime, Paul Burns, playing offensive guard, not only blocked the Carolina player who had made the crack about the Hail Marys, but drove him to the ground several yards into the end zone.

When the blocked Carolina player got to his feet, he was evidently so embarrassed by the block that he started to chase one of the Notre Dame players down the sideline to get some retribution. Burns, seeing this, took off after the Carolina player to protect his teammate. Near the Notre Dame bench the Carolina player slowed down and Burns grabbed him and started to pound him on the headgear before the fight was broken up.

At the noon meeting the following Monday, Leahy said, "Oh, lads, I like the loyalty on this team protecting your teammates, but for Heaven's sake, Paul Burns, if you're going to hit him—take his helmet off."

Iowa

Notre Dame defeated an always tough Iowa team, 28-7, for its eighth victory. Williams tossed a 20-yard touchdown pass to Spaniel for the first score. Iowa came right back and tied it in the second quarter, but Notre Dame's Barrett scored on a seven-yard end run before halftime. In the fourth quarter, backed up on his own five-yard line, Williams hit Spaniel on a pass that covered 55 yards. Spaniel, on the same drive, scored from close in to make it 21-7, Notre Dame. Hart ended the scoring on a 15-yard pass from Williams.

Southern California

The Notre Dame team was anxious to play the Trojans to erase from their minds the 14-14 tie from the previous season. Williams opened the scoring by throwing a beautiful touchdown pass to Hart, covering 40 yards. The Trojans, trying to mount an attack, had a pass intercepted by Petitbon, who ran 48 yards down the sideline to score. When Barrett recovered a fumble, Leahy unveiled the secret weapon that the team had been working on all week in practice—Hart playing fullback. On the first play after the fumble, Williams handed off to Hart, who rammed into the line carrying three defenders for seven yards. On the next play, Williams again appeared to handoff to Hart, who faked into the line, allowing Sitko to go wide for the score. Spaniel and Barrett each scored on short plunges to make the final score, ND 32, USC 0.

Southern Methodist

With SMU's star halfback, Doak Walker, out of the game because of injuries, Kyle Rote was the dominant player for the Mustangs, scoring all three of their touchdowns. SMU was in the game right to the finish, but Notre Dame prevailed, 27-20, to keep its 38-game undefeated streak intact. The Irish took the lead on Williams' 42-yard pass to Wightkin and his 35-yard pass to Zalejski. Rote brought SMU back with his brilliant running and passing. Barrett scored from the three to give Notre Dame a 20-7 lead after three quarters, but Rote scored twice early in the fourth period to get the Mustangs even at 20-20. Spaniel ran the ensuing kickoff back to the Irish 44 and Notre Dame moved down the field on the running of Sitko and Barrett and the bull-like rushes of Hart playing fullback. As Williams recalls, "Leon wasn't that familiar with the fullback plays. In the huddle, I'd just tell him 'go to my left' or 'go to my right,' so I wouldn't get killed." After a fake to Hart up the middle, Williams handed off to Barrett, who scored the winning touchdown by sweeping left end from the six.

Because of Rote's play in that game, he was a unanimous All-Opponent selection by the Notre Dame team. Years later, when the 1949 team celebrated the 25th anniversary of its National Championship season, Kyle Rote was the guest of the players and was named an honorary team member.

259

The 1949 Irish led the nation in total offense with 434.8 yards per game. Based on their record of 10-0-0 and their outstanding year, Notre Dame was awarded the National Championship by the largest margin of votes ever accorded any team in the history of the Associated Press poll.

For those members of the team who had started in 1946—Bill Wightkin, Jim Martin, Al Zmijewski (later Al Adam), Bob Lally, Ralph McGehee, Gus Cifelli, Leon Hart, Ray Espenan, Frank Spaniel, Ernie Zalejski, Larry Coutre, Red Sitko, Ed Hudak, Steve Oracko, Mike Swistowicz, Gerry Begley, George Dickson, and Jack Connor—it had been quite a ride; they'd gone four years without a defeat and had won three National Championships.

Martin, McGehee, Hart, Coutre, Sitko, Oracko, Swistowicz, Doug Waybright (1944, 1947, 1948, and 1949) and Walter Grothaus (1944, 1947, 1948, and 1949) joined the very select group of Notre Dame football players that had won four football monograms.

Sitko was named to the All-America team for the second straight year as well as placing eighth in the Heisman balloting. He also led the team in rushing for an unprecedented fourth year in a row, a Notre Dame record that is still intact. Emil "Red" Sitko died in 1971; he was elected to the Hall of Fame posthumously in 1984. Red was a great teammate, fun to be with, and without a doubt the most modest player on the squad.

Jim Martin, who unselfishly switched to tackle after starting at end for three years, made the All-America team—a much deserved honor. Martin could do it all. He was a devastating blocker on offense, especially downfield, and more than most players could handle on defense. He was as tough on the field as he was pleasant off the field. Currently he is on the ballot for election to the Hall of Fame— a much deserved and overdue honor.

Bob Williams, in his first year as the starting quarterback, was sensational. He was elected to the All-America team and placed fifth in the Heisman balloting. He led the team in passing by completing 83 of 147 attempts for 1,347 yards and 16 touchdowns, breaking Angelo Bertelli's 1942 records for yardage and touchdowns. John Huarte broke Williams' pass yardage record in 1964 and tied his touchdown pass record.

In 1970, Joe Theismann also passed for 16 touchdowns and, in 1991, Rick Mirer set the existing record with 18 touchdown passes.

Williams' single season Passing Efficiency Rating (passes, completions, yardage, touchdowns, and interceptions) of 161.4 is still the Notre Dame record. He was an All-American again in 1950 and was sixth in the Heisman voting. Bob was elected to the Hall of Fame in 1988. He was the sixth Notre Dame quarterback to be so honored (Carideo, Stuhldreyer, Lujack, Bertelli, Hornung, and Williams).

The name "Bob Williams" has no unique ring to it like "Marchy Schwartz" or "Bill Shakespeare" and he is by far the most anonymous of Notre Dame's Hall-of-Famers. He is often confused with the Bob Williams who quarterbacked the Irish in the late 1950s and was the architect of ND's monumental 7-0 victory over Oklahoma in 1957. "Many times when I've been introduced as a former Notre Dame quarterback, people have asked about the Oklahoma game," Williams says.

He also tells an amusing story about what happened in 1988 when the public announcement of his Hall of Fame induction was to be made at halftime of a Notre Dame game. "That morning, a friend was looking for me and went into the athletic offices to ask where I was. They asked him, 'Who's Bob Williams?'"

Leon Hart made the All-America team for the third consecutive year. He led the team in receiving for the second consecutive year and was awarded the Heisman Trophy as the outstanding player in the nation. In winning the award, he became the third Notre Dame player to receive the Heisman and only the second lineman in the history of the award ever to be so honored (Larry Kelly of Yale won it in 1936).

Hart was voted the Associated Press Male Athlete of the Year. In addition, he received the following awards: the Maxwell Trophy, Philadelphia Sportswriters Trophy, *Los Angeles Times* Award, and the *Detroit Times* Award. He was elected to the National Football Foundation Hall of Fame on January 7, 1973.

Bill Wightkin, the other end, had an outstanding year. He caught some clutch passes during the season and was tremendous on both offense and defense. Many of the sportswriters who covered the Irish games were of the opinion that Wightkin would have been a surefire All-American if it were not for the fact that Leon Hart was the other end. His teammates agreed with this assessment of Wightkin.

Bill Gay led the team in punt return average and interceptions for the second straight year. Sophomore Bill Barrett and Red Sitko tied for the team lead in points scored with 54.

Walter Grothaus had a difficult time eating for several days following the final game because of 23 stitches required to close a gash in his mouth. As an understudy for Bill Walsh in his first three years, Grothaus played excellent football. As the starting center on the 1949 team, he came into his own as one of the best blocking centers in the nation. When I see him at our reunions, I always remind him that he was offside on almost every offensive play.

Grothaus worked hard at perfecting his craft. He refined the technique for centering the ball and getting off the line to a point where he did it all in one motion and a half count ahead of the actual snap count. The effect of his innovation was that he actually started moving as he was snapping the ball, so that his body preceded the ball by a fraction of a second. Grothaus was an outstanding blocker without any advantage, but, with his technique, he was unbeatable to the man playing opposite him.

Leahy's move of switching Martin to tackle and starting Wightkin at left end proved to be a brilliant stroke, as Wightkin and Martin had outstanding years. The move of McGehee to right tackle also proved to be the right move, as he was outstanding blocking both on the line and downfield. McGehee was not as big as most tackles, but what he lacked in size, he made up for with a fierce determination to get his man.

Rodney Johnson was solid at left guard, filling the big shoes of the departed All-American, Bill Fischer, as were Wallner and Lally, playing the other guard for the departed Marty Wendell.

Newcomers Toneff, Petitbon, Burns, Mutscheller, and Barrett had great years, as did the veterans, Coutre, Spaniel, Zalejski, Groom, Landry, Gay, and Swistowicz.

Individually, the players performed at a higher level than even the coaches had anticipated. But more than that, was the way the team performed as a whole. Although there were individual stars, the thing that impressed everyone was the way the players played as a unit. They pulled together and had the type of chemistry that made them the champions that they were. Every victory was truly a team victory.

After the season was over, the team suffered a tremendous blow when Ray Espenan, a three-year monogram winner, died as a result of an accident. Espenan, a senior from New Orleans, was student teaching in South Bend when he suffered a broken neck practicing on the trampoline. He lived only days before he succumbed to the severity of his injury. Ray was a superb athlete, participating in football and track for four years. Along with Bill Higgins and several other members of the squad, I had the pleasure of sharing his company on many occasions during the off-time of summer practice that year. He was a delight to be with and, as we learned, a deeply spiritual man.

The spirit of that team is still going strong some 44 years later. Leon Hart, the co-captain, conscientiously keeps in contact with his teammates with the able assistance of another of the players, Dan Modak, who puts out a timely newsletter. Each of us tries to help in keeping the spirit alive, not just for the sake of nostalgia, but knowing the men of that team were—and are—a great group of men.

The conclusion of the 1949 season brought to an end the Golden Age of Notre Dame football (1946-49)—38 consecutive games without a defeat and three National Championships. It also concluded the era of the 1940s that saw Leahy coach seven years and lose only three games.

The Old-Timers' Game

At the conclusion of spring practice following the 1949 season, the traditional Old-Timers' Game was played. Ziggie, as usual, was up to mischief that had Coach Leahy talking to himself.

Ziggie, who had made the trip from Chicago for the game, wanted to have the entrance of the Old-Timers' squad as dramatic as the one in the hearse two years before. He managed to borrow one of the city's fire engines for his pre-game antics. He also arranged to have a long rod attached to the front of the engine with a child-sized toy fire engine attached in front of the rod. This would give the appearance of the toy engine pulling the regular engine, when, in reality, it was being pushed by the big engine. The stage was set.

George Connor, Ziggie's frequent cohort in crazy stunts, also traveled from Chicago to see his pal make his grand entrance. George, who had not practiced since the Chicago Bears' season ended that previous fall, had no intention of playing in the game. As he walked across the campus, he encountered Bob Dove, another Notre Dame all-time great who had been an All-American end in 1941 and 1942. Bob, too, was playing professional football and had not practiced since the fall.

"Are you going to play today?" Dove asked George.

"I'll play if you play," responded George, thinking that there was no way Dove would play.

A short time later when George went into the locker room to visit with some of his old buddies, he was surprised to see Dove drawing his football equipment. To honor his word, George went to MacAllister and drew his gear. Typical of MacAllister, he did not have to ask either Connor or Dove their sizes; he remembered their exact size for every piece of equipment.

Connor and Dove joined Ziggie and the rest of the team to get Ziggie's instructions for their entrance. Following Ziggie's plan, the team assembled at the ramp leading to the field. Ten of the starters for the Old-Timers took their positions on the fire engine while Ziggie sat on the engine.

The varsity squad was on the field and ready for the kickoff, but the Old-Timers' squad was not yet in sight. Leahy was having a fit on the sidelines. He yelled at the referee to get the game started. Seeing the ref approaching the ramp, Ziggie, with his flair for timing, knew the time was now. With a shrill blast from the fire engine siren to alert the crowd, Ziggie gave the word for the two engines to proceed onto the field. The crowd went wild with laughter and cheers as Ziggie, sitting on the little engine, waved to the crowd as the engines made their way to midfield. Leahy, who believed that a football field was sacred ground and not to be used for pranks, had to turn his back on Ziggie's grand entrance.

Despite the pre-game antics by the Old-Timers, they put their game faces on when the whistle blew to signal the kickoff. As with the game two years before, the Old-Timers again defeated the varsity. Connor caught a tackle-eligible pass to score the winning touchdown. Ziggie, of course, saved his energy to star at the Old-Timers' party held that evening.

Chapter Fourteen

LOOKING BACK—THE COACHES

Frank Leahy

After the 1949 season, Leahy would go on to coach for four more years, but not with the success he had enjoyed during the 1940s. With the loss of 16 monogram winners, three All-Americans, and a Heisman winner from the 1949 team, the next season (1950) was the worst season in Leahy's career (record of 4-4-1). He lost more games in that one year than in his seven previous seasons.

It was not just the loss of so many top players from the 1949 team that caused Leahy's problem in 1950; he was the victim of the numbers game in recruiting going back to 1947. He was only allowed 18 football scholarships that year and for most of the succeeding years. Five of those recruited in 1947 left Notre Dame to play elsewhere. Some got hurt and some just quit football altogether, leaving only 10 players that stayed on to become seniors in 1950. The entire varsity football squad had fewer than 50 players that year. There was not a sufficient number of experienced players to lead the team to a successful season.

Leahy continued coaching until the end of the 1953 season. During the 1953 Georgia Tech game, the fourth game of the season, he collapsed at halftime, causing deep concern at the time that he might die. He even received the last rites of the Catholic Church.

Leahy was taken to a hospital where his ailment was diagnosed as gastroenteritis. Fortunately, he recovered and was able to make it through the season. On January 31, 1954, however, at the age 45, he officially resigned.

There is no question that Leahy was asked to resign by Father Hesburgh and Father Joyce when they met with him at Father

Hesburgh's request in late January 1954. Leahy, never one to embarrass his beloved university, acquiesced. Leahy had every intention of returning for the 1954 season. A week before the announcement of his retirement, Bob Kelly (1943-44) stopped at school to have lunch with Bill Earley, the backfield coach. As it turned out, Leahy went with them and, while at lunch, gave Earley instructions on what he wanted him to do in preparation for spring practice. It was evident by his remarks that he planned to be back, but the university had other ideas.

Whether Leahy should have been asked to resign because of his health problems, no doubt brought about because of his intense involvement in coaching, or whether he could have continued on in the profession he loved so much, is not a matter for this book. Suffice it to say—Leahy was never the same after leaving Notre Dame.

Despite his relative youth, Leahy had secured his place in the annals of college football. Leahy coached at Notre Dame a total of 11 years, winning four undisputed National Championships (1943, 1946, 1947, and 1949—the 1953 team, with a record of 9-0-1, was second to Maryland in the AP and UP polls, but was first in other polls). His 87-11-9 record at Notre Dame is second only to that of Knute Rockne.

As head coach of Boston College and Notre Dame, Leahy led the Eagles and the Irish to 107 victories; far outweighing their 13 losses and nine ties. Only Rockne had compiled a higher won-lost percentage among major college football coaches.

In addition, Leahy's teams went undefeated in 39 straight games—a Notre Dame record. His teams were unbeaten six of the 11 years he coached at Notre Dame. Thirty-six players at Notre Dame won All-American honors during his tenure. Four of Leahy's players—Angelo Bertelli, John Lujack, Leon Hart, and Johnny Lattner were named Heisman Award winners. Eleven of his former players have been selected for the National Football Foundation's Hall of Fame. They are: Angelo Bertelli, Creighton Miller, John Lujack, George Connor, Ziggie Czarobski, Red Sitko, Bill Fischer, Leon Hart, Bob Williams, John Lattner, and Jerry Groom. As of this date, two more are under consideration for selection: Bob Dove and Jim Martin.

Among Leahy's many accomplishments are: five Coach of the Year awards, coach four times of the College All-Stars (twice as an assistant and twice as head coach), and entry into the National Football Foundation's Hall of Fame on December 8, 1970. Outside the sphere of athletics, he enjoyed several other honors. He is believed to be the first person in the field of athletics to be named a Knight of Malta (in 1951 he was so honored by Pope Pius XII), and he seconded the nomination of General Eisenhower at the Republican Convention in 1956.

Some of his coaching innovations include: the first college team to run from an erect stance; the first college team to use the pro-type zone defense; the double quarterback; optional blocking assignments for linemen on the same running play; audible signals from the line; and the open huddle.

Although Leahy never again coached after the 1953 season, his mind was never far away from the game he loved. In 1958, he came close to getting back into coaching when he considered the head coaching position at Texas A&M. While visiting the school officials on the campus of Texas A&M, Leahy and the school authorities reached an understanding that he would become the head football coach. At Leahy's suggestion, there would be no publicity surrounding the agreement until he had time to go to the Mayo Clinic for a physical checkup.

While at Mayo's, just the thought of getting back into coaching caused his blood pressure to soar. On the basis of his elevated blood pressure, the doctors advised him not to coach. Leahy reluctantly agreed and so notified the Texas A&M officials, thus canceling their tentative agreement. He never realistically entertained the idea of coaching again.

How good a coach was Leahy? His record speaks for itself. Not even the greats among the ancients such as Dobie, Yost, Haughton, Warner, Stagg, Howard Jones, or Zuppke achieved the results that Leahy did. Even his contemporaries, Bernie Bierman, Earl Blaik, Fritz Crisler, Carl Snavely, Wallace Wade, Bob Neyland, Lou Little, and Jock Sutherland, could not match Leahy's record.

The question becomes—did he have more football talent to work with than the coaches he competed against, or was the difference his ability as a coach? There is no question that Notre Dame attracted excellent material during Leahy's tenure, but it is equally true that other coaches were at schools that attracted excellent material too. Added to this is the fact that the Irish always had the more difficult schedule. Despite this, other coaches lost games on a regular basis. When Notre Dame lost, it was sensational news.

In 1949, Red Grange, the legendary "Galloping Ghost" of Illinois and Chicago Bear fame who kept abreast of college football in the times when Leahy coached, summarized best the opinions of most football experts about Leahy. When asked why Notre Dame was the number one team in the country, Grange responded, "Because of Frank Leahy. Frank gets good material. But that isn't the answer. I think other universities get comparable talent, especially big schools like Michigan, Ohio State, California, Minnesota, and Illinois. Leahy gets more out of his material than other coaches."

He went on to say that Leahy produced better players because of long hours of hard work, training, and instruction. "Look at the succession of outstanding quarterbacks Frank has had," continued Grange. "That isn't an accident. It's the result of hard work. He takes equal pains with candidates for every other position. Frank is a perfectionist—his players seldom make a mistake. Conversely, if an opponent makes a mistake against Notre Dame, it likely will cost the game."

Vince Lombardi, recognized as one of football's greatest coaches, also said that Leahy was a superb teacher of football. In the early 1970s, Jerry Groom ran into Lombardi in the airport in St. Louis. As Groom tells it, "He and his wife, Marie, and I spent an hour visiting. We got to talking about Leahy. Vince told me Leahy was the single most important influence on his life in football. [Lombardi was one of the Seven Blocks of Granite at Fordham—Leahy was his line coach.] He said everything he knew—all the basics, the philosophy, all the intricate parts of football, he learned from Leahy."

Certain characteristics signaled Leahy's teams. A hallmark of a Leahy coached team was that it was in superb condition. From the first day of summer practice until the last day of the season, you ran, ran, and ran. You started by running from the entrance gate of Cartier Field to midfield. You paused only to pick up your helmet before you reached your assigned group. When you ran plays, whether live or dummy scrimmage, you had to run not only full speed, you had to turn up field and sprint another 30 to 40 yards. No matter the position played, you had to run full speed at all times.

This constant running produced a group of players that were in superb condition. As the season wore on, the players seemed to get stronger as they were honed to a fine edge. Leahy liked speed in his linemen and through this constant sprinting, all the linemen could really move out going downfield. As you watch old films, it is amazing to see four and five men downfield on all but the quick openers. There is nothing more demoralizing for a defensive back than to see two or three big, fast, tough linemen bearing down on him.

As Bernie Crimmins once said, "Remember, we scrimmaged a great deal. We evaluated every player over and over, hour after hour. It was the same for every position. Frank had his own evaluations, but he always gave the assistant coaches the opportunity to express their feelings about the players they thought had the ability plus the desire to work hard and to win football games. He always felt that going into the fourth quarter you rely on a guy who was out there giving it everything he had and was in a little better condition. He felt if you were willing to give a little extra all the time it would pay off in the games. He said a lot of games are won in the fourth quarter because of the ability to out-hit the other guy."

Leahy played tackle during his student days under Knute Rockne and later coached the line at Fordham. With this background he knew and appreciated line play as well as any coach in football. He wanted all his linemen not only to be hard-nosed blockers, but also to master the techniques of blocking for the player's particular position.

Leahy never believed in running up the score on an opponent. However, he did believe in holding the opposing team to as few points as possible. Leahy loved defense and was known by his fellow coaches as a genius in defensive strategy.

He was a master at designing defenses to counter whatever type of offense the other team used. Immediately after a Saturday game, he began work on next week's game. By Sunday night, Leahy usually had his defense in place. He had learned that his Monday mornings were interrupted constantly by calls from his coaching friends around the country. They would be seeking advice about the defense they should use for their opposition that coming Saturday. Leahy could be seen in his office with the phone in one hand and with a pad of paper covered by X's and O's in the other. Jim Tatum, the head coach at Maryland, and Wally Butts of Georgia were regular Monday-morning callers.

From 1941-49, Leahy coached seven seasons (missing two, 1944 and 1945, because of the war). In those seven seasons his teams compiled a record of 60 wins, three losses, and five ties. The statistics that are most amazing for these 68 games are the defensive ones. In 24 of the games the opponents were held scoreless; or to put it another way, in over one-third of the games, the opposing team could not score a point. In another 24 of these games the opposing team scored seven or fewer points. Combining these two statistics reveals that in 48 of the 68 games played, or slightly over 70 percent, the opponents scored an average of fewer than five points a game.

In the 1946 season there was a total of 24 points scored against Notre Dame in the nine games played. No one scored more than six points—which means there was not an extra point or field goal scored against the team for the entire season. That team was nationally ranked as the number one team on defense with a scoring defense of 2.7 points per game. This team still holds the modern Notre Dame record for the fewest points scored by opponents in a single season.

It was not that Leahy's defenses were so complicated. On the contrary, they were simple in design geared to stop the main thrust of the opponent's attack. In preparing for an upcoming game, Leahy would have John Druze scout the other team. The first thing Leahy would ask him when he returned for their Sunday coaches' meeting was how did he think the team would do against that opponent. One time Druze said, "I think we can beat them by three or four touchdowns."

Leahy shot back, "Oh, Coach Druze, don't say things like that. We haven't played them yet. No, you're not supposed to talk that way."

Then Leahy would ask Druze this question. "What three things do we have to do to defeat our enemy?" Eventually the coaches would agree on the three main parts of the opposing offense they had to stop. Once they had that decided, they put in the defensive scheme that they would use for that game. Once designed, the main ingredients of the defense were: execution, tough one-on-one battles, and discipline to protect the area of responsibility assigned.

Leahy would instruct the scout, usually Druze, to embellish the size and abilities of the opposition for the team scouting report given on Mondays at the noon meeting. If a player was 6-foot-3, he became 6-foot-5, and if a passer was pretty good, he became the greatest passer ever to come out of the particular conference he played in. Crimmins said, "If one listened to the reports the scouts gave the coaches, and then listened to the one the team heard, it wasn't even close."

Like most coaches, Leahy loved the offensive side of football, and it is there that his real genius as a coach could be seen. He was innovative in his design of plays to exploit the other team's weakness, or to take advantage of his team's strengths. A good example of the latter was the use of Hart as a fullback. When Hart played fullback, Sitko would take his place at right end. Hart would pound the middle for yardage, but the follow-up play, an end-around with Sitko carrying the ball, was the big gainer and game breaker.

For every game he would design special plays. More often than not, the special plays were not needed. By the end of the season we would have a notebook full of these special plays.

However, Leahy knew that a championship team must first have a strong defense. The record bears him out. His four National Championship teams allowed the opponents an average of slightly less than 58 points a season as contrasted to the teams of the 1950s which allowed 151 points. In the 1960s, opponents averaged 131 points per season. It is interesting to note that Ara Parseghian's 1966 National Championship Notre Dame team allowed the opponents only 38 total points—proving again that championship teams start with a good defense.

It was obvious to any observer of a Notre Dame team in those years that all Leahy's players were well trained in the fundamentals of football—namely blocking, tackling, recovering a fumble, handling the ball, snapping the football, and all the other basics. He used to say, "Every time you apply a block or tackle, I want you to thump him. Thump him so hard that he will wish he was up in the stands watching the game with his parents."

According to Bernie Crimmins, "Everything he did was detailed. As far as playing quarterback was concerned, every movement was orchestrated starting with the snap of the ball and the way you took the ball from center and got it into your body to precisely how the ball was handed off. Each maneuver—a spin, reverse spin, a pitch-out, no matter what—was planned down to the exact number of inches the quarterback would move his feet. We made the quarterbacks spin and then spin faster using their hips and shoulders. Everything was timed. These details were important to Frank.

"He put an awful lot of stress on technique at every position. He used to say, 'In order to get the point across, you have to stress your point through constant repetition. Even if you think you have gone over it enough, do it again. Then they will get the job done.' Another thing Leahy stressed was asking why. 'Why did you do that, why?' Even with the coaching staff he would ask, 'Why did you do that?'

"I have watched workouts at different universities and they just don't go through the fundamentals that well. They don't stress that anymore, but Frank sure did and it paid off for him."

Leahy once told Leon Hart, years after Hart had played, when they were discussing coaching philosophy, "Leon, some coaches forget there are three phases to coaching. You tell the young lad what to do and how to do it. That's where most coaches stop. The great coaches will tell the player why he is doing it that way."

On a Leahy-coached team there was discipline. Not just the matters one usually thinks about concerning discipline—being on time, staying in condition, and following the rules laid down by the coaches—but mental discipline. Rarely, for example, did one see a Leahy-coached player miss the snap count and go offside, forget or mix up his assignment, loaf at any time, or fail to hold his position on defense.

Leahy demanded sacrifice from his players. He worked them hard, but he worked as hard himself, often working into the wee hours of the morning. He was a meticulous planner and never wanted to leave any detail unattended. He understood all facets of the game down to the last detail. He studied the basics of each position, always thinking of small ways to improve the technique involved. For example, when he installed the T-formation he put the foot movements in chalk on the floor down to the last eighth of an inch. He then taught his assistants the details and expected them to impart this knowledge to the players on the practice field. After partaking of one spring practice, every quarterback could spin, reverse spin, and do all the moves exactly as Leahy had drawn the move. He left nothing to chance.

He planned each game as a general would prepare for a battle, and that is exactly what it was to him—a battle between two forces. He thought in terms of a fighter in the ring—always prepared to go the distance, but always alert to apply the knockout punch that would put his opponent away.

Leahy's one discernible weakness as a coach was his inability, at times, to keep his composure on the sidelines during a game. He would get so hyper that he oftentimes would lose his concentration and get confused. A good example of his mental lapses occurred in the 1949 SMU game. George Dickson, a reserve quarterback who would later go on to coach for many years in the NFL, explains what happened: "There were about five minutes to play with the score tied at 20-20. Jack Landry was in the game in place of Red Sitko. I saw the way their defense was spread out, so I suggested to Bill Earley that a 32 counter up the middle should go like hell. I spotted Sitko, our best back, on the bench.

"I said to Earley, 'You should put Sitko in the game,' thinking he was the perfect one to run the 32 counter. Earley asked, 'Did the old man say so?'

"I told him no. He suggested I tell Leahy. So I went up to Leahy, who didn't seem to be with it, and asked, 'Coach, don't you want Sitko in the game?'

"Leahy seemed to come out of his haze and almost shouted, 'Oh my God, yes, get him in the game!'

"Sitko did go in and was mainly responsible for our getting the ball down inside their 10-yard line, where Billy Barrett scored the winning touchdown."

There are numerous examples of Leahy's lapses on the sidelines, but usually it played no significant role in the outcome. The meticulous preparation for a game for which Leahy was known more than made up for his sideline failings. The one notable exception was his mental lapse during the 1948 Southern California game which might have cost the team a victory and a possible National Championship.

Apart from the more obvious aspects of Leahy's teams, the Irish enjoyed another advantage because of Leahy's inclination to disguise the true weight, and sometimes the height, of his players. In the Notre Dame football program and other press releases, most of the linemen, and occasionally a back, were listed at weights substantially below their actual weights. Leahy did this deliberately to confuse the opponents. This type of deception was consistent with his pattern of pessimism in dealing with the press. He seemed to be saying, "See, we are not that big either."

Leahy's underreporting of the players' weights continues to play havoc with football historians. Consider the writer who conscientiously reviews the old programs and press releases in an effort to be accurate. He is tricked into thinking the players were lighter than they were and this inevitably leads to faulty conclusions when comparing the size of these teams to others. Unfortunately, as these writers write about the weights of players of that era, they perpetuate the myth that these players were not very big.

It seems that Leahy never forgot anything he ever heard. In 1940, he went to West Warwick, Rhode Island, to recruit Jim Mello for Boston College where he was then coaching. After Leahy eloquently expounded on the virtues of a college education, Mello's father, a Portuguese grocery store owner, retorted in his broken English, "Mr. Leahy, that's a fine—ed-u-ca-shun—but you know a man's a best friend is money in his pocket."

Upon graduation from Notre Dame in 1947, Mello went to see Leahy to say goodbye. According to Mello, Leahy congratulated him on his stay at Notre Dame and added, "Never forget your dad's philosophy on money in the pocket."

Norman (Jack) Barry, the son of Norman Barry Sr., a teammate of George Gipp's on the 1920 National Championship team, played end on the 1940 and 1941 teams. After the war, Jack returned to the Notre Dame campus to attend law school. Leahy appointed Jack as coach of the Notre Dame B squad. Jack recently recalled a story about Leahy:

"I took the B team to East Lansing to play the Michigan State B team. We lost, 21-13. On Monday morning I was in my 8 A.M. Tort class when the senior football manager came into the classroom saying that Coach Leahy wanted to see me. I told him I would go after class. 'He said he wants to see you now!' I went to Breen-Phillips Hall and was ushered into his office immediately. He said, 'What happened to you up there?' I replied, 'Coach, they had a large number of very large and good football players.' For the next half hour he gave me a thorough critique of why one does not use a five-man defense against the Z-formation.

"Several years later, I went to East Lansing to see Notre Dame play Michigan State. It was one of the worst losses he had ever suffered. After the press had cleared out, I went to the locker room and told him how sorry I was about the game. He immediately replied, 'Jack, you were right. They have a lot of good players.' I was amazed that the loss of a B-team game would still be in his memory bank."

Leahy not only recalled what he heard but also what he saw. His memory was phenomenal. It was not just the games he remembered, but he seemed to remember in detail every practice session. One Sunday in 1946, when I was a freshman and had played a season on the B team, I was on the South Shore train on my way back to South Bend from my home in Chicago. Leahy boarded the train at Michigan City and sat next to me. After exchanging pleasantries, his first comment was, "That was quite a block you threw on Corwin Clatt early in the season."

It was one of my shining moments and I remember it vividly, but I couldn't believe that Leahy remembered it. He was referring to a scrimmage during the second week of the season when the B team was running the next opponent's plays against the varsity. I was flanked wide and had a crack-back block on the linebacker who was Clatt. Here I was, a B-team player, which meant that in relation to the ranking of talent on the practice field, I was as about as far down the line as could be, and yet he could recall that one good block from the thousands of such blocks that were executed on Cartier Field during the course of the season. I am quite confident he could have recalled the others if put to the test.

Leahy's biggest fault was his inability to relax and enjoy life. He thought about football constantly, all during the year, not just the spring practice and the fall, but all year. According to Crimmins, "He rarely loosened up with the assistant coaches. Once in a great while, maybe after a great victory he'd loosen up a little bit, but nine out of 10 times, no. He was strictly business."

Leahy was a worrier and a pessimist. As far back as when he coached at Boston College, he was a worrier. On the day of one of the BC games while Leahy was coach, Jack Leahy, his nephew, and Bill Sullivan, the sports information director (later owner of the New England Patriots), were sitting in the kitchen in Leahy's Waban, Massachusetts, home. Leahy came over to the table and said, "I don't know how you two can sit here and eat bacon and eggs and all that food when we have this tough game today. How can you do it? I can't even get a cup of coffee down." (Boston College was playing St. Anslem's that day.)

It seems that his obsession with football caused Leahy not to be interested in food, at least during the football season. Bernie Crimmins, John Druze, Moose Krause, and the other coaches had very healthy appetites and enjoyed eating. Crimmins recalls, "After living with him at the firehouse for quite a while, I would get up with him and say, 'Let's go to breakfast,' and he would answer, 'Just get me some coffee and bring me a doughnut.'

"Then at lunchtime, I'd say, 'Coach, you need some food,' and he would say, 'Bernard, someday you are going to weigh 400 pounds the way you like to eat.' I would volunteer to bring him back something and his reply would be, 'Bring me a bean sandwich or just a few slices of bread and a can of beans, that would be great.'

"The next time at lunch he would say, 'I'd like to have a couple of scoops of vanilla ice cream with some chocolate on it, and bring me a bag of peanuts.' That would be his lunch. Maybe once a week, usually on Thursday, he would go downtown and have a steak dinner. Other than that, he was not very interested in food."

He could think of all kinds of ways an opponent could beat him and, as a result, he worried about each game no matter what the record of the opposing team. As the season progressed, he seemed to get more and more tense, as if waiting for some form of bad news to take its toll. Even when the season was over, and the team had gone undefeated and won the National Championship, he still could not allow himself the luxury of enjoying his success, even for a short while.

William Butler Yeats, the Irish poet, once wrote, "Being Irish, he had an abiding sense of tragedy which sustained him through temporary periods of joy." In that sense, Leahy was Irish to the core.

It was this all-consuming devotion to football that eventually drove him from the game he loved and devoted his life to. What a loss it was to the game of football. And, how sad that, for his own personal well-being, he could not take to heart and act on the advice of his coaching staff and other friends who tried to get him to ease up and take more time for himself and his family.

At one of our reunions, Moose Krause commented. "Players say that Leahy was tough—really mean. He worked the hell out of you every day, Monday, Tuesday, Wednesday, Thursday, and even Friday, but remember how happy you were Saturday night? In my opinion, the way to judge a football coach like Bear Bryant or Frank Leahy— great coaches—is to ask how do the players feel about him…"

Taking my cue from Krause, I have asked over 70 former Notre Dame players who played in the 1940s under Coach Frank Leahy for their assessment of him. The overwhelming majority are of the opinion that Frank Leahy was, as a coach, the best they had ever known, and perhaps the best of all time. These players cite his complete knowledge of the game, his ability to innovate, to motivate, to teach all aspects of the game, to recruit, to organize, to bring out the very best of a player's abilities. He was seen by the players as a perfectionist, a taskmaster, an outstanding teacher, a psychologist, and a winner.

There are a few of the former players who have some reservations about Leahy, either because of his tactics and his perceived win-at-all-cost attitude, or his aloofness, which irritated some of them. However, most of these players readily acknowledge that as strategist, teacher, and innovator, he was in a class by himself.

The following is a sample of what Leahy's former players think about him:

Bernie Crimmins, number 44, halfback, fullback, guard, and coach

"He was a phenomenal individual. He was a great coach and everybody recognized that. Playing under him and coaching under him was fantastic, a real delight. He was a hard-nosed guy who expected you to give far beyond what you thought you had."

Lank Smith, number 20, halfback

"Coach Leahy won and had undefeated seasons at Boston College. His record is unequaled, even when compared with Rockne's, when you consider the stronger competition Leahy played against. He was a coaching genius.

"Leahy had a profound, positive effect on my life. In my opinion, Leahy's 'Lads' who played for him during the decade of the 1940s are the most loyal single group in the history of Notre Dame."

Bill Walsh, number 46, center

"The coaching staff we played for was the best you could have. Leahy was a great coach. It was so good to have him signal you out in front of the squad for a good block. I was scared to death of him—all I ever said to him in my three years was, 'Yes, sir' or 'No, sir.'"

Ralph McGehee, number 74, tackle

"Being part of three National Championship teams is a lifetime accomplishment still of importance to me, my family, friends, and associates. Unfortunately, playing football under Leahy [four spring practices, etc.], was a most difficult period not only physically, but emotionally. One former guard told me Coach McArdle's injunction, 'Get McGehee.' This sort of approach to a sport ruined my enjoyment of the game and frequently made it an agony rather than a joy. The emphasis on winning, rather than winning coupled with encouragement, may have damaged many players under Leahy."

Bob McBride, number 47, guard and coach

"Frank Leahy was a man who possessed the qualities of deep dedication, loyalty, and very strong character to their zenith. He loved Notre Dame with a passion I have never seen matched by any man. He believed Notre Dame deserved all of, and only, the very best from any person who represented Her—in any way. And, he most certainly got that point across to all the young men he coached.

"He did want to win—and win he did! But not at all costs. He coached people to 'pay the price' for victory, to give all they had, to be gentlemen—men, representatives of Notre Dame, and he gave them the tools to win. He was an innovator, a student of the game, a teacher of the highest caliber, and a very hard driver. Frank Leahy won because he was the greatest coach of his time, possibly of ALL TIME!"

Larry Sullivan, number 72, tackle

"Coach Leahy was a winner. He was a leader who demanded the best from all his players and in return gave his best back to them. He taught us the importance of intestinal fortitude. When you were exhausted, you could reach down and continue. After playing at Notre Dame with two years under Leahy, then playing for the Marines at Camp Lejuene, I learned that the teaching of Coach Leahy prepared me much better than my teammates from other colleges how to win and play aggressively. I was prepared to play the game and to carry on the traditions of Notre Dame."

Chet Ostrowski, number 87, end

"Frank Leahy was the greatest coach I ever played for. He taught me not only to play the game, but to live by the rules that were set forth. I will always remember him tenderly."

Jerry Groom, number 50, center, (captain of the 1950 team)

"In my estimation, Leahy was the greatest football coach in the history of the game. You can talk about Rockne and all the other great coaches, but having played for coaches in the East-West Game and five different coaches in pro ball, I can say that they couldn't touch, not even come close to touching Leahy.

"The sad thing about Leahy is that people will never know what a really great guy Frank was. They have talked about his weaknesses, maybe some of them are true, but I'll tell you the guy was one of the most honest individuals I have ever met. He absolutely loved his players—loved his ex-players. He would do anything for any one of them, and he didn't care if they were on the seventh string. I am sure the deal about his retirement could have been handled better. He wasn't ready to retire at age 45. Think of it. Parseghian came in at about that age. How old was Holtz when he started at Notre Dame? It hurt Frank badly, so badly that he never really recovered or bounced back from that."

Angelo Bertelli, number 48, quarterback

"Frank Leahy was a very formal man and a very, very talented man. One of the most embarrassing moments of my life occurred while I was still in the Marine Corp after the war ended. I went back to visit the coach and Lujack was there at the same time. The coach had both Lujack and I in his office and we were chatting. We are having a great chat and, for some reason or another, I made the mistake of calling him Frank instead of coach. He turned to Lujack and said, 'Oh Johnny, has Angelo changed?' I felt like crawling in a hole and never coming out. That's how formal he was.

"He visited me while I was on Guam. While he was there, I took him to regimental headquarters and introduced him to at least 20 officers. When he was leaving, he went up to each one and called him by name. How nice to meet you Captain White—how nice to see you Major Jones—his mind used to work that way.

"He didn't have the personality of a Rockne, who could beat a team's brains out and still be loved. Leahy beat your brains out and the opposition hated him for it. The players respected him, there was no question about that. Our respect for him was as a great coach and a great man. Those were great times [1941-43] and he did a great job. I was hoping somewhere along the way that Notre Dame would recognize that and name a field or something after him."

John Lujack, number 32, quarterback

"I only played for two coaches in college and in pro ball, Frank Leahy and George Halas. I think Leahy was 10 times better than Halas. Leahy had it over everybody as a preparatory coach, as a fundamentals coach, as a motivator, and as an innovator. I thought Leahy was the all-time greatest coach who ever came down the pike.

"I think that Frank Leahy helped us in a lot of the things that are important in life. He taught you dedication. He taught you sacrifice so that you must be willing to pay the price for success. Success doesn't come easy, you must work at it. Don't be disappointed or discouraged when you have a downturn. The real character of a person is measured by the ability to come back after a disappointment. These are the things that he taught us. I think the priests and professors at Notre Dame might not have taught the identical things, but they all had a purpose that blended right in. I have always been so pleased that I was able to go to Notre Dame. I feel I am a very fortunate man to have gotten a scholarship to Notre Dame, playing under Leahy, and being with all the fine people that represent Notre Dame."

Larry Coutre, number 24, halfback

"I was awed by Leahy—his speech and mannerisms. You had to respect him. He was a good coach and, I don't take anything away from him, but he surrounded himself with great assistant coaches. Leahy had the system and he was a motivator."

Bill Fischer, number 72, guard

"The players under Leahy were disciples of the Rockne-Hunk Anderson style of coaching. Each day the individual coaches would take on the players at that particular position. That concept of 'hands-on' teaching was unique to Notre Dame. When Terry Brennan took over as head coach from Frank Leahy, he hired all Leahy-trained people. That tradition of hands-on teaching continued. After Terry left, it was the end of the Rockne style of coaching. I always thought it was significant because we were the beneficiaries of some marvelous teachers who knew how to evaluate us and physically show us the correct techniques.

"The demanding part of Leahy on himself filtered down to the coaching staff. They naturally hammered it into us. This gave us that simple philosophy that we had to work harder and be in better shape than our opponents. We had to take the fight to them and punish them in the first, second, and third quarters so we would own them by the fourth quarter. We had the desire to do the necessary things to win.

"Leahy was right when he told us every team we faced was potentially the toughest team in the country and it's true today. We had that driven into us. Every team is tough until you prove otherwise. Take them out of the game, beat them up, block and run, play tough defense, wear them down. The good football team will now become a mediocre team and you will win. That's the way Leahy taught it."

Bill Gay, number 22, halfback

"Attending Notre Dame and having the opportunity to play football was a dream come true. Being coached by the master, Frank Leahy, and playing with so many All-Americans is something I will treasure forever. Every member of our football teams were class guys—not really thinking about themselves—only about the good of the team."

Frank Tripucka, number 8, quarterback

"To me, Leahy was so much smarter than other coaches. As far as the basics and fine points of the T-formation, everything came from Leahy. Little things, the automatic exchange from center, drop backs, setting up. Leahy was at all the quarterback meetings and he would run them. He would demonstrate what he wanted done. We worked on faking hour after hour in practice. By game time, it was second nature. Coaches today don't work on those details the way Leahy did. He would say, 'Is it comfortable for you to do it this way?' Or, 'Would you rather do it this way?' Great coaches do that. Leahy knew the details perfectly. How your feet should be planted, how you should hold the ball when passing, where your hands should be. Even today in the NFL you see quarterbacks who don't know how to make the exchange and what to do with their hands. Leahy knew it all."

Creighton Miller, number 37, halfback

"After I was through playing, I had a very good relationship with Leahy. He would call me in Cleveland and we would play golf. As a coach, he was as good as I have ever seen. I just don't think there was anybody better. He lost three games his first seven years at Notre Dame. I don't think any school, and I'm sure that goes for Notre Dame, wants a National Championship every year, and that's understandable. Other schools and other coaches don't want to play you if you beat the hell out of them all the time. So, you can't really get too good for everybody. All he was doing is what they hired him to do."

Leahy was a complicated person. Despite being in the limelight most of his career and having the opportunity to mingle with famous people, he was essentially an introvert. As Creighton Miller put it, "I think his reputation as being somewhat aloof came from having an inferiority complex."

An example of this is how he behaved at coaches' clinics. Time permitting, he happily went to these clinics to impart his knowledge of the game to other coaches. During these sessions he never held back his vast knowledge of the game, but would pass along his insights to anyone who would listen. He would answer all questions fully—oftentimes staging a half-speed drill with one of his assistant coaches in order to make a point.

When the teaching sessions were over for the day, however, he rarely joined the other coaches in their usual bull sessions. He preferred instead to retire to his hotel room where access was limited to a few trusted friends. Friends who knew him well said that he did not avoid his fellow coaches out of any lack of feeling for them, but rather he did this because of his natural reluctance to mingle in such an informal setting.

Leahy did not want to have a close relationship with a player while he was in school. He never socialized with the players, he was not their buddy, he did not have a drink with them, dinner with them, or partake in any activity that could possibly denote a personal relationship. That does not mean he was unfriendly. On the contrary, he was cordial off the field in his relations with the players, and every inch a gentleman at all times. He never used profanity on the field or at any other time. He had a rule that there be no profanity on the practice field or at anytime in his presence, and he insisted that his coaches and players follow the rule to the letter. They did.

If he wanted to talk to an individual player, he would ask that player to meet him in his office where the business at hand could be dispatched as quickly as possible. In some instances, the meeting could be about a personal matter such as the player's family, his studies, or his future, and the meeting could be in a friendly manner, but it was always on the basis of a subordinate talking to his boss. Leahy liked it that way and kept it that way. It was possible to play under Leahy for three or four years and, except for an initial meeting, never meet with him personally again.

Leahy wasn't the type to holler during practice; he left that up to the assistant coaches. His way of showing his disapproval was through sarcasm. If one of the players, for example Joe Signaigo, missed a block, he might say, "Oh, Joseph Signaigo, you missed that block. Do you really want to play ball for the University of Notre Dame? Let's run that play over again and see if Joseph wants to protect his teammate."

No player liked to be singled out like that so Leahy's ploy usually had the desired effect as Signaigo would not only block the man the next time, but probably put the poor guy on his back. Leahy would then comment, "That's the way to block, Joseph." He might turn to an assistant coach and say, "Coach McArdle, you leave Joseph Signaigo in the lineup. I think he wants to play football."

You knew you were in trouble when he talked in front of you to an assistant coach. When he saw an end drop a pass, he liked to say, "Coach Druze, can that player see all right? You better take him to the doctor and have his eyes examined." Or, if a quarterback had a pass intercepted, he might say, "Coach Crimmins, is that man color blind? He can't seem to tell the difference between the jerseys."

In one of the games, Bill Wightkin dropped a pass and Leahy called out, "Oh, William Wightkin, you don't love your mother and father. They're up in the stands and you dropped a pass."

From his perch in the tower or as he patrolled the practice area, he seemed to have eyes in the back of his head—he never missed a thing. He was forever the teacher making comments as he saw something that needed correcting. When Leahy spotted a particularly good play on the practice field, the scenario went like this: He would ask the assistant coach nearest to the play, "Coach Krause, who made that tackle?" Krause would yell back, "Bob Lally," or whoever it was. Leahy would respond in a loud voice, "That's the way to tackle, Bob Lally." On an outstanding play he would bypass his usual question to the assistant coach, like the day Leon Hart hit one of the young backs so hard on a blind-side block, the guy flew up in the air, did a cartwheel and landed in a heap, unconscious. Leahy, from his tower, yelled out, "God bless you, Leon Hart, for that block."

The fact that the poor back was laying out cold on the field did not seem to bother Leahy, he was more interested in the devastating block. His reaction was, "Oh Coach McArdle, get that man off the field so we can continue practice."

That is not to say he was without feelings for his players and coaches, but he rarely expressed these feelings about them while he was at Notre Dame. In later years, Jerry Groom and Leahy became very close and saw each other often. Groom says Leahy talked constantly and with great feeling about his former players and assistant coaches.

After talking to so many of the players of that era in researching this book, I have concluded that there is a different perception of Leahy among those who later got to know him on a personal basis as opposed to those who did not. Those who got to know him discovered a different Leahy than the one they knew as a coach. The "new" Leahy was warm, friendly, gracious, and had a delightful sense of humor. This side of him was concealed from the players, and to some extent his coaches, while he was active in coaching.

My brothers, Chuck and George, and I had a very personal experience which attests to Leahy's feelings about his players. In 1971, our father, Dr. Charles H. Connor, died after a long and fruitful life. Frank Leahy at that time was himself very ill with a form of leukemia. This condition required that his blood be drained and new blood transfused on a monthly basis. Leahy had just had such a procedure done in Portland, Oregon, where he was living at the time, when he heard about our father's death. Despite his weakened condition and protests from his brother, Tom, Leahy insisted that he fly to Chicago to attend the funeral.

On the morning of the funeral, Chuck, George, and our sister Mary Ellen, and I rode in a limousine with our mother from our home to St. Philip Neri Church on Chicago's south side where the funeral Mass for my father was to be said. As the limousine came to a halt in front of the church and we disembarked, we saw a car pull up across the street. Jack Leahy, Frank's nephew and close companion, and Tom Leahy exited the car and began to help a man in the back seat who was having some difficulty getting out of the car. To our complete amazement it was Coach Leahy.

We had heard that the coach just had a complete transfusion, and we knew from talking to Jack Leahy, who was a close friend of ours, that it always took several days for the coach to get his strength back before he could get around at all. We could not believe he had come to Chicago so soon after his treatment.

We waited on the sidewalk in front of the church as we watched Jack and Tom Leahy assist the coach across the street to where we were standing. Coach Leahy, always the gentleman, immediately offered his condolences to my mother and sister, then turned to face Chuck, George, and me. Chuck spoke up and said, "Coach, you didn't have to make this difficult trip; we know how weak you must be."

Coach Frank Leahy shook hands with the three of us and said, "The three of you played ball for me and, when you did, you gave it everything you had. There is not much I can do to help you or to repay you, except to be here with you today and let you know how much I care." He went on to say some nice things about our dad before we all went into the church for the service. I know from first-hand experience that he really did care about his "lads."

In his eulogy at the funeral of Frank Leahy, Pat O'Malley, chairman of the board of Canteen Corporation, said, "Frank's interest in and friendship with his 'Lads,' as he fondly called them, did not end with graduation, nor was it affected by material success. In every city of this country there lives a colony of men who are endeared to this man with a devotion that rivals their love of family. Until a month ago, Frank traveled extensively, and, if he only paused in a city, he was on the telephone renewing friendships with his 'Lads,' with Notre Dame alumni, and with business associates. As a molder of men he had no equal."

At the time of Moose Krause's funeral, some of the teammates and I were having one of our sessions at the Ramada Inn in South

Bend. Jack Leahy, Frank's nephew, was in the group. He intro-duced us to Frank's grandson, Ryan Leahy, a tackle on the Notre Dame football team, who had stopped by to visit with Jack. As I looked at this handsome, 6-foot-4, 290-pound, well-spoken, polite young man, I could not help but think how proud the coach would have been of his grandson—another Leahy carrying on the family football tradition at Notre Dame.

Moose Krause

Edward W. (Moose) Krause, a Notre Dame legend, died in his sleep on December 11, 1992, at the age of 79.

Moose, the son of a Chicago butcher, was born in the Back of the Yards neighborhood of Chicago as Edward Kraucuinas. His coach at De La Salle Institute, Norman Barry (the other halfback with George Gipp on the 1920 Notre Dame National Championship team) shortened the name to Krause when he found Kraucuinas too hard to pronounce. It was Barry who chided the newcomer Krause, "You are big enough to be a moose and you can't even block that little guy." From that day until the day he died, Krause was known to the world as "Moose."

Moose and his brother, Phil, dominated the sports scene at De La Salle during the late 1920s. Moose won All-City honors in football, basketball, baseball, and track, and led De La Salle to two national Catholic basketball championships.

Moose began what turned out to be a lifetime commitment to Notre Dame when he enrolled there as a freshman in 1930. As a tackle, he became an All-American while playing on the 1932 and 1933 teams. He was an All-American center on the basketball team for three years.

After graduation, Moose was named captain of the College All-Star football squad in the first ever All-Star Game played against the professional champions, the Chicago Bears. In recalling the game, he said, "On the first play of the game, the Bear player opposite me threw a punch that landed on my jaw and said, 'So you're the hotshot guy from Notre Dame.' On the second play, I punched him square in the mouth and said, 'Yeah, I'm from Notre Dame. What do you want to do about it?' He never said another word and I had no trouble with him the rest of the game."

Moose went on to coach football, basketball, track, and baseball at St. Mary's College in Winona, Minnesota, before going to Holy Cross College in Worcester, Massachusetts. He stayed at Holy Cross for six years, coaching football and basketball until he was summoned by Notre Dame's athletic director, Frank Leahy, to return to his alma mater in 1942.

In 1942, Krause became the tackle coach under Leahy and also the assistant basketball coach under the legendary George Keogan. When Keogan died in 1943, Moose became the head basketball coach. He served as an officer in the Marine Corps during the war before returning to Notre Dame in 1946 to assume his duties as head basketball coach and the number one football assistant to Frank Leahy.

In 1948, Moose gave up his football duties to become assistant athletic director under Leahy while continuing his basketball coaching. In 1949, he was named athletic director, a position he held with distinction until his retirement in 1981. In 1951, he was "fired" by the athletic director (himself) as head basketball coach. In typical Moose style he used to say, "Best move I ever made—we needed a change."

After his retirement, Moose maintained an office in the Joyce Athletic and Convocation Center—one which probably has had more visitors through the years than any other place on campus. All the former athletes loved to stop in and chat with Moose, who was always a gracious and delightful host.

Those who should know say that there was the largest collection of former athletes ever assembled at one time at Moose's funeral with the exception of a Monogram Club gathering. In a fitting tribute to Moose, his son, Fr. Edward Krause, CSC, characterized him as a "gentle giant" in his heartfelt homily.

He told of how, for more than 20 years, his father cared for his wife, Elise, who had suffered brain damage and paralysis in a automobile accident. For the last eight years before she died in 1990, Moose would visit her twice daily in a nursing home to spoon-feed her. In the last months before she died, Moose would go to the nursing home a third time every day to sing her to sleep.

Father Ed captured the spirit of Moose when he said, "My father lived the way he played ball. He never gave up, he never stopped trying. He was faithful and he was loyal."

Ara Parseghian, riding in the limousine with the other pallbearers, got off the quip of the day when he said to his fellow pallbearers, "Who recruited this group of pallbearers? It's the worst recruiting job I've ever seen. I forgot my cane, George Connor has trouble walking, Lou Holtz has a hernia, George Kelly can't breathe, Dick Rosenthal has two balloons for knees, and Colonel Stephens is so short his feet don't touch the ground. Moose in the casket is in better shape than any of us."

According to Bill Fischer, there is one of Moose's accomplishments for which he has never received credit. "When Notre Dame was looking for a new head coach, they discovered that Lou Holtz had an escape clause in his contract with Minnesota. I asked Father Reihle, 'Who do you suppose whispered in Holtz's ear about a Notre Dame escape clause? Nobody has the kind of foresight to have such a clause put in a contract.' Reihle didn't know. I asked around and never got an answer. Then one day I asked Moose Krause who it was that whispered to Holtz. Moose answered, 'You're talking to the man. I had been fighting to get Holtz for the last 10 years, but nobody would listen to me. I told Lou, "I'm still fighting for you and I may win. And when I do, and Notre Dame calls on you to become its head coach, I want you to be able to get out of your contract."'

"One day I told that story to Bernie Crimmins, who said, 'Bill, that story you just told about Moose is one hundred percent correct. Moose is the man and nobody gives him credit for it.'"

Moose was a delight to be around whether it was on the golf course, just visiting, or in his booth at Notre Dame Stadium. It was there that Moose was at his best. He would hold court with the variety of friends he entertained as his guests. George and I, along with Creighton Miller and Buddy and Mike Romano, called his booth "Heaven," because it was not only the highest point in the stadium, but because it was so enjoyable; we thought this must be a glimpse of heaven. There was a time when George and I thought we were going to be banished from "Heaven."

Several years ago my brother George called me and said, "I am really in deep trouble."

"What's wrong?" I inquired.

"Moose just called me and chewed me out for forgetting his birthday [February 2, Groundhog Day]."

About a week later I was at a Notre Dame function in Chicago and saw Moose. I said, "I hear George is in deep trouble." Moose said, "He forgot my birthday, no cigar, no gift, not even a card. And you're in trouble too, I didn't hear from you either."

Later that same evening I reported the conversation to George, who said, "We have to do something to get back in Moose's good graces. He might ban us from going to 'Heaven' and we can't let that happen."

George planned a delayed birthday celebration for Moose to be held the day before the Monogram outing in early June. We came up with the idea that we would honor Moose with an award entitled, "The First Annual Groundhog Day Award." George purchased a double-extra-large-sized white jacket and had the groundhog symbol with Moose's name put on the left breast of the jacket. I wrote a tongue-in-cheek award and had it framed. George had about 20 T-shirts made with the symbol of the groundhog on the front with the words, "Moose Krause Groundhog Day" on the front of the shirts.

On the appointed day, George and Mike Smith took Moose to lunch at the Ramada Inn in South Bend, for what Moose thought was a lunch just for the three of them. In the dining room there were about 20 of his former players gathered to surprise Moose. After a fun-filled lunch and at George's signal, we all put on our T-shirts. With George acting as emcee, we had our awards ceremony—Moose loved it. While Moose was standing and giving a thank-you speech, I leaned over to George and whispered, "If he goes on the attack, we'll know we made a hit."

Moose was very gracious in thanking everyone for his day, and particularly George and me. As soon as he sat down, he turned to the two of us and said, "And don't be late next year." We both burst out laughing. George said, "You're right, we're in, he's on the attack."

As a student, coach, athletic director, goodwill ambassador, and in his emeritus status, Moose consistently enhanced the reputation of the university by his unswerving loyalty to his family, the university, and his legion of friends. When many of us think of Notre Dame and what it stands for, we have only to look at Moose Krause for our model.

Other Coaches

The players of the 1940s were very fortunate in playing under some of the finest assistants coaches in the country. Of Leahy's three original coaches, Johnny Druze, Ed McKeever, and Joe McArdle, whom he brought with him from Boston College, only McKeever departed. Druze and McArdle stayed with Leahy his entire coaching career. Moose Krause, who joined the Leahy staff in 1942, stayed on the staff until his duties as assistant athletic director forced him, in 1948, to devote full-time to that office. Wally Ziemba, who became an assistant coach under Leahy in 1943, stayed on Leahy's staff until 1953, when Leahy ended his coaching career.

Bernie Crimmins, who signed on as an assistant in 1946, stayed with Leahy until 1951, when he accepted the head coaching position at Indiana University. Bill Earley, who also joined Leahy's staff in 1946, stayed with Leahy until he quit coaching in 1953, as did Bob McBride, who took Krause's place in early 1949. The continuity of the coaching staff was, in itself, a significant factor in the success of the program.

All the teammates agree that the assistant coaches throughout the 1940s, including the war years, were the best group of coaches anyone could possibly want. Leahy, with all his genius, never would have been able to field such superbly trained teams if it were not for the caliber of the assistants.

In talking about the assistant coaches, Bill Fischer said, "On my own I would never have thought of looking for a second man to hit after going downfield and throwing a block. The coaches demanded it and taught us how to give more that we thought we could. When we thought we had given everything we had, they asked for another 10 to 15 percent. They made us perform, overperform, do far better that we could ever imagine.

"We had a center coach, a guard coach, a tackle coach, an end coach, and a couple of backfield coaches. We played offense and defense and they had to coach offense and defense. We had what they call speciality teams today, punting team, punt return team, and the same for kickoffs. Our coaches had to teach the fundamentals and techniques for all phases of the game. I can say this without question—I cannot think of any coaching staff that I have ever seen from that time, college or pro, and all through the years, that was as good at teaching in a hands-on style all the right techniques that are required to make proficient ballplayers."

Each of the assistants had a different approach in the way he handled the players. McArdle played the role of the tough guy, which earned him the nickname "Captain Bligh" (behind his back, of course). He worked his players relentlessly, which Leahy loved. Underneath the gruff exterior, he cared deeply about all the players.

One day in spring practice before my sophomore year, he got me aside and said, "Jack, you're the first one out on the practice field and often the last to leave. I know you are working your butt off to try and get some recognition. You hit as hard as anyone for your size [5-foot-11, 190 pounds], you have good technique, but I'm afraid it isn't enough, and I don't want you to get your hopes too high. I know you don't like to be compared to your brother, but the difference between you and George, Bill Fischer, Marty Wendell, and those guys is, if you are playing on offense, your idea is to block the man opposite you. Those guys assume they're going to block the guy, so they want to knock him down and trample him on their way to knock down a second or third guy—you just don't have the killer instinct."

From that time on, no matter how hard he worked us, or how much he hollered, I always knew he was just doing his job the best way he could. It did not surprise me to later learn from Dick Leous (the quarterback of our B team), that it was McArdle who comforted him when he broke his cheekbone and suffered a severe concussion, which ended his playing career.

Druze was almost the opposite of McArdle in his approach to the players. He was even-tempered and never seemed to get mad. Rather than holler or put you down, Druze accomplished the goal of making his players better by calmly correcting their mistakes and giving words of encouragement when it was done right. One day Leahy asked his nephew, Jack Leahy, "What do the players think of McArdle?" Jack replied, "They think he is a tough sonovabitch." Leahy just smiled. He then asked Jack, "What do the players think of Druze?" Jack replied, "They think he is a great guy—they really like him." Leahy frowned and said, "Oh, I'm going to have to speak to Coach Druze about that."

Crimmins was somewhere between McArdle and Druze in style of coaching. He could holler with the best of them and could chew a player out for a mistake, but he could praise him as well when the player got it right. He was known for his very strong voice. He never needed an amplifier to project his voice across the practice field—he could be heard on the far side of the field during a practice session, yelling at one of the backs. Even when you were up close to him, he would speak in a voice about three decibels louder than the average person. One day at practice, he leaned into the offensive huddle to give some sort of instruction in his usual loud voice. As he walked away, Red Sitko said to the group, "I thought we got rid of that deaf fellow."

Not only was the coaching staff unchanged for so many years, but the coaches, with their diverse personalities, got along very well with each other. More than that, they were good friends and maintained their friendships through the years. This type of harmony on the coaching staff did not go unnoticed by the players. The way the coaches worked together and their obvious caring for one another also played a role in the teams' success. More than that, it served as a good example for all the players in how they treated each other.

Unfortunately, as of this writing, only Druze and McBride are still with us. As each of the others died, it was a tremendous blow to the teammates. These men were not only respected and admired, but were loved by the players who played for them.

The Players: Life After Football

As the players of the 1940s graduated, they found that the lessons learned while students at Notre Dame and the discipline and teamwork instilled in them by Leahy and the assistant coaches were sources of strength that would serve them well as they married, raised children, and got on with their chosen careers.

As might be expected, considering the great Notre Dame teams of the 1940s, 68 of the players from that era entered the professional football ranks. There was a great demand for players as pro football became more popular. This popularity created a demand which was accelerated when the All-American Football Conference was founded in 1946 to compete with the already existing National Football League. (The All-American Conference was absorbed by the National Football League in 1950.)

One of the things I am most proud of in my association with the players of the 1940s is the way in which they have helped the less fortunate in our society. These men not only gave everything they had to give while playing at Notre Dame, but many of them have channeled the energy that made them so great on the gridiron into pursuits to help their fellow human beings.

I have been told by guests who are invited to attend one of our yearly reunions that they are immediately aware of and impressed by several attributes of our group. First is the modesty of each member of the group. If one did not know the names, there is no way to tell who was an All-American, a Heisman, or Outland winner, or who was in the Hall of Fame. When we gather, we tell our stories, of course. But you never hear someone tell a story about some good play he made. Rarely do you hear a story about any game. Rather, the stories center around the funny incidents that occurred, usually on the practice field.

A second characteristic of the group that impresses people is the way we get along with each other and our obvious care and concern for one another. The teammates have always been very supportive of each other down through the years.

We have a network among the teammates that is amazing. Let me give an example. When Moose Krause's wife, Elise, died, Buddy Romano received a call from the athletic department at Notre Dame. He called me and George, and I called Ed Mieszkowski. Between us, we started the calls and asked others to call. About an hour later, I made a check and found that almost everyone on the list for our Ziggie reunions had been called. Naturally, a few couldn't be reached. I called Joe O'Brien, the associate director of athletics at Notre Dame, to tell him our group had been contacted and to check them off the list. He couldn't believe we could do it so quickly.

Many of the teammates stay in touch with each other on a regular basis—not just with those that live near them, but all across the country and in Canada (Blackie Johnston and Zeke O'Connor live in Toronto). If there is news about a teammate or help is needed, the network gets busy. (One of the greatest at this was Moose Krause.) It is inspiring to witness the teammates in action when the need arises. Now I know why Ziggie used the word "teammate" as he did. As we have advanced in age, we have learned that being a "teammate" is more than being a fellow player—it is a love and concern for one another that adds an extra dimension to our lives.

There are some beautiful and touching stories of how the teammates have rallied to help a fellow teammate. The stories are numerous—and of such a personal nature—that telling them here does not seem appropriate. Suffice it to say that all of us have learned some wonderful lessons of life in witnessing our teammates' care for each other.

Marty Brutz, one of Ziggie's great pals, said, "The love, mutual respect, and strong friendship that the players of the 1940s share with one another has continued for 50 years, as evidenced by our reunions. Has there ever been such a group so bonded together for so long a time?"

This concern for one another has grown and deepened through the years. Lujack once said that coming back to Notre Dame for our reunions was like a retreat. He explained what he meant. "I have always said that coming back to Notre Dame—getting into the spirit of the things on campus, visiting the Grotto—brings back pleasant memories for me. When I hear the Notre Dame Victory March, I still get goose pimples—I can't recall a time when I didn't. I enjoy the people. We get together as former players and that is always a delight for me. I called it a retreat because it cleanses your soul."

Chapter Fifteen

ZIGGIE AND REUNIONS

Ziggie was the one who kept the team loose during the years he played, and in later years, when the playing days were over, he was the driving force that brought the team together year after year.

He made it his business to stay in close touch with as many of his teammates as possible. Those of us in Chicago saw him often. My brother George saw him the most—they were like brothers. They must have been on the program together at more than 1,000 banquets. They had lunch together several times a week and talked by phone almost every day.

Ziggie was like part of our family. He once sent a picture of himself, my brothers Chuck and George, and me to my mother, signed, "Your Polish son Ziggie, one of your four boys." It was my mother's favorite picture.

George was the best man and Marty Brutz was an usher at Ziggie's wedding.

Some time before the wedding, Ziggie and George met at a downtown restaurant in Chicago to have lunch before they went to nearby Gingess Brothers to be measured for their tuxes. Brutz, who lived in Youngstown, Ohio, could not make it in to be measured. Ziggie called him from a phone close to the table where George was seated.

George reported hearing the following from Ziggie's end of the conversation:

"Marty, what size shirt do you wear?"

"That big? Are you sure? How about the waist? My God, Marty, what's happened to you? How about your coat size?"

"Geez Marty, this is really bad. Oh well, don't concern yourself, I'll just order two my size."

Another story about Ziggie's wedding concerns the telegram

Terry Brennan sent to Doris' parents before the wedding. Brennan could not make the wedding and sent his apologies along with his best wishes. Instead of the usual "You are not losing a daughter, you are gaining a son," Brennan's telegram read, "You are not losing a daughter, you're gaining a ton."

When Ziggie would call me, the conversation would always start the same way, "Jack, this is '76.' " Most calls were to arrange a get-to-gether of his Chicago teammates—he loved gatherings of the teammates. Those of us he called would juggle our schedules to make sure we could attend. No one wanted to miss a Ziggie lunch no matter what its ostensible purpose.

One day during the early 1960s, I ran into Ziggie at a restaurant in downtown Chicago. I asked how he was doing. His face was clouded by a sad look (which was unusual for him) and he told me that his doctor suspected he had diabetes.

I didn't see Ziggie again for about four months. When we met at a sports function, I immediately inquired about his diabetes.

"Oh, that's fine, I don't have it anymore."

"How can that be?" I pressed.

"My doctor died." He replied.

In 1971, Ziggie decided that it was about time his teammates had an official reunion. We had been meeting in small groups in Chicago, New York, and at Notre Dame for years. Now the timing was ripe for a big reunion because that year marked the 25th anniversary of the 1946 team's National Championship.

As was typical of Ziggie, he planned a reunion that included not only the 1946 team, but also the 1943 and 1947 teams as well. This made sense—many of the players were on all three teams, plus all three had won National Championships. Why not celebrate together? Besides, with Ziggie, the more teammates he could gather together the better.

Most individuals with such a plan would immediately form a committee composed of players from all three teams to assure maximum participation. Not Ziggie. He didn't need a committee—he *was* a committee.

He drove to South Bend and reserved 60 rooms at Randall's Inn for several nights during the football season (a few years later the re-union was switched to Frank Meloy's Ramada Inn). While there, he selected the menu and hired a band. Ziggie then went to the university's athletic office and convinced Bob Cahill, the Notre Dame ticket manager, to reserve one hundred tickets for the game to be played the weekend of the reunion. A visit to the publicity department resulted in a commitment to publicize the event and to include a half-time introduction of the players attending the reunion.

With all the essentials for the reunion in place, Ziggie mailed an invitation letter to more than one hundred of his teammates. Every custom-designed invitation was handwritten in green ink. The letter began, "Dear Teammate…[the player's first name]." He outlined the events, supplying all the appropriate details, and closed with a plea to respond by a certain date. He then added a personal note to each teammate.

To Ziggie, the word "teammate" was a term of endearment. He loved his teammates and made no effort to hide behind some false macho image. Rather, he openly used this word with great affection. As he journeyed through life, Ziggie began to call anyone who played at Notre Dame, regardless of the year, his teammate—and later, as a special designation for any friend who was a loyal Notre Dame follower.

Several months after Ziggie's first communication to the teammates about the reunion, he mailed a second letter to those who had not responded to the original invitation. Again, the green ink issued an update on who was coming and an urging to get your check in as soon as possible. If there was no response to the this letter, a third letter was not far behind. This third letter prompted my brother George to comment, "I see that '76's' Polish mimeograph machine is working overtime."

As the reunion approached, Ziggie mailed another letter to each player updating them on who was coming and telling them to make sure they were on time for the "scrimmage" (cocktail hour) Friday afternoon. When you total the letters that Ziggie had handwritten, there must of been close to three hundred.

When the actual event took place, Ziggie would not take any special credit for all his work. He acted very nonchalant, as if the whole thing just somehow happened.

As the players arrived that Friday at the motel for the pre-dinner "scrimmage," most of them with their wives, Ziggie, with his wife Doris at his side, greeted each couple with a big hug, all the while wearing his famous wide-brim hat and his ever present smile. For the entertainment immediately after the dinner, Ziggie told the group he had imported the finest emcee in the country to run the program. Ziggie modestly admitted later that this top emcee was—himself.

The dinner and the program that followed were a big hit with everyone. During the program, Ziggie read a telegram from their former coach, Frank Leahy:

> Dear Lads and your fortunate brides:
>
> Words cannot adequately express the depth of my sadness over not being with you during the most unique gathering in athletic history.
>
> Four National Championship teams together after 28 years, which proves conclusively your love for each other and Notre Dame. Never lose contact with that famous Lady who reigns so serenely over our beautiful campus. Give Her a chance not to forget you by seeking assistance when necessary. She stands ready and willing to reciprocate for your unsurpassed representation during and since graduation.
>
> A privilege of attending Notre Dame has given you an enviable mark of distinction. People everywhere expect more from you because you are a Notre Dame man, because you were a Notre Dame team, and at all times you have and will continue to measure up.
>
> While attending our Mother's school, you had indelibly inscribed in your minds and hearts certain qualities that set you apart and above most others. Thank God you are cognizant of the awesome monumental challenge and responsibility.
>
> You are men endowed with the qualities that forged our nation to greatness. Notre Dame leadership is more important now than ever before. You, and others like you, are in a position to restore America to a position of pride, power, prestige, and popularity. You have learned many invaluable lessons at Notre Dame, especially, the realization that games can never be won, character developed, that nothing of lasting value can be achieved without desire, hard work, loyalty, self-discipline, and depravation.
>
> Thanks profoundly players and assistant coaches for your incredible performances. I shall forever be deeply in

your debt. A special salute to Ziggie for the effort and time he has poured into his unforgettable collection of wonderful people. Congratulations in advance to our brilliant coach, Ara, [Parseghian] on his victory this afternoon.

As some of you know, I was almost called to meet my Maker a short while ago. During, and immediately following the operation, many of your faces floated across my mind and I kept stressing to myself that you men never knew the meaning of the word quit, so I readily admit that enough of you rubbed off on me to help keep me in the game. My sincere thanks to the greatest.

Coach Leahy

(Coach Leahy never had the opportunity to meet with his former players and coaches at one of these reunions. On June 21, 1973 Frank Leahy died of leukemia.)

Then, as with all of Ziggie's reunions, the festivities ended with Ziggie serenading the group with his rendition of "Thanks for the Memories."

All the players had such a great weekend at that first official reunion that it was decided (or maybe Ziggie decided) that we should meet again as a team in five years, in 1976. Naturally, since we were meeting in the year '76, "76" made sure that reunion was extra special. He had programs printed listing all the committees. But as usual, Ziggie had done all the work, so the committee listings were just a gesture. It was Ziggie's way of listing all the players and wives, while also having a little fun. One of the listings was typical Ziggie—it was "The Pom-Pom Committee."

All the teammates had such a great time that it was the unanimous opinion that we should not wait for another anniversary to meet again. The teammates opted instead to select one Notre Dame home football game each year as the time we would meet. This started the tradition of our yearly reunions, which have continued unbroken to the present. Ziggie continued to orchestrate the entire operation on his own until his death in 1984.

For Ziggie, bringing people together was a task not reserved for just his Notre Dame teammates or coaches. He also made sure his teammates from his high school days at Mt. Carmel met often and remained close friends. They say that Ziggie's graduating class of 1941 always had terrific attendance at the school's alumni banquets.

Ziggie had other groups he would bring together. His birthday parties were good examples. And I do mean "parties," as Ziggie would throw birthday parties for himself four times a year. Ziggie had so many friends he wanted to see and be with on his birthday that no one party could accommodate them all. He made going to his own birthday parties practically a full-time job.

He would call everyone slated for his "downtown" party and inform them there was to be a birthday party for him at a designated restaurant at an appointed date and time. Ziggie would then go out and buy 30 or so different birthday cards to correspond with the number of guests expected that day. As each person entered the restaurant, Ziggie would greet him and say, "Would you sign this card?" Not knowing what he was signing, the person would, of course, sign. Ziggie would then hit the guy for a small donation to "cover expenses" for the day.

After a few drinks and lunch, Ziggie would rise and thank everyone for coming—as if the party was a surprise to him. Then he would start reading the cards he'd had everyone sign. "Here is a nice card," Ziggie would say as he read the entire verse. When he finished he would say, "It's signed, 'Your pal "71." ' What a nice card, Moose, thanks." George Connor would laugh because he had no knowledge of anything other than signing a card at the beginning of the party. Ziggie would go through all 30 cards to the delight of everyone there.

Just as Ziggie finished, perhaps at his signal, a waiter would bring in a birthday cake. Ziggie would feign embarrassment as the crowd rose to sing "Happy Birthday." Naturally, as with most Ziggie gatherings, the group would adjourn to the bar for many stories and laughs as Ziggie and George held court.

Thus, Ziggie enjoyed four wonderful birthday parties a year, instigated at no expense to him—even including, of course, the cost of the birthday cards. No one felt pressured. On the contrary, everyone had such a special time that they would have been disappointed had they not been invited.

Ziggie gave many speeches over the years for various groups and was well known for his ability to delight any audience. Once he gave a talk in Chicago to a major food company at the request of one of his pals. As always, he was a success. That same pal later asked Ziggie if he would be willing to travel to Albuquerque, New Mexico, to be the speaker at the company's dinner following their national sales meeting. He told Ziggie that the company would pay the travel expenses for Ziggie and Doris, plus a nice fee. Ziggie accepted.

Jim Nerad, Ziggie's lifelong pal and his wife, Evelyn, accompanied Ziggie and Doris on the trip. Nerad tells what happened the night of the dinner.

"The dinner was held at this beautiful club and everything about it was first-class. The president of the company and all the directors were there, as well as many local dignitaries, including the lieutenant governor of the state. Since this was the big party for the food company, they went to great lengths to make sure the food was of the highest quality.

"When it came time for Ziggie to speak, his first words at the microphone to the large audience were, 'I've got to tell you something. That meal we just had was the lousiest meal I ever had in my life.' The Lieutenant Governor almost fell out of his chair with laughter, as did most of the audience. Ziggie then went on to have the audience laughing the rest of the talk. The lieutenant governor liked Ziggie so much that the next day he made Ziggie an honorary colonel, aide-de-camp to the governor of New Mexico."

Each year in early December the National Football Foundation and Fall of Fame has its annual induction ceremonies at a black-tie dinner at the Waldorf-Astoria Hotel in New York City. My brother George, inducted into the Hall of Fame in 1963, liked to attend the event every year to renew acquaintances with his fellow inductees.

As in some previous years, I planned to attend, since I had to be in New York anyway for business reasons. George and I invited Ziggie to go with us as our guest for a few days.

The three of us met at O'Hare Airport in Chicago on the morning of departure. As we checked our luggage and started to walk to the appropriate terminal, George noticed that Ziggie was carrying a large brown paper bag. "76, what's in the bag?" George inquired.

"Some Fannie May candy for the stewardesses."

George and I knew Ziggie's routine with the candy, but George loved to needle Ziggie, so he said, "76, you're a passenger. You don't have to bring the stewardesses candy when you go on a plane ride."

Ziggie replied, "Moose, these girls work hard, so I just want to show them I appreciate what they do."

We were the first to board the plane and Ziggie immediately called the closest stewardess over to where he was seated, which was across the aisle from George and me. "My dear," Ziggie began as he kissed her hand, "my name is Ziggie [he ignored George and me], here is a box of candy for you for the wonderful service I know you will provide during the trip. If you will send the other girls over, I would like to meet them and also give them a gift."

The stewardess had a baffled look on her face that reflected what must have been in her mind. "Is this guy for real?"

Within a few minutes, three other stewardesses came to Ziggie and he went through the routine with each of them. "Look at him," said George, "here we are paying his way and he'll end up with all the service."

Sure enough, George and I were lucky if we got a drink, while Ziggie was being waited on throughout the flight.

Also on the flight was Bill Wirtz, the owner of the Chicago Blackhawks hockey team. Wirtz was a good friend of George's, but had never met Ziggie. After George introduced them, Ziggie entertained Wirtz for most of the flight with his many stories. You could tell, Wirtz was really enjoying his time with Ziggie.

I had been warned by my New York office that there was currently a cab strike in the city. Accordingly, they had a limousine waiting at LaGuardia Airport for the transportation downtown. I told George and Ziggie about this.

As we were about to leave the plane, Ziggie asked Wirtz, "Bill, are you aware there is a cab strike in New York?"

Wirtz said, "No, I didn't know that. That means I'll probably be late for the league meeting."

"Don't worry Bill," Ziggie said, "I knew about the strike, so I have my driver and limousine at the airport and I'll be glad to drop you off wherever you want to go."

George poked me and whispered, "Now it's his limo. We might as well have some fun with this." As we departed the plane, the four stewardesses were lined up to give Ziggie a hug and one of them said, "Thank you for the candy, Mr. Ziggie. We hope you fly with us again." George and I did not even get a smile.

George and I arrived at the limousine before Ziggie and Wirtz. George told the driver what he should say and he agreed to go along. As Ziggie and Wirtz approached the limousine, the driver went directly to Ziggie and said, "Good morning boss, I hope you had a nice flight."

Without batting an eye, as if he did this every day, Ziggie said, "Good morning, Henry [he did not have the slightest idea what the driver's name was]. Yes, we had a delightful flight. I would like you to drive direct to Madison Square Garden to drop off my good friend, Mr. Wirtz, who has an important meeting there."

"Henry" drove directly to the Garden. As we stopped at the curb, Ziggie got out first. Joey Giardello, the former middleweight champion, happened to be at the curb and, when he saw Ziggie, rushed to him and gave him a big hug. "Ziggie, my old pal, so good to see you."

Later, Wirtz talked to George and said, "Who is this guy Ziggie? What does he do? He seems to know everybody. I never met anyone like him." As life would have it, because of meeting Ziggie, Wirtz later became a close friend to Fr. John Smyth, the director of Maryville Academy. Wirtz's association with Father John and Maryville has proven to be very beneficial for the welfare of the young people of Maryville.

A few years later, George and I again were with Ziggie at the annual National Football Hall of Fame dinner in New York. Since the dinner included the presentation of the new inductees, it was, naturally an emotional evening. To offset the seriousness of the evening, the dinner committee interjected some comic relief into the program by having some celebrity known for his wit give a short talk.

George, who was well known to the committee, recommended his pal "76" for the task of providing the comedy. The dinner was a sellout, as usual, with over one thousand men in black-tie dress and the usual four-tiered dais, with Terence Cardinal Cooke, the archbishop of New York, and other church and civic dignitaries in attendance.

After Ziggie was introduced, he began:

"Mr. Toastmaster, Your Eminence, Distinguished Clergy, Honored guests, Fellow Football Players:

"Your Eminence, seeing you here tonight reminds me of my good friend Father Paul. Father was having some problems with his vocation, so he asked his bishop if he could have a leave of absence from his duties in order to sort out his life. He explained to the bishop that his sister had a cabin in the mountains outside of Denver where he could go and meditate. The bishop granted his request.

"Several months later the bishop was in Denver on some church business when he recalled that Father Paul was in the area. He found the phone number of the cabin and called. Father Paul was delighted to hear from the bishop and invited him to make the drive up the side of a mountain to the cabin. When the bishop arrived at the cabin, he was greeted by Father Paul, who now had a beard, was dressed in a toga with a string of beads around his neck, and wearing sandals. When Father Paul and the bishop settled into the two chairs on the porch of the cabin with the great view of the mountains, the bishop said, 'Father Paul, how is your time of meditation coming along?' "Father Paul replied, 'It's wonderful, Bishop, I have this beautiful view, my rosary, and my wine. Speaking of wine, would you like some?'

" 'Yes, I would,' said the bishop. Father Paul called out, 'Rosary, would you bring us two glasses of wine?' "

There was a moment of silence as all eyes went to the cardinal. Cardinal Cooke started to smile and then erupted in laughter that spread throughout the audience. Ziggie owned the audience the rest of his talk. The committee must have loved him because two years later he was inducted into the Hall of Fame.

Ziggie was a great pal of Mike Souchock, one of the leading money winners on the professional golf circuit in the late 1950s. Souchock was in Chicago to participate in one of the tour events during that time and spent much of his time with Ziggie.

At the practice tee of Beverly Country Club where the event was played, Souchock was hitting balls while his pal Ziggie sat behind the tee in a comfortable lounge chair watching him. Every 10 minutes or so, Souchock would take a break and go back to Ziggie and chat. After about 40 minutes, Souchock had had enough practice. He went to Ziggie and told him he would meet him in the clubhouse.

A young golfer, who was playing in his first professional tournament, observed Souchock and Ziggie and assumed Ziggie was Souchock's instructor. As soon as Souchock departed the young golfer approached Ziggie and said, "Excuse me, sir. I couldn't help but notice how Mr. Souchock improved his shots after he talked to you. I wonder if you would give me some advice."

"Certainly young man," replied Ziggie. "Why don't you take a few shots so I can observe you." (Ziggie did not know the first thing about golf.)

The golfer hit about 10 shots and looked back at Ziggie. "What do you think?"

Ziggie frowned, but did not say a word.

"It's in my hands? Right?"

That's the only hint Ziggie needed. He could improvise in any situation.

"It's definitely your hands, move your left hand over," ordered Ziggie. (Hc had heard about the left hand somewhere.)

"I knew it," said the happy young golfer. "Thanks very much."

"Anytime," responded Ziggie magnanimously as he left for the clubhouse.

The young golfer whom Ziggie had given a lesson to, shot in the 80s that day—the worst game of golf that he had shot since high school days.

Frank Tripucka recently recalled some of his favorite recollections of Ziggie. "After an away game, Ziggie would head straight for the club car when we were headed home. Typical of Ziggie, he would stand in the middle of the car, usually shoulder to shoulder with people, and ask in a loud voice, 'Can I have your attention please?' Once he had their attention, he would continue, 'I would like to buy you all a drink, but to tell you the truth, I'm broke.' Money would come flying at him from the different alumni and fans. Ziggie would walk out of there with his pockets full of bills. People just couldn't do enough for Ziggie. But I'll guarantee that if you talked to Ziggie leaving the club car and told him you needed $200, Ziggie would give it to you without hesitation.

"In 1972 Angelo Bertelli was inducted into the National Football Foundation Hall of Fame. I was chairman of a dinner committee to honor Bert. I thought the ideal guy to emcee the affair would be Ziggie. He was a teammate of Bert's on the 1943 team and a good friend.

"I called Ziggie and asked if he would come. He said, 'Are you kidding? Of course I would love to come in.' The dinner committee had the head table set up in front of a screen. Behind the screen we had different gifts which we were going to present to Bert during the program. We had a woman mayor in the community who was very staid—a very strait-laced type of person. Her job was to present a bouquet of roses to Jill, Bert's wife. Ziggie heard me making the arrangements with the mayor, so I suspected he might pull some kind of trick. When she got up on the podium, she was to say, 'And now for Mrs. Bertelli, a bouquet of roses.' Then she was to put her hands behind the screen and someone would put the bouquet in her hand.

"When the program progressed to that point, the mayor said, 'And now for Mrs. Bertelli, a bouquet of roses.' She put her hand behind the screen as planned, but instead of a bouquet of roses, the stagehand, at Ziggie's instructions, put a bottle of Four Roses whiskey in the mayor's hand. When she brought her hand forward and the audience saw the bottle, they roared with laughter, to the embarrassment of the mayor. Ziggie then took over the program and had the audience laughing the rest of the evening. A typical Ziggie performance."

Probably the Ziggie story most often repeated is the one concerning Omar Bradley, the famous five-star general of World War II. It is also one that is told incorrectly most times—particularly the punch line. Since I was with Ziggie at the time, let me set the record straight as to what happened and what was said.

Again it was Hall of Fame time in New York. George, Ziggie, and I were together for the annual black-tie, men-only event held in the grand ballroom at the famous Waldorf-Astoria Hotel. The evening of the dinner, George and I donned our tuxedos in our room at the Drake Hotel. Ziggie joined us from his room down the hall.

When it was time to go, we boarded the elevator at the end of our hall. We traveled just one floor and stopped. As the doors opened, a very distinguished-looking couple entered. Ziggie immediately said, as he put out his hand in greeting, "General Omar Bradley!"

The general looked up and extended his hand to shake Ziggie's, as Ziggie continued, "Ziggie Czarobski, Notre Dame, and these are my teammates, George Connor and Jack Connor."

"Happy to meet you," responded the general. He then introduced us to his wife. We had a delightful conversation with the general for the remainder of the brief ride down.

When we reached the lobby floor and the elevator doors opened, the general said, "Men, I sure enjoyed meeting you." He then looked at Ziggie and said, "Ziggie, I enjoyed all your games."

Without a second's hesitation, Ziggie immediately shot back, "General, I enjoyed all your wars."

The general barely made it out of the elevator he was laughing so hard.

Ziggie was continuously involved in some charity and always had a big heart, especially when it came to helping children. In 1968 he became involved in the first Special Olympics for Exceptional Children held in Chicago. This charitable work was always one of Ziggie's favorites.

However, it was his association with Fr. John Smyth, the administrator of Maryville Academy in Des Plaines, Illinois, that started Ziggie on what was to be his life's work. In 1969, Father Smyth, or Father John, as he is called by most of the teammates, was desperately in need of funds to operate the state's largest residential child care facility that he had been running since his assignment there in 1962. Father John was well known to all the players from Notre Dame because he was not only a graduate, but had been a star basketball player there in the mid-'50s. At the time he did not know Ziggie well, but he had run into him at a function in Chicago. During their encounter, Ziggie had said he would help him raise some funds for the kids of Maryville.

Father John did not hear from Ziggie for four or five months. Then out of the blue, Ziggie called and said, "I have to have a meeting with you and some of the guys—we're going to make a lot of money for you." Father John and some Maryville board members, plus George Connor and Johnny Lattner, met to discuss Ziggie's plan for raising money. As Father John describes it, "I had never done a fundraiser before that time—I was green. They had given me Maryville and I knew I was going down the tube. That's all I was sure of. Ziggie said, 'We're going to have a picnic and were going to make a lot of money for you.'

"I'll never forget my words. I said, 'Ziggie, how are you going to make any money on a picnic? This is the dumbest idea I ever heard.'

"Ziggie never took no for an answer, so he keep right on going. 'We're going to have a picnic and it will be on the last Sunday in June and we'll call it the Chuckwagon Day.' I asked, 'What's a Chuckwagon?'

"He said, 'That's where you eat off the wagon.' I said, 'Fine, let's have a picnic.' That's how the first Chuckwagon Day was born."

The event was held in the Maryville gym and about 1,000 people came. Father John thought at first it was a disaster, but when he saw the crowd, he knew Ziggie was onto something. To Father John's surprise and delight, the first Chuckwagon Day made $24,000. "After the first year we moved outside," recalled Father John. "It is now the single largest fundraiser in the state of Illinois and possibly the United States. We grossed $2.2 million last year and this year it will probably be $2.3 or $2.4 million."

In late June 1993, the 22nd annual Chuckwagon Day was held on the grounds of Maryville Academy. This marvelous event to raise needed funds for the orphans of Maryville, started and nurtured by "76," is a continuing tribute to our teammate, Ziggie Czarobski.

Ziggie's impact on Maryville did not end with his death. The original group of men who Ziggie gathered for the first Maryville Chuckwagon Day are still involved in the annual event. Their generosity over the years is astounding, and it is all because of Ziggie. As you drive through the grounds of Maryville you see the "Ben Stein Social Center" and the "Jack Leahy Athletic Field," named in honor of two dear friends of Ziggie who were part of the original group.

It was only about a week before he died that Ziggie attended his last Maryville Chuckwagon Day. As Father John recalls, "He came to the last Chuckwagon and rode around in a golf cart. He looked about one-tenth of what he did normally. He suffered a lot, but never complained. I really admired him for that. He came to me with Doris and said he wanted to be waked at Maryville because this is his real home. I said, 'I'll do anything you want.'

"It was the first wake we ever had at Maryville. The people came, and came and came—helicopters were landing on the grounds. It was the biggest wake I have ever seen. At one time, in one of our conference rooms we had six Heisman Trophy winners [Jay Berwanger, Angelo Bertelli, John Lujack, Leon Hart, John Lattner, and Paul Hornung]. Ziggie had that way of developing such loyalty that people would run through a wall for him."

The funeral Mass was at St. Emily's, down the street from Maryville. Ziggie's former teammates and coaches acted as honorary pallbearers. These men took up the first four or five pews at church—it looked like a Who's Who of sports. Father John gave the homily and it was a masterpiece. He began by saying that Ziggie was always in charge and planned everything. He said, "His number was 76, he is being buried in the seventh month on the sixth day [7/6], and it is 76 degrees out."

Just then a wind blew through the church, the candles flickered, and the pages of Father John's notes flipped over. At first Father John was stunned, then he got a big smile on his face, shook his head, and said, "See what I mean? Ziggie is still in charge and he's letting me know it."

When the Mass was over and people filed out of church, George was talking to Doris, Ziggie's wife. He started to laugh. Doris said, "George, what's wrong?"

"Ziggie did it again," replied George. "The pallbearers left the casket in the church and Ziggie must be laughing."

It was true. As the whole congregation sang the Notre Dame Victory March, the honorary pallbearers filed out of the pews and the regular pallbearers, Ziggie's nephews, no doubt caught up in all the emotion, followed the others out of the church, leaving the casket behind.

Ziggie always seemed to get the last laugh in any circumstance—even in death. He did it again when the new community center to be named after him was about to be dedicated. The building was complete and the last detail was putting the name, "Zygmont 'Ziggie' Czarobski Community Center," on its front.

Father John had inspected the building at every stage of construction and was confident that all was in order for the dedication the following day. He thought he would go by one more time to see how it looked with Ziggie's name on it.

As he came around the corner, with the building now in full view, he looked up at the large bold letters that had just been put there by the workmen. At first he could not believe what he saw, then the irony of it hit him and he started to laugh. The workers had spelled Czarobski incorrectly. Ziggie was still getting the last laugh.

In reminiscing about Ziggie, Father John said, "Ziggie never wanted to hurt anybody. In my 21 years with him, I never heard him bum rap anyone. Some guys let him down, or didn't come through for Maryville, and Ziggie would say, 'It's a bad time for him, but we'll get him back in the fold.' He was a very sensitive, wonderful person. The most important thing in his life was charity. You don't get that too often. He let his charity take over. He seemed to say, 'I've got to do this,' and, in his way, he got it accomplished.

"He had a knack of being a catalyst for bringing people together. He could entertain them and that was the secret of his talent. If I brought people together, they would fall asleep—what am I going to tell them? But, with Ziggie, you never knew what was going to happen. He kept everyone off guard—his timing was perfect. He had a God-given ability that he developed—a great sense of humor. He was refreshing every time you met him—it was always something new."

Ziggie is buried on a hill overlooking his beloved Maryville. Father John said, "I go up on the hill to see him all the time—he is still giving me orders."

There are literally a thousand Ziggie stories that could be told. Some of them have been related during the course of this book. For all his nuttiness, Ziggie was a very good football player, a great friend, and a deeply sentimental man. By virtue of his personality alone, Ziggie's impact on his teammates was profound. By keeping the teammates together and entertaining them through the years, he played a major role in shaping the way the players of that era feel about each other.

Had Ziggie not graced our scene, the teams might have won the championships they did, but it would not have been the same—there would not have been the fun, the laughs, and the inspiration he provided. All the teammates will tell you that the players would not be as close today if it were not for "76" keeping us all together.

When the teammates gather next fall at one of the Notre Dame home football games for our annual Ziggie reunion, at the end of the party on Friday night, as the nostalgic evening comes to a close, a strange phenomenon will take place, as it does every year. I swear that if you pause and reflect for a moment, you can hear in your heart our departed and never to be forgotten teammate, Ziggie Czarobski, singing the song he always sang for us at the close of the party.

To the tune of "Thanks for the Memories," from the old Bob Hope radio show, Ziggie would belt this parody (in a surprisingly good singing voice), with a catch in his voice:

Thanks for the memories
Beneath that golden dome,
Those haunts we used to roam,
Breakfast buns and Mello runs,
And packages from home,
We thank you, Notre Dame.

Thanks for the memories
Of Lujack and of Gipp

310

And dear old Brother Zip,
Sorin Hall, the senior ball,
And all those student trips,
We thank you so much.

We had the time of our lives there,
Together whatever the odds were,
And if we could we'd be back there,
For we sure had fun with no harm done.

So, thanks for the memories
Of Rock on Cartier
And days without a care,
Though they're gone, they linger on,
We thank you Notre Dame.

God willing, the teammates will continue to meet at Notre Dame for our yearly Ziggie reunion in the years to come, and at the yearly Monogram Club outing, and in other smaller groups around the country.

When we meet the next time, I am sure I will take some good-natured ribbing about omitting someone's favorite story from this book, or having the "grave story" in the wrong year, or some flaw in another story. And that's the way it should be—that's the fun of it all.

We will continue to rehash the old stories and maybe hear some new ones. If need be, we will invent some new ones—after all, age does have its privileges. The important thing is that we continue to meet and enjoy each other's company and be nourished by the love that abounds when the teammates get together.

Lastly, I am sure I speak for all my teammates in saying to each other, to the University of Notre Dame, and to all our departed team-mates and coaches, especially to Moose and Ziggie—"Thanks for the Memories."

Epilogue

As he was dying of cancer, Fr. Mike Hart (Msgr. Michael Hart), our Ziggie reunion chaplain, wrote a letter encouraging me to write this book. There is a part of the letter that I have used as my guide. In it, Father Mike said, "I can't suggest anything to you except this—Humor, obvious, easy, plentiful, spontaneous, has got to be the thread that holds it together and reflects the generous and genuine friendship of the gang, because that's how, over the years, the friendship [maybe even love for one another] has been expressed… So you have to be our translator, Jack—an interpreter, and that's not easy, but I figured I throw it in the pot for your consideration. The project is worth it, very much so."

Speaking for myself, the project indeed has been worth it. More than that, it has been one of the best experiences of my life. I have had the opportunity to talk to so many of the teammates and get to know them better, and to get acquainted with some whom I did not know very well prior to this undertaking. For someone who loves football, Notre Dame, and my teammates, what could be better?

My one regret about the book is that I am sorry I did not get the opportunity to interview Joe McArdle, my guard coach, before he died. He was a marvelous man.

Joe, who was one of Leahy's assistants since their days at Boston College, was a great coach and a wonderful person. He was a tough coach on the field and a very caring person off the field. He loved the former players and his fellow coaches, and they loved him in return. He and his wife, Eleanor, never missed one of our reunions as long as he was able to attend. I am sure he would have shared the wealth of information he had from his years of coaching had I had the chance to interview him.

Since Moose Krause's death, no matter what I was trying to

write, my thoughts constantly drifted to Moose and particularly to the wonderful times my brother George and I had with him in his booth at the Notre Dame home games. George and I have commented that losing him was like losing a father, a brother, a pal, a confidant, all rolled into one.

Shortly after his death, I tried to express my feelings and those shared by George, and our dear friends and fellow booth participants, Buddy and Mike Romano, by writing the following:

In Heaven With Moose

High above the field
Where the Irish play each fall
Are wooden booths lined in a row
That number ten in all

Among the ones is a special place
Reserved for you know who
It belongs to Moose so he can watch
His team and good friend Lou

Moose gathers his friends and former players
To meet in that place up high
We cheer the team and we coach at times
You'd think it was do or die

Moose commands the booth and sets the drill
He keeps us all in line
He sets the tone that begins the same
"George, tell them about the time..."

The stories start and last all game
Ziggie's there and Leahy too
We laugh and cry as we reminisce
With the Golden Dome in view

We call the place Heaven it's got to be
We're up so high above
We tell our stories and share the laughs
We're with our Moose the one we love

The Moose is gone but not really so
He'll be with us every day
His spirit lives on we know for sure
It's our belief it's what we say

We'll meet again and be with the Moose
He'll be in charge and we'll toe the line
He'll show us his booth and say again
"George, tell them about the time..."

Recently, George and I learned by experience that Moose is still in charge of things and looking out for us. George, Buddy Romano, and I drove to South Bend to attend a Friday night dinner sponsored by the Moose Krause Chapter of the National Football Foundation and Hall of Fame. The dinner, in addition to honoring the student-athletes of the area, also honored the memory of Moose Krause. The following day was the traditional Notre Dame Blue-Gold Game, the inter-squad game that ended spring practice.

During the course of the evening, George asked me several times, "What are we going to do tomorrow about the game? Without Moose, we're going to have to sit in the stands, and I am not sure my hip can handle the stairs."

After about the fourth time I said, "George, I have the solution. Moose is in Heaven, right?"

"Of course, Moose is in Heaven," replied George.

"I went on, "Moose always looked after us, so why don't we leave it up to him?"

"That's a great idea," replied George. With his face looking up, he said, "Moose, it's up to you, you have to take care of us."

For the rest of the evening we did not give a thought to where we would sit for the game the next day. The following morning, Buddy and I preceded George to the dining room at the Ramada Inn to have some breakfast. I saw George come into the room with a big smile on his face. "Moose did it," he said as he approached the table. "I was passing the front desk and they read me a message from Dick Rosenthal [Notre Dame's athletic director]. 'Three passes for the press booth waiting for you at the pass gate, compliments of Moose Krause.' "

As the poem says, "He'll be with us every day."

Leahy's Lads, 1941-1949
Team Rosters

1941

Ashbaugh, Russell (Pete)

Barry, Norm
Bereolos, Hercules
Bertelli, Angelo
Bolger, Matt
Brock, Tom
Brutz, Jim

Creevy, Dick
Crimmins, Bernie

Dove, Bob

Earley, Bill
Ebli, Ray
Evans, Fred (Dippy)

Filley, Pat

Hargrave, Bob
Hines, Mike
Hogan, Don

Juzwik, Steve

Kovatch, John
Kudlacz, Stan

Laiber, Joe
Lanahan, John
Lillis, Paul (C)

Maddock, Bob
McBride, Bob
McLaughlin, Dave

McNeill, Chuck
Miller, Creighton
Miller, Tom
Murphy, George

Neff, Bob

O'Brien, Dick

Pattan, Paul
Prokop, Joe

Riordan, Will
Rymkus, Lou

Sullivan, Larry

Walsh, Bob
Warner, Jack
Wright, Harry

Ziemba, Wally

1942

Adams, John (Tree)
Ashbaugh, Russell (Pete)

Bertelli, Angelo
Brock, Tom
Brutz, Marty

Clatt, Corwin, (Cornie)
Coleman, Herb
Cowhig, Garry
Creevey, John
Creevy, Dick
Creevy, Tom
Cusick, Frank
Czarobski, Zygmont (Ziggie)

Dove, Bob
Dwyer, Gene

Earley, Bill
Evans, Fred (Dippy)

Filley, Pat
Frawley, George

Higgins, Luke
Huber, Bill

Krupa, Ed
Kudlacz, Stan

Lanahan, John
Limont, Paul
Livingstone, Bob

McBride, Bob
McGinnis, John
Mello, Jim
Meter, Bernie (Bud)
Miller, Creighton
Miller, Tom
Murphy, George (C)

Neff, Bob

O'Connor, Bill (Bucky)

Peasenelli, John
Piccone, Cammille (Pic)

Rymkus, Lou

Sullivan, Larry

Tobin, George

White, Jim
Wright, Harry

Yonakor, John

Ziemba, Wally

1943

Adams, John (Tree)
Angsman, Elmer

Berezney, Pete
Bertelli, Angelo

Cibula, George
Coleman, Herb
Curley, Bob
Czarobski, Zygmont (Ziggie)

Dancewicz, Frank
Davis, Ray

Earley, Bill

Filley, Pat (C)
Flanagan, Jim
Ford, Gerald

Ganey, Mike

Hanlon, Bob

Kelly, Bob
Krupa, Ed
Kuffel, Ray
Kulbitski, Vic

Limont, Paul
Lujack, Johnny
Lyden, Mike

Maggioll, Achille (Chick)
Mello, Jim
Meter, Bernie (Bud)
Mieszkowski, Ed
Miller, Creighton

Nemeth, Steve

Paladino, Bob
Perko, John

Rellas, Chris
Renaud, Charles
Ruggerio, Frank
Rykovich, Julie

Signaigo, Joe
Skat, Al
Snyder, Jim
Statuto, Art
Sullivan, George
Szymanski, Frank

Terlep, George
Tharp, Jim
Todorovich, Mike
Trumper, Ed

Urban, Gasper

Waldron, Ronayne
White, Jim

Yonakor, John

Zilly, Jack

1944

Adams, John W.
Angsman, Elmer J., Jr.
Archer, Arthur

Benigni, George
Berezney, Peter, Jr.
Bernhardt, Richard
Brennan, James
Bush, Roy A.

Cash, Anthony
Chandler, William

Dailer, James H.
D'Alonzo, Alfred
Dancewicz, Frank J.
Dee, John

Eilers, Carl
Endress, Frank

Fallon, John J.
Fay, Edward
Filley, Patrick J. (C)
Fitzgerald, Arthur
Franklin, Raymond

Ganey, Michael J.
Gasparella, Joseph R.
Glaab, John
Guthrie, Thomas F., Jr.

Iliff, Robert

Kelly, Joseph
Kelly, Robert J.
LeBrou, John F.
Limont, Mark

Manzo, Michael B., Jr.
Marino, Nunzio R.
Martz, George
Mastrangelo, John B.
McGurk, James S.
Mergenthal, Arthur
Mieszkowski, Edward T.

Nemeth, Steve J.

O'Connor, William F.

Rovai, Fred J.
Ruggerio, Frank A.

Schreiber, Thomas
Schuster, Kenneth R.
Scott, Vince
Skoglund, Robert W.
Slovak, Emil
Stewart, Ralph
Sullivan, George A.
Szymanski, Francis S.

Toczylowski, Stephen

Waybright, Douglas G.
Welch, Robert F.
Wendell, Martin P.
Westenkirchner, Joseph

Yokemonis, Charles

1945

Agnone, John J., Jr.
Angsman, Elmer J., Jr.

Berezney, Peter, Jr.
Brennan, Terence P.
Bush, Roy A.

Cadieux, Roger E.
Colella, Philip J.
Cronin, Richard M.

Dancewicz, Francis J. (C)
DeBuono, Richard F.

Fallon, John A.
Fay, Edward J.
Fischer, William
Flynn, William J.P.

Gasparella, Joseph R.
Glaab, John
Gompers, William G.
Grothaus, Walter J., Jr.

Herman, Richard D.

Kane, Charles J.
Krivik, Stanley
Kurzynske, James R.

LeBrou, John F.
Leonard, William
Lesko, Alexander

Malec, Robert
Maryanski, Matthew S.
Mastrangelo, John B.
McGurk, James S.
Mieszkowski, Edward T.

O'Connor, Philip
Opela, Bruno P.
Oracko, Stephen F.

Panelli, John R.
Pantera, Leroy P.
Potter, Thomas A.

Ratterman, George W.
Rovai, Fred J.
Ruggerio, Frank A.
Russell, Willmer

Schmid, Alfred L.
Schreiber, Thomas P.
Scott, Vincent J.
Skoglund, Robert W.
Slovak, Emil
Stanczyak, Alphonse
Stelmazek, Edward T.

Vainisi, Jack A.
Virok, Ernest S.
Walsh, William H.
White, Robert T.

Yonto, Joseph

Zehler, William D.

1946

Ashbaugh, Russell

Brennan, Terence
Brown, Roger
Brutz, Martin
Budynkiewicz, Ted

Cifelli, August
Clatt, Corwin
Connor, George
Coutre, Lawrence
Cowhig, Gerald
Creevey, John
Czarobski, Zygmont (Ziggie)

Dougherty, James

Earley, Fred
Espenan, Ray

Fallon, John
Fischer, William

Gasparella, Joseph
Gompers, William

Hart, Leon
Heywood, William
Higgins, Luke

Kelly, Robert
Kosikowski, Frank

Limont, Paul
Livingstone, Robert
Lujack, John

Martin, James
Mastrangelo, John
McBride, Robert
McGehee, Ralph
McGurk, James
Mello, James
Meter, Bernard
Michaels, William
Murphy, John

O'Connor, William (Bucky)
O'Connor, William (Zeke)

Panelli, John
Potter, Thomas

Ratterman, George
Rovai, Fred
Russell, Willmer

Scott, Vincent
Signaigo, Joseph
Simmons, Floyd
Sitko, Emil
Skoglund, Robert
Slovak, Emil
Smith, William L.
Statuto, Arthur
Strohmeyer, George
Sullivan, George
Swistowicz, Michael

Tobin, George
Tripucka, Frank

Urban, Gasper

Vangen, Willard

Walsh, Robert
Walsh, William
Wendell, Martin
Wightkin, William

Zalejski, Ernest
Zilly, John
Zmijewski, Al

1947

Ashbaugh, Russell

Begley, Gerald
Brennan, James
Brennan, Terence
Brown, Roger
Budynkiewicz, Ted
Burnett, Albert

Carter, Donald
Ciechanowicz, Emil
Cifelli, August
Clatt, Corwin
Connor, George (C)
Connor, John
Couch, Leo
Coutre, Lawrence
Czarobski, Zygmont (Ziggie)

Dailer, James

Earley, Frederick
Espenan, Raymond

Fallon, John
Fallon, Joseph
Fischer, William
Flanagan, James
Frampton, John

Gaul, Francis
Gay, William
Gompers, William
Grothaus, Walter

Hart, Leon
Harty, Frank
Heywood, William
Hudak, Edward

Jeffers, John

Kosikowski, Frank

Lally, Robert
LeCluyse, Leonard
Leonard, William
Leous, Richard

Livingstone, Robert
Lujack, John

Martin, James
McCarty, Thomas
McGee, Coy
McGehee, Ralph
Michaels, William

O'Connor, William (Bucky)
O'Connor, William (Zeke)
O'Neil, John
Oracko, Steve

Panelli, John

Ramsberger, Gerald
Russell, Willmer

Saggau, Thomas
Signaigo, Joseph
Simmons, Floyd
Sinkovitz, John
Sitko, Emil
Smith, Lancaster
Spaniel, Frank
Statuto, Arthur
Strohmeyer, George
Sullivan, George
Swistowicz, Michael

Tripucka, Frank

Urban, Gasper

Vangen, Willard

Walsh, William
Waybright, Douglas
Wendell, Martin
Wightkin, William
Wilke, Clifford

Yanoschik, Phillip C.

Zalejski, Ernest
Zmijewski, Al

1948

Begley, Gerald
Brennan, Terence
Brown, Roger
Budynkiewicz, Ted

Cantwell, Philip
Ciechanowicz, Emil
Cifelli, August
Connor, John
Cotter, Richard A.
Coutre, Lawrence

Dailer, James
Dickson, George

Espenan, Charles

Fallon, John
Fallon, Joseph
Fischer, William (C)
Flynn, William
Frampton, John

Gaul, Francis
Groom, Jerome
Grothaus, Walter

Hart, William
Helwig, John
Hudak, Edward

Jeffers, John
Johnston, Frank

Kuh, Richard

Lally, Robert
Landry, John
Leonard, William
Lesko, Alexander

Martin, James
McGee, Coy
McGehee, Ralph
McKillip, William

O'Neil, John
Oracko, Steve

Palmisano, Frank
Panelli, John

Saggau, Thomas
Ste. Marie, Vincent
Sitko, Emil
Smith, Eugene
Smith, William
Spaniel, Frank
Swistowicz, Michael

Thomas, Deane
Tripucka, Frank

Vangen, Willard

Walsh, William
Waybright, Douglas
Wendell, Martin
Wightkin, William
Wilke, Clifford
Williams, Robert

Yanoschik, Phillip C.

Zalejski, Ernest
Zmijewski, Al

1949

Banicki, Frederick
Barrett, William C.
Bartlett, James
Begley, Gerald C.
Boji, Byron B.
Burns, Paul E.
Bush, John L.
Butz, Jean

Carter, Thomas L.
Cifelli, August B.
Connor, John F.
Cotter, Richard A.
Coutre, Lawrence E.

Dailer, James
Daut, John D.
Dickson, George C.
Dolmetsch, Robert E.

Espenan, Charles R.

Flood, David M.
Flynn, William J.
Fox, Francis J.

Gander, Fidel J.
Gay, William T.
Groom, Jerome P.
Grothaus, Walter J.

Hamby, James H.
Hart, Leon J. (co-C)
Helwig, John F.
Higgins, William P.
Holmes, Thomas P.
Hovey, William A.
Huber, Thomas E.
Hudak, Edward J.

Jeffers, John T.
Johnston, Frank
Jonardi, Raymond

Kapish, Robert J.
Kiousis, Martin J.
Koch, David A.

Lally, Robert J.
Landry, John W.
Layden, Elmer F.

Mahoney, James E.
Martin, James E. (co-C)
Mazur, John E.
McGehee, Ralph W.
McKillip, William L.
Modak, Daniel
Mutscheller, James F.

O'Neil, John D.
Oracko, Steve
Ostrowski, Chester C.

Perry, Arthur R.
Petitbon, John E.

Saggau, Thomas H.
Schwartz, Phillip
Sitko, Emil M.
Smith, Eugene F.
Spaniel, Francis J.
Swistowicz, Michael P.

Toneff, Robert

Wallner, Frederick W.
Waybright, Douglas G.
Whiteside, William A.
Wightkin, William J.
Williams, Robert

Yanoschik, Phillip C.

Zalejski, Ernest R.
Zambrowski, Anthony J.
Zancha, John D.
Zmijewski, Al

About the Author

Jack Connor, a native of Chicago's south side, attended De LaSalle High School, where he earned an athletic scholarship to Notre Dame. As a student athlete he played basketball for one year, was a member of the Irish football squad for four years (1945-49), and graduated cum laude with a Bachelor of Arts degree in Economics.

Connor was commissioned a Second Lieutenant in the U.S. Marine Corps in July 1951, and served on active duty as an Anti-Aircraft Artillery Officer, a legal officer, a football coach and player before being honorably discharged with a rank of captain in the Marine Corps Reserves in early 1954.

From 1955 to 1960, Connor was a special agent in the Federal Bureau of Investigation, twice earning personal commendations from FBI Director J. Edgar Hoover. In 1960, he joined the world of investment banking where he worked for 23 years. Connor is currently a self-employed financial consultant.

While always interested in writing, *Leahy's Lads* is Connor's first book. He has written several poems about Notre Dame players and coaches, which include tributes to Bernie Crimmins, Johnny Druze, and "Motts" Tonelli. Connor's poem, "In Heaven With Moose," honors the 1943 team on the occasion of the 50th anniversary of their National Championship, and was inscribed on a plaque and donated to the University of Notre Dame. It is currently on display in the Moose Krause section of the Monogram Room in the Joyce Athletic and Convocation Center.

Jack and Alice, his wife of 37 years, have four children and eight grandchildren and, with the exception of time in the military and the FBI, have been lifelong residents of Chicago.